POLITICS AND ECONOMICS OF THE MIDDLE EAST

IRAN: ISSUES AND PERSPECTIVES

POLITICS AND ECONOMICS OF THE MIDDLE EAST

Additional books in this series can be found on Nova's website
under the Series tab.

Additional E-books in this series can be found on Nova's website
under the E-book tab.

POLITICS AND ECONOMICS OF THE MIDDLE EAST

IRAN: ISSUES AND PERSPECTIVES

STEPHEN D. CALHOUN
EDITOR

Nova Science Publishers, Inc.
New York

Copyright © 2010 by Nova Science Publishers, Inc.

All rights reserved. No part of this book may be reproduced, stored in a retrieval system or transmitted in any form or by any means: electronic, electrostatic, magnetic, tape, mechanical photocopying, recording or otherwise without the written permission of the Publisher.

For permission to use material from this book please contact us:
Telephone 631-231-7269; Fax 631-231-8175
Web Site: http://www.novapublishers.com

NOTICE TO THE READER

The Publisher has taken reasonable care in the preparation of this book, but makes no expressed or implied warranty of any kind and assumes no responsibility for any errors or omissions. No liability is assumed for incidental or consequential damages in connection with or arising out of information contained in this book. The Publisher shall not be liable for any special, consequential, or exemplary damages resulting, in whole or in part, from the readers' use of, or reliance upon, this material. Any parts of this book based on government reports are so indicated and copyright is claimed for those parts to the extent applicable to compilations of such works.

Independent verification should be sought for any data, advice or recommendations contained in this book. In addition, no responsibility is assumed by the publisher for any injury and/or damage to persons or property arising from any methods, products, instructions, ideas or otherwise contained in this publication.

This publication is designed to provide accurate and authoritative information with regard to the subject matter covered herein. It is sold with the clear understanding that the Publisher is not engaged in rendering legal or any other professional services. If legal or any other expert assistance is required, the services of a competent person should be sought. FROM A DECLARATION OF PARTICIPANTS JOINTLY ADOPTED BY A COMMITTEE OF THE AMERICAN BAR ASSOCIATION AND A COMMITTEE OF PUBLISHERS.

LIBRARY OF CONGRESS CATALOGING-IN-PUBLICATION DATA

Iran : issues and perspectives / editor, Stephen D. Calhoun.
    p. cm.
  Includes index.
  ISBN 978-1-61728-007-8 (hardcover)
 1. Iran--Strategic aspects. 2. Iran--Military policy. 3. Iran--Foreign
relations--1997- 4. Nuclear weapons--Iran. 5. Nuclear arms control--Iran.
6. Iran--Politics and government--1997- 7. United States--Foreign
relations--Iran. 8. Iran--Foreign relations--United States. I. Calhoun,
Stephen D.
 DS318.9.I7265 2010
 955.06'1--dc22
                          2010013758

Published by Nova Science Publishers, Inc. † New York

CONTENTS

Preface		vii
Chapter 1	Iran: U.S. Concerns and Policy Responses *Kenneth Katzman*	1
Chapter 2	Iran: Regional Perspectives and U.S. Policy *Casey L. Addis, Christopher M. Blanchard, Kenneth Katzman,* *Carol Migdalovitz, Jim Nichol, Jeremy M. Sharp and Jim Zanotti*	59
Chapter 3	Iran's Nuclear Program: Status *Paul K. Kerr*	107
Chapter 4	Iran's Nuclear Program: Tehran's Compliance with International Obligations *Paul K. Kerr*	131
Chapter 5	Iran Sanctions *Kenneth Katzman*	145
Chapter 6	Iran's 2009 Presidential Elections *Casey L. Addis*	175
Chapter 7	Iran's Activities and Influence in Iraq *Kenneth Katzman*	189
Index		201

PREFACE

As the Obama administration and Congress move forward to pursue engagement, harsher sanctions, or both, regional actors are evaluating their policies and priorities with respect to Iran. Iran's neighbors share many U.S. concerns, but often evaluate them differently than the United States when calculating their own relationship with or policy toward Iran. This book provides a description of Iran's neighbors' policies and interests, options for Congressional consideration, and an analysis of potential regional implications. Also explored is Iran's nuclear program status, sanctions, Iran's 2009 presidential elections and influence on Iraq.

Chapter 1 - President Obama has said his Administration shares the goals of previous Administrations to contain Iran's strategic capabilities and regional influence. The Administration has not changed the previous Administration's characterization of Iran as a "profound threat to U.S. national security interests," a perception generated not only by Iran's nuclear program but also by its military assistance to armed groups in Iraq and Afghanistan, to the Palestinian group Hamas, and to Lebanese Hezbollah. The Obama Administration formulated approaches to achieve those goals that differ from those of its predecessor by expanding direct diplomatic engagement with Iran's government and by downplaying discussion of potential U.S. military action against Iranian nuclear facilities. However, the domestic unrest in Iran that has burgeoned since alleged fraud in Iran's June 12, 2009, presidential election has presented the Administration with a choice of whether to continue to engage Iran's government or to back the growing ranks of the Iranian opposition.

Although Administration statements in December 2009 were more supportive of the student-led protests than previously, the Administration remained open to negotiating a nuclear deal with Iran along the lines of an October 1, 2009, multilateral agreement with Iran. Under that framework, Russia and France would reprocess some of Iran's low-enriched uranium for medical use. However, Iran has not, to date, agreed to the stipulated technical details of such a reprocessing program, casting doubts on Iran's commitment to the tentative deal and sparking renewed discussions of new U.N. sanctions, particularly those that would target members and companies of Iran's Revolutionary Guard Corps. The Guard is the main element used by the regime to crack down against the protesters.

Any additional U.N. Security Council sanctions would build on those put in place since 2006. These sanctions generally are targeted against WMD-related trade with Iran, but also ban Iran from transferring arms outside Iran and restrict dealings with some Iranian banks. Separate U.S. efforts to persuade European governments to curb trade with, investment in, and credits for Iran, and to convince foreign banks not to do business with Iran, are intended to compound the U.N. pressure. Some in Congress believe that additional unilateral U.S. sanctions that try to curb sales to Iran of gasoline could help pressure Iran into a nuclear settlement. Others believe that sanctioning Iran's ability to monitor the Internet—or clearer statements of U.S. support for the demonstrators—would help the domestic opposition materially change or even topple the regime. Others believe that new U.S. unilateral or U.N. measures would cause Iran to resist compromise, fracture the U.S.-led coalition that is trying to curb Iran's program, or hurt the cause of the opposition. For further information, see CRS Report RS2087 1, *Iran Sanctions*, by Kenneth Katzman; CRS Report R40849, *Iran: Regional Perspectives and U.S. Policy*, coordinated by Casey L. Addis; and CRS Report RL34544, *Iran's Nuclear Program: Status*, by Paul K. Kerr.

Much of the debate over U.S. policy toward Iran has centered on the nature of the current regime; some believe that Iran, a country of about 70 million people, is a threat to U.S. interests because hardliners in Iran's regime dominate and set a policy direction intended to challenge U.S. influence and allies in the region. President George W. Bush, in his January 29, 2002, State of the Union message, labeled Iran part of an "axis of evil" along with Iraq and North Korea.

Chapter 2 - As the Administration and Congress move forward to pursue engagement, harsher sanctions, or both, regional actors are evaluating their policies and priorities with respect to Iran. Iran's neighbors share many U.S. concerns, but often evaluate them differently than the United States when calculating their own relationship with or policy toward Iran. Because Iran and other regional concerns—the Arab-Israeli peace process, stability in Lebanon and Iraq, terrorism, and the ongoing war in Afghanistan—have become increasingly intertwined, understanding the policies and perspectives of Iran's neighbors could be crucial during the consideration of options to address overall U.S. policy toward Iran.

Chapter 3 - Although Iran claims that its nuclear program is exclusively for peaceful purposes, it has generated considerable concern that Tehran is pursuing a nuclear weapons program. Indeed, the UN Security Council has responded to Iran's refusal to suspend work on its uranium enrichment and heavy-water nuclear reactor programs by adopting several resolutions which imposed sanctions on Tehran.

Despite this pressure, Iran continues to enrich uranium, install additional centrifuges, and conduct research on new types of centrifuges. Tehran has also continued work on its heavy-water reactor and associated facilities.

Whether Iran is pursuing a nuclear weapons program is, however, unclear. A National Intelligence Estimate made public in December 2007 assessed that Tehran "halted its nuclear weapons program," defined as "Iran's nuclear weapon design and weaponization work and covert uranium conversion-related and uranium enrichment-related work," in 2003. The estimate, however, also assessed that Tehran is "keeping open the option to develop nuclear weapons" and that any decision to end a nuclear weapons program is "inherently reversible." Intelligence community officials have reaffirmed this judgment on several occasions. Iranian efforts to produce fissile material for nuclear weapons by using its known nuclear facilities would almost certainly be detected by the IAEA.

Although Iran has cooperated with the International Atomic Energy Agency (IAEA) to an extent, the agency says that Tehran's action's have not been sufficient to alleviate all of the IAEA's concerns about Iran's enrichment and heavy-water reactor programs. The IAEA continues to investigate the program, particularly evidence that Tehran may have conducted procurement activities and research directly applicable to nuclear weapons development.

Chapter 4 - In 2002, the International Atomic Energy Agency (IAEA) began investigating allegations that Iran had conducted clandestine nuclear activities. Ultimately, the agency reported that some of these activities had violated Tehran's IAEA safeguards agreement. The IAEA has not stated definitively that Iran has pursued nuclear weapons, but has also not yet been able to conclude that the country's nuclear program is exclusively for peaceful purposes. The IAEA Board of Governors referred the matter to the U.N. Security Council in February 2006. Since then, the council has adopted five resolutions, the most recent of which (Resolution 1835) was adopted in September 2008.

The Security Council has required Iran to cooperate fully with the IAEA's investigation of its nuclear activities, suspend its uranium enrichment program, suspend its construction of a heavy-water reactor and related projects, and ratify the Additional Protocol to its IAEA safeguards agreement. However, a November 2009 report from then-IAEA Director-General Mohamed ElBaradei to the agency's Board of Governors indicated that Tehran has continued to defy the council's demands by continuing work on its uranium enrichment program and heavy-water reactor program. Iran has signed, but not ratified, its Additional Protocol.

Iran and the IAEA agreed in August 2007 on a work plan to clarify the outstanding questions regarding Tehran's nuclear program. Most of these questions have essentially been resolved, but ElBaradei told the agency's board in June 2008 that the agency still has questions regarding "possible military dimensions to Iran's nuclear programme." The IAEA has reported for some time that it has not been able to make progress on these matters.

This chapter provides a brief overview of Iran's nuclear program and describes the legal basis for the actions taken by the IAEA board and the Security Council.

Chapter 5 - Iran is subject to a wide range of U.S. sanctions, restricting trade with, investment, and U.S. foreign aid to Iran, and requiring the United States to vote against international lending to Iran. Several laws and Executive Orders authorize the imposition of U.S. penalties against foreign companies that do business with Iran, as part of an effort to persuade foreign firms to choose between the Iranian market and the much larger U.S. market. Most notable among these sanctions is a ban, imposed in 1995, on U.S. trade with and investment in Iran. That ban has since been modified slightly to allow for some bilateral trade in luxury and humanitarian-related goods. Foreign subsidiaries of U.S. firms remain generally exempt from the trade ban since they are under the laws of the countries where they are incorporated. Since 1995, several U.S. laws and regulations that seek to pressure Iran's economy, curb Iran's support for militant groups, and curtail supplies to Iran of advanced technology have been enacted. Since 2006, the United Nations Security Council has imposed some sanctions primarily attempting to curtail supply to Iran of weapons-related technology but also sanctioning some Iranian banks.

U.S. officials have identified Iran's energy sector as a key Iranian vulnerability because Iran's government revenues are approximately 80% dependent on oil revenues and in need of substantial foreign investment. A U.S. effort to curb international energy investment in Iran began in 1996 with the Iran Sanctions Act (ISA), but no firms have been sanctioned under it and the precise effects of ISA—as distinct from other factors affecting international firms' decisions on whether to invest in Iran—have been unclear. While international pressure on Iran to curb its nuclear program has increased the hesitation of many major foreign firms to invest in Iran's energy sector, hindering Iran's efforts to expand oil production beyond 4.1

million barrels per day, some firms continue to see opportunity in Iran. This particularly appears to be the case for companies in Asia that appear eager to fill the void left by major European and American firms and to line up steady supplies of Iranian oil and natural gas.

Some in Congress express concern about the reticence of U.S. allies, of Russia, and of China, to impose U.N. sanctions that would target Iran's civilian economy. In an attempt to strengthen U.S. leverage with its allies to back such international sanctions, several bills in the 111th Congress would add U.S. sanctions on Iran. For example, H.R. 2194 (which passed the House on December 15, 2009), H.R. 1985, H.R. 1208, and S. 908 would include as ISA violations selling refined gasoline to Iran; providing shipping insurance or other services to deliver gasoline to Iran; or supplying equipment to or performing the construction of oil refineries in Iran. Several of these bills would also expand the menu of available sanctions against violators. A bill reported by the Senate Banking Committee, S. 2799, contains these sanctions as well as a broad range of other measures against Iran, including reversing previous easings of the U.S. ban on trade with Iran, and protecting investment funds from lawsuits for divesting from companies active in Iran. A growing trend in Congress is to alter some U.S. sanctions laws in order to facilitate the access to information of a growing student-led opposition movement in Iran, and to sanction firms that sell the regime internet-monitoring gear. Some see the various legislative proposals as supporting Obama Administration policy by threatening Iran with further isolation, while others believe such legislation would reduce European cooperation with the United States on Iran. Still others say these proposals could backfire by strengthening the political control exercised by Iran's leaders. For more on Iran, see CRS Report RL3 2048, *Iran: U.S. Concerns and Policy Responses*, by Kenneth Katzman.

Chapter 6 - On June 12, 2009, following a heated campaign between reformist candidate Mir Hussein Musavi and incumbent President Mahmoud Ahmadinejad, Iranians turned out in record numbers to vote in the presidential election. Shortly after the polls closed, the Interior Minister announced that President Ahmadinejad had been reelected by a 62% margin. The announcement was followed by allegations of vote rigging and election fraud and prompted supporters of leading reformist candidate Mir Hussein Musavi and others to hold public demonstrations in several major cities of a size and intensity unprecedented since the Iranian Revolution of 1979.

Despite a government ban on unauthorized public gatherings, protests reportedly have continued since the election. Restrictions on foreign and domestic journalists, reported disruptions of mobile phone networks, limited accessibility of some internet sites, mass arrests, and clashes between civilian protestors and Basij forces have garnered international attention and increased concerns about the Iranian government's apparent disregard for human rights and basic civil liberties.

Regardless of the actual election results, the Supreme Leader Khamenei, along with the Revolutionary Guard and the Basij, appear determined to impose the election outcome by force. The government crackdown on protestors appears to be effective, even as smaller gatherings have continued in Tehran and other major cities. Attention has now focused on the potential long-term effects of the post-election unrest on Iranian government and society, and what the outcome might mean for U.S. efforts to resolve the issues of Iran's nuclear program, its support for terrorism, and other national security concerns.

The Obama Administration's response has been cautious, but somewhat has hardened as reports of deaths, injuries, and mass arrests of Iranian citizens have increased. Many observers believe that President Obama is attempting to balance the need to condemn the violence against the protestors with the need to avoid the perception of U.S. interference, which some worry could prompt the Iranian government to clamp down further on freedom of expression or jeopardize U.S. efforts to engage Iran on the issue of its nuclear program.

Chapter 7 - With a conventional military and weapons of mass destruction (WMD) threat from Saddam Hussein's regime removed, Iran seeks to ensure that Iraq can never again become a threat to Iran, either with or without U.S. forces present in Iraq. Some believe that Iran's intentions go well beyond achieving Iraq's "neutrality"—that Iran wants to try to harness Iraq to Iran's broader regional policy goals and to help Iran defend against international criticism of Iran's nuclear program. Others believe Iran sees Iraq as providing lucrative investment opportunities and a growing market for Iranian products and contracts. The violent unrest in Iran surrounding that country's June 12, 2009, presidential election has given Iran another reason to exercise influence in Iraq—to try to suppress Iranian dissidents located over the border inside Iraq.

Iran has sought to achieve its goals in Iraq through several strategies: supporting pro-Iranian factions and armed militias; attempting to influence Iraqi political leaders and faction leaders; and building economic ties throughout Iraq that might accrue goodwill to Iran. It is Iran's support for armed Shiite factions that most concerns U.S. officials. That Iranian activity has hindered—and continues to pose a threat to—U.S. efforts to stabilize Iraq, and has heightened the U.S. threat perception of Iran generally.

While some see Iran as having accomplished many of its key objectives in Iraq, others maintain that Iran has suffered key setbacks over the past year. Its protégé Shiite factions, formerly united, are increasingly competing with each other politically, and several are losing support among the Iraqi public. The most pro-Iranian factions generally fared poorly in the January 31, 2009, provincial elections.

In: Iran: Issues and Perspectives
Editor: Stephen D. Calhoun

ISBN: 978-1-61728-007-8
© 2010 Nova Science Publishers, Inc.

Chapter 1

IRAN: U.S. CONCERNS AND POLICY RESPONSES[*]

Kenneth Katzman

SUMMARY

President Obama has said his Administration shares the goals of previous Administrations to contain Iran's strategic capabilities and regional influence. The Administration has not changed the previous Administration's characterization of Iran as a "profound threat to U.S. national security interests," a perception generated not only by Iran's nuclear program but also by its military assistance to armed groups in Iraq and Afghanistan, to the Palestinian group Hamas, and to Lebanese Hezbollah. The Obama Administration formulated approaches to achieve those goals that differ from those of its predecessor by expanding direct diplomatic engagement with Iran's government and by downplaying discussion of potential U.S. military action against Iranian nuclear facilities. However, the domestic unrest in Iran that has burgeoned since alleged fraud in Iran's June 12, 2009, presidential election has presented the Administration with a choice of whether to continue to engage Iran's government or to back the growing ranks of the Iranian opposition.

Although Administration statements in December 2009 were more supportive of the student-led protests than previously, the Administration remained open to negotiating a nuclear deal with Iran along the lines of an October 1, 2009, multilateral agreement with Iran. Under that framework, Russia and France would reprocess some of Iran's low-enriched uranium for medical use. However, Iran has not, to date, agreed to the stipulated technical details of such a reprocessing program, casting doubts on Iran's commitment to the tentative deal and sparking renewed discussions of new U.N. sanctions, particularly those that would target members and companies of Iran's Revolutionary Guard Corps. The Guard is the main element used by the regime to crack down against the protesters.

---

[*] This is an edited, reformatted and augmented version of a CRS Report for Congress publication dated January 2010.

Any additional U.N. Security Council sanctions would build on those put in place since 2006. These sanctions generally are targeted against WMD-related trade with Iran, but also ban Iran from transferring arms outside Iran and restrict dealings with some Iranian banks. Separate U.S. efforts to persuade European governments to curb trade with, investment in, and credits for Iran, and to convince foreign banks not to do business with Iran, are intended to compound the U.N. pressure. Some in Congress believe that additional unilateral U.S. sanctions that try to curb sales to Iran of gasoline could help pressure Iran into a nuclear settlement. Others believe that sanctioning Iran's ability to monitor the Internet—or clearer statements of U.S. support for the demonstrators—would help the domestic opposition materially change or even topple the regime. Others believe that new U.S. unilateral or U.N. measures would cause Iran to resist compromise, fracture the U.S.-led coalition that is trying to curb Iran's program, or hurt the cause of the opposition. Much of the debate over U.S. policy toward Iran has centered on the nature of the current regime; some believe that Iran, a country of about 70 million people, is a threat to U.S. interests because hardliners in Iran's regime dominate and set a policy direction intended to challenge U.S. influence and allies in the region. President George W. Bush, in his January 29, 2002, State of the Union message, labeled Iran part of an "axis of evil" along with Iraq and North Korea.

POLITICAL HISTORY

The United States was an ally of the late Shah of Iran, Mohammad Reza Pahlavi ("the Shah"), who ruled from 1941 until his ouster in February 1979. The Shah assumed the throne when Britain and Russia forced his father, Reza Shah Pahlavi (Reza Shah), from power because of his perceived alignment with Germany in World War II. Reza Shah had assumed power in 1921 when, as an officer in Iran's only military force, the Cossack Brigade (reflecting Russian influence in Iran in the early 20th century), he launched a coup against the government of the Qajar Dynasty. Reza Shah was proclaimed Shah in 1925, founding the Pahlavi dynasty. The Qajars had been in decline for many years before Reza Shah's takeover. That dynasty's perceived manipulation by Britain and Russia had been one of the causes of the 1906 constitutionalist movement, which forced the Qajars to form Iran's first Majles (parliament) in August 1906 and promulgate a constitution in December 1906. Prior to the Qajars, what is now Iran was the center of several Persian empires and dynasties, but whose reach shrunk steadily over time. Since the 16th century, Iranian empires lost control of Bahrain (1521), Baghdad (1638), the Caucasus (1828), western Afghanistan (1857), Baluchistan (1872), and what is now Turkmenistan (1894). Iran adopted Shiite Islam under the Safavid Dynasty (1500-1722), which brought Iran out from a series of Turkic and Mongol conquests.

The Shah was anti-Communist, and the United States viewed his government as a bulwark against the expansion of Soviet influence in the Persian Gulf and a counterweight to pro-Soviet Arab regimes and movements. Israel maintained a representative office in Iran during the Shah's time and the Shah supported a peaceful resolution of the Arab-Israeli dispute. In 1951, under pressure from nationalists in the Majles (parliament) who gained strength in the 1949 Majles elections, he appointed a popular nationalist parliamentarian, Dr. Mohammad Mossadeq, as Prime Minister. Mossadeq was widely considered left-leaning, and the United States was wary of his policies, which included his drive for nationalization of the oil industry. Mossadeq's followers began an uprising in August 1953 when the Shah tried to dismiss Mossadeq, and the Shah fled. The Shah was restored in a successful CIA-supported uprising against Mossadeq.

The Shah tried to modernize Iran and orient it toward the West, but in so doing he also sought to marginalize Iran's Shiite clergy. He exiled Ayatollah Ruhollah Khomeini in 1964 because of Khomeini's active opposition, which was based on the Shah's anti-clerical policies and what Khomeini alleged was the Shah's forfeiture of Iran's sovereignty to the United States. Khomeini fled to and taught in Najaf, Iraq, a major Shiite theological center that contains the Shrine of Imam Ali, Shiism's foremost figure. There, he was a peer of senior Iraqi Shiite clerics and, with them, advocated direct clerical rule or *velayat-e-faqih* (rule by a supreme Islamic jurisprudent). In 1978, three years after the March 6, 1975, Algiers Accords between the Shah and Iraq's Baathist leaders, which settled territorial disputes and required each party to stop assisting each other's oppositionists, Iraq expelled Khomeini to France, from which he stoked the Islamic revolution. Mass demonstrations and guerrilla activity by pro-Khomeini forces, allied with a broad array of anti-Shah activists, caused the Shah's government to collapse in February 1979. Khomeini returned from France and, on February 11, 1979, declared an Islamic Republic of Iran, as enshrined in the constitution that was adopted in a public referendum in December 1979 (and amended in 1989). Khomeini was strongly anti-West and particularly anti-U.S., and relations between the United States and the Islamic Republic turned hostile even before the November 4, 1979, seizure of the U.S. Embassy by pro-Khomeini radicals.

REGIME STRUCTURE, STABILITY, AND OPPOSITION

About a decade after founding the Islamic republic, Ayatollah Ruhollah Khomeini died on June 3, 1989. Iran's regime has always been considered authoritarian, but with a degree of popular input and checks and balances among power centers. The regime Khomeini established—enshrined in an Islamic republican constitution adopted in October 1979 and amended in a national referendum of April 1989—consists of some elected and some appointed positions. National elections under the Islamic republic have always been held, and on time, even during the eight- year Iran-Iraq war, although there are limitations on who is allowed to run.

Until the serious popular and intra-regime unrest that followed the June 12, 2009, presidential election, the regime had appeared relatively stable and faced only low-level and episodic unrest from minorities, intellectuals, students, labor groups, and women. Since the elections, the regime has struggled to contain the unrest, which some believe is evolving into a revolutionary movement that will be satisfied only with the outright replacement of the regime with a secular democracy. An increasing number of Iran experts believe this opposition movement—calling itself "The Green Path of Hope"—will eventually lead to a toppling or major alteration of the current regime.

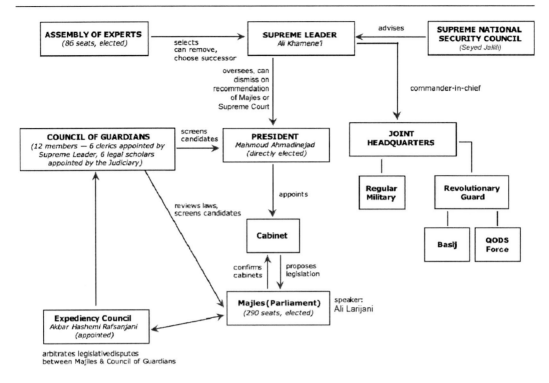

Figure 1. Structure of the Iranian Government

The Supreme Leader, His Powers, and Other Ruling Councils

Upon Khomeini's death, one of his disciples, Ayatollah Ali Khamene'i, was selected Supreme Leader by an elected 86-seat *"Assembly of Experts."*[1] Although he has never had Khomeini's undisputed authority, Khamene'i has vast formal powers as Supreme Leader that have helped him maintain his grip on power. Amid reports Khamene'I believes that major concessions to the opposition will lead to regime demise, the protest movement is nonetheless increasingly bold in denouncing him and in defying his authority. Some of his peers have criticized his handling of the protest movement, while experts say he is now almost completely dependent on regime security forces, most notably the Islamic Revolutionary Guard Corps (IRGC).

Formally, the Supreme Leader is Commander in Chief of the armed forces, giving him the power to appoint commanders and to be represented on the highest national security body, the Supreme National Security Council, composed of top military and civilian security officials. He appoints half of the 12-member *Council of Guardians*;[2] and the head of Iran's judiciary (currently Ayatollah Sadeq Larijani). Headed by Ayatollah Ahmad Jannati, the conservative-controlled Council of Guardians reviews legislation to ensure it conforms to Islamic law, and it screens election candidates and certifies elections results. The Supreme Leader also has the power, under the constitution, to remove the elected President if either the judiciary or the elected *Majles* (parliament) say the President should be removed, with cause. The Supreme Leader appoints members of the 42-member *Expediency Council*, set up in 1988 to resolve legislative disagreements between the *Majles* and the Council of Guardians but its powers were expanded in 2006 to include oversight of the executive branch (cabinet) performance. Expediency Council members serve five-year terms. The Council, appointed most recently in February 2007, is still headed by Rafsanjani; its executive officer is former Revolutionary Guard commander-in-chief Mohsen Reza'i.

The *Assembly of Experts* is empowered to oversee the work of the Supreme Leader and replace him if necessary, as well as to amend the constitution. The Assembly serves a six-year term; the fourth election for that Assembly was held on December 15, 2006. After that election, Akbar Hashemi-Rafsanjani, still a major figure having served two terms as president himself (1989- 1997), was named deputy leader of the Assembly. After the death of the leader of the Assembly, Rafsanjani was selected its head in September 2007, outpointing a harder line competitor, Ayatollah Ahmad Jannati. (See Figure 1 for a chart of the Iranian regime.)

Table 1. Major Factions and Personalities

Conservatives	
Supreme Leader Ali Khamene'i	Born in July 1939 to an Azeri (Turkic) family from Mashhad. Lost the use of his right arm in an assassination attempt in June 1981. Helped organize the Revolutionary Guard and other post-revolution security organs. Served as elected president during 1981-1989 and was selected Khomeini's successor in June 1989 upon the Ayatollah's death. Upon that selection, his religious ranking was advanced in the state-run press and official organs to "Ayatollah" from the lower predecessor, founder of the revolutionary regime Ayatollah Ruhollah Khomeini. Like Khomeini, Khamene'i generally stays out of day-to-day governmental business but saves his prestige to resolve factional disputes or to quiet popular criticism of regime performance. Has taken more interventionist role to calm ranking "Hojjat ol-Islam." Has all the formal powers but not the undisputed authority of his internal infighting in wake of June 2009 election dispute. Considered moderate- conservative on domestic policy but hardline on foreign policy and particularly toward Israel. Seeks to challenge U.S. hegemony and wants Israel defeated but respects U.S. military power and fears military confrontation with United States. Generally supports the business community (bazaaris), and opposes state control of the economy. Senior aides in his office include second son, Mojtaba, who is said to be acquiring increasing influence. Has made public reference to purported letters to him from President Obama that he asserts have asked for renewed U.S.-Iran relations.
Expediency Council and Assembly of Experts Chair Ali Akbar Hashemi-Rafsanjani	Long a key strategist of the regime, and longtime advocate of "grand bargain" to resolve all outstanding issues with United States, although on Iran's terms. A mid-ranking cleric, now leads both Expediency Council and Assembly of Experts, although generally perceived as waning in influence generally. Heads moderate-conservative faction known as Executives of Construction. Was Majles speaker during 1981-89 and President 1989- 1997. One of Iran's richest men, family owns large share of Iran's total pistachio nut production. Supported Musavi in June 2009 election, purportedly financed much of his campaign, and played behind-the-scenes role trying to persuade Supreme Leader to nullify the June 2009 election. Now considered essentially an opponent of the Supreme Leader, the arrest of five Rafsanjani family members in June 2009, may have reflected Khamene'I pressure on him. Daughter Faizah has participated in several opposition protests.
President Mahmoud Ahmadinejad	Declared re-elected on June 12, 2009, and inaugurated August 5, but results still not accepted by his election challengers and protesters. See box on page 8.
Majles Speaker Ali Larijani	Overwhelming winner for Majles seat from Qom on March 14, 2008, and selected Majles Speaker on May 25 (237 out of 290 votes). Former state broadcasting head (1994-2004) and Minister of Culture and Islamic Guidance (1993), was head of Supreme National Security Council and chief nuclear negotiator from August 2005 until October 2007 resignation. Sought to avoid U.N. Security Council isolation. Politically close to Khamene'i but highly critical of Ahmadinejad and criticized

Table 1. (Continued)

Conservatives	
	election officials for the flawed June 12, 2009, election and subsequent crackdown. However, has grown increasingly threatening against protesters as the opposition has gained strength. Brother of judiciary head.
Tehran Mayor Mohammad Baqer Qalibaf	Former Revolutionary Guard Air Force commander and police chief, but a moderate-conservative and ally of Larijani. Encourages comparisons of himself to Reza Shah, invoking an era of stability and strong leadership, while also making use of modern media tools. Lost in the 2005 presidential elections, but supporters won nine out of 15 seats on Tehran city council in December 2006 elections, propelling him to current post as mayor of Tehran. Recruited moderate conservatives for March 2008 Majles election.
Senior Clerics in Qom	The most senior clerics in Qom, including several Grand Ayatollahs, are generally "quietist"—they believe that the senior clergy should refrain from direct involvement in politics. These include Grand Ayatollah Nasser Makarem Shirazi, Grand Ayatollah (former judiciary chief) Abdol Karim Musavi-Ardabili, and Grand Ayatollah Yusuf Sanei, all of whom have criticized regime crackdown against opposition protests. Others believe in political involvement, including Ayatollah Mohammad Taqi Mesbah Yazdi. He is founder of the hardline Haqqani school, and spiritual mentor of Ahmadinejad. Fared poorly in December 2006 elections for Assembly of Experts. An assertive defender of the powers of the Supreme Leader and a proponent of an "Islamic state" rather than the current "Islamic republic," and advocates isolation from the West. May seek to replace Khamene'i. Another politically active senior cleric is Ayatollah Kazem Haeri, mentor of radical Iraqi cleric Moqtada Al Sadr.
Judiciary Chief/ Ayatollah Sadeq Larijani	Larijani named in late August 2009 as Judiciary head, replacing Ayatollah Mahmoud Shahrudi, who had headed the Judiciary since 1999. Larijani is brother of Majles Speaker Ali Larijani; both are close to the Supreme Leader. Was appointed primarily to curb Ahmadinejad's aggressive prosecutions of reformist leaders following June 2009 election dispute. Another Larijani brother, Mohammad Javad, was deputy Foreign Minister during the 1980s.
Militant Clerics Association	Longtime organization of hardline clerics headed by Ayatollah Mohammad Mahdavi-Kani. Not to be confused with an organization with almost the same name, below. Did not back Ahmadinejad in June 12 presidential elections.
Opposition/"Green Path Hope" All of the blocs and personalities below can be considered part of the Green Path of Hope opposition/revolutionary movement. However, overall leadership of the opposition is unclear, with several components competing for pre-eminence and the ability to determine the direction of the protest movement.	
Mohammad Khatemi/ Mir Hossein Musavi	Khatemi—reformist president during 1997-2005 and declared he would run again for President in June 2009 elections, but withdrew when allied reformist Mir Hossein Musavi entered the race in late March 2009. Khatemi elected May 1997, with 69% of the vote; re-elected June 2001with 77%. Rode wave of sentiment for easing social and political restrictions among students, intellectuals, youths, and women that seeks reform but not outright replace-ment of the regime, but became disillusioned with Khatemi failure to stand up to hardliners on reform issues. Now heads International Center for Dialogue Among Civilizations. Visited U.S. in September 2006 to speak at Harvard and the Washington National Cathedral on "dialogue of civilizations." Has hewed to staunch anti-Israel line of most Iranian officials, but perceived as open to accepting a Palestinian-Israeli compromise. Musavi has views similar to Khatemi on political and social freedoms and on reducing Iran's international isolation, but supports strong state intervention in the economy to benefit workers, lower classes. Khatemi supported Musavi challenge to 2009 election legitimacy. Continues to appear at some protests, sometimes intercepted or constrained by regime security agents, but may be losing ground to harder line student opposition leaders who criticize his January 2010 statements indicating regime reconciliation is possible and who want to completely replace the current system. Some Green supporters have left Iran for Europe, Asia, or the United States. Some IRGC and parliamentary hardliners continue to urge his arrest.

Table 1. (Continued)

Conservatives	
Society of Militant Clerics/Mehdi Karrubi	Reformist grouping once led by Mehdi Karrubi. Karrubi formed a separate "National Trust" faction after losing 2005 election. Ran again in 2009, but received few votes and subsequently has emerged, along with Musavi, as a symbol of the opposition.
Student Opposition Leaders/Confederation of Iranian Students/Office of Consolidation of Unity (Daftar Tahkime-Vahdat)	Staunch oppositionists and revolutionaries, many now favor replacement of the regime with secular democracy. One key bloc in this group is the Confed-eration of Iranian Students (CIS), led by Amir Abbas Fakhravar, who was jailed for five years for participating in July 1999 student riots. CIS, committed to non-violent resistance, is successor of Office of Consolidation Unity, which led those riots. CIS supports international efforts to sanction the regime. At the time of those riots, the students had been strong Khatemi supporters, but turned against him for failing to challenge hardliners, particularly after July 1999 violent crackdown on student riots, in which four students were killed. Student leaders attempting—and increasingly succeeding—in gaining support of older generation, labor, clerics, and other segments to topple regime.
Conservatives	
Islamic Iran Participation Front (IIPF).	The most prominent and best organized pro-reform grouping, but has lost political ground to more active and forceful student core of Green Path opposition movement. Its leaders include Khatemi's brother, Mohammad Reza Khatemi (a deputy speaker in the 2000-2004 Majles) and Mohsen Mirdamadi. Backed Musavi in June 12 election; several IIPF leaders, including Mirdamadi, detained and prosecuted in postelection dispute.
Mojahedin of the Islamic Revolution Organization (MIR)	Composed mainly of left-leaning Iranian figures who support state control of the economy, but want greater political pluralism and relaxation of rules on social behavior. A major constituency of the reformist camp. Its leader is former Heavy Industries Minister Behzad Nabavi, who supported Musavi in 2009 election and was remains jailed for post-election unrest.
Shirin Abadi	A number of dissidents have struggled against regime repression for many years, long before the election dispute. One major longtime dissident and human rights activist is Nobel Peace Prize laureate (2003) and Iran human rights activist lawyer Shirin Abadi. Subsequent to the passage of the U.N. General Assembly resolution above, Iranian authorities raided the Tehran office of the Center for Defenders of Human Rights, which she runs. Shehas often represented clients persecuted or prosecuted by the regime. She left Iran for Europe, fearing arrest in connection with the postelection dispute. In December 2009, the regime confiscated her Nobel Prize award.
Grand Ayatollah Hosein Ali Montazeri	Died December 20, 2009 of natural causes and has become a symbol of some oppositionists. Montazeri was Khomeini's designated successor until 1989, when Khomeini dismissed him for allegedly protecting intellectuals and opponents of clerical rule He was released in January 2003 from several years of house arrest, and, despite being under close watch, issued statements highly critical of the postelection crackdown.
Other Long Term Dissidents	Other leading dissidents have challenged the regime long before the presidential election. For example, joournalist Akbar Ganji conducted hunger strikes to protest regime oppression; he was released on schedule on March 18, 2006, after sentencing in 2001 to six years in prison for alleging high-level involvement in 1999 murders of Iranian dissident intellectuals that the regime had blamed on "rogue" security agents. Another prominent dissident is Abdol Karim Soroush, who challenged the doctrine of clerical rule. Others in this category include former Revolutionary Guard organizer Mohsen Sazegara, former Culture Minister Ataollah Mohajerani, and Mohsen Kadivar.

The Presidency/Mahmoud Ahmadinejad

The President, a position held since 2005 by Mahmoud Ahmadinejad, appoints and supervises the work of the cabinet. Cabinet appointments are subject to confirmation by the Majles (parliament), and the Supreme Leader is believed to have significant input into key security cabinet appointments, including ministers of defense, interior, and intelligence. Although subordinate to the Supreme Leader, the presidency is a coveted and intensely fought-over position which provides vast opportunities for the President to empower his political base and to affect policy.

After suffering several election defeats at the hands of President Mohammad Khatemi and the reformists in the 1997 and 2001 presidential elections, hardliners successfully moved to regain the sway they held when Khomeini was alive. Conservatives won the February 20, 2004, Majles elections (which are always held one year prior to each presidential election), although the conservative win was the result of the Council of Guardians' disqualification of 3,600 reformist candidates, including 87 Majles incumbents. That helped conservatives win 155 out of the 290 seats. The George W. Bush Administration and the Senate (S.Res. 304, adopted by unanimous consent on February 12, 2004) criticized the elections as unfair.

As the reformist faction suffered setbacks, the Council of Guardians narrowed the field of candidates for the June 2005 presidential elections to 8 out of the 1,014 persons who filed. Rafsanjani [3] was considered the favorite against several opponents more hardline than he is—three had ties to the Revolutionary Guard: Ali Larijani (see **Table 1**); Mohammad Baqer Qalibaf (see Table 1); and Tehran mayor Mahmoud Ahmadinejad. In the June 17, 2005, first round, turnout was about 63% (29.4 million votes out of 46.7 million eligible voters). With 21% and 19.5%, respectively, Rafsanjani and Ahmadinejad, who did unexpectedly well because of tacit backing from Khamene'i, moved to a runoff. Reformist candidates (Mehdi Karrubi and Mostafa Moin) fared worse than expected. Ahmadinejad won in the June 24 runoff, receiving 61.8% to Rafsanjani's 35.7%. He first took office on August 6, 2005.

Ahmadinejad's Policies and Popularity

Well before the June 2009 election unrest, Ahmadinejad had been a controversial figure for his inflammatory statements. He attracted significant world criticism for an October 26, 2005, Tehran conference entitled "A World Without Zionism" by stating that "Israel should be wiped off the map." He insisted on holding a December 2006 conference in Tehran questioning the Holocaust, a theme he has returned to several times since, including at a September 2007 speech at Columbia University. A U.N. Security Council statement and Senate and House resolutions (H.Res. 523 and S.Res. 292), passed by their respective chambers, condemned the statement. On June 21, 2007, the House passed H.Con.Res. 21, calling on the U.N. Security Council to charge Ahmadinejad with violating the 1948 Convention on the Prevention and Punishment of the Crime of Genocide; the Convention includes "direct and public incitement" to commit genocide as a punishable offense.

Even before the 2009 presidential election campaign, several Iranian leaders, and portions of the population, were expressing concern that Ahmadinejad's defiance of the international community on the nuclear issue—as well as his frequent visits and meetings with such anti-U.S. figures as Venezuela's Hugo Chavez—was isolating Iran. These perceptions contributed to a split within his conservative "Principalist" faction in the March

2008 Majles elections. Supreme Leader Khamene'i has publicly supported Ahmadinejad for refusing to bow to international demands on the nuclear issue. At other times, such as April 2009, Khamene'i has upbraided Ahmadinej ad—in this case for incorporating the position of coordinator of the Hajj (major pilgrimage to Mecca) into the Tourism Ministry; the move was reversed. Khamene'i was perceived as favoring Ahmadinej ad's reelection but, perhaps sensing that this outcome was not assured, he was publicly neutral in the campaign.

On economic matters, many Iranians criticized Ahmadinejad for raising some wages and lowering interest rates for poorer borrowers, cancelling some debts of farmers, and increasing some social welfare payments. These moves fed inflation, but poorer Iranians saw Ahmadinejad as attentive to their economic plight and this support appears to have been key to his reelection. Iranian economists say that these programs began to deplete Iran's reserve fund ("Oil Stabilization Fund," which had been as high as about $10 billion) even when oil prices were high in mid-2008, leaving Iran now unable to cope with the fall in oil prices. Others say he has not moved to curb the dependence on oil revenues, which account for about 20% of Iran's gross domestic product (GDP). On the other hand, he has attempted to persuade the Majles to pass legislation to greatly reduce state subsidies.

Major economic sectors or markets are controlled by the quasi-statal "foundations" (*bonyads*), run by powerful former officials, and there are special trading privileges for them and the bazaar merchants, a key constituency for some conservatives. The same privileges—and more— reportedly apply to businesses run by the Revolutionary Guard, as discussed below, leading to criticism that the Guard is using its political influence to win business contracts.

Ahmadinejad has generally been opposed by affluent and educated urbanites. Even before the post June 2009 election unrest, educated, urban sentiment against him was evident in several student protests against him. The most recent of these, prior to the June 12 election, was in late February 2009, when authorities tried to rebury on Amir Kabir University of Technology grounds the bodies of some killed in the Iran-Iraq war.

June 12, 2009, Presidential Elections

The opposition movement grew out of severe disappointment and suspicion of fraud in the June 12, 2009, presidential election. Prospects for reformists to unseat Ahmadinejad seemed to brighten in February 2009, when Khatemi—who is still highly popular among reform-minded Iranians—said that he would run. However, on March 18, 2009, Khatemi withdrew from the race in favor of another reformist, former Prime Minister Mir Hossein Musavi. Musavi was viewed as somewhat less divisive—and therefore more acceptable to the Supreme Leader—because Musavi had served as Prime Minister during the 1980-88 Iran-Iraq war. Khatemi backed Musavi enthusiastically.

Table 2. Factions in the Eighth Majles (Elected March 14-April 25, 2008)

Pro-Ahmadinejad Conservatives (United Front of Principalists)	117
Anti-Ahmadinejad Conservatives (Coalition of Principalists)	53
Reformists (39 seats in seventh Majles)	46
Independents	71
Seats annulled or voided	3

> **MAHMOUD AHMADINEJAD**
>
> First non-cleric to be president of the Islamic republic since the assassination of then president Mohammad Ali Rajai in August 1981. About 56, he asserts he is a "man of the people," the son of a blacksmith who lives in modest circumstances, who would promote the interests of the poor and return government to the original principles of the Islamic revolution. Has burnished that image as president through regular visits to poor areas and through subsidies directed at the lower classes. His official biography says he served with the "special forces" of the Revolutionary Guard, and he served subsequently (late 1980s) as a deputy provincial governor. Has been part of the "Isargaran" faction composed of former Guard and Basij (volunteer popular forces) leaders and other hardliners. U.S. intelligence reportedly determined he was not one of the holders of the 52 American hostages during November 1979-January 1981. Other accounts say Ahmadinejad believes his mission is to prepare for the return of the 12th Imam—Imam Mahdi—whose return from occultation would, according to Twelver Shiite doctrine, be accompanied by the establishment of Islam as the global religion. Earned clerical criticism in May 2008 for again invoking intervention by Imam Mahdi in present day state affairs. Regularly attends U.N. General Assembly sessions in New York each September. In an October 2006 address, Ahmadinejad said, "I have a connection with God." Sent letter of congratulation to President-elect Barack Obama for his election victory, but has only tepidly responded to subsequent Obama Administration outreach initiatives. Following limited recount, declared winner of June 12, 2009, election. Many diplomats walked out on or did not attend Ahmadinejad's speech before the U.N. General Assembly on September 23, 2009.

A total of about 500 candidates for the June 12, 2009, presidential elections registered their names during May 5-10, 2009. The Council of Guardians decide on the final candidates on May 20— permitting only four to run: Ahmadinejad, Musavi, Mehdi Karrubi, and Mohsen Reza'i. The Interior Ministry, which runs the election, also instituted during this campaign season a series of one-on-one debates among the candidates, which were acrimonious, including Ahmadinejad's accusations of corruption against Rafsanjani and against Musavi's wife. If no candidate received more than 50% of the vote on June 12, there would have been a runoff one week later.

The challengers and their backgrounds and platforms were:

- Mir Hosein Musavi. The main reformist candidate. Non-cleric. About 67. Architect and disciple of Ayatollah Khomeini, he served as Foreign Minister (1980), then Prime Minister (1981-89), at which time he successfully managed the state rationing program during the privations of the Iran-Iraq war but often feuded with Khamene'i, who was then President. At that time, he was an advocate of state control of the economy. His post was abolished in the 1989 revision of the constitution. Later moderated his views, including the need to avoid confrontation with the international community, but publicly opposed— and continues to oppose—U.N.-demanded curbs on Iran's nuclear program. Musavi's campaign made extensive use of his high profile wife, Zahra Rahnevard, a well-known women's activist and professor.

- Mehdi Karrubi. Some feared he might split the reformist vote because of his attentiveness to economic policies that favor the lower classes, but official results showed him a minor factor in the voting.
- Mohsen Reza'i. As noted above, he was Commander in Chief of the Revolutionary Guard for almost all of the Iran-Iraq war period. About 58 years old, he is considered an anti-Ahmadinejad conservative. Reza'i dropped out just prior to the 2005 presidential election due to perceived insufficient support, and he apparently did not build substantial support since then. He attended Khamene'i's June 19, 2009, speech and later dropped his formal challenge of the election results, but he criticized elements of the government crackdown.

Election Dispute and Aftermath

The outcome of the election was always difficult to foresee. Polling results were inconsistent. Musavi supporters held large rallies in Tehran, but pro-Ahmadinejad rallies were large as well. During the campaign, Khamene'i met with Musavi and, in mid-May 2009, visited Musavi's father at his home, suggesting neutrality, although the two were often at odds during the Iran-Iraq war, when Khamene'i was President and Musavi was Prime Minister. Turnout was high at about 85%; 39.1 million valid (and invalid) votes were cast. The Interior Ministry announced two hours after the polls closed that Ahmadinejad had won, although in the past results have been announced the day after. The totals were announced on Saturday, June 13, 2009, as follows:

Ahmadinejad: 24.5 million votes—62.6% Musavi: 13.2 million votes—33.75% Reza'i: 678,000 votes—1.73%

Invalid: 409,000 votes—1%

Karrubi: 333,600 votes—0.85%

Almost immediately after the results were announced, Musavi supporters began protesting the results on June 13, as he, Karrubi, and Reza'i, asserted outright fraud and called for a new election, citing the infeasibility of counting 40 million votes so quickly; the barring of candidate observers at many polling stations; regime shut-down of Internet and text services; and repression of postelection protests. Khamene'i declared the results a "divine assessment," appearing to certify the results even though formal procedures require a three day complaint period. While several outside analysts say the results appeared to represent widespread fraud.[4], others said the announced results tracked preelection polls and reflected Ahmadinejad's perceived strong support in rural areas and among the urban poor.

Protests built throughout June 13-19, large in Tehran but also held in other cities, exposing regime divisions and posing the most significant threat to the regime's grip on power to date. Security forces used varying amounts of force to control them, causing 27 protester deaths for the period of active protests, according to official Iranian statements (with figures from opposition groups running over 100). The protesters' hopes of having Khamene'i annul the election were dashed by his major Friday prayer sermon on June 19 in which he refuted allegations of vast fraud and threatened a crackdown on further protests. Such a crackdown was evident on Saturday, June 20, with state media reporting at least 10 protesters killed that day.

Protests lessened by June 22, but continued sporadically thereafter, including on the July 9 anniversary of the suppression of the 1999 student riots; the August 5, 2009, official inauguration of Ahmadinejad; and September 18 "Jerusalem Day." The sporadic nature of the protests created the impression that the regime would gain the upper hand. However, the opposition has proved resilient, making use of Internet-based sites (Facebook, Twitter) and timing their demonstrations to official holidays when people can gather easily. The most recent demonstrations have been large and marked by resistance to the security forces as well as the spreading to smaller cities and the involvement of older generation and even religious persons. These were the hallmarks of protests on November 4, 2009, the 30th anniversary of the takeover of the U.S. embassy in Tehran, and particularly on the occasion of the Ashura Shiite holy day (December 27, 2009, which also marked the seventh day since the death of Ayatollah Montazeri, a major critic of Khamene'i). On December 27, some anti-riot police are said to have refused to beat protesters.

The regime, particularly the Supreme Leaders, at first tried to at least appear to address complaints about the election and the crackdown. On June 29, 2009, the Council of Guardians performed a televised recount of 10% of the votes of Tehran's districts and some provincial ballots and, finding no irregularities, certified the results. Musavi and Karrubi, joined by Khatemi, have continued to call the election fraudulent. In response to complaints even by hardline clerics about the amount of force used against the protests, in late July Khamene'i ordered 140 more released and a prison closed (Khazirak) where some protesters purportedly died or were beaten in custody. In December 2009, however, regime leaders and parliamentarians have increasingly threatened arrests of senior opposition leaders and even executions of protesters. Some regime officials are said to believe that the hardening of anti-opposition tactics has caused the opposition to radicalize into a revolutionary movement that will not reconcile with the regime.

How Shaken and Divided Is the Regime?

Some say that the most serious effects have been the exposure and widening of cracks within the regime, the most serious internal rift in Iran since the early 1 980s. The composition of the regime has narrowed significantly—reformists and even some senior clerics have left the regime fold and are now supporting the opposition. Senior longtime regime stalwart Rafsanjani, discussed extensively above, is backing the Green movement, and he and others did not attend

Ahmadinej ad's inauguration. In a speech on December 6, 2009, he criticized the use of the Basij and IRGC against unarmed civilians. Larijani, Qalibaf, and several senior Ayatollahs in Qom, such as Grand Ayatollah Yusuf Sanei, Grand Ayatollah Abdol Karim Musavi Ardabili, and the Association of Researchers and Teachers of Qom Seminary, have also criticized the use of violence against the protesters. Others of the most senior clerics appeared to lean toward that position as well.

U.S. and Allied Reaction

The burgeoning unrest has complicated policy for President Obama, who has tried to balance non-interference in Iranian affairs (a sensitive issue in Iran)—and preserve the possibility of a nuclear deal with Iran—with calls for him to focus entirely on pressuring the regime. Some believe that President Obama might have missed, or is missing, an opportunity to bring the regime down by siding more decisively with the opposition movement. As the crackdown has progressed, the statements of President Obama and other U.S. officials have become progressively more critical of the regime. Some presidential statements appear to have been influenced, to some extent by House and Senate passage of resolutions on June 19 (H.Res. 560 and S.Res. 193, respectively), condemning violence against demonstrators and the government's suppression of electronic communication. Another resolution passed by the Senate that day, S.Res. 196, calling on the Iranian regime to permit free expression, free speech, and a free press. On December 23, 2009, the Senate passed S.Res. 386, condemning Iran's use of violence against the demonstrators and its use of Internet censorship and monitoring to counter the opposition. Other legislation, such as the "Voice Act" (Subtitle D of the FY20 10 Defense Authorization, P.L. 111-84), contain provisions to potentially penalize companies that are selling Iran technology equipment that it can use to suppress or monitor the Internet usage of Iranians.[5] On December 28, 2009, President Obama continued to shift toward public support for the opposition outright by saying, in regard to the unrest in Iran, "Along with all free nations, the United States stands with those who seek their universal rights."[6]

Several European governments, such as France, Britain, and Germany, were even more critical of Iran's crackdown than was the United States. A joint statement of the July 8-9, 2009, G-8 summit meeting, held in Italy, deplored Iran's treatment of protesters but also renewed the call for diplomacy with Iran on the nuclear issue.

Exiled Opposition Groups

Some groups have been committed to the replacement of the regime virtually since its inception, and remain mostly in exile. Their linkages to the Green Path movement are unclear, and some indications are these movements want to dominate any coalition that might topple the current regime.

People's Mojahedin Organization of Iran (PMOI)/Camp Ashraf

One of the best known exiled opposition groups is the People's Mojahedin Organization of Iran (PMOI).[7] Secular and left-leaning, it was formed in the 1960s to try to overthrow the Shah of Iran and advocated Marxism blended with Islamic tenets. It allied with pro-Khomeini forces during the Islamic revolution and supported the November 1979 takeover of the U.S. Embassy in Tehran but was later driven into exile. Even though it is an opponent of Tehran, since the late 1 980s the State Department has refused contact with the PMOI and its umbrella organization, the National Council of Resistance (NCR). The State Department designated the PMOI as a foreign terrorist organization (FTO) in October 1997[8] and the NCR was named as an alias of the PMOI in the October 1999 re-designation. The FTO designation was prompted by PMOI attacks in Iran that sometimes kill or injure civilians—although the group does not appear to purposely target civilians. In August 14, 2003, the State Department designated the NCR offices in the United States an alias of the PMOI, and NCR and Justice Department authorities closed down those offices. The regime accuses the group of involvement in the post June 2009 presidential election violence.

The State Department report on international terrorism for 2007 asserts that the organization— and not just a radical element of the organization as the group asserts—was responsible for the alleged killing of seven American defense advisers to the former Shah in

1975-1976. The report again notes the group's promotion of women in its ranks and again emphasizes the group's "cult- like" character, including indoctrination of its members and separation of family members, including children, from its activists. The group's alliance with Saddam Hussein's regime in the 1 980s and 1 990s has contributed to the U.S. shunning of the organization.

Some advocate that the United States not only remove the group from the FTO list but also enter an alliance with the group against Iran. The FTO designation was up for formal review in October 2008, and, in July 2008, the PMOI formally petitioned to the State Department that its designation be revoked, on the grounds that it renounced any use of terrorism in 2001. However, the State Department announced in mid-January 2009 that the group would remain listed; the next review of the FTO list is in October 2009.

The group is trying to build on recent legal successes in Europe; on January 27, 2009, the European Union (EU) removed the group from its terrorist group list; the group had been so designated by the EU in 2002. In May 2008, a British appeals court determined that the group should no longer be considered a terrorist organization on the grounds that the British government did not provide "any reliable evidence that supported a conclusion that PMOI retained an intention to resort to terrorist activities in the future." Currently, the governments that still list the group as a "terrorist organization," include the United States, Canada, Australia. In June 2003, France arrested about 170 PMOI members, including its co-leader Maryam Rajavi (wife of PMOI founder Masoud Rajavi, whose whereabouts are unknown). She was released and remains based in France, and is occasionally received by European parliamentarians and other politicians.

The issue of group members in Iraq is increasingly pressing. U.S. forces attacked PMOI military installations in Iraq during Operation Iraqi Freedom and negotiated a ceasefire with PMOI military elements in Iraq, requiring the approximately 3,400 PMOI fighters to remain confined to their Ashraf camp near the border with Iran. Its weaponry is in storage, guarded by U.S. personnel. In July 2004, the United States granted the Ashraf detainees "protected persons" status under the 4th Geneva Convention, meaning they will not be extradited to Tehran or forcibly expelled as long as U.S. forces have a mandate to help secure Iraq. Another 200 PMOI fighters have taken advantage of an arrangement between Iran and the ICRC for them to return to Iran if they disavow further PMOI activities; none are known to have been persecuted since returning.

The U.S.-led security mandate in Iraq was replaced on January 1, 2009, by a bilateral U.S.-Iraq agreement that limits U.S. flexibility in Iraq. The group fears that, now that Iraqi forces have taken control of the camp, Iraq will expel the group to Iran. The Iraqi government tried to calm those fears in January 2009 by saying that it would adhere to all international obligations not do so, but that trust was lost on July 27, 2009, when it set up a police post in the Camp, which was resisted by PMOI residents. The PMOI says about a dozen were killed in the clashes. Some observers say Iraq might move the camp to Iraq's interior, away from the Iran border. The EU "de-listing" might help resolve the issue by causing EU governments to take in those at Ashraf. In December 2009, Iraq announced the group would be relocated to a detention center near Samawah, in southern Iraq; substantial resistance by the Ashraf residents is expected if and when Iraq attempts to implement that decision.

Other Armed Groups

Some armed groups are operating in Iran's border areas, and are generally composed of ethnic or religious minorities. One such group is *Jundullah*, composed of Sunni Muslims primarily from the Baluchistan region bordering Pakistan. Since mid-2008, it has conducted several successful attacks on Iranian security personnel, apparently including in May 2009, claiming revenge for the poor treatment of Sunnis in Iran. On October 18, 2009, it claimed responsibility for killing five Revolutionary Guard commanders during a meeting they were holding with local groups in Sistan va Baluchistan Province.

An armed Kurdish group operating out of Iraq is the Free Life Party, known by its acronym PJAK. PJAK was designated in early February 2009 as a terrorism supporting entity under Executive order 13224, although the designation statement indicated the decision was based mainly on PJAK's association with the Turkish Kurdish opposition group Kongra Gel, also known as the PKK. Another militant group, the "*Ahwazi Arabs*," operates in the largely Arab inhabited areas of southwest Iran, bordering Iraq.

The Son of the Former Shah

Some Iranian exiles, as well as some elites still in Iran, want to replace the regime with a constitutional monarchy led by Reza Pahlavi, the U.S.-based son of the late former Shah and a U.S.-trained combat pilot. In January 2001, the Shah's son, who is about 54 years old, ended a long period of inactivity by giving a speech in Washington, DC, calling for unity in the opposition and the institution of a constitutional monarchy and democracy in Iran. He has since broadcast messages into Iran from Iranian exile-run stations in California,[9] and delivered a statement condemning the regime for the post-2009 election crackdown. He does not appear to have large- scale support inside Iran, but he may be trying to capitalize on the opposition's growing popularity. In January 2010, he called for international governments to withdraw their representation from Tehran.

Other Outside Activists

Numerous Iranians-Americans in the United States want to see a change of regime in Tehran. Many of them are based in California, where there is a large Iranian-American community, and there are about 25 small-scale radio or television stations that broadcast into Iran. While many Iranian-Americans protested Ahmadinej ad's visit to the United Nations in September 2009, and many others sport green bracelets indicating sympathy with the Green movement, it is not clear the degree to which Iranian-American or other Iranians outside Iran are in touch with oppositionists inside Iran or are influencing events in Iran.

Some organizations, such as The National Iranian American Council (NIAC) and the Public Affairs Alliance of Iranian-Americans (PAAIA), are not necessarily seeking change within Iran. The mission of NIAC, composed largely of Iranian-Americans, is to promote discussion of U.S. policy and the group has advocated engagement with Iran. PAAIA's mission is to discuss issues affecting Iranian-Americans, such as discrimination caused by public perceptions of association with terrorism or radical Islam.

Table 3. Human Rights Practices

Group/Issue	Regime Practice/Recent Developments
Ethnic and Religious Breakdown	Persians are about 51% of the population, and Azeris (a Turkic people) are about 24%. Kurds are about 7% of the population, and about 3% are Arab. Of religions, Shiite Muslims are about 90% of the Muslim population and Sunnis are about 10%. About 2% of the population is non-Muslim, including Christians, Zoroastrians (an ancient religion in what is now Iran), Jewish, and Baha'i.
Media	Since 2000, judicial hardliners have closed hundreds of reformist newspapers, although many have tended to reopen under new names. Even before the election-related unrest, Iran blocked proreform websites and blogs supportive of the reformist candidates. In August 2007, the government closed a major reformist daily, *Shargh*, which had previously been suspended repeatedly. In February 2008, the regime closed the main women's magazine, Zanan (women in Farsi) for allegedly highlighting gender inequality in Islamic law. In November 2008, the regime arrested famed Iranian blogger Hossein Derakshan. Canadian journalist (of Iranian origin) Zahra Kazemi was detained in 2003 for filming outside Tehran's Evin prison and allegedly beaten to death in custody. The intelligence agent who conducted the interrogation/beating was acquitted July 25, 2004.
Labor Unions/ Students/ Other Activists	Independent unions are technically legal but not allowed in practice. The sole authorized national labor organization is a state-controlled "Workers' House" umbrella. However, some activists show independence and, in 2007, the regime arrested labor activists for teachers' associations, bus drivers' unions, and a bakery workers' union. A bus drivers union leader, Mansur Osanloo, has been in jail since July 2007. The regime reportedly also dissolved student unions and replaced them with regime loyalists following student criticism of Ahmadinejad. In September 2008, Iran arrested several HIV/AIDs researchers for alleged anti-government activities.
Women	Regime strictly enforcing requirement that women fully cover themselves in public, generally with a garment called a *chador*, including through detentions. In March 2007, the regime arrested 31 women activists who were protesting the arrest in 2006 of several other women's rights activists; all but 3 of the 31 were released by March 9. In May 2006, the Majles passed a bill calling for increased public awareness of Islamic dress, an apparent attempt to persuade women not to wear Western fashion. The bill did not contain a requirement that members of Iran's minority groups wear badges or distinctive clothing. In April 2006, Ahmadinejad directed that women be allowed to attend soccer matches, but the Supreme Leader reversed that move. Women can vote and run in parliamentary and municipal elections. Iranian women can drive, and many work outside the home, including owning their own businesses. There are 9 women in the 290-seat Majles.
Religious Freedom	Each year since 1999, the State Department religious freedom report has named Iran as a "Country of Particular Concern" under the International Religious Freedom Act. No sanctions added, on the grounds that Iran is already subject to extensive U.S. sanctions. Continued deterioration in religious freedom noted in the International Religious Freedom report for 2000 (October 26, 2009).
Baha'is	Iran repeatedly cited for repression of the Baha'i community, which Iran's Shiite Muslim clergy views as a heretical sect. It numbers about 300,000 – 350,000. The State Department cited Iran on February 13, 2009, for charging seven Bahai's with espionage; thirty other Bahai's remain imprisoned. In the 1990s, several Baha'is were executed for apostasy (Bahman Samandari in 1992; Musa Talibi in 1996; and Ruhollah Ruhani in 1998). Another, Dhabihullah Mahrami, was in custody since 1995 and died of unknown causes in prison in December 2005. A wave of Baha'i arrests occurred in May 2006 and two-thirds of university students of the Baha'i faith were expelled from university in 2007. Several congressional resolutions have condemned Iran's treat-ment of the Baha'is, including in 1982, 1984, 1988, 1990, 1992, 1994, 1996, 2000, and 2006. In the 110th Congress, H.Res. 1008 condemned Iran's treatment of the Baha'is (passed House August 1, 2008).

Table 3. (Continued)

Jews	Along with Christians, a "recognized minority," with one seat in the Majles, the 30,000-member Jewish community (the largest in the Middle East aside from Israel) enjoys somewhat more freedoms than Jewish communities in several other Muslim states. However, in practice the freedom of Iranian Jews to practice their religion is limited, and Iranian Jews remain reluctant to speak out for fear of reprisals. During 1993-1998, Iran executed five Jews allegedly spying for Israel. In June 1999, Iran arrested 13 Jews (mostly teachers, shopkeepers, and butchers) from the Shiraz area that it said were part of an "espionage ring" for Israel. After an April-June 2000 trial, ten of the Jews and two Muslims accomplices were convicted (July 1, 2000), receiving sentences ranging from 4 to 13 years. An appeals panel reduced the sentences, and all were released by April 2003. On November 17, 2008, Iran hanged businessman Ali Ashtari (a Muslim), who was arrested in 2006, for allegedly providing information on Iran's nuclear program to Israel.
Sunnis	The cited reports note other discrimination against Sufis and Sunni Muslims, although abuses against Sunnis could reflect that minority ethnicities, including Kurds, are mostly Sunnis. No reserved seats for Sunnis in the *Majles* but several are usually elected in their own right.
Human Trafficking	The June 16, 2009, (latest annual), State Department "Trafficking in Persons" report continues to place Iran in Tier 3 (worst level) for failing to take action to prevent trafficking in persons. Girls are trafficked for sexual exploitation within Iran and from Iran to neighboring countries.
Executions/ Juvenile Executions	Human rights groups say executions have increased sharply since the dispute over the June 2009 election. A Kurdish activist was executed in November 2009 for opposition activities. Iran executed six persons under the age of 18 in 2008, the only country to do so. As a party to the International Covenant on Civil and Political Rights and the Convention on the Rights of the Child, Iran is obligated to abolish such executions.
Stonings	In 2002, the head of Iran's judiciary issued a ban on stoning. However, Iranian officials later called that directive "advisory" and could be ignored by individual judges. On December 2, 2008, Iran confirmed the stoning deaths of two men in Mashhad who were convicted of adultery.
Azeris	Azeris are one quarter of the population, but they complain of ethnic and linguistic discrimination. In 2008, there were several arrests of Azeri students and cultural activists who were pressing for their right to celebrate their culture and history.
Arrests of Dual Nationals and Foreign Nationals	An Iranian-American journalist, Roxanna Saberi, was arrested in January 2009 allegedly because her press credentials had expired; she was charged on April 9, 2009, with espionage, apparently for possessing an Iranian military document. Sentenced to eight years in jail, she was released on appeal on May 12, 2009, but barred from practicing journalism, and has left Iran. Another dual national, Esha Momeni, arrested in October 2008, is unable to leave Iran. U.S. national, former FBI agent Robert Levinson, remains missing after a visit in 2005 to Kish Island. Iran was given a U.S. letter on these cases at a March 31, 2009, meeting in the Netherlands on Afghanistan. Three American hikers remain under detention in Iran; they were arrested in August 2009 after crossing into Iran, possibly mistakenly, from a hike in northern Iraq.

Sources: Most recent State Department reports on human rights (February 25, 2009), trafficking in persons (June 16, 2009), and on religious freedom (October 26, 2009). http://www.state.gov.

HUMAN RIGHTS PRACTICES

The sections below discuss various aspects of Iran's human rights record. **Table 3** discusses the regime's record on a number of human rights issues and its repression of certain groups. The table is based largely on the latest State Department human rights report (released February 25, 2009) and the 2009 State Department "International Religious

Freedom" report (released October 26, 2009). These reports cite Iran for widespread serious abuses, including unjust executions, politically motivated abductions by security forces, torture, arbitrary arrest and detention, and arrests of women's rights activists. The State Department human rights reports said the government's "poor human rights record worsened" during 2008. An October 1, 2008, report on Iran by the U.N. Secretary General became the basis of a U.N. General Assembly resolution, finalized on December 18, 2008, by a vote of 69-54, calling on Iran to allow visits by U.N. personnel investigating the status of human rights practices in Iran.

IRAN'S STRATEGIC CAPABILITIES AND WEAPONS OF MASS DESTRUCTION PROGRAMS

Many in the Obama Administration view Iran, as the Bush Administration did, as one of the key national security challenges facing the United States.[10] This assessment is based largely on Iran's weapons of mass destruction (WMD) programs—and particularly in light of revelations in September 2009 that Iran is building at least one more nuclear site than it had previously declared—and its ability to exert influence in the region counter to U.S. objectives.[11] Many experts agree that Iran's core national security goals are to protect itself from foreign, primarily U.S., interference or attack, and to exert regional influence that Iran believes is commensurate with its size and concept of nationhood. On the other hand, some see the internal unrest as distracting Iranian leaders from exerting influence outside Iran and from making key decisions that might be needed to further accelerate WMD programs.

Conventional Military/Revolutionary Guard/Qods Force

Iran's armed forces are extensive but they are widely considered relatively combat ineffective against a well-trained, sophisticated military such as that of the United States or a regional power such as Turkey, and Iran lacks the logistical ability to project power much beyond its borders. Still, Iranian forces could still cause damage to U.S. forces and allies in the Gulf region, and they are sufficiently effective to deter or fend off conventional threats from Iran's weaker neighbors such as post-war Iraq, Turkmenistan, Azerbaijan, and Afghanistan. Iran's armed forces have few formal relationships with foreign militaries, but Iran and India have a "strategic dialogue" and some Iranian naval officers reportedly have undergone some training in India. Iran and Turkey agreed in principle in April 2008 to jointly fight terrorism along their border. Most of Iran's other military-to-military relationships, such as with Russia, Ukraine, Belarus, North Korea, and a few others, generally center on Iranian arms purchases or upgrades.

Iran's armed forces are divided organizationally. The Islamic Revolutionary Guard Corps (IRGC, known in Persian as the *Pasdaran*)[12] controls the *Basij* (Mobilization of the Oppressed) volunteer militia that enforces adherence to Islamic customs and has been the main instrument to repress the postelection protests in Iran. The IRGC and the regular military report to a Joint Headquarters, headed by Hassan Firuzabadi. In line with some congressional and Administration ideas to try to weaken the IRGC by addressing its vulnerabilities, a provision of the National Defense Authorization Act for FY2010 (Section 1224, P.L. 111-84) calls for a report on Iran's conventional military strategy and power, in particular the capabilities of the IRGC.

Table 4. The Revolutionary Guard

The IRGC is generally loyal to Iran's hardliners politically and is clearly more politically influential than is Iran's regular military, which is numerically larger but was held over from the Shah's era. Its influence has, by all accounts, grown sharply over the past few years as the regime has relied on it to suppress dissent. As described in a 2009 Rand Corporation study, " Founded by a decree from Ayatollah Khomeini shortly after the victory of the 1978-1979 Islamic Revolution, Iran's Islamic Revolutionary Guards Corps (IRGC) has evolved well beyond its original foundations as an ideological guard for the nascent revolutionary regime. Today the IRGC functions as an expansive socio-political-economic conglomerate whose influence extends into virtually every corner of Iranian political life and society. Bound together by the shared experience of war and the socializa-tion of military service, the Pasdaran have articulated a populist, authoritarian, and assertive vision for the Islamic Republic of Iran that they maintain is a more faithful reflection of the revolution's early ideals. The IRGC's presence is particularly powerful in Iran's highly factionalized political system, in which [many senior figures] hail from the ranks of the IRGC. Outside the political realm, the IRGC oversees a robust apparatus of media resources, training activities, education programs designed to bolster loyalty to the regime, prepare the citizenry for homeland defense, and burnish its own institutional credibility vis-a-vis other factional actors. It is in the economic sphere, however, that the IRGC has seen the greatest growth and diversification—strategic industries and commercial services ranging from dam and pipeline construction to automobile manufacturing and laser eye surgery have fallen under its sway, along with a number of illicit smuggling and black market enterprises."
Through its Qods (Jerusalem) Force, the IRGC has a foreign policy role in exerting influence throughout the region by supporting pro-Iranian movements, as discussed further below. The Qods Force numbers approximately 10,000-15,000 personnel who provide advice, support, and arrange weapons deliveries to pro-Iranian factions in Lebanon, Iraq, Persian Gulf states, Gaza/West Bank, Afghanistan, and Central Asia. It also operates a worldwide intelligence network to give Iran possible terrorist option and to assist in procurement of WMD-related technology. The Qods Force commander, Brig. Gen. Qassem Soleimani, is said to have his own independent channel to Supreme Leader Khamene'i, bypassing the IRGC and Joint Staff command structure. The Qods Force commander during 1988-1995 was Brig. Gen. Ahmad Vahidi, confirmed as Defense Minister on September 3, 2009. He led the unit during several major initiatives such as its alleged assistance to two bombings of Israeli and Jewish targets in Buenos Aires (the 1994 bombing he is wanted by Interpol for a role in it; the buildup of Lebanese Hezbollah's rocket capabilities; the recruitment of Saudi Hezbollah activists later accused of the June 1996 Khobar Towers bombing; and the assassination of Iranian dissident leaders in Europe in the early 1990s.
IRGC leadership developments are significant because of the political influence of the IRGC. On September 2, 2007, Khamene'i replaced Rahim Safavi with Mohammad Ali Jafari as Commander In Chief of the Guard; Jafari is considered a hardliner against political dissent and is reputedly close to the Supreme Leader and less so to Ahmadinejad. The *Basij* reports to the IRGC Commander in Chief; its leadership was changed in October 2009, to Brig. Gen. Mohammad Reza Naqdi (replacing Hossein Taeb). It operates from thousands of positions in Iran's institutions. Command reshuffles in July 2008 that integrated the Basij more closely with provincially-based IRGC units furthered the view that the Basij is playing a more active role in uncovering suspected plotting by Iran's minorities and others. In November 2009, the regime gave the IRGC's intelligence units greater authority, perhaps surpassing those of the Ministry of Intelligence, in monitoring dissent. More information on how the Iranian military might perform against the United States is discussed later. The IRGC Navy now has responsibility to patrol the entire Persian Gulf, and that the regular Navy is patrolling the Strait of Hormuz and Gulf of Oman.
As noted, the IRGC is also increasingly involved in Iran's economy, acting through a network of contracting businesses it has set up, most notably *Ghorb* (also called *Khatem ol-Anbiya*, Persian for "Seal of the Prophet"). Active duty IRGC senior commanders reportedly serve on Ghorb's board of directors. In late September 2009, the Guard boutht a 50% stake in Iran Telecommunication Company at a cost of \$7.8 billion. In the past five years, Guard affiliated firms have won 750 oil and gas and construction contracts, and the Guard has its own civilian port facilities (New York Times, September 29, 2009). On October 21, 2007, the Treasury Department designated several IRGC companies as proliferation entities under Executive Order 13382. Also that day, the IRGC as a whole, the Ministry of Defense, several IRGC commanders, and several Iranian banks were sanctioned under that same executive order. Simultaneously, the Qods Force was named as a terrorism supporting entity under Executive Order 13224. Both orders freeze the U.S.-based assets and prevent U.S. transactions with the named entities, but these entities are believed to have virtually no U.S.-based assets that could be frozen. The designations stopped short of concurring with provisions of bills in the 110th Congress—H.R. 1400 (passed by the House on September 25), S. 970, and the FY2008 defense authorization bill (P.L. 110-181, Senate amendment adopted September 6, 2007, by vote of 76-22)— for the Revolutionary Guard to be designated a foreign terrorist organization, or FTO. **Sources:** Frederic Wehrey et al. "The Rise of the Pasdaran." Rand Corporation. 2009. Katzman, Kenneth. "The Warriors of Islam: Iran's Revolutionary Guard." Westview Press, 1993.

Nuclear Program and Related International Diplomacy

Since 2005, Iran and the international community have been seeking to limit Iran's nuclear program. U.S. officials say they are operating under the assumption that Iran intends to develop a nuclear weapon from that program. Then International Atomic Energy Agency (IAEA) Director Mohammad El Baradei[13] said in a press interview on June 17, 2009, that "My gut feeling is that Iran definitely would like to have the technology ... that would enable it to have nuclear weapons if they decided to do so." In February 2009, the Director of National Intelligence (DNI) Dennis Blair reiterated previous assessments that it is likely that Iran will eventually try to develop a nuclear weapon. These assessments were given additional weight on September 25, 2009, when President Obama and French and British leaders revealed purported longstanding intelligence that Iran is developing a uranium enrichment site on a Revolutionary Guard base near Qom that appears unsuitable for purely civilian use. Iran had formally notified the IAEA of the site in prior days and asserted that, because the site was not operational, the site was not a violation of its Safeguards Agreement with the IAEA, although IAEA and U.S. officials maintain this violates agreed reporting requirements of Iran.

The Obama Administration faces policy choices in light of IAEA reports (February 19, 2009) that Iran has now enriched enough uranium for a nuclear weapon, although only if enriched to 90%. An IAEA report of June 5, 2009, reiterated that Iran's enrichment thus far has been 5%, which is a level that would permit only civilian uses, but added that Iran has now installed over 7,000 centrifuges, of which over 5,000 are being fed with uranium feedstock. There continues to be no evidence that Iran has diverted any nuclear material for a nuclear weapons program, but the IAEA asserts that it cannot verify that Iran's current program is purely peaceful. Several of its reports (January 31, 2006, February 27, 2006, May 26, 2008, and September 15, 2008) describe Iranian documents that show a possible involvement of Iran's military in the program.

Some U.S. officials, including Secretary of Defense Gates, have signaled less urgency, saying on March 1, 2009, that Iran is "not close" to a nuclear weapon. The George W. Bush Administration's December 2007 NIE assessed that Iran will likely be technically capable of producing enough highly enriched uranium for a nuclear weapon some time during 2010-2015. This time frame was reiterated in February 12, 2009, testimony by Director of National Intelligence Dennis Blair and by him again since then.[14] Because of the Qom site revelation, it is no longer clear that Iran's weaponization efforts are on hold, as the 2007 NIE had said they have been (since 2003). On the other hand, some experts say that there has been some slowdown in Iran's program in recent months, possibly due to the turmoil resulting from the domestic unrest, and/or technical difficulties.

Iran's Arguments and the International Response

International scrutiny of Iran's nuclear program intensified in 2002, when Iran confirmed PMOI allegations that Iran was building two facilities that could potentially be used to produce fissile material useful for a nuclear weapon: a uranium enrichment facility at Natanz and a heavy water production plant at Arak,[15] considered ideal for the production of plutonium. It was revealed in 2003 that the founder of Pakistan's nuclear weapons program, A.Q. Khan, sold Iran nuclear technology and designs.[16]

Iranian leaders have addressed the scrutiny by saying that Iran's nuclear program is for electricity generation and that enrichment is its "right" as a party to the NPT. Iran professes that WMD is inconsistent with its ideology and says that its leaders, including the late Ayatollah Khomeini, have issued formal pronouncements (*fatwas*) that nuclear weapons are un-Islamic. Iran says its oil resources are finite and that enriching uranium to make nuclear fuel is allowed under the 1968 Nuclear Non-Proliferation Treaty,[17] to which Iran is a party. An analysis was published by the National Academy of Sciences challenging the U.S. view that Iran is petroleum rich and therefore has no need for a nuclear power program. According to the analysis, the relative lack of investment could cause Iran to have negligible exports of oil by 2015.[18] The United States and its partners now accept Iran's right to purely peaceful uses of nuclear energy. In the past, U.S. officials have said that Iran's gas resources make nuclear energy unnecessary.

There is widespread belief among experts that Iran's governing factions perceive a nuclear weapons capability as a means of ending Iran's perceived historic vulnerability to invasion and domination by great powers, and as a symbol of Iran as a major nation. Others believe a nuclear weapon represents the instrument with which Iran intends to intimidate its neighbors and dominate the Persian Gulf region. There are also fears Iran might transfer WMD to extremist groups or countries. On the other hand, some Iranian strategists maintain that a nuclear weapons will bring Iran only further sanctions, military containment, U.S. attempted interference in Iran, and efforts by neighbors to develop countervailing capabilities. Some members of the domestic opposition, such as Musavi, have positions on the nuclear issue similar to those of regime leaders, but some opposition factions see the nuclear program as an impediment to eventual re-integration with the West and might be willing to significantly limit the program.

U.S. officials have generally been less concerned with Russia's work, under a January 1995 contract, on an $800 million nuclear power plant at Bushehr. Russia insisted that Iran sign an agreement under which Russia would provide reprocess the plant's spent nuclear material; that agreement was signed on February 28, 2005. The plant was expected to become operational in 2007, but Russia had insisted (including during President Putin's visit to Iran in October 2007) that Iran first comply with the U.N. resolutions discussed below. In December 2007, Russia began fueling the reactor, and Iran says it expects the plant to become operational in 2009. Some preliminary tests of the plant began in February 2009, but, possibly as a sign of Russian cooperation with international pressure on Iran, Russia has not brought the plant to operational status to date. As part of this work, Russia has trained 1,500 Iranian nuclear engineers.

Diplomatic Efforts in 2003 and 2004/Paris Agreement

In 2003, France, Britain, and Germany (the "EU-3") opened a separate diplomatic track to curb Iran's program. On October 21, 2003, Iran pledged, in return for peaceful nuclear technology, to (1) fully disclose its past nuclear activities, (2) to sign and ratify the "Additional Protocol" to the NPT (allowing for enhanced inspections), and (3) to suspend uranium enrichment activities. Iran signed the Additional Protocol on December 18, 2003, although the *Majles* has not ratified it. Iran discontinued abiding by the Protocol after the IAEA reports of November 10, 2003, and February 24, 2004, stated that Iran had violated its NPT reporting obligations over an 18-year period.

In the face of the U.S. threat to push for Security Council action, the EU-3 and Iran reached a more specific November 14, 2004, "Paris Agreement," committing Iran to suspend uranium enrichment (which it did as of November 22, 2004) in exchange for renewed trade talks and other aid.[19] The Bush Administration did not openly support the track until March 11, 2005, when it announced it would drop U.S. objections to Iran applying to join the World Trade Organization (it applied in May 2005) and to selling civilian aircraft parts to Iran. The Bush Administration did not participate directly in the talks.

Reference to the Security Council

The Paris Agreement broke down just after Ahmadinejad's election; Iran rejected as insufficient an EU-3 offer to assist Iran with peaceful uses of nuclear energy and provide limited security guarantees in exchange for Iran's (1) permanently ending uranium enrichment; (2) dismantling the Arak heavy-water reactor;[20] (3) no-notice nuclear inspections; and (4) a pledge not to leave the NPT (it has a legal exit clause). On August 8, 2005, Iran broke the IAEA seals and began uranium "conversion" (one step before enrichment) at its Esfahan facility. On September 24, 2005, the IAEA Board declared Iran in non-compliance with the NPT and decided to refer the issue to the Security Council,[21] but no time frame was set for the referral. After Iran resumed enrichment activities, on February 4, 2006, the IAEA board voted 27-3[22] to refer the case to the Security Council. On March 29, 2006, the Council agreed on a presidency "statement" setting a 30-day time limit (April 28, 2006) for ceasing enrichment.[23]

Establishment of "P5+1" Contact Group/June 2006 Incentive Package

Taking a multilateral approach, the George W. Bush Administration offered on May 31, 2006, to join the nuclear talks with Iran if Iran first suspends its uranium enrichment. Such talks would center on a package of incentives and possible sanctions—formally agreed on June 1, 2006—by a newly formed group of nations, the so-called "Permanent Five Plus 1" (P5+1: United States, Russia, China, France, Britain, and Germany). EU representative Javier Solana formally presented the P5+1 offer to Iran on June 6, 2006. (The package is Annex I to Resolution 1747.)

Incentives:

- Negotiations on an EU-Iran trade agreements and acceptance of Iran into the World Trade Organization.
- Easing of U.S. sanctions to permit sales to Iran of commercial aircraft/parts.
- Sale to Iran of a light-water nuclear reactor and guarantees of nuclear fuel (including a five year buffer stock of fuel), and possible sales of light-water research reactors for medicine and agriculture applications.
- An "energy partnership" between Iran and the EU, including help for Iran to modernize its oil and gas sector and to build export pipelines.
- Support for a regional security forum for the Persian Gulf, and support for the objective of a WMD free zone for the Middle East.
- The possibility of eventually allowing Iran to resume uranium enrichment if it complies with all outstanding IAEA requirements.

Sanctions:[24]

- Denial of visas for Iranians involved in Iran's nuclear program and for high-ranking Iranian officials.
- A freeze of assets of Iranian officials and institutions; a freeze of Iran's assets abroad; and a ban on some financial transactions.
- A ban on sales of advanced technology and of arms to Iran; and a ban on sales to Iran of gasoline and other refined oil products.
- An end to support for Iran's application to the WTO.

Resolution 1696

Iran did not immediately respond to the offer. On July 31, 2006, the Security Council voted 14-1 (Qatar voting no) for U.N. Security Council Resolution 1696, giving Iran until August 31, 2006, to fulfill the longstanding IAEA nuclear demands (enrichment suspension, etc). Purportedly in deference to Russia and China, it was passed under Article 40 of the U.N. Charter, which makes compliance mandatory, but not under Article 41, which refers to economic sanctions, or Article 42, which would authorize military action. It called on U.N. member states not to sell Iran WMDuseful technology. On August 22, 2006, Iran responded, but Iran did not offer enrichment suspension, instead offering vague proposals of engagement with the West.

Resolution 1737

With the backing of the P5+1, chief EU negotiator Javier Solana negotiated with Iran to try arrange a temporary enrichment suspension, but talks ended on September 28, 2006, without agreement. The Security Council adopted U.N. Security Council Resolution 1737 unanimously on December 23, 2006, under Chapter 7, Article 41 of the U.N. Charter. It prohibits sale to Iran— or financing of such sale—of technology that could contribute to Iran's uranium enrichment or heavy-water reprocessing activities. It also required U.N. member states to freeze the financial assets of 10 named Iranian nuclear and missile firms and 12 persons related to those programs. It called on—but did not mandate—member states not to permit travel by these persons. In deference to Russia, the Resolution did not apply to the Bushehr reactor.

Resolution 1747 and Results

Resolution 1737 demanded enrichment suspension by February 21, 2007. With no Iranian compliance, on March 24, 2007, after only three weeks of P5+1 negotiations, Resolution 1747 was adopted unanimously, which

- added 10 military/WMD-related entities; 3 Revolutionary Guard entities; 8 persons, and 7 Revolutionary Guard commanders. Bank Sepah is among the entities sanctioned.
- banned arms transfers by Iran, a provision targeted at Iran's alleged arms supplies to Lebanese Hezbollah and to Shiite militias in Iraq.
- required all countries to report to the United Nations when sanctioned Iranian persons travel to their territories.

- called for (but did not require) countries to avoid selling arms or dual use items to Iran and to avoid any new lending or grants to Iran.

Resolution 1747 demanded Iran suspend enrichment by May 24, 2007. Iran did not comply, but, suggesting it wanted to avoid further isolation, in August 2007, Iran agreed to sign with the IAEA an agreement to clear up outstanding questions on Iran's past nuclear activities by the end of 2007. On September 28, 2007, the P5+1 grouping—along with the EU itself—agreed to a joint statement pledging to negotiate another sanctions resolution if there is no progress reported by the IAEA in implementing the August 2007 agreement or in negotiations with EU representative Javier Solana. The IAEA and Solana indicated that Iran's responses fell short; Solana described a November 30, 2007, meeting with Iranian negotiator Sayid Jallili as "disappointing."

Resolution 1803 and Additional Incentives

After several months of negotiations, Resolution 1803 was adopted by a vote of 14-0 (Indonesia abstaining) on March 3, 2008. It (1) bans sales of dual use items to Iran; (2) authorizes, but does not require, inspections of cargo, carried by Iran Air Cargo and Islamic Republic of Iran Shipping Line, suspected of shipping WMD-related goods; (3) imposes a firm travel ban on five Iranians named in Annex II to the Resolution and requires reports on international travel by 13 individuals named in Annex I; (4) calls for, but does not impose, a prohibition on financial transactions with Iran's Bank Melli and Bank Saderat; and (5) adds 12 entities to those sanctioned under Resolution 1737. (On June 23, 2008, the EU, acting under Resolution 1803, froze the assets of Bank Melli and several IRGC entities and commanders.)

Resolution 1803 also stated the willingness of the P5+1 to consider additional incentives to resolve the Iranian nuclear issue through negotiation "on the basis of their June 2006 proposals." The Bush Administration agreed to expand the June 2006 incentive package at a meeting in London on May 2, 2008, resulting in an offer to Iran to add political cooperation and enhanced energy cooperation to prior incentive packages. EU envoy Solana presented the package (which included a signature by Secretary of State Rice) on June 14, 2008, but Iran was non-committal.

Sensing increasing pressure, in July 2008, Iran indicated it might be ready to first accept a six week "freeze for freeze," i.e., the P5+1 would freeze further sanctions efforts and Iran would freeze any expansion of uranium enrichment (though not suspend outright). To try to take advantage of what appeared to be an Iranian willingness to compromise, the Bush Administration sent Undersecretary of State for Political Affairs William Burns to join Solana and the other P5+1 representatives at a meeting in Geneva on July 19, 2008. Iran did not accept the "freeze for freeze" idea by an extended deadline of August 2, 2008.

Resolution 1835

As a result of the lack of progress, the P5+1 began discussing another sanctions resolution. Ideas reportedly considered included adding more Iranian banks to those sanctioned, or banning insurance for Iran's tanker fleet. On August 7, 2008, the EU implemented the sanctions specified in Resolution 1803, including asserting the authority to inspect suspect shipments, and called on its members to refrain from providing new credit guarantees on exports to Iran. However, the August 2008 crisis between Russia and Georgia set back U.S.-Russia relations, and Russia opposed new U.N. sanctions on Iran. In an effort to demonstrate to Iran continued unity, the Council did adopt (September 27, 2008) Resolution 1835, calling on Iran to comply with previous resolutions, but restating a willingness to negotiate and imposing no new sanctions.

With Iran still not complying, the P5+1 met again in October and in November of 2008. However, with U.S. partner officials uncertain about what U.S. policy toward Iran might be under a new U.S. Administration, there was no consensus on new sanctions.

The P5+1 Process Under President Obama

After President Obama was inaugurated, the P5+1 met in Germany (February 4, 2009), reportedly focusing on the new U.S. Administration's approach on Iran. It recommitted to the "two track" strategy of incentives and sanctions.[25] Another P5+1 meeting was held in London on April 8, 2009, during which Undersecretary Burns told the other members of the group that, henceforth, a U.S. diplomat would attend all of the group's meetings with Iran. Iran put off new meetings until after the Iranian June 12, 2009, election.[26] In order to try to show good faith to Iran, the Obama Administration did not press for new sanctions.

As far as a time frame for an Iranian response, on May 18, 2009, in the context of a meeting with visiting Israeli Prime Minister Benjamin Netanyahu, President Obama said he expect a positive response by Iran to the U.S. outreach "by the end of [2009]," but that the United States would not entertain the idea of endless talks that yield no result. The July 9, 2009, G-8 summit statement, which included Russian concurrence, mentioned late September 2009 (G-20 summit on September 24) as a time by which the P5+1 would expect Iran to come to new talks and offer constructive proposals for a settlement, lest the P5+1 consider "crippling sanctions" on Iran's economy.

October 1 Tentative Agreement and Subsequent Developments

Perhaps sensing the pressure, on September 1, 2009, Iran's senior negotiator, Sayed Jallili, said Iran would come to new talks. On September 9, 2009, Iran distributed its long anticipated proposals to settle the nuclear issue. To P5+1 representatives in Iran (Swiss Ambassador represented the United States).[27] The Iranian proposals were criticized by many as vague but the United States and its partners considered it a sufficient basis to schedule a meeting with Iran for October 1, 2009, in Geneva.

In light of September 25 revelations about the previously unreported Iranian nuclear site—and despite Iran's insistence that it would allow the facility to be inspected—little progress was expected at the meeting. However, the seven hour session, in which U.S. Under Secretary of State William Burns, representing the United States, also met privately with Iranian negotiator Sayed Jallili, resulted in tentative agreements to (1) meet again later in October; (2) allow the IAEA to inspect the newly revealed Iranian facility near Qom; and (3) allow Russia and France, subject to technical talks to begin by mid-October, to re-process about 75% of Iran's low-enriched uranium for medical use.

The technical talks were held October 19-21, 2009, at IAEA headquarters in Vienna, Austria, and chaired on the U.S. side by Deputy Energy Secretary Daniel Poneman. A draft agreement was approved by the P5+1 countries and the IAEA. Iran has not accepted the draft, instead offering tentative counter-proposals to ship its enriched uranium to France and Russia in increments. On the other hand, some Iranian officials have floated the concept of having the uranium sent to Turkey for enrichment, a proposal that U.S. officials reportedly offered a substitute for Russian or French enrichment. All of Iran's proposals were deemed insufficiently specific or responsive to meet P5+1 demands by the end of 2009. Some attribute the Iranian refusal to agree to the October 1 terms as due to the internal political pressure from reformist leaders, such as Musavi, who are trying to paint Ahmadinejad as so politically weak that he is forced to accept a deal that disadvantages Iran. The Qom facility was inspected during October 25-29, 2009, as agreed.

Because Iran did not accept the October 1 terms by the end of 2009, the P5+1 countries have returned to considering sanctions against Iran. The P5+1 met in Brussels on November 21, 2009, issuing a statement calling on Iran to accept the October 1 proposal. Later, with reported help from China, which had received an NSC briefing on the likely adverse implications for the oil market if Iran's nuclear program proceeds apace, the IAEA Board adopted a resolution on November 27, 2009. China and Russia voted for the Resolution.[28] The Resolution (Gov/2009/82) urged Iran to suspend construction at the Qom site; and called on Iran to confirm it had not decided to construct any other undeclared nuclear facility. As a response to the Resolution, which Iran viewed as contrary to the spirit of negotiated resolution of the nuclear disputes, Iranian officials announced they would construct 10 new uranium enrichment sites, and Ahmadinejad, in early December, declared Iran would enrich uranium to 20% purity for medical uses (but which could be taken as an intent to later make weapons grade uranium).

Some of the specific sanctions ideas under consideration before the latest phase of the dispute included those previously considered: cutting Iran's banks off from the international banking system; banning insurance or re-insurance to carry gasoline products to Iran; and a ban on arms sales to Iran. In light of the unrest in Iran, several December 2009 and January 2010 press reports say the Administration is focusing on sanctioning the Revolutionary Guard and other security organs that are suppressing the Iranian protesters. (See further in "Further International and Multilateral Sanctions" section below.) However, the support of Russia and China for any new sanctions remains uncertain. Despite comments by Secretary Clinton on January 4, 2010, that new sanctions are needed, China's Ambassador to the United Nations said on January 6, 2010, that diplomacy is still possible and that, therefore, "some more time and patience" are needed before new sanctions should be enacted. The reluctance of the two countries to sanction Iran has increased discussion of a group of "like-minded" countries enacting additional sanctions on Iran.

Chemical Weapons, Biological Weapons, and Missiles

Official U.S. reports and testimony continue to state that Iran is seeking a self-sufficient chemical weapons (CW) infrastructure, and that it "may have already" stockpiled blister, blood, choking, and nerve agents—and the bombs and shells to deliver them. This raises questions about Iran's compliance with its obligations under the Chemical Weapons Convention (CWC), which Iran signed on January 13, 1993, and ratified on June 8, 1997. These officials and reports also say that Iran "probably maintain[s] an offensive [biological weapons] BW program ... and probably has the capability to produce at least small quantities of BW agents."

Ballistic Missiles/Warheads

At the February 2009 Annual Threat Assessment of the Intelligence Community, Director of National Intelligence, Dennis Blair, testified "although many of their statements are exaggerations, Iranian officials throughout the past year have repeatedly claimed greater ballistic missile capabilities that could threaten U.S. and allied interests."[29] Tehran appears to view its ballistic missiles as an integral part of its strategy to deter or retaliate against forces in the region, including U.S. forces. However, Iran's technical capabilities are a matter of some debate among experts, and Iran appears to be focus more on missiles capable of hitting regional targets rather than those of intercontinental range. The chart below contains some details on Iran's missile programs and recent tests.

In August 2008, the George W. Bush Administration reached agreements with Poland and the Czech Republic to establish a missile defense system to counter Iranian ballistic missiles. These agreements were reached over Russia's opposition, which was based on the belief that the missile defense system would be used to neutralize Russian capabilities. However, reportedly based on assessments of Iran's focus on missiles of regional range, on September 17, 2009, the Obama Administration reoriented this missile defense program to focus, at least initially, on ship-based systems, possibly later returning to the idea of Poland and Czech-based systems. Some saw this as an effort to win Russia's support for additional sanctions on Iran, and Russian statements did shift somewhat toward the U.S. position on Iran after the Obama missile defense announcement.

FOREIGN POLICY AND SUPPORT FOR TERRORIST GROUPS

Iran's foreign policy is a product of the ideology of Iran's Islamic revolution, blended with longstanding national interests. Some interpret Iran's objectives as the overturning of the power structure in the Middle East, which Iran believes favors the United States, Israel, and their "collaborators"—Sunni Muslim regimes such as Egypt, Jordan, and Saudi Arabia. The State Department report on international terrorism for 2008 released April 30, 2009, again stated (as it has for more than a decade) that Iran "remained the most active state sponsor of terrorism" in 2008, and it again attributed the terrorist activity primarily to the Qods Force of the Revolutionary Guard. The report focused particular attention on Iran's lethal support to Shiite militias in Iraq as well as on shipments to and training of "selected" Taliban fighters in Afghanistan.[31] On October 27, 2008, the deputy commander of the Basij became the first top Guard leader to publicly acknowledge that Iran supplies weapons to "liberation armies" in the region, a reference to pro- Iranian movements discussed below. The appointment of Brig. Gen. Ahmad Vahidi, the former Qods Forces commander, as Defense Minister in September 2009 (who got the highest number of Majles votes for his confirmation) caused concern in some neighboring states.

Some experts believe that Iran has been ascendant in the region because of the installation of pro- Iranian regimes in Iraq and Afghanistan, and the strength of Hezbollah in Lebanon and Hamas in Gaza. Iran might, according to this view, seek to press its advantage to strengthen regional Shiite movements and possibly drive the United States out of the Gulf. During a visit to the Middle East in March 2009, Secretary of State Clinton said, after meeting with several Arab and Israeli leaders in the region, that "There is a great deal of concern about Iran from this whole region."

Others reach an opposite conclusion, stating that Iran now feels more encircled than ever by proU.S. regimes. Elections in Lebanon in 2009 that boosted pro-U.S. factions, U.S. engagement with Syria, stability in Iraq, and an influx of U.S. troops to Afghanistan have rendered Iran weaker than it has been in recent years.

Relations with the Persian Gulf States

The Persian Gulf monarchy states (Gulf Cooperation Council, GCC: Saudi Arabia, Kuwait, Bahrain, Qatar, Oman, and the United Arab Emirates) fear the strategic influence of Iran but they do not openly support U.S. conflict with Iran that might cause Iran to retaliate against Gulf state targets. The Gulf states privately welcome Iran's postelection turmoil because it means that Iran might be strategically weakened and consumed by internal infighting. However, there is concern in the Gulf that Iran might assert itself in the region to focus public attention outside Iran. Commercial relations between the Gulf states and Iran are normal, and several of the Gulf states, particularly Kuwait and UAE, have excess oil refining capacity and sell gasoline to Iran.

Since the mid-1990s, Iran has tried to blunt Gulf state fears of Iran by curtailing activity, conducted during the 1 980s and early 1 990s, to sponsor Shiite Muslim extremist groups in these states, all of which are run by Sunni governments. Iran found, to its detriment, that such activity caused the Gulf states to ally closely with the United States. In part to counter Iran's perceived growing influence in the Gulf, in December 2006 the summit of the GCC leaders announced that the GCC states might jointly study their own development of "peaceful nuclear technology." On the other hand, seeking to avoid further tensions with Iran, the GCC leaders invited Ahmadinejad to speak at the December 2007 summit of the GCC leaders in Doha, Qatar, marking the first time an Iranian president had been invited since the GCC was formed in 1 98 1. His speech reiterated a consistent Iranian theme that the Gulf countries, including Iran, should set up their own security structure without the help of "outside powers" but also called for a "new chapter" in Iran-GCC relations.

- *Saudi Arabia.* Many observers closely watch the relationship between Iran and Saudi Arabia because of Saudi alarm over the emergence of a pro-Iranian government in Iraq and Iran's nuclear program. Saudi Arabia sees itself as leader of the Sunni Muslim world and views Shiite Muslims as heretical and disloyal internally. However, the Saudis, who do not want a repeat of Iran's sponsorship of disruptive and sometimes violent demonstrations at annual Hajj pilgrimages in Mecca in the 1980s and 1990s—or an increase in Iranian support for Saudi Shiite dissidents—are receptive to easing tensions with Iran. The Saudis continue to blame a pro-Iranian movement in the Kingdom, Saudi Hezbollah, for the June 25, 1996, Khobar Towers housing complex bombing, which killed 19 U.S. airmen.[32] After restoring relations in December 1991 (after a four-year break), Saudi-Iran ties progressed to high-level contacts during Khatemi's presidency, including Khatemi visits in 1999 and 2002, and Ahmadinejad has visited on several occasions.

- *United Arab Emirates* (UAE) concerns about Iran never fully recovered from the April 1992 Iranian expulsion of UAE security forces from the Persian Gulf island of Abu Musa, which it and the UAE shared under a 1971 bilateral agreement. (In 1971, Iran, then ruled by the U.S.-backed Shah, seized two other islands, Greater and Lesser Tunb, from the emirate of Ras al-Khaymah, as well as part of Abu Musa from the emirate of Sharjah.) In general, the UAE (particularly the federation capital, Abu Dhabi, backs U.S. efforts to dissuade Iran from developing its nuclear capability through international sanctions. Abu Dhabi generally takes a harder line against Iran than does the emirate of Dubai, which has an Iranian-origin resident community as large as 300,000 and business ties to Iran). On the islands dispute, the UAE wants to refer the dispute to the International Court of Justice (ICJ). Iran insists on resolving the issue bilaterally. The UAE formally protested Iran's setting up of a maritime and ship registration office on Abu Musa in July 2008. The United States supports UAE proposals but takes no formal position on sovereignty. Still seeking to avoid antagonizing Iran, in May 2007 the UAE received Ahmadinejad (the highest level Iranian visit since the 1979 revolution) and allowed him to lead an anti-U.S. rally of a reported several hundred Iranian-origin residents of Dubai at a soccer stadium there.

- *Qatar*, like most of the other Gulf states, does not seek confrontation and seeks to accommodate some of its interests, yet Qatar remains wary that Iran might eventually seek to encroach on its large North Field (natural gas). It shares that field with Iran (called South Pars on Iran's side) and Qatar earns large revenues from natural gas exports from it. Qatar's fears were heightened on April 26, 2004, when Iran's deputy Oil Minister said that Qatar is probably producing more gas than "her right share" from the field and that Iran "will not allow" its wealth to be used by others. Possibly to try to ease such implied threats, Qatar invited Ahmadinejad to the December 2007 GCC summit there.

- *Bahrain* is about 60% Shiite, many of whom are of Persian origin, but its government is dominated by the Sunni Muslim Al Khalifa family. In 1981 and again in 1996, Bahrain publicly accused Iran of supporting Bahraini Shiite dissidents (the Islamic Front for the Liberation of Bahrain, Bahrain-Hezbollah, and other Bahraini dissident groups) in efforts to overthrow the ruling Al Khalifa family. Bahraini fears that Iran would try to interfere in Bahrain's November 25, 2006, parliamentary elections by providing support to Shiite candidates did not materialize, although the main Shiite opposition coalition won 18 out of the 40 seats of the elected body. Tensions have flared several times since July 2007 when Iranian editorialists asserted that Bahrain is part of Iran—that question was the subject of the 1970 U.N.-run referendum in which Bahrainis opted for independence. The issued flared again after a February 20, 2009, statement by Ali Akbar Nateq Nuri, an adviser to Khamene'i, that Bahrain was at one time an Iranian province. The statement caused major criticism of Iran throughout the region, and contributed to a decision by Morocco to break relations with Iran.

Still, Bahrain has sought not to antagonize Iran and has apparently allowed Iran's banks to establish a presence in Bahrain's vibrant banking sector. On March 12, 2008, the Treasury Department sanctioned the Bahrain-based Future Bank under Executive order 13382 that sanctions proliferation entities. Future Bank purportedly is controlled by Bank Melli. The bank remains in operation.

- *Oman.* Of the GCC states, the Sultanate of Oman is closest politically to Iran and has refused to ostracize or even harshly criticize Iranian policies. Some press reports say local Omani officials routinely turn a blind eye to or even cooperate in the smuggling of western goods to Iran. Sultan Qaboos made a state visit to Iran in August 2009, coinciding with the inauguration of Ahmadinejad.

Iranian Policy in Iraq

The U.S. military ousting of Saddam Hussein benefitted Iran strategically,[33] and during 2004- 2008, U.S.-Iran differences in Iraq widened to the point where some were describing the competition as a U.S.-Iran "proxy war" inside Iraq. The acute source of tension was evidence, detailed on several occasions by U.S. commanders in Iraq, that the *Qods* Force was providing arms (including highly lethal "explosively forced projectiles," EFPs, which have killed U.S. soldiers), training, guidance, and financing to Shiite militias involved in sectarian violence.

However, recent Defense Department reports on Iraq stability—most recently in September 2009—corroborate a widespread perception that Iranian interference in Iraq has lessened, including fewer Iranian weapons shipments. In Iraq itself, the Shiite militias and political parties that benefit most from Iranian support fared poorly in the January 31, 2009, provincial elections in Iraq, and the results were viewed as a setback for Iran's influence in Iraq. One Shiite militia, Asa'ib al Haq (League of the Righteous) has reconciled with the government and its leaders (Khazali brothers) have been released from U.S. custody. Iran was unable to derail the U.S.-Iraq defense pact (which took effect January 1, 2009). In January 2009, Iraqi Prime Minister Nuri al

Maliki visited Iran for the fourth time since he became Prime Minister, reportedly to assure Iran that the pact did not threaten Iran.

Iran also has signed a number of agreements with Iraq on transportation, energy cooperation, free flow of Shiite pilgrims, border security, intelligence sharing, and other cooperation; several more agreements, including a $1 billion credit line for Iranian exports to Iraq, were signed during Ahmadinejad's March 2-3, 2008, visit to Iraq; implementing agreements were signed in April 2008. The two countries now do about $4 billion in bilateral trade.

After at first rejecting dialogue with Iran on the Iraq issue, the George W. Bush Administration supported and attended several regional conferences on Iraq, attended by Iran, and undertook bilateral talks with Iran on the Iraq issue. Several meetings were held in Baghdad in 2007, with no concrete results, according to former Ambassador to Iraq Crocker, who led the U.S. side at the talks. A round of talks was tentatively scheduled for December 18, 2007, but Iran repeatedly postponed them because of differences over the agenda and the level of talks (Iran wanted them to be at the ambassador level). On May 5, 2008, Iran indefinitely suspended this dialogue, and, in February 2009, Iran said there was no need to resume it.

A provision of the FY2008 defense authorization bill (P.L. 110-181) required a report to Congress on Iran's interference in Iraq. On several occasions since January 2008, the Treasury Department has taken action against suspected Iranian and pro-Iranian operatives in Iraq by designating individuals and organizations as a threat to stability in Iraq under the July 17, 2007, Executive Order 13438, which freezes the assets and bans transactions with named individuals. The named entities, which includes a senior Qods Forces leader, are in the tables on sanctioned entities in CRS Report RS20871, *Iran Sanctions*, by Kenneth Katzman. On July 2, 2009, a pro-Iranian militia offshoot, Khata'ib Hezbollah (Hezbollah Battalions) was named under the order, and was also designated a Foreign Terrorist Organization (FTO) under the Immigration and Naturalization Act. On July 9, 2009, the United States military turned over to Iraqi custody five Iranian Qods Forces operatives (Iran claims they are diplomats) arrested in 2007 in Irbil, northern Iraq. The men returned to Iran.

Supporting Palestinian Militant Groups

Iran's support for Palestinian militant groups has long concerned U.S. Administrations, as part of an apparent effort by Tehran to obstruct an Israeli-Palestinian peace, which Iran believes would strengthen the United States and Israel. Ahmadinejad's various statements on Israel were discussed above, although Supreme Leader Khamene'i has repeatedly called Israel a "cancerous tumor." He used that term again during a March 4, 2009, press conference in Tehran. In December 2001, Rafsanjani said that it would take only one Iranian nuclear bomb to destroy Israel, whereas a similar strike against Iran by Israel would have far less impact because Iran's population is large.

Iran has hosted numerous conferences to which anti-peace process terrorist organizations were invited (for example: April 24, 2001, and June 2-3, 2002). During his presidency, Khatemi also issued sharp criticisms and recriminations against Israel, but he also conversed with Israel's president at the 2005 funeral of Pope John Paul II. The formal position of the Iranian Foreign Ministry, considered a bastion of moderates, is that Iran would not seek to block an Israeli- Palestinian settlement but that the peace process is too weighted toward Israel to result in a fair settlement.

Iran and Hamas

The State Department report on terrorism for 2007 (mentioned above) again accused Iran of providing "extensive" funding, weapons, and training to Hamas, Palestinian Islamic Jihad (PIJ), the Al Aqsa Martyr's Brigades, and the Popular Front for the Liberation of Palestine-General Command (PFLP-GC). All are named as foreign terrorist organizations (FTO) by the State Department for their use of violence to undermine the Arab-Israeli peace process. Some saw Iran's regional policy further strengthened by Hamas's victory in the January 25, 2006, Palestinian legislative elections, and even more so by Hamas's June 2007 armed takeover of the Gaza Strip. The Hamas gains potentially positioned it to block any peace settlement with Israel. Hamas activists downplay Iranian influence on them, asserting that Iran is mostly

Shiite, while Hamas members are Sunni Muslims.[34] Hamas was reputed to receive about 10% of its budget in the early 1990s from Iran, although since then Hamas has cultivated funding from wealthy Persian Gulf donors and supporters in Europe and elsewhere.

Still, it was evident from the December 27, 2008-January 17, 2009, Israel-Hamas war in Gaza, that Iran provides material support to Hamas. Joint Chiefs Chairman Adm. Mike Mullen said on January 27, 2009, that the United States boarded but did not seize a ship carrying light arms to Hamas from Iran; the ship (the Monchegorsk) later went to Cyprus. On March 11, 2009, a U.N. committee monitoring Iran's compliance with Resolution 1747, which bans Iranian arms exports, said Iran might have violated that resolution with the alleged shipment. Hamas appeared to corroborate allegations of Iranian weapons supplies when its exiled leader, Khaled Meshal, on February 1, 2009, publicly praised Iran for helping Hamas achieve "victory" over Israel in the conflict.[35] On December 29, 2008, Khamene'i said that Muslims worldwide were "duty-bound" to defend Palestinians in the Gaza Strip against the Israeli offensive against the Hamas-run leadership there, but the Iranian leadership did not attempt to send Iranian volunteers to Gaza to fight on Hamas' behalf. Iranian weaponry might also have been the target of a January 2009 strike on a weapons delivery purportedly bound for Gaza in transit via Sudan (presumably via Egypt).

Sunni Arab leaders in Egypt, Jordan, Saudi Arabia, and throughout the region apparently fear Iran's reported attempts to discredit these leaders for what Iran considers insufficient support for Hamas in its recent war with Israel. Some Iranian efforts reportedly involve establishing Hezbollah cells in some of these countries, particularly Egypt, purportedly to stir up opposition to these governments and build public support for Hezbollah and Hamas.[36] These countries are also said to fear that President Obama's outreach to Iran might lead the United States to downplay their concerns about Iran—a sentiment that Secretary of Defense Gates tried to allay during his visit to the Middle East in May 2009.

Lebanese Hezbollah and Syria

Iran has maintained a close relationship with Hezbollah since the group was formed in 1982 by Lebanese Shiite clerics who were sympathetic to Iran's Islamic revolution and belonged to the Lebanese Da'wa Party. Hezbollah was responsible for several acts of anti-U.S. and anti-Israel terrorism in the 1980s and 1990s.[37] Hezbollah's attacks on Israeli forces in southern Lebanon contributed to an Israeli withdrawal in May 2000, but, despite United Nations certification of Israel's withdrawal, Hezbollah maintained military forces along the border. Hezbollah continued to remain armed and outside Lebanese government control, despite U.N. Security Council Resolution 1559 (September 2, 2004) that required its dismantlement. In refusing to disarm, Hezbollah says it was resisting Israeli occupation of some Lebanese territory (Shib'a Farms).

Although Iran likely did not instigate Lebanese Hezbollah to provoke the July-August 2006 war, Iran has long been its major arms supplier. Hezbollah fired Iranian-supplied rockets on Israel's northern towns during the fighting. Reported Iranian shipments to Hezbollah prior to the conflict included the "Fajr" (dawn) and Khaybar series of rockets that were fired at the Israeli city of Haifa (30 miles from the border), and over 10,000 Katyusha rockets that were fired at cities within 20 miles of the Lebanese border.[38] Iran also supplied

Hezbollah with an unmanned aerial vehicle (UAV), the *Mirsad*, which Hezbollah briefly flew over the Israel-Lebanon border on November 7, 2004, and April 11, 2005; at least three were shot down by Israel during the conflict. On July 14, 2006, Hezbollah apparently hit an Israeli warship with a C-802 sea-skimming missile probably provided by Iran. (See **Table 5** above for information on Iran's acquisition of that weapon from China.) Iran als purportedly provided advice during the conflict; about 50 Revolutionary Guards Qods Force personnel were in Lebanon (down from about 2,000 when Hezbollah was formed, according to a *Washington Post* report of April 13, 2005) when the conflict began; that number might have increased during the conflict to help Hezbollah operate the Iran-supplied weaponry. In November 2009, Israel intercepted a ship that it asserted was carrying 500 tons of arms purportedly for Hezbollah.

Even though Hezbollah reduced its overt military presence in southern Lebanon in accordance with the conflict-related U.N. Security Council Resolution 1701 (July 31, 2006), Hezbollah was perceived as a victor in the war for holding out against heavy Israeli air-strikes and some ground action. Iran supported Hezbollah's demands and provided it with leverage by resupplying it, after the hostilities, with 27,000 rockets, more than double what Hezbollah had at the start of the 2006 war.[39] Among the post-war deliveries were 500 Iranian-made "Zelzal" (Earthquake) missiles with a range of 186 miles, enough to reach Tel Aviv from south Lebanon. Iran also made at least $150 million available for Hezbollah to distribute to Lebanese citizens (mostly Shiite supporters of Hezbollah) whose homes were damaged in the Israeli military campaign.[40] The State Department terrorism report for 2008, referenced above, specifies Iranian aid to Hezbollah as exceeding $200 million in 2008, and says that Iran trained over 3,000 Hezbollah fighters in Iran during the year.

Table 5. Iran's Conventional Military Arsenal

Military Personnel	Tanks	Surface- Air Missiles	Combat Aircraft	Ships	Defense Budget (billions U.S. $)
545,000 (regular military and Revolutionary Guard Corps (IRGC). IRGC is about one- third of total force.	1,693 (incl. 480 T- 72)	150 I-Hawk plus some Stinger	280 (incl. 25 MiG-29 and 30 Su- 24)	200 (incl. 10 Chinese-made Hudong, 40 Boghammer, 3 frigates) Also has 3 Kilo subs	6.6
Ship-launched cruise missiles. Iran is able to arm its patrol boats with Chinese-made C-802 cruise missiles. Iran also has Chinese-supplied HY-2 Seerseekers emplaced along Iran's coast.					
Midget Subs. Iran is said to possess several, possibly purchased assembled or in kit form from North Korea. Iran claimed on November 29, 2007, to have produced a new small sub equipped with sonar-evading technology.					
Anti-aircraft missile systems. Russia has sold and now delivered to Iran (January 2007) 30 anti-aircraft missile systems (Tor M1), worth over $1 billion. In September 2006, Ukraine agreed to sell Iran the Kolchuga radar system that can improve Iran's detection of combat aircraft. In December 2007, Russia agreed to sell the even more capable S-300 (also known as SA-20 "Gargoyle") air defense system, purportedly modeled after the U.S. Patriot system, which U.S. officials say would greatly enhance Iran's air defense capability. The value of the deal is estimated at $800 million. Amid unclear or weak denials by Iranian and Russian officials, U.S. officials told journalists on December 11, 2008, that Iran has indeed contracted for the missile. It is reportedly was due for delivery by March 2009 and to be operational by June 2009, but Russian press reports in February 2009 about the visit of Iran's Defense Minister to Moscow indicate that Russia has placed delivery on hold due to "political considerations"—expectations of possible adverse reaction by the Obama Administration. Delivery has not taken place to date, by all accounts, and Israel said in August 2009 that Russia had agreed not to deliver any equipment to Iran that would upset the regional balance of power.					

Neither Israel nor the United States opposed Hezbollah's progressively increased participation in peaceful Lebanese politics. In March 2005, President George W. Bush indicated that the United States might accept Hezbollah as a legitimate political force in Lebanon if it disarms. In the ebanese parliamentary elections of May—June 2005, Hezbollah expanded its presence in the parliament to 14 out of the 128-seat body, and it gained two cabinet seats. In mid May 2008, Hezbollah, for the first time ever, used its militia wing for domestic purposes. Its fighters took over large parts of Beirut in response to an attempt by the U.S. and Saudi-backed Lebanese government to curb Hezbollah's media and commercial operations. The success of its fighters contributed to a Qatar-brokered settlement on May 21, 2008, in which the majority coalition agreed to give Hezbollah and its allies enough seats in a new cabinet (one Hezbollah cabinet seat and seven allies holding cabinet seats as well) to be able to veto government decisions. Hezbollah agreed to the compromise candidate of Lebanese Army commander Michel Suleiman to become president.

Based on the strength, Hezbollah was viewed as a likely winner in June 7, 2009, parliamentary elections in Lebanon. However, its coalition won 57 seats in the elections, failing to overturn the majority of the pro-U.S. factions led by Sa'd al-Hariri, son of assassinated leader Rafiq Hariri, which won 71 seats (one more than they had previously). A new cabinet was formed in November 2009, but Hezbollah's political strength in that government was reduced only slightly compared to the pre-election government. Nonetheless, the election defeat for Hezbollah allies set back Tehran's regional influence. As a matter of policy, the United States does not meet with any Hezbollah members, even those in the parliament or cabinet. Hezbollah is a designated FTO, but that designation bars financial transactions with the group and does not specifically ban meeting members of the group.

Syria

Iran's support for Hezbollah is linked in many ways to its alliance with Syria. Syria is the transit point for the Iranian weapons shipments to Hezbollah and both countries see Hezbollah as leverage against Israel to achieve their regional and territorial aims. In order to preserve its links to Syria, which is one of Iran's few real allies, Iran purportedly has acted as an intermediary with North Korea to supply Syria with various forms of WMD and missile technology. Some see Israel-Syria negotiations—and recent Obama Administration engagement with Syria—as means to wean Syria away from its alliance with Iran. However, Iran is a major investor in the Syrian economy, which attracts very little western investment, and some believe the Iran-Syria alliance is not easily severed. On December 13, 2009, the Syrian and Iranian defense ministers signed a defense agreement to "face common enemies and challenges."

Central Asia and the Caspian

Iran's policy in Central Asia has thus far emphasized Iran's rights to Caspian Sea resources, particularly against Azerbaijan. That country's population, like Iran's, is mostly Shiite Muslim, but its leadership is secular. In addition, Azerbaijan is ethnically Turkic, and Iran fears that Azerbaijan nationalists might stoke separatism among Iran's large Azeri Turkic population, which demonstrated some unrest in 2006. These factors could explain why Iran has generally tilted toward Armenia, which is Christian, even though it has been at odds with Azerbaijan over territory and control of ethnic Armenians. In July 2001, Iranian warships and combat aircraft threatened a British Petroleum (BP) ship on contract to Azerbaijan out of an area of the Caspian that Iran considers its own. The United States called that action provocative, and it is engaged in border security and defense cooperation with Azerbaijan directed against Iran (and Russia). The United States successfully backed construction of the Baku-Tblisi-Ceyhan oil pipeline, intended in part to provide alternatives to Iranian oil. Along with India and Pakistan, Iran has been given observer status at the Central Asian security grouping called the Shanghai Cooperation Organization (SCO—Russia, China, Kazakhstan, Kyrgyzstan, Uzbekistan, and Tajikistan). In April 2008, Iran applied for full membership in the organization, which opposes a long-term U.S. presence in Central Asia.

Afghanistan and Pakistan[41]

Iran is viewed by U.S. officials as pursuing a multi-track strategy—attempting to help develop Afghanistan and enhance its influence there, while also building leverage against the United States by arming anti-U.S. militant groups. Iran is particularly interested in restoring some of its traditional sway in eastern, central, and northern Afghanistan where Persian-speaking Afghans predominate. Iran may want to be in position to threaten the air base at Shindand, in Herat Province, which is now used by U.S. and allied forces and which Iran believes could be used for surveillance of or strikes on Iran.

The State Department terrorism report for 2008 again accused the Qods Force of supplying various munitions, including 107mm rockets, to Taliban and other militants in Afghanistan; some Taliban commanders openly say they are obtaining Iranian weapons. The 2008 reports also, and for the first time, accuses Iran of training Taliban fighters in small unit tactics, small arms use, explosives, and indirect weapons fire. Among specific shipments noted by the United States: on April 17, 2007, U.S. military personnel in Afghanistan captured a shipment of Iranian weapons that purportedly was bound for Taliban fighters. On several occasions in 2007, NATO officers said they directly intercepted Iranian shipments of heavy arms, C4 explosives, and advanced roadside bombs (explosively forced projectiles, or EFPs, such as those found in Iraq) to Taliban fighters in Afghanistan. U.S. commanders in Afghanistan maintain that the intercepted shipments are large enough that the Iranian government would have to have known about them. U.S. and Afghan officials say the shipments continue, but are not consistent or necessarily decisive in the Afghanistan war.

These shipments and contacts have caused debate over Iran's goals because Iran long opposed the regime of the Taliban in Afghanistan on the grounds that it oppressed Shiite Muslim and other Persian-speaking minorities. Iran nearly launched a military attack against the Taliban in September 1998 after Taliban fighters captured and killed nine Iranian diplomats based in northern Afghanistan, and Iran provided military aid to the Northern Alliance factions. During the major combat phase of the post-September 11 U.S.-led war in Afghanistan, Iran offered search and rescue of any downed service persons and the transshipment to Afghanistan of humanitarian assistance. Iran and U.S. diplomats were in continuous contact in forging a post-Taliban government in Afghanistan at the December

2001 "Bonn Conference." In March 2002, Iran expelled Gulbuddin Hikmatyar, an Afghan militant leader; it froze his assets in January 2005.

After 2004, Iran's influence waned somewhat as Northern Alliance figures were marginalized in Afghan politics. To build financial and alternative political influence in Afghanistan, Iran has funded projects that total about $1.2 billion million since 2001 (close to a pledged amount in international donors conferences), mostly in neighboring Herat but also in Kabul (Shiite theological seminaries there). Afghan officials and observers in Herat Province say Iran's influence is substantial there but not necessarily against the Afghan government.[42] Iran's construction of Shiite mosques and seminaries could indicate Iran is trying to support Afghanistan's Shiite (Hazara tribe) minority, and Iran has funded several media outlets in Afghanistan catering to Shiites.

At the same time, some commanders, including CENTCOM Commander Gen. David Petraeus, have said that U.S. engagement with Iran on Afghanistan might help U.S. stabilization efforts there. Others say that working with Iran on Afghanistan might help build a broader understanding with Iran on other issues, including the nuclear issue.

Perhaps in recognition of Iran's role in Afghanistan, or as part of a broader effort to build dialogue with Iran, the United States invited Iran to an international conference on Afghanistan held in the Netherlands on March 31, 2009. Iran's representatives there had a brief side exchange there with U.S. special representative for Afghanistan and Pakistan Ambassador Richard Holbrooke. At the meeting, Iran pledged cooperation on preventing drug smuggling out of Afghanistan and in helping economically develop that country.

Pakistan

Iran's relations with Pakistan have been partly a function of events in Afghanistan, although relations have worsened somewhat in late 2009 as Iran has accused Pakistan of supporting Sunni Muslim rebels in Iran's Baluchistan region. These Sunni guerrillas have conducted a number of attacks on Iranian regime targets in 2009, as discussed above ("Jundullah").

Iran had a burgeoning military cooperation with Pakistan in the early 1 990s, and as noted Iran's nuclear program benefitted from the A.Q. Khan network. However, Iran-Pakistan relations became strained in the 1 990s when Pakistan was supporting the Taliban in Afghanistan, which committed alleged atrocities against Shiite Afghans (Hazara tribe), and which seized control of Persian-speaking areas of Afghanistan. Currently, Iran remains suspicious that Pakistan might want to again implant the Taliban in power in Afghanistan— and Iran itself is aiding the Taliban to some extent—but Iran and Pakistan now have a broad agenda that includes a potential major gas pipeline project, discussed further below.

Al Qaeda

Iran is not a natural ally of Al Qaeda, largely because Al Qaeda is an orthodox Sunni Muslim organization. However, some experts believe that hardliners in Iran might want to use Al Qaeda activists as leverage against the United States and its allies. Some say Iran might want to exchange them for a U.S. hand-over of PMOI activists under U.S. control in Iraq. The 9/11 Commission report said several of the September 11 hijackers and other plotters, possibly with official help, might have transited Iran, but the report does not assert that the Iranian government cooperated with or knew about the plot. Another bin Laden ally, Abu Musab al-Zarqawi, killed by U.S. forces in Iraq on June 7, 2006, reportedly transited Iran after the September 11 attacks and took root in Iraq, becoming an insurgent leader there.

However, Iran might see possibilities for tactical alliance with Al Qaeda. Iran asserted on July 23, 2003, that it had "in custody" senior Al Qaeda figures. On July 16, 2005, Iran's Intelligence Minister said that 200 Al Qaeda members are in Iranian jails.[43] U.S. officials have said since January 2002 that Iran has not prosecuted or extradited any senior Al Qaeda operatives. The three major Al Qaeda figures believed to have been in Iran include spokesman Sulayman Abu Ghaith, top operative Sayf Al Adl, and Osama bin Laden's son, Saad.[44] although some U.S. officials said in January 2009 that Saad bin Laden might have left Iran and could be in Pakistan. That information was publicized a few days after the Treasury Department (on January 16, 2009) designated four Al Qaeda operatives in Iran, including Saad bin Laden (and three lesser known figures) as terrorist entities under Executive Order 13224. (U.S. officials blamed Saad bin Laden, Adl, and Abu Ghaith for the May 12, 2003, bombings in Riyadh, Saudi Arabia, against four expatriate housing complexes on these operatives, saying they have been able to contact associates outside Iran.[45]) Saad bin Laden was subsequently said to have possibly been killed in a U.S. air strike against Al Qaeda locations in Pakistan, although there has been no confirmation of that.

In December 2009, Iran's Foreign Minister confirmed that a teenage daughter of Osama bin Laden had sought refuge in the Saudi embassy in Tehran—the first official confirmation that members of bin Laden's family have been in Iran. Other family members are said to have been living in a compound in Iran since the September 11, 2001, attacks. Some family members have said the young bin Ladens have never been affiliated with Al Qaeda.

Latin America

A growing concern has been Iran's developing relations with countries and leaders in Latin America considered adversaries of the United States, particularly Cuba and Venezuela's Hugo Chavez. Ahmadinejad made a high profile visit to five Latin American countries in November 2009, including Brazil but also including, as expected, Venezuela. On January 27, 2009, Secretary of Defense Gates said Iran was trying to build influence in Latin America by expanding front companies and opening offices in countries there. Recent State Department terrorism reports have said that Cuba maintains "close relationships with other state sponsors of terrorism such as Iran." Iran has offered Bolivia $1 billion in aid and investment, according to an *Associated Press* report of November 23, 2008.

Chavez has visited Iran on several occasions, offering Iran additional gasoline during Iran's fuel shortages in 2007 as well as joint oil and gas projects. A firm deal for Petroleos de Venezuela to supply Iran with gasoline was signed in September 2009, apparently in a joint effort to circumvent any potential worldwide ban on sales of gasoline to Iran. The two countries have established direct air links, and 400 Iranian engineers have reportedly been sent to Venezuela to work on infrastructure projects there. However, many accounts say that most of the agreements between Iran and Venezuela are agreements in principle that have not been implemented in reality. On October 30, 2007, then Secretary of Homeland Security

Michael Chertoff said that Iran's relationship with Venezuela is an emerging threat because it represents a "marriage" of Iran's extremist ideology with "those who have anti-American views."

India

Iran and India have cultivated good relations with each other in order to enable each to pursue its own interests and avoid mutual conflict. The two backed similar anti-Taliban factions in Afghanistan during 1996-2001 and have a number of mutual economic and even military-tomilitary relationships and projects, discussed further in CRS Report RS22486, *India-Iran Relations and U.S. Interests*, by K. Alan Kronstadt and Kenneth Katzman.

One aspect of the relationship involves not only the potential building of a natural gas pipeline from Iran, through Pakistan, to India, but also the supplies of gasoline to Iran. A key supplier is Reliance Industries Ltd., which by some accounts supplies up to 40% of Iran's imports of gasoline. In December 2008, some Members of Congress expressed opposition to a decision by the Export-Import Bank to provide up to $900 million in loan guarantees to Reliance, because of its gasoline sales to Iran. A provision of H.R. 3081, a FY20 10 foreign aid appropriation, would end provision of such export credits to companies that sell gasoline to Iran. Another source of U.S. concern has been visits to India by some Iranian naval personnel.

Africa

Some Members of Congress are concerned that Iran is support radical Islamist movements in Africa. In the 111th Congress, H.Con.Res. 16 cites Hezbollah for engaging in raising funds in Africa by trafficking in "conflict diamonds." Iran also might have supplied Islamists in Somalia with anti-aircraft and anti-tank weaponry. The possible transfer of weaponry to Hamas via Sudan was discussed above.

U.S. POLICY RESPONSES, OPTIONS, AND LEGISLATION

The February 11, 1979, fall of the Shah of Iran, a key U.S. ally, opened the long and deep rift in U.S.-Iranian relations. On November 4, 1979, radical "students" seized the U.S. Embassy in Tehran and held its diplomats hostage until minutes after President Reagan's inauguration on January 20, 1981. The United States broke relations with Iran on April 7, 1980 (just after the failed U.S. military attempt to rescue the hostages) and the two countries had only limited official contact thereafter.[46] The United States tilted toward Iraq in the 1980-1988 Iran-Iraq war, including U.S. diplomatic attempts to block conventional arms sales to Iran, providing battlefield intelligence to Iraq[47] and, during 1987-1988, direct skirmishes with Iranian naval elements in the course of U.S. efforts to protect international oil shipments in the Gulf from Iranian mines and other attacks. In one battle on April 18, 1988 ("Operation Praying Mantis"), Iran lost about a quarter of its larger naval ships in a one-day engagement with the U.S. Navy, including one frigate sunk and another badly damaged. Iran strongly disputed the U.S. assertion that the July 3, 1988, U.S. shoot-down of Iran Air Flight 655 by the *U.S.S. Vincennes* over the Persian Gulf (bound for Dubai, UAE) was an accident.

In his January 1989 inaugural speech, President George H.W. Bush laid the groundwork for a rapprochement, saying that, in relations with Iran, "goodwill begets goodwill," implying better relations if Iran helped obtain the release of U.S. hostages held by Hezbollah in Lebanon. Iran reportedly did assist in obtaining their releases, which was completed in December 1991, but no thaw followed, possibly because Iran continued to back groups opposed to the U.S.-sponsored Middle East peace process, a major U.S. priority.

Policy During the Clinton and George W. Bush Administrations

Upon taking office in 1993, the Clinton Administration moved to further isolate Iran as part of a strategy of "dual containment" of Iran and Iraq. In 1995 and 1996, the Clinton Administration and Congress added sanctions on Iran in response to growing concerns about Iran's weapons of mass destruction, its support for terrorist groups, and its efforts to subvert the Arab-Israeli peace process. The election of Khatemi in May 1997 precipitated a U.S. shift toward engagement; the Clinton Administration offered Iran official dialogue, with no substantive preconditions. In January 1998, Khatemi publicly agreed to "people-to-people" U.S.-Iran exchanges as part of his push for "dialogue of civilizations, but he ruled out direct talks. In a June 1998 speech, then Secretary of State Albright called for mutual confidence building measures that could lead to a "road map" for normalization. Encouraged by the reformist victory in Iran's March 2000 *Majles* elections, Secretary Albright, in a March 17, 2000, speech, acknowledged past U.S. meddling in Iran, announcing some minor easing of the U.S. trade ban with Iran, and promised to try to resolve outstanding claims disputes. In September 2000 U.N. "Millennium Summit" meetings, Albright and President Clinton sent a positive signal to Iran by attending Khatemi's speeches.

George W. Bush Administration Policy

The George W. Bush Administration policy priority was to prevent Iran from obtaining a nuclear weapons capability, believing that a nuclear Iran would be even more assertive in attempting to undermine U.S. objectives in the Middle East than it already is. The George W. Bush Administration undertook multi-faceted efforts to limit Iran's strategic capabilities through international diplomacy and sanctions—both international sanctions as well as sanctions enforced by its allies, outside Security Council mandate. At the same time, the Administration engaged in bilateral diplomacy with Iran on specific priority issues, such as Afghanistan and Iraq. The policy framework was supported by maintenance of a large U.S. conventional military capabilities in the Persian Gulf and through U.S. alliances with Iran's neighbors.

At times, the George W. Bush Administration considered or pursued more assertive options. Some Administration officials, reportedly led by Vice President Cheney, believed that policy should focus on using the leverage of possible military confrontation with Iran or on U.S. efforts to change Iran's regime.[48] Legislation in the 110th Congress indicated support for steps to compel other foreign companies to curtail business dealings with Iran.[49]

Overview of Obama Administration Policy

President Obama came into office articulating a policy of engagement with Iran as a means of persuading it to verifiably limit its nuclear program to purely peaceful uses and to curb Iran's propensity to fund and arm militant movements in the region. The policy is undergoing evolution as Iran has cracked down on democracy protesters and refused to accept proposals to limit its nuclear program. He said in his inaugural speech that the United States would be responsive to an Iranian "unclenched fist," and that the Administration would pursue consistent and broad direct diplomacy with Iran. In concert with that approach, Obama Administration officials have not indicated support for military action should Iran continue to pursue its nuclear program— although that option has not been explicitly "taken off the table." No Administration official has publicly supported "regime change" in Iran to accomplish U.S. goals, even at the height of the election-related protests.

Some Obama Administration officials, including Secretary of State Clinton and Secretary of Defense Gates, well before the unrest in Iran, expressed public skepticism that engagement would yield changes in Iran's policies. Others, including Dennis Ross, who was named in late February 2009 as an adviser to Secretary of State Clinton for "Southwest Asia" (a formulation understood to center on Iran), and then assigned to a similar capacity in the White House in June 2009, believe that the United States and its partners need to present Iran with clearer incentives and clearer punishments if Iran continues to refuse cooperation on the nuclear issue.

Implementation of the Engagement Policy

Prior to the June 12 election in Iran, the steps to engage Iran included:

- The message to the Iranian people by President Obama on the occasion of Nowruz (Persian New Year), March 21, 2009. Experts noted particularly the President's reference to "The Islamic Republic of Iran," a formulation that appears to suggest that the United States fully accepts the Islamic revolution in Iran and is not seeking "regime change."
- President Obama reportedly sent a letter to Iran's leadership expressing the Administration's philosophy in favor of engagement with Iran. (According to Iran's "Tabnak" website, which is close to the Revolutionary Guard, a second letter was sent to Iran in August 2009.)
- The major speech to the "Muslim World" in Cairo on June 4, 2009, in which President Obama said the United States had played a role in the overthrow of Mossadeq, and said that Iran had a right to peaceful nuclear power if it complies with its responsibilities under the NPT.
- The public invitation for Iran to attend the March 31, 2009, conference on Afghanistan in the Netherlands, discussed above.
- The U.S. announcement on April 8 that it would attend all future P5+1 meetings with Iran, and suspension of seeking new P5+1 agreement on additional U.N. sanctions.
- The loosening of restrictions on U.S. diplomats to meet their Iranian counterparts at international meetings, and the message to U.S. embassies abroad that they can invite

Iranian diplomats to upcoming celebrations of U.S. Independence Day. (The July 4 invitations did not get issued because of the Iran unrest.)
- On the other hand, President Obama issued a formal one year extension of the U.S. ban on trade and investment with Iran on March 15, 2009, (see "U.S. Ban on Trade and Investment with Iran," below).

The election-related unrest in Iran did not, initially, alter the Administration's commitment to engagement. As Iran has resisted nuclear compromise, and as democracy protests have grown, the Administration has begun to push for "crippling sanctions"— sanctions that bite into Iran's civilian economy. In particular, as of January 2010, the Administration has formulated proposals to target the Revolutionary Guard for sanctions, in part as a symbol of support for the pro- democracy demonstrators, and perhaps also in recognition that it cannot obtain international agreement for crippling sanctions on Iran's economy. The Administration continues to assert that it is open to further talks with Iran on the nuclear issue, but it appears to be lowering its expectations of a nuclear deal and shifting to greater support to the pro-democracy movement in Iran.

Enhanced U.S. Interests Section

On specific future steps toward greater engagement, the George W. Bush Administration said in late 2008 that it would leave to the Obama Administration a decision on whether to staff the U.S. interests section in Tehran with U.S. personnel, who would mostly process Iranian visas and help facilitate U.S.-Iran people-to-people contacts. The current interests section is under the auspices of the Swiss Embassy. The Obama Administration appeared inclined toward that step as well but no decision has been announced, to date, and was likely delayed or derailed outright by the Iranian response to the postelection protests.

Engagement Efforts During the George W. Bush Administration

Prior to 2008, the George W. Bush Administration directly engaged Iran on specific regional priority (Afghanistan and Iraq) and humanitarian issues. The United States had a dialogue with Iran on Iraq and Afghanistan from late 2001 until May 2003, when the United States broke off the talks following the May 12, 2003, terrorist bombing in Riyadh. At that time, the United States and Iran publicly acknowledged that they were conducting direct talks in Geneva on those two issues,[50] the first confirmed direct dialogue between the two countries since the 1979 revolution. The United States briefly resumed some contacts with Iran in December 2003 to coordinate U.S. aid to victims of the December 2003 earthquake in Bam, Iran, including a reported offer— rebuffed by Iran—to send a high-level delegation to Iran including Senator Elizabeth Dole and reportedly President George W. Bush's sister, Dorothy.

Prior to the July 2008 decision to have Undersecretary Burns attend the July 19, 2008, P5+1 nuclear negotiations with Iran, the George W. Bush Administration maintained it would join multilateral nuclear talks, or even potentially engage in direct bilateral talks, only if Iran suspended uranium enrichment. Some believe the Administration position was based on a view that offering to participate in a nuclear dialogue with Iran would later increase international support for sanctions by demonstrating U.S. willingness to negotiate.

The George W. Bush Administration did indicate that it considers Iran a great nation and respects its history; such themes were prominent in speeches by President George W. Bush such as at the Merchant Marine Academy on June 19, 2006, and his September 18, 2006, speech to the U.N. General Assembly. Then Secretary of State Rice said in January 2008 that the United States does not consider Iran a "permanent enemy." An amendment by then Senator Biden (adopted June 2006) to the FY2007 defense authorization bill (P.L. 109-364) supported the Administration's offer to join nuclear talks with Iran.

"Grand Bargain Concept"

The George W. Bush Administration did not offer Iran an unconditional, direct U.S.-Iran bilateral dialogue on *all* issues of U.S. concern: nuclear issues, Iranian support of militant movements, involvement in Iraq, and related issues. Some argue that the issues that divide the United States and Iran cannot be segregated, and that the key to resolving the nuclear issue is striking a "grand bargain" on all outstanding issues. The Obama Administration outreach appears to suggest a willingness to consider such a comprehensive agreement, if such agreement could be reached.

Some say the George W. Bush Administration "missed an opportunity," saying that U.S. officials rebuffed a reported comprehensive overture from Iran just before the May 12, 2003, Riyadh bombing, along the lines of a so-called "grand bargain." The *Washington Post* reported on February 14, 2007 (*"2003 Memo Says Iranian Leaders Backed Talks"*), that the Swiss Ambassador to Iran in 2003, Tim Guldimann, had informed U.S. officials of a comprehensive Iranian proposal for talks with the United States. However, State Department officials and some European diplomats based in Tehran at that time question whether that proposal represented an authoritative Iranian communication. Others argue that the offer was unrealistic because an agreement would have required Iran to abandon key tenets of its Islamic revolution.

Containment and Possible Military Action

The George W. Bush Administration consistently maintained that military action to delay or halt Iran's nuclear program was an option that was "on the table." The Obama Administration has not ruled this option out but has not indicated any inclination toward it. Secretary of Defense Gates said in interviews on September 27, 2009, that military action could only temporarily set back Iran's program, not end it. Although some oppose most forms of military action against Iran, others fear that military action might be the only means of preventing Iran from acquiring a working nuclear device. A U.S. ground invasion to remove Iran's regime has not, at any time, appeared to be under serious consideration in part because of the likely resistance an invasion would meet in Iran.

Proponents of U.S. air and missile strikes against suspected nuclear sites argue that military action could set back Iran's nuclear program because there are only a limited number of key targets, and these targets are known to U.S. planners and vulnerable, even those that are hardened or buried.[51] Estimates of the target set range from 400 nuclear and other WMD-related targets, to potentially a few thousand targets crucial to Iran's economy and military. Those who take an expansive view of the target set argue that the United States would need to reduce Iran's potential for retaliation by striking not only nuclear facilities but also Iran's conventional military, particularly its small ships and coastal missiles.

Still others argue that there are military options that do not involve air or missile strikes. Some say that a naval embargo or related embargo is possible that could pressure Iran into reconsidering its stand on the nuclear issue. Such action was "demanded" in H.Con.Res. 362. Others say that the imposition of a "no-fly zone" over Iran might also serve that purpose. Either action could still be considered acts of war, and could escalate into hostilities.

Most U.S. allies in Europe, not to mention Russia and China, oppose military action. These states tend to agree with experts who maintain that any benefits would be temporary, and are not justified by the risks. Some believe that a U.S. strike would cause the Iranian public to rally around Iran's regime, others say a strike would provoke a new regional war.

An Israeli Strike?

Israeli officials view a nuclear armed Iran as an existential threat and have repeatedly refused to rule out the possibility that Israel might strike Iran's nuclear infrastructure. Speculation about this possibility increased in March and April 2009 with statements by Israeli Prime Minister Benjamin Netanyahu to *The Atlantic* magazine stating that "You don't want a messianic apocalyptic cult controlling atomic bombs," which generated testimony in Congress by CENTCOM commander General Petraeus indicating that Israel has become so frightened by a prospect of a nuclear Iran that it might decide to launch a strike on Iran's nuclear facilities. Adding to the prospects for this scenario, in mid-June 2008, Israeli officials confirmed reports that Israel had practiced a long range strike such as that which would be required. In 2008, the George W. Bush Administration reportedly strongly discouraged an Israeli plan to conduct such a strike, and it denied Israel's requests for certain equipment useful to that operation. The issue was again highlighted in comments on July 5, 2009, by Vice President Biden when he indicated Israel had the right, as a sovereign country, to decide when its own national security was threatened to the point where it felt military action was the only viable option. Several senior U.S. officials (Secretary of Defense Gates, and National Security Advisor James Jones) visited Israel in late July 2009 to express the view that the Obama Administration is committed to strict sanctions on Iran—with the implication that Israeli or U.S. military action should not be undertaken, at least as of this time.

Although Israeli strategists say this might be a viable option, several experts doubt that Israel has the capability to make such action sufficiently effective to justify the risks. U.S. military leaders are said by observers to believe that an Israeli strike would inevitably draw the United States into a conflict with Iran but without the degree of planning that would be needed for success.

Iranian Retaliatory Scenarios[52]

Some officials and experts warn that a U.S. military strike on Iran could provoke unconventional retaliation. At the very least, such conflict is likely to raise world oil prices significantly out of fear of an extended supply disruption. Others say such action would cause Iran to withdraw from the NPT and refuse any IAEA inspections. Other possibilities include firing missiles at Israel— and Iran's July 2008 missile tests could have been intended to demonstrate this retaliatory capability—or directing Lebanese Hezbollah or Hamas to fire rockets at Israel. Iran could also try to direct anti-U.S. militias in Iraq and Afghanistan to attack U.S. troops.

Iran has developed a strategy for unconventional warfare that partly compensates for its conventional weakness. Then CENTCOM commander Gen. John Abizaid said in March 2006 that the Revolutionary Guard Navy, through its basing and force structure, is designed to give Iran a capability to "internationalize" a crisis in the Strait of Hormuz. On January 30, 2007, his replacement at CENTCOM, Admiral William Fallon, said that "Based on my read of their military hardware acquisitions and development of tactics ... [the Iranians] are posturing themselves with the capability to attempt to deny us the ability to operate in [the Strait of Hormuz]." (General David Petraeus became CENTCOM commander in September 2008.) In July 2008 Iran again claimed it could close the Strait in a crisis but the then commander of U.S. naval forces in the Gulf, Admiral Kevin Cosgriff, backed by Joint Chiefs Chairman Mullen, said U.S. forces could quickly reopen the waterway.

Iran has nonetheless tried to demonstrate that it is a capable force in the Gulf. Iran has conducted at least five major military exercises since August 2006, including exercises simultaneous with U.S. exercises in the Gulf in March 2007. Iran has repeatedly stated it is capable of closing the Strait of Hormuz and would do so, if attacked. In early 2007, Iranian ships were widening their patrols, coming ever closer to key Iraqi oil platforms in the Gulf. In February 2007, Iran seized 15 British sailors that Iran said were patrolling in Iran's waters, although Britain says they were in Iraqi waters performing coalition-related searches. They were held until April 5, 2007. On January 6, 2008, the U.S. Navy reported a confrontation in which five IRGC Navy small boats approached three U.S. Navy ships to the point where they manned battle stations. The IRGC boats veered off before any shots were fired. In October 2008, Iran announced it is building several new naval bases along the southern coast, including at Jask, indicating enhanced capability to threaten the entry and exit to the Strait of Hormuz. In late November 2009, Iran seized and held for about one week a British civilian sailing vessel and its crew that Iran said had strayed into its waters.

A recent study published by the Office of Naval Intelligence says that Iran has developed new capabilities and tactics over the past few years, backed by new acquisitions, that could pose a threat to U.S. naval forces in the Gulf. If there were a conflict in the Gulf, some fear that Iran might try to use large numbers of boats to attack U.S. ships, or to lay mines, in the Strait. In April 2006, Iran conducted naval maneuvers, including test firings of what Iran claims are underwater torpedoes that can avoid detection, presumably for use against U.S. ships in the Gulf, and a surface-to-sea radar-evading missile launched from helicopters or combat aircraft. U.S. military officials said the claims might be an exaggeration. The Gulf states fear that Iran will fire coastal- based cruise missiles at their oil loading or other installations across the Gulf, as happened during the Iran-Iraq war.

Containment and the Gulf Security Dialogue

The Obama Administration is continuing the efforts of its predecessor to strengthen containment of Iran by enhancing the military capabilities of U.S. regional allies. The policy may have been enhanced somewhat in May 2009 when France inaugurated a small military base in UAE, its first in the region, and which was clearly a signal that France is committed to containing Iran.

An assertive military containment component of George W. Bush Administration policy was signaled in the January 10, 2007, Iraq "troop surge" statement by President George W. Bush. In that statement, he announced that the United States was sending a second U.S. aircraft carrier group into the Gulf,[53] extending deployment of Patriot anti-missile batteries in the Gulf, reportedly in Kuwait and Qatar, and increasing intelligence sharing with the Gulf states. Secretary of Defense Gates said at the time that he saw the U.S. buildup as building leverage against Iran that could bolster diplomacy.

The U.S. Gulf deployments built on a containment strategy inaugurated in mid-2006 by the State Department, primarily the Bureau of Political-Military Affairs ("Pol-Mil"). It was termed the "Gulf Security Dialogue" (GSD), and represented an effort to revive some of the U.S.-Gulf state defense cooperation that had begun during the Clinton Administration but had since languished as the United States focused on the post-September 11 wars in Afghanistan and Iraq.

One goal of the GSD is to boost Gulf state capabilities through new arms sales to the GCC states. The emphasis of the sales is to improve Gulf state missile defense capabilities, for example by sales of the upgraded Patriot Advanced Capability-3 (PAC-3),[54] as well as to improve border and maritime security equipment through sales of combat littoral ships, radar systems, and communications gear. Several GSD-inspired sales include PAC-3 sales to UAE and Kuwait, and Joint Direct Attack Munitions (JDAMs) to Saudi Arabia and UAE (notified to Congress in December 2007 and January 2008). A sale to UAE of the very advanced "THAAD" (Theater High Altitude Area Defense) has also been notified.

Presidential Authorities and Legislation

A decision to take military action might raise the question of presidential authorities. In the 109th Congress, H.Con.Res. 391, introduced on April 26, 2006, called on the President to not initiate military action against Iran without first obtaining authorization from Congress. A similar bill, H.Con.Res. 33, was introduced in the 110th Congress. An amendment to H.R. 1585, the National Defense Authorization Act for FY2008, requiring authorization for force against Iran, was defeated 136 to 288. A provision that sought to bar the Administration from taking military action against Iran without congressional authorization was taken out of an early draft of an FY2007 supplemental appropriation (H.R. 1591) to fund additional costs for Iraq and Afghanistan combat (vetoed on May 1, 2007). Other provisions, including requiring briefings to Congress about military contingency planning related to Iran's nuclear program, is in the House-passed FY2009 defense authorization bill (H.R. 5658). In the 111th Congress, H.Con.Res. 94 calls for the United States to negotiate an "Incidents at Sea" agreement with Iran.

Regime Change

A major early feature of George W. Bush Administration policy—promotion of "regime change"—receded in the latter stages of the Administration. The Obama Administration has clearly distanced itself from the prior Administration's attraction to this option, for example by explicitly referring to Iran by its formal name—"the Islamic Republic of Iran." Judging from statements by President Obama in December 2009 that seem to support pro-democracy demonstrators, there are indications that the Obama Administration might see the resiliency of the opposition as providing a realistic opportunity to change the regime.

There has been some support in the United States for regime change since the 1979 Islamic revolution; the United States provided some funding to anti-regime groups, mainly pro- monarchists, during the 1980s.[55] The George W. Bush Administration's belief in this option became apparent after the September 11, 2001, attacks, when President George W. Bush described Iran as part of an "axis of evil" in his January 2002 State of the Union message. President George W. Bush's second inaugural address (January 20, 2005) and his State of the Union messages of January 31, 2006, stated that "our nation hopes one day to be the closest of friends with a free and democratic Iran." Other indications of affinity for this option included increased public criticism of the regime's human rights record and the funding of Iranian pro- democracy activists. However, the George W. Bush Administration shifted away from this option as a strategy employing multilateral sanctions and diplomacy took form in 2006, in part because U.S. partners believe regime change policies harm diplomacy.

Although it was clearly hoping for opportunities to change the regime, the George W. Bush Administration said that the democracy promotion programs discussed below were intended to promote political evolution in Iran and change regime behavior, not to overthrow the regime. A few accounts, such as *"Preparing the Battlefield"* by Seymour Hersh in the New Yorker (July 7 and 14, 2008) say that President George W. Bush authorized U.S. covert operations to destabilize the regime,[56] involving assistance to some of the ethnic-based armed groups discussed above. CRS has no way to confirm assertions in the Hersh article that up to $400 million was appropriated and/or used to aid the groups mentioned. In January 2009, Iran tried four Iranians on charges of trying to overthrow the government with U.S. support.

Democracy Promotion Efforts

The George W. Bush Administration's efforts to promote democracy in Iran began in FY2004 and were supported by many in Congress. Clear congressional sentiment in favor of this effort came in the 109th Congress with enactment of the Iran Freedom Support Act (P.L. 109-293, signed September 30, 2006, which authorized funds (no specific dollar amount) for Iran democracy promotion and modified the Iran Sanctions Act.[57]

Table 6. Summary of Provisions of U.N. Resolutions on Iran Nuclear Program (1737, 1747, and 1803)

Require Iran to suspend uranium enrichment
Prohibit transfer to Iran of nuclear, missile, and dual use items to Iran, except for use in light-water reactors
Prohibit Iran from exporting arms or WMD-useful technology
Freeze the assets of 40 named Iranian persons and entities, including Bank Sepah.
Require that countries exercise restraint with respect to travel of 35 named Iranians and ban the travel of 5 others
Calls on states not to export arms to Iran or support new business with Iran
Calls for "vigilance" (a non-binding call to cut off business) with respect to all Iranian banks, particularly Bank Melli and Bank Saderat
Calls on countries to inspect cargoes carried by Iran Air Cargo and Islamic Republic of Iran Shipping Lines if there are indications they carry cargo banned for carriage to Iran.

Table 7. Iran's Ballistic Missile Arsenal

Shahab-3 ("Meteor")	800-mile range. Two of first three tests (July 1998, July 2000, and September 2000) reportedly unsuccessful. After successful test in June 2003, Iran called missile operational (capable of hitting Israel). Despite claims, some U.S. experts say the missile not completely reliable—some observers said Iran detonated in mid-flight a purportedly more accurate version on August 12, 2004. On May 31, 2005, Iran announced it had tested a solid-fuel version. Iran tested several of the missiles on September 28, 2009, in advance of the October 1 meeting with the P5+1.
Shahab-4 /Sijj	1,200-1,500-mile range. In October 2004, Iran announced it had extended range of the Shahab-3 to 1,200 miles, and it added in early November 2004 that it is capable of "mass production" of it. *Agence France Presse* report (February 6, 2006) said January 2006 test succeeded. Related missiles claimed by Iran to have 1,200 mile range, include the "Ashoura" (claimed in November 2007); the "Ghadr" (displayed at military parade in September 2007); and the "Sijil," tested on November 12, 2000 (solid fuel). "Sijil 2" tested successfully on May 20, 2009 and December 16, 2009, but Secretary Gates said the range is likely closer to 1,200 miles than to 1,500. Still, this test potentially puts large portions of the Near East and Southeastern Europe in range, including U.S. bases in Turkey.
BM-25	1,500-mile range. On April 27, 2006, Israel's military intelligence chief said that Iran had received a shipment of North Korean-supplied BM-25 missiles. Missile said to be capable of carrying nuclear warheads. The *Washington Times* appeared to corroborate this chaptering in a July 6, 2006, story, which asserted that the North Korean-supplied missile is based on a Soviet-era "SS-N-6" missile.
ICBM	U.S. officials believe Iran might be capable of developing an intercontinental ballistic missile (3,000 mile range) by 2015. In February 2008 Iran claimed to have launched a probe into space, suggesting its missile technology might be improving to the point where an Iranian ICBM is realistic.
Other Missiles	On September 6, 2002, Iran said it successfully tested a 200 mile range "Fateh 110" missile (solid propellent), and Iran said in late September 2002 that it had begun production. Iran also possesses a few hundred short-range ballistic missiles, including the *Shahab-1* (Scud-b), the *Shahab-2* (Scud-C), and the *Tondar-69* (CSS-8). In January 2009, Iran claimed to have tested a new air-to-air missile.
Space Vehicle	Following an August 2008 failure, in early February 2009, Iran successfully launched a small, low- earth satellite on a Safir-2 rocket (range about 155 miles). The Pentagon said the launch was "clearly a concern of ours" because "there are dual-use capabilities here which could be applied toward the development of long-range missiles."
Warheads	*Wall Street Journal* report of September 14, 2005, said that U.S. intelligence believes Iran is working to adapt the Shahab-3 to deliver a nuclear warhead. Subsequent press reports say that U.S. intelligence captured an Iranian computer in mid-2004 showing plans to construct a nuclear warhead for the Shahab.[30] The IAEA is seeking additional information from Iran.

The Obama Administration has not announced a discontinuation of the democracy promotion efforts, but has shifted toward working directly with Iranians inside Iran who are organized around certain issues such as health care, the environment, science, and like issues.[58] There is less emphasis than previously on sponsoring visits by Iranians to the United States.

Another part of the effort is broadcasting to Iran. As noted below, the Voice of America and Radio Free Europe/Radio Liberty have been expanding broadcasts to Iran of information about Iran and about the United States. The Department has also formed a Persian-language website. Some oppositionists have criticized these broadcasting services for covering longstanding exiled opposition groups such as supporters of the Shah's son, and downplaying some of the newer, emerging pro-democracy groups inside Iran.

Until the post-election unrest, many questioned the prospects of U.S.-led Iran regime change because of the weakness of opposition groups. Providing overt or covert support to anti-regime organizations, in the view of many experts, would not make them materially more viable or attractive to Iranians. Even before the post-election crackdown, Iran was arresting civil society activists by alleging they are accepting the U.S. democracy promotion funds, while others have refused to participate in U.S.-funded programs, fearing arrest.[59] In May 2007—Iranian-American scholar Haleh Esfandiari, of the Woodrow Wilson Center in Washington, DC, was imprisoned for several months, on the grounds that the Wilson Center was part of this effort. The Center has denied being part of the democracy promotion effort in Iran.

The State Department has been the implementer of U.S. democracy promotion programs. The Department has used funds in appropriations (see **Table 8** below) to support pro-democracy programs run by 26 organizations based in the United States in Europe; the Department refuses to name grantees for security reasons.

In 2006, the George W. Bush Administration also began increasing the presence of Persian- speaking U.S. diplomats in U.S. diplomatic missions around Iran, in part to help identify and facilitate Iranian participate in U.S. democracy-promotion programs. The Iran unit at the U.S. consulate in Dubai has been enlarged significantly into a "regional presence" office, and "Iran- watcher" positions have been added to U.S. diplomatic facilities in Baku, Azerbaijan; Istanbul, Turkey; Frankfurt, Germany; London; and Ashkabad, Turkmenistan, all of which have large expatriate Iranian populations and/or proximity to Iran.[60] An enlarged (eight person) "Office of Iran Affairs" has been formed at State Department, and it is reportedly engaged in contacts with U.S.-based exile groups such as those discussed earlier. Iran asserts that funding democracy promotion represents a violation of the 1981 "Algiers Accords" that settled the Iran hostage crisis and provide for non-interference in each others' internal affairs.

Funding

As shown below, $67 million has been appropriated for Iran democracy promotion ($19.6 million through DRL and $48.6 million through the Bureau of Near Eastern Affairs/USAID). (Of these amounts, $58 million has been obligated as of July 2009). Additional funds, discussed in the chart below, have been appropriated for cultural exchanges, public diplomacy, and broadcasting to Iran. The Obama Administration requested funds for Near East regional democracy programs in its FY20 10 budget request, but no specific request for funds for Iran were delineated. This could be an indication that the new Administration views this effort as inconsistent with its belief in dialogue with Iran. No U.S. assistance has been provided to exile-run stations. (The conference report on the FY2006 regular foreign aid

Table 8. Iran Democracy Promotion Funding

FY2004	Foreign operations appropriation (P.L. 108-199) earmarked $1.5 million for "educational, humanitarian and non-governmental organizations and individuals inside Iran to support the advancement of democracy and human rights in Iran." The State Department Bureau of Democracy and Labor (DRL) gave $1 million to a unit of Yale University, and $500,000 to National Endowment for Democracy.
FY2005	$3 million from FY2005 foreign aid appropriation (P.L. 108-447) for democracy promotion. Priority areas: political party development, media, labor rights, civil society promotion, and human rights.
FY2006	$11.15 for democracy promotion from regular FY2006 foreign aid appropriation (P.L. 109-102). $4.15 million administered by DRL and $7 million for the Bureau of Near Eastern Affairs.
FY2006 supp.	Total of $66.1 million (of $75 million requested) from FY2006 supplemental (P.L. 109-234): $20 million for democracy promotion ($5 million above request); $5 million for public diplomacy directed at the Iranian population (amount requested); $5 million for cultural exchanges (amount requested); and $36.1 million for Voice of America-TV and "Radio *Farda*" broadcasting ($13.9 million less than request). Of all FY2006 funds, the State Department said on June 4, 2007, that $16.05 million was obligated for democracy promotion programs, as was $1.77 million for public diplomacy and $2.22 million for cultural exchanges (bringing Iranian professionals and language teachers to the United States). Broadcasting funds provided through the Broadcasting Board of Governors; began under Radio Free Europe/Radio Liberty (RFE/RL), in partnership with the VOA, in October 1998. *Farda* ("Tomorrow" in Farsi) received $14.7 million of FY2006 funds; now broadcasts 24 hours/day. VOA Persian services (radio and TV) combined cost about $10 million per year. VOA-TV began on July 3, 2003, and now is broadcasting to Iran 12 hours a day. (Farda began when Congress funded it at $4 million in the FY1998 Commerce/State/Justice appropriation, P.L. 105-119. It was to be called Radio Free Iran but was never formally given that name by RFE/RL.)
FY2007	FY2007 continuing resolution provided $6.55 million for Iran (and Syria) to be administered through DRL. $3.04 million was used for Iran. No funds were requested.
FY2008	$60 million (of $75 million requested) is contained in Consolidated Appropriation (H.R. 2764, P.L. 110-161), of which, according to the conference report $21.6 million is ESF for pro-democracy programs, including non-violent efforts to oppose Iran's meddling in other countries. $7.9 million is from a "Democracy Fund" for use by DRL. The Appropriation also fully funded additional $33.6 million requested for Iran broadcasting: $20 million for VOA Persian service; and $8.1 million for Radio Farda; and $5.5 million for exchanges with Iran.
FY2009	Request was for $65 million in ESF "to support the aspirations of the Iranian people for a democratic and open society by promoting civil society, civic participation, media freedom, and freedom of information." H.R. 1105 (P.L. 111-8) provides $15 million for democracy promotion programs in Iran
FY2004	Foreign operations appropriation (P.L. 108-199) earmarked $1.5 million for "educational, humanitarian and non-governmental organizations and individuals inside Iran to support the advancement of democracy and human rights in Iran." The State Department Bureau of Democracy and Labor (DRL) gave $1 million to a unit of Yale University, and $500,000 to National Endowment for Democracy. and several other countries.
FY2010	No specific democracy promotion request, but some funds (out of $40 million requested for Near East democracy programs) likely to fund continued human rights research and public diplomacy in Iran.

Further International and Multilateral Sanctions

There are a number of options available for additional U.N. or multilateral sanctions against Iran. U.S. officials have said that sanctions such as those below might also be considered by a "coalition" of countries, outside Security Council authorization. Such a coalition might include major U.S. allies in Europe, Asia, and the Middle East. U.S. allies tend to oppose the unilateral imposition by the United States of sanctions, especially when such sanctions seek to prevent European or other foreign companies from transacting business with Iran. Among the further U.N. or multilateral sanctions widely discussed (and some of these ideas are appearing in U.S. legislation to increase U.S. sanctions on Iran) are

- *Mandating Reductions in Diplomatic Exchanges with Iran or Prohibiting Travel by Iranian Officials.* As noted above, Resolution 1803 imposes a ban on travel by some named Iranian officials. One option is to further expand that list of Iranian officials. A further option is to limit sports or cultural exchanges with Iran, such as Iran's participation in the World Cup soccer tournament. However, many experts oppose using sporting events to accomplish political goals.

- *Banning International Flights to and from Iran.* Bans on flights to and from Libya were imposed on that country in response to the finding that its agents were responsible for the December 21, 1988, bombing of Pan Am 103 (now lifted). There are no indications that a passenger aircraft flight ban is under consideration among the P5+1. As noted above, inspections of Iranian international cargo flights and shipping is authorized in Resolution 1803.

- *A Ban on Exports to Iran of Refined Oil Products or of Other Products.* This sanction appears to be under P5+1 and Security Council consideration because such a ban might seriously hurt Iran's economy and thereby meet the definition of a "crippling" sanction. However, some members of the U.N. Security Council oppose this sanction as likely to halt prospects for a diplomatic solution to Iran's nuclear program. Iran imports about 25%-40% of its gasoline needs due to a lack of domestic refining capacity. Some experts believe Iran would be able to circumvent this sanction by offering premium prices to suppliers willing to defy such a U.N. resolution or by raising prices to discourage consumption by Iranian drivers. A version of this option would prevent companies of U.N. member states from shipping to Iran parts or technology needed to construct oil refineries or related installations.

- *Financial and Trade Sanctions, Such as a Freeze on Iran's Financial Assets Abroad.* Existing U.N. resolutions do not freeze all Iranian assets abroad, and such a broad freeze does not appear to be under Security Council consideration at this time. However, what appears to be under consideration is an extensive, or possibly comprehensive, ban on financial transactions with Iranian banks. Fearing this possibility, Iran moved $75 billion out of European banks in May 2008.

- *Limiting Lending to Iran by Banks or International Financial Institutions.* Another option is to ban lending to Iran by international financial institutions, or to mandate a reduction of official credit guarantees. British Prime Minister Brown indicated British support a limitation of official credits on November 12, 2007. As discussed below, EU countries and their banks have begun taking these steps, even without a specific U.N. mandate.

- *Banning Worldwide Investment in Iran's Energy Sector.* This option would represent an "internationalization" of the U.S. "Iran Sanctions Act," which is discussed in CRS Report RS20871, *Iran Sanctions*, by Kenneth Katzman. On November 12, 2007, comments, British Prime Minister Brown expressed support for a worldwide financing of energy projects in Iran as a means of cutting off energy development in Iran, and British officials have told CRS in August 2009 that the British government continues to favor this option.

- *Banning Insurance for Iranian Shipping.* One option, reportedly under consideration by the P5+1, is to ban the provision of insurance, or re-insurance, for any shipping to Iran. Shipments of Iranian oil require insurance against losses from military action, accidents, or other causes. A broad ban on provision of such insurance could make it difficult for Iran to Islamic Republic of Iran Shipping Lines (IRISL) to operate and force Iran to rely on more expensive shipping options. Iran said in September 2008 that it would have ways to circumvent the effect of this sanction if it is imposed. (The United States has imposed sanctions on IRISL.)

- *Imposing a Worldwide Ban on Sales of Arms to Iran.* Resolution 1747 called for—but did not require—U.N. member states to exercise restraint in selling arms to Iran. A future resolution might mandate an arms sales ban. Another option under discussion is to eliminate the Resolution 1737 exemption from sanctions for the Bushehr nuclear reactor project.

- *Imposing an International Ban on Purchases of Iranian Oil or Other Trade.* This is widely considered the most sweeping of sanctions that might be imposed, and would be unlikely to be considered in the Security Council unless Iran was found actively developing an actual nuclear weapon. Virtually all U.S. allies conduct extensive trade with Iran, and would oppose sanctions on trade in civilian goods with Iran. A ban on oil purchases from Iran is unlikely to be imposed because of the potential to return world oil prices to the high levels of the summer of 2008.

European/Japanese/Other Foreign Country Policy on Sanctions and Trade Agreements

U.S. allies supported the initial Obama Administration approach toward Iran more so than the George W. Bush Administration approach, which was perceived as primarily punitive. During 1992-1997, when the United States was tightening its own sanctions against

Iran, the European Union (EU) countries maintained a policy of "critical dialogue" with Iran, and the EU and Japan refused to join the 1995 U.S. trade and investment ban on Iran. The European dialogue with Iran was suspended in April 1997 in response to the German terrorism trial ("Mykonos trial") that found high-level Iranian involvement in killing Iranian dissidents in Germany, but resumed in May 1998 during Khatemi's presidency.

With Iran defiant on nuclear issues, the European countries, Japan, and other countries moved closer to the U.S. position since 2005. This trend has accelerated as Iran's leaders have responded violently to the post-election protests. The EU is no longer negotiating new trade agreements and other economic interaction with Iran, but rather has begun to implement some sanctions that exceed those mandated in Security Council resolutions. For example, several EU countries are discouraging their companies from making any new investments in or soliciting any new business with Iran. In addition, several EU countries report that civilian trade with Iran is down because Iran's defiance on the nuclear issue is introducing more perceived risk to trading with Iran. As noted above, some EU countries say they have reduced credit guarantee exposure to Iran since Resolution 1737 was passed, as shown in Table 6 above. Previously, the EU countries and their banks maintained that financing for purely civilian goods is not banned by any U.N. resolution and that exporters of such goods should not be penalized.

Negotiations with Iran on a "Trade and Cooperation Agreement" (TCA) are not currently being held; such an agreement would have lowered the tariffs or increased quotas for Iranian exports to the EU countries.[61] Similarly, there is insufficient international support to grant Iran membership in the World Trade Organization (WTO) until there is progress on the nuclear issue. Iran first attempted to apply to join the WTO in July 1996. On 22 occasions after that, representatives of the Clinton and then the George W. Bush Administration blocked Iran from applying (applications must be by consensus of the 148 members). As discussed above, as part of an effort to assist the EU-3 nuclear talks with Iran, at a WTO meeting in May 2005, no opposition to Iran's application was registered, and Iran formally began accession talks.

In the 1990s, European and Japanese creditors—over U.S. objections—rescheduled about $16 billion in Iranian debt. These countries (governments and private creditors) rescheduled the debt bilaterally, in spite of Paris Club rules that call for multilateral rescheduling. Iran's improved external debt led most European export credit agencies to restore insurance cover for exports to Iran. In July 2002, Iran tapped international capital markets for the first time since the Islamic revolution, selling $500 million in bonds to European banks.

World Bank Loans

The EU and Japan appear to have made new international lending to Iran contingent on Iran's response to international nuclear demands. This represents a narrowing of past differences between the United States and its allies on this issue. Acting under provisions of successive foreign aid laws (which require the United States to vote against international loans to countries named by the United States as sponsors of international terrorism), in 1993 the United States voted its 16.5% share of the World Bank against loans to Iran of $460 million for electricity, health, and irrigation projects, but the loans were approved. To block that lending, the FY1994- FY1996 foreign aid appropriations (P.L. 103-87, P.L. 103-306, and P.L. 104-107) cut the amount appropriated for the U.S. contribution to the Bank by the amount of those loans. The legislation contributed to a temporary halt in new Bank lending to Iran.

During 1999-2005, Iran's moderating image had led the World Bank to consider new loans over U.S. opposition. In May 2000, the United States' allies outvoted the United States to approve $232 million in loans for health and sewage projects. During April 2003-May 2005, a total of $725 million in loans were approved for environmental management, housing reform, water and sanitation projects, and land management projects, in addition to $400 million in loans for earthquake relief.

U.S. Sanctions

Any additional international or U.S. sanctions would add to the wide range of U.S. sanctions in place since the November 4, 1979, seizure of the U.S. hostages in Tehran.[62] Some experts believe that, even before U.S. allies had begun to impose some sanctions on Iran, U.S. sanctions alone were slowing Iran's economy.[63] However, the Obama Administration is said to oppose new U.S. unilateral sanctions because of their potential to offend U.S. allies whose companies would be the likely targets of such sanctions, although some Administration officials believe that the threat of new U.S. sanctions gives the Administration added leverage with Iran. Supporters of some new U.S. sanctions believe that allied firms should be compelled to choose between business with Iran and business with the United States.

As expected, there have been congressional efforts to push forward on proposed sanctions legislation because Iran has not agreed to implement the October 1, 2009, tentative nuclear agreement discussed above. The U.S. sanctions below are discussed in far greater depth in CRS Report RS20871, *Iran Sanctions*, by Kenneth Katzman.

Terrorism/Foreign Aid Sanctions

Several U.S. sanctions are in effect as a result of Iran's presence on the U.S. "terrorism list." The list was established by Section 6(j) of the Export Administration Act of 1979, sanctioning countries determined to have provided repeated support for acts of international terrorism. Sanctions imposed as a consequence include a ban on U.S. foreign aid to Iran; restrictions on U.S. exports to Iran of dual use items; and requires the United States to vote against international loans to Iran.

The separate, but related, Executive Order 13224 (September 23, 2001) authorizes the President to freeze the assets of and bar U.S. transactions with entities determined to be supporting international terrorism.

Proliferation Sanctions

Iran is prevented from receiving advanced technology from the United States under relevant and Iran-specific anti-proliferation laws[64] and by Executive Order 13382 (June 28, 2005). The laws include The Iran-Iraq Arms Nonproliferation Act (P.L. 102-484), and The Iran Nonproliferation Act (P.L. 106-178, now called the Iran-Syria-North Korea Non-Proliferation Act). These sanctions impose penalties on foreign firms that sell equipment to or assist Iran's WMD programs.

Targeted Financial Measures by Treasury Department

U.S. officials, particularly Undersecretary of the Treasury Stuart Levey (who has remained in the Obama Administration), say the United States is having substantial success in separate unilateral efforts ("targeted financial measures") to persuade European governments and companies to stop financing commerce with Iran on the grounds that doing so entails financial risk and furthers terrorism and proliferation.

U.S. Ban on Trade and Investment with Iran

On May 6, 1995, President Clinton issued Executive Order 12959 banning U.S. trade and investment in Iran.[65] This followed an earlier March 1995 executive order barring U.S. investment in Iran's energy sector. The provisions of the trade and investment ban, exemptions, and the debate over its application to foreign subsidiaries are discussed in substantial depth in CRS Report RS20871, *Iran Sanctions*, by Kenneth Katzman.

The Iran Sanctions Act (ISA)

The Iran Sanctions Act penalizes foreign (or U.S.) investment of more than $20 million in one year in Iran's energy sector.[66] No projects have actually been sanctioned under ISA, and numerous investment agreements with Iran since its enactment have helped Iran slow deterioration of its energy export sector. This Act is discussed in substantial depth in CRS Report RS2087 1, *Iran Sanctions*, by Kenneth Katzman, which contains a chart on foreign energy investments in Iran, and discusses pending legislation to expand ISA's authorities to include sanctions on companies that sell gasoline to Iran. This chapter contains extended discussion of several major pieces of legislation, including the House-passed H.R. 2194, and the "Dodd-Shelby Comprehensive Iran Sanctions, Accountability, and Divestment Act" (S. 2799). Both bills would expand the authorities of ISA to authorize sanctions against companies that sell gasoline or refinery-related equipment or services to Iran. The Dodd-Shelby bill has numerous provisions beyond that, including a broad ban on imports from Iran; freezing the assets of Revolutionary Guard Corps officials; authorizing divestment (see below); and prohibiting U.S. government procurement from firms that do business in Iran's energy sector or sell equipment that Iran could use to monitor or jam the Internet.

Divestment

A growing trend not only in Congress but in several states is to require or call for or require divestment of shares of firms that have invested in Iran's energy sector (at the same levels considered sanctionable under the Iran Sanctions Act).[67] For a discussion of pending legislation on this issue, see CRS Report RS2087 1, *Iran Sanctions*, by Kenneth Katzman.

Counter-Narcotics

In February 1987, Iran was first designated as a state that failed to cooperate with U.S. anti-drug efforts or take adequate steps to control narcotics production or trafficking. U.S. and U.N. Drug Control Program (UNDCP) assessments of drug production in Iran prompted the Clinton Administration, on December 7, 1998, to remove Iran from the U.S. list of major drug producing countries. This exempts Iran from the annual certification process that kept drug-related U.S. sanctions in place on Iran. According to several governments, over the past few years Iran has augmented security on its border with Afghanistan in part to prevent the flow of narcotics from that country into Iran. Britain has sold Iran some night vision equipment and body armor for the counter-narcotics fight.

Travel-Related Guidance

Use of U.S. passports for travel to Iran is permitted. Iranians entering the United States are required to be fingerprinted, and Iran has imposed reciprocal requirements. In May 2007, the State Department increased its warnings about U.S. travel to Iran, based largely on the arrests of the dual Iranian-American nationals discussed earlier.

Status of Some U.S.-Iran Assets Disputes

Iranian leaders continue to assert that the United States is holding Iranian assets, and that this is an impediment to improved relations. This is discussed in CRS Report RS20871, *Iran Sanctions*, by Kenneth Katzman.

Source: Map Resources. Adapted by CRS (April 2005).

Figure 2. Map of Iran

CONCLUSION

Mistrust between the United States and Iran's Islamic regime has run deep for almost three decades. Many argue that a wholesale replacement of the current regime would produce major strategic benefits for the United States, including a dramatic lessening of concerns about Iran's nuclear program, and an end to Iran's effort to obstruct a broad Arab-Israeli peace.

Others argue that many Iranians are united on major national security issues and that a new regime would not necessarily align with the United States. Some believe that many Iranians fear that alignment with the United States would produce a degree of U.S. control and infuse Iran with Western culture that many Iranians find un-Islamic and objectionable.

Others say that, now matter who is in power in Tehran, the United States and Iran have a common long-term interest in stability in the Persian Gulf and South Asia regions in the aftermath of the defeat of the Taliban and the regime of Saddam Hussein. According to this view, major diplomatic overtures toward the regime, if it survives the unrest, might yield fruit.

End Notes

[1] The Assembly also has the power to amend Iran's constitution.
[2] The Council of Guardians consists of six Islamic jurists and six secular lawyers. The six Islamic jurists are appointed by the Supreme Leader. The six lawyers on the Council are selected by the judiciary but confirmed by the Majles.
[3] Rafsanjani was constitutionally permitted to run because a third term would not have been consecutive with his previous two terms. In the 2001 presidential election, the Council permitted 10 out of the 814 registered candidates.
[4] A paper published by Chatham House and the University of St. Andrews strongly questions how Ahmadinejad's vote could have been as large as reported by official results, in light of past voting patterns throughout Iran. "Preliminary Analysis of the Voting Figures in Iran's 2009 Presidential Election." http://www.chathamhouse.org.uk.
[5] For more discussion of such legislation, see CRS Report RS20871, *Iran Sanctions*.
[6] White House, Office of the Press Secretary. "Statement by the President on the Attempted Attack on Christmas Day and Recent Violence in Iran." December 28, 2009.
[7] Other names by which this group is known is the Mojahedin-e-Khalq Organization (MEK or MKO) and the National Council of Resistance (NCR).
[8] The designation was made under the authority of the Anti-Terrorism and Effective Death Penalty Act of 1996 (P.L. 104-132).
[9] Kampeas, Ron. "Iran's Crown Prince Plots Nonviolent Insurrection from Suburban Washington." Associated Press, August 26, 2002.
[10] A March 16, 2006 "National Security Strategy" document stated that the United States "may face no greater challenge from a single country than from Iran."
[11] See http://www.whitehouse.gov/nsc/nss/2006/.
[12] For a more extensive discussion of the IRGC, see Katzman, Kenneth. "The Warriors of Islam: Iran's Revolutionary Guard," *Westview Press*, 1993.
[13] A new IAEA Director, Japanese official Yukiya Amano, took office December 2009.
[14] Text at http://www.dni.gov/press_releases/20071203_release.pdf.
[15] In November 2006, the IAEA, at U.S. urging, declined to provide technical assistance to the Arak facility on the grounds that it was likely for proliferation purposes.
[16] Lancaster, John and Kamran Khan. "Pakistanis Say Nuclear Scientists Aided Iran." *Washington Post*, January 24, 2004.
[17] For Iran's arguments about its program, see Iranian paid advertisement "An Unnecessary Crisis—Setting the Record Straight About Iran's Nuclear Program," in the *New York Times*, November 18, 2005. P. A11.

[18] Stern, Roger. "The Iranian Petroleum Crisis and United States National Security," *Proceedings of the National Academy of Sciences of the United States of America*. December 26, 2006.

[19] For text of the agreement, see http://www.iaea.org/NewsCenter/Focus/IaeaIran/eu_iran14112004.shtml. EU-3—Iran negotiations on a permanent nuclear pact began on December 13, 2004, and related talks on a trade and cooperation accord (TCA) began in January 2005.

[20] In November 2006, the IAEA, at U.S. urging, declined to provide technical assistance to the Arak facility.

[21] Voting in favor: United States, Australia, Britain, France, Germany, Canada, Argentina, Belgium, Ghana, Ecuador, Hungary, Italy, Netherlands, Poland, Portugal, Sweden, Slovakia, Japan, Peru, Singapore, South Korea, India. Against: Venezuela. Abstaining: Pakistan, Algeria, Yemen, Brazil, China, Mexico, Nigeria, Russia, South Africa, Sri Lanka, Tunisia, and Vietnam.

[22] Voting no: Cuba, Syria, Venezuela. Abstaining: Algeria, Belarus, Indonesia, Libya, South Africa.

[23] See http://daccessdds.un.org/doc/UNDOC/GEN/N06/290/88/PDF/N0629088.pdf?OpenElement.

[24] One source purports to have obtained the contents of the package from ABC News: http://www.basicint.org/pubs/Notes/BN060609.htm.

[25] Dempsey, Judy. "U.S. Urged to Talk With Iran." *International Herald Tribune*, February 5, 2009.

[26] CRS conversations with European diplomats in July 2009.

[27] "Cooperation for Peace, Justice, and Progress." Text of Iranian proposals. http://enduringamerica.com/2009/09/11/ irans-nukes-full-text-of-irans-proposal-to-5 1-powers/

[28] Three countries voted no: Malaysia, Cuba, and Venezuela. Six abstained: Afghanistan, Pakistan, Turkey, Brazil, Egypt, and South Africa. Azerbaijan left the meeting before voting.

[29] Annual Threat Assessment of the Intelligence for the Senate Select Committee on Intelligence, Dennis C. Blair, Director of National Intelligence, February 12, 2009.

[30] Broad, William and David Sanger. "Relying On Computer, U.S. Seeks to Prove Iran's Nuclear Aims." *New York Times*, November 13, 2005.

[31] U.S. Department of State. *Country Reports on Terrorism 2008*. Released April 30, 2009. http://www.state.gov/s/ct/rls/crt/2008/index.htm

[32] Walsh, Elsa. "Annals of Politics: Louis Freeh's Last Case." *The New Yorker*, May 14, 2001. The June 21, 2001, federal grand jury indictments of 14 suspects (13 Saudis and a Lebanese citizen) in the Khobar bombing indicate that Iranian agents may have been involved, but no indictments of any Iranians were announced. In June 2002, Saudi Arabia reportedly sentenced some of the eleven Saudi suspects held there. The 9/11 Commission final report asserts that Al Qaeda might have had some as yet undetermined involvement in the Khobar Towers attacks.

[33] This issue is covered in greater depth in CRS Report RS22323, *Iran's Activities and Influence in Iraq*, by Kenneth Katzman.

[34] CNN "Late Edition" interview with Hamas co-founder Mahmoud Zahar, January 29, 2006.

[35] Hamas Leader Praises Iran's Help in Gaza 'Victory.' CNN. February 1, 2009.

[36] Slackman, Michael. "Egypt Accuses Hezbollah of Plotting Attacks in Sinai and Arms Smuggling to Gaza." New York Times, April 14, 2009

[37] Hezbollah is believed responsible for the October 1983 bombing of the U.S. Marine barracks in Beirut, as well as attacks on U.S. Embassy Beirut facilities in April 1983 and September 1984, and for the hijacking of TWA Flight 847 in June 1985 in which Navy diver Robert Stetham was killed. Hezbollah is also believed to have committed the March 17, 1992, bombing of Israel's embassy in that city, which killed 29 people. Its last known terrorist attack outside Lebanon was the July 18, 1994, bombing of a Jewish community center in Buenos Aires, which killed 85. On October 31, 2006, Argentine prosecutors asked a federal judge to seek the arrest of Rafsanjani, former Intelligence Minister Ali Fallahian, former Foreign Minister Ali Akbar Velayati, and four other Iranian officials for this attack.

[38] "Israel's Peres Says Iran Arming Hizbollah." Reuters, February 4, 2002.

[39] Rotella, Sebastian. "In Lebanon, Hezbollah Arms Stockpile Bigger, Deadlier." *Los Angeles Times*, May 4, 2008.

[40] Shadid, Anthony. "Armed With Iran's Millions, Fighters Turn to Rebuilding." *Washington Post*, August 16, 2006.

[41] See CRS Report RL3 0588, *Afghanistan: Post-Taliban Governance, Security, and U.S. Policy*, by Kenneth Katzman.

[42] Conversations with observers and officials in Herat during CRS visit there. October 2009.

[43] "Tehran Pledges to Crack Down on Militants." Associated Press, July 18, 2005.

[44] Gertz, Bill. "Al Qaeda Terrorists Being Held by Iran." *Washington Times*, July 24, 2003.

[45] Gertz, Bill. "CIA Points to Continuing Iran Tie to Al Qaeda." *Washington Times*, July 23, 2004.

[46] An exception was the abortive 1985-1986 clandestine arms supply relationship with Iran in exchange for some American hostages held by Hezbollah in Lebanon (the so-called "Iran-Contra Affair"). Iran has an interest section in Washington D.C. under the auspices of the Embassy of Pakistan; it is staffed by Iranian-Americans. The U.S. interest section in Tehran has no American personnel; it is under the Embassy of Switzerland.

[47] Sciolino, Elaine. *The Outlaw State: Saddam Hussein's Quest for Power and the Gulf Crisis*. New York: John Wiley and Sons, 1991. p. 168.

[48] Cooper, Helene and David Sanger. "Strategy on Iran Stirs New Debate at White House." *New York Times*, June 16, 2007.

[49] The FY2007 defense authorization law (P.L. 109-364) called for a report by the Administration on all aspects of U.S. policy and objectives on Iran (and required the DNI to prepare a national intelligence estimate on Iran, which was released on December 3, 2007 as discussed above).

[50] Wright, Robin. "U.S. In 'Useful' Talks With Iran." *Los Angeles Times*, May 13, 2003.

[51] For an extended discussion of U.S. air strike options on Iran, see Rogers, Paul. *Iran: Consequences Of a War*. Oxford Research Group, February 2006.

[52] See also, Washington Institute for Near East Policy. The Last Resort: Consequences of Preventive Military Action Against Iran, by Patrick Clawson and Michael Eisenstadt. June 2008.

[53] Shanker, Thom. "U.S. and Britain to Add Ships to Persian Gulf in Signal to Iran," *New York Times*, December 21, 2006.

[54] "New Persian Gulf Security Effort Expected to Fuel Arms Sales in FY-07." *Inside the Pentagon*, November 9, 2006.

[55] CRS conversations with U.S. officials responsible for Iran policy. 1980-1990. After a period of suspension of such assistance, in 1995, the Clinton Administration accepted a House-Senate conference agreement to include $18-$20 million in funding authority for covert operations against Iran in the FY1996 Intelligence Authorization Act (H.R. 1655, P.L. 104-93), according to a *Washington Post* report of December 22, 1995. The Clinton Administration reportedly focused the covert aid on changing the regime's behavior, rather than its overthrow.

[56] Ross, Brian and Richard Esposito. Bush Authorizes New Covert Action Against Iran. http://blogs.abcnews.com/theblotter/2007/05/bush_authorizes.html.

[57] This legislation was a modification of H.R. 282, which passed the House on April 26, 2006, by a vote of 397-21, and S. 333, which was introduced in the Senate.

[58] CRS conversation with U.S. officials of the "Iran Office" of the U.S. Consulate in Dubai. October 2009.

[59] Three other Iranian Americans were arrested and accused by the Intelligence Ministry of actions contrary to national security in May 2007: U.S. funded broadcast (Radio Farda) journalist Parnaz Azima (who was not in jail but was not allowed to leave Iran); Kian Tajbacksh of the Open Society Institute funded by George Soros; and businessman and peace activist Ali Shakeri. Several congressional resolutions called on Iran to release Esfandiari (S.Res. 214 agreed to by the Senate on May 24; H.Res. 430, passed by the House on June 5; and S.Res. 199). All were released by October 2007. Tajbacksh was re-arrested in September 2009 and remains incarcerated.

[60] Stockman, Farah. "'Long Struggle' With Iran Seen Ahead." *Boston Globe*, March 9, 2006.

[61] During the active period of talks, which began in December 2002, there were working groups focused not only on the TCA terms and proliferation issues but also on Iran's human rights record, Iran's efforts to derail the Middle East peace process, Iranian-sponsored terrorism, counter-narcotics, refugees, migration issues, and the Iranian opposition PMOI.

[62] On November 14, 1979, President Carter declared a national emergency with respect to Iran, renewed every year since 1979.

[63] "The Fight Over Letting Foreigners Into Iran's Oilfields." *The Economist*, July 14, 2001.

[64] Such laws include the Atomic Energy Act of 1954 and the Energy Policy Act of 2005 (P.L. 109-5 8).

[65] An August 1997 amendment to the trade ban (Executive Order 13059) prevented U.S. companies from knowingly exporting goods to a third country for incorporation into products destined for Iran.

[66] Originally called the Iran-Libya Sanctions Act, or ILSA; P.L. 104-172, August 5, 1996. It was renewed by P.L. 107- 24, August 3, 2001; renewed again for two months by P.L. 109-267; and renewed and amended by P.L. 109-293.

[67] For information on the steps taken by individual states, see National Conference of State Legislatures. State Divestment Legislation.

In: Iran: Issues and Perspectives
Editor: Stephen D. Calhoun

ISBN: 978-1-61728-007-8
© 2010 Nova Science Publishers, Inc.

Chapter 2

IRAN: REGIONAL PERSPECTIVES AND U.S. POLICY[*]

Casey L. Addis, Christopher M. Blanchard, Kenneth Katzman, Carol Migdalovitz, Jim Nichol, Jeremy M. Sharp and Jim Zanotti

SUMMARY

As the Administration and Congress move forward to pursue engagement, harsher sanctions, or both, regional actors are evaluating their policies and priorities with respect to Iran. Iran's neighbors share many U.S. concerns, but often evaluate them differently than the United States when calculating their own relationship with or policy toward Iran. Because Iran and other regional concerns—the Arab-Israeli peace process, stability in Lebanon and Iraq, terrorism, and the ongoing war in Afghanistan—have become increasingly intertwined, understanding the policies and perspectives of Iran's neighbors could be crucial during the consideration of options to address overall U.S. policy toward Iran.

Iran's neighbors seek to understand and influence changes in the following areas:

- Iran's regional influence,
- Iran's nuclear program,
- Iran's role as an energy producer, and
- Iran's support for terrorism and non-state actors.

Although the Obama Administration may share many goals of the previous administration on Iran, it also sees the need for new strategies and approaches. The Obama Administration has advocated a policy of engagement with Iran to determine the nature of its nuclear program and address other subjects of international concern. While post-election turmoil in Iran delayed these efforts temporarily, it appears that the Administration is

---

[*] This is an edited, reformatted and augmented version of a CRS Report for Congress publication dated January 2010.

committed to pursue engagement through the P5+1 framework. At the same time, some Members of Congress have called for increased sanctions on Iran.

The United States, Israel, and the EU proposed the end of 2009 as a deadline for Iran to demonstrate its willingness to cooperate on the nuclear issue. That deadline has lapsed with no visible progress toward a resolution and the Administration is now working with its P5+1 partners to determine a course of action for 2010. Regardless of how they decide to proceed, any actions on the part of the Obama Administration, Congress, or the international community, and any developments in or provocations by Iran, will have implications for U.S. interests in the region as Iran's neighbors react and reevaluate their policies accordingly.

This chapter provides a description of Iran's neighbors' policies and interests, options for Congressional consideration, and an analysis of potential regional implications

INTRODUCTION: U.S. AND REGIONAL INTERESTS[1]

As the Administration and Congress move forward to pursue engagement, harsher sanctions, or both, regional actors are evaluating their policies and priorities with respect to Iran. Iran's neighbors share many U.S. concerns, but often evaluate them differently than the United States when calculating their own relationship with or policy toward Iran. Because Iran and other regional concerns—the Arab-Israeli peace process, stability in Lebanon and Iraq, terrorism, and the ongoing war in Afghanistan—have become increasingly intertwined, understanding the policies and perspectives of Iran's neighbors could be crucial during the consideration of options to address overall U.S. policy toward Iran.

Iran's neighbors seek to understand and influence changes in the following areas:

- Iran's regional influence,
- Iran's nuclear program,
- Iran's role as an energy producer, and
- Iran's support for terrorism and non-state actors.

Iran's Regional Influence

The United States and Iran's neighbors have expressed concerns about Iran's regional ambitions, its ability to influence the domestic political circumstances of its neighbors, and its ability to act as a spoiler in the peace process. Many analysts have cast events in the region as a power struggle between Sunni-ruled Arab states, led by Egypt and Saudi Arabia, and Iran and its allies and proxies, namely Syria, Hamas, and Hezbollah.[2] Others reject this paradigm as overly simplistic, pointing to Iran's physical and demographic attributes as an explanation for its regional role. Iran is a country of considerable size and resources[3] and, as a result, exerts a natural level of influence, both in positive and negative ways, they argue. Some observers have argued that Iran's soft power has diminished since the June 2009 presidential election and ongoing unrest.

For some of Iran's neighbors, Iran's regional influence is a domestic political concern. For example, Bahrain and Kuwait—Gulf states with signification Shiite populations—often express concerns that Iran is fomenting unrest among Shiites, highlighting fears about their own internal stability. In recent years, Morocco, Egypt, and Yemen have expressed similar concerns. Iran also uses proxies that at times are a destabilizing force, as is the case with Hezbollah in Lebanon. Others view Iran's regional aspirations in a broader sense. Saudi Arabia, for example, criticizes Iran's interference in what it perceives as "Arab causes," like the Israeli-Palestinian issue, and reportedly confronts Iran's proxies in Lebanese politics with material support of Sunni political parties and candidates.

Iran's Nuclear Program

The primary goal of U.S. and international engagement with Iran is to gain a clear understanding of Iran's nuclear activities through inspections and safeguards, and to limit Iran's uranium enrichment capacity to mitigate future concerns about the nature of its program and its possible weaponization. Some argue that uncertainty over Iran's nuclear program centers on the regime's political will to develop a nuclear weapon and are uncertain whether that will exists. Many analysts, however, perceive the weaponization of Iran's nuclear program as a certainty unless the international community acts to stop it. The disclosure on September 21, 2009 of a second uranium enrichment facility near Qom raised concerns on all sides (see "Caspian Neighbors" below). Iran's intentions are difficult to discern, but most analysts and observers agree that if Iran was seeking enriched fuel for nuclear energy and other civilian purposes, then it would not need to conceal an enrichment facility or restrict access of International Atomic Energy Agency (IAEA) inspectors to existing sites.

Most of Iran's neighbors share the concern of the United States and the international community over the nature of Iran's nuclear program, but some perceive it as a more imminent threat than others. Others recognize the threat but have competing economic and political interests that may prevent them from publicly expressing their concerns. Almost all of Iran's neighbors share the primary concern that uncertainty over Iran's nuclear program could lead to a regional arms race or war that could spill over into their territories, complicate their relationships with the United States, and/or badly damage their economies.

Iran's Role as an Energy Producer

Iran's energy resources serve as both a source of funds for its nuclear program, support for terrorism, and other activities, and as leverage over international players who might otherwise condemn those activities. According to the Energy Information Administration (EIA), Iran holds an estimated 10% of proven global oil reserves, the third largest proven reserves following Saudi Arabia and Canada. It is the fourth largest exporter of crude oil by volume, behind Saudi Arabia, Russia, and Norway. Perhaps just as valuable is Iran's strategic location along the Strait of Hormuz, a narrow chokepoint through which more than 40% of the world's traded oil transits. In addition to its oil reserves, Iran holds an estimated 15% of the world's natural gas reserves, the second largest globally. (Russia is first.)[4] Iran's vast energy resources, some argue, are underexploited and with continued investment could become more vital as world demand also grows.[5] This fact is increasingly relevant to regional and U.S. approaches to Iran, as nations n Asia develop stronger energy partnerships with Iran as a means of capitalizing on its potential.

For some of Iran's neighbors, economic and security concerns are in conflict when it comes to their relationships with Iran, and their policy priorities are shaped by whether they perceive potential economic benefits to outweigh security concerns. While almost all of Iran's neighbors share the view that a nuclear Iran is not desirable, especially if its development leads to a regional arms race or military conflict, some likely are unwilling to publicly challenge Iran on the issue because of their economic dependence on or relationships with Iran.

Source: Map Resources, Adapted by CRS (10/2009)

Figure 1. Iran and its Neighbors

Iran's Support for Terrorism

The United States and Iran's neighbors are concerned about Iran's support for terrorism in the region. According to the U.S. State Department Country Reports on Terrorism, Iran supports an array of U.S.-designated terrorist organizations and militant groups, including Lebanese Hezbollah, Hamas, Palestinian terrorist groups, Iraqi militants, and Taliban fighters in Afghanistan.[6] This support has at times undermined the political stability of Iran's neighbors, like Iraq, and poses direct military threats to others, like Israel and Lebanon. It also directly challenges U.S. efforts to advance the peace process, stabilize Iraq and Afghanistan, and promote regional stability.

Terrorist groups supported by Iran have perpetrated attacks in the Middle East, Europe, and Central Asia. While these attacks have targeted U.S. or Israeli interests, the presence of terrorist groups often limits the options available to Iran's neighbors to act together to address other regional concerns. By creating internal divisions and exploiting existing political and sectarian discord in places like the Palestinian territories and Lebanon, and by maintaining a proxy military presence on Israel's northern border (Hezbollah), Iran can perpetuate conflict without directly involving its own troops while using continued Arab-Israeli strife to justify its own militant, revolutionary rhetoric at home to shore up domestic support.

IRAN: REGIONAL PERSPECTIVES AND POLICIES

Saudi Arabia[7]

Perspectives and Interests

As the two most politically and religiously influential states in the Gulf region, Saudi Arabia and Iran have long maintained a binary balance of power, with each seeking to maximize its position relative to the other and relative to important outside players. Knit together by a common Islamic history but divided by sectarian, ethnic, and linguistic differences, the two Gulf energy giants leverage their economic resources and political power competitively to shape policy outcomes across the region and around the world. During the Cold War, the shared anti-Communist positions of the late King Faisal bin Abdul Aziz Al Saud and the late Shah Mohammed Reza Pahlavi made each a key regional ally of the United States under the so-called Twin Pillar policy, in spite of their latent rivalry. Iran's Islamic revolution accentuated core strategic tensions between the two regional powers by bringing religious and ideological differences into sharp contrast. In the 1980s, Iran's revolutionary clerical regime produced anti-Al Saud propaganda that questioned Saudi custodianship of the holy cities of Mecca and Medina, while official Saudi clerics and Salafi activists amplified their anti-Shiite rhetoric. Sectarian clashes in Saudi Arabia's Eastern Province and the holy city of Mecca underscored Saudi fears of potential subversion from Iran, and Saudi Arabia led other Gulf Arab states in supporting Iraq in its eight year war against Iran.

In the 1990s, Saudi Arabia served as the key hub for the implementation of the U.S. "dual containment" strategy, which was designed to maintain United Nations sanctions and no-fly zones in Iraq and to deter potential Iranian or Iraqi aggression. During this period Saudi Arabia viewed Iran in less hostile terms in light of Iraq's invasion of neighboring Kuwait. The U.S.-led invasion of Iraq in 2003 and the subsequent empowerment of Iraqi Shiites via the ballot box upended the prevailing security balance in the Gulf: in Saudi Arabia's view, Iran was the main beneficiary of the removal of Saddam Hussein. The potential for insecurity and sectarian violence in Iraq to draw Saudi Arabia and Iran into proxy warfare appears to have subsided at present. However, the fundamental reorientation of Iraq's political scene has created a new field of competition that continues to shape the views of Iranian and Saudi leaders about regional dynamics. The outcome of the pending national elections in Iraq will affect the relative interests of Saudi Arabia and Iran and the prospects for future engagement or competition among them.

Elsewhere, Iran and Saudi Arabia remain engaged in a direct competition for influence, at times pursuing diametrically opposed policies with regard to Lebanon and the Israeli-Palestinian peace process. Whereas Saudi Arabia previously placed great emphasis on positioning itself as the spiritual, if not political defender, of Sunni Islamic orthodoxy and a transnational Muslim community, its leaders' current focus appears to be on strengthening national and pan-Arab solidarity in an attempt to undercut domestic extremist threats and contain Iran. While sectarian rhetoric continues to enflame Saudi-Iranian relations, the dynamic between the two governments has reverted to basic strategic competition, overlaid with official assurances of mutual respect and periodic consultation. Saudi authorities have become less wary about asserting a leadership role in the Arab world and have asked Iranian leaders not to unduly interfere in what the Saudi Arabian government now considers to be strictly "Arab causes," including Palestinian political disputes.[8] Iran's nuclear program is a source of concern for Saudi Arabia, as is the potential for regional conflict resulting from the international community's confrontation with Iran. More recently, Saudi Arabia's military campaign against the Shiite Al Houthi rebel group in northern Yemen has brought fears of proxy conflict back into focus. Yemeni and Saudi sources have alleged that Iran has provided material support to the Houthis, while Iranian figures have condemned Saudi and Yemeni military operations as anti-Shiite.

Policy Priorities

Iran may no longer be working overtly to destabilize or overturn neighboring governments, but Iranian politicians nevertheless advocate for and support actors that have opposed Saudi policy and disrupted regional security in recent years, such as Hamas and Hezbollah. Combined with the perceived influence Iran has gained in Iraq and from its nuclear program, these trends have led the Saudi government to adopt a cautious policy approach that seeks to avoid direct confrontation while limiting the further spread of Iranian influence through coordination with other Arab governments and, to a lesser extent, with the United States. In general, Saudi officials have pursued limited engagement with their Iranian counterparts and have avoided exacerbating sectarian tensions with official public statements. Saudi media outlets, including government owned television channels and newspapers, have taken a more critical line toward Tehran, and have capitalized on controversies such as the early 2009 flare-up over Bahrain (see below) and the ongoing confrontation with the Al Houthi rebels in Yemen to fan popular opposition to perceived Iranian interference in the region. On the nuclear issue, Saudi Foreign Minister Prince Saud Al Faisal said in April 2009 that Saudi Arabia welcomed,

> "the US Government's positive approach of wishing to deal with the Iranian nuclear dossier crisis diplomatically and through dialogue. We are very hopeful that the Iranian Government will respond to these efforts for solving the crisis in a way that spares the Arab Gulf region and the Middle East the dangers of the proliferation of nuclear weapons and ensures the right of all the region's countries to the peaceful use of nuclear energy in accordance with the International Atomic Energy Agency's standards."[9]

At the United Nations General Assembly in September 2009, Prince Saud linked Israel's nuclear program to Iran's in arguing that the international community's response to Israel's presumed nuclear capabilities "has motivated some states to push ahead with the development of nuclear capabilities, using the pretext of double standards to justify non-compliance with international resolutions in this regard."[10]

Economic and Security Concerns

The value of Saudi-Iranian trade remains relatively limited, estimated by the International Monetary Fund at $1.42 billion in 2007 and $1.87 billion in 2008.[11] The limits imposed on the productivity of Iran's oil sector by U.S. and international sanctions and the difficulties foreign firms have found working in Iran benefit Saudi Arabia by helping to preserve its global market share. As an oil producer with significant excess production capacity, Saudi Arabia is able to exert some pressure on global oil prices and thereby has the power to affect the potential oil export revenue available to its fellow OPEC member Iran.

Economic and security concerns are linked for both parties, as regional security disruptions have the potential to threaten the viability of oil exports and necessary imports. Saudi Arabia's military forces possess more sophisticated modern equipment than those of Iran, in spite of the Iranian military's larger overall manpower. Saudi military spending also far outpaces that of Iran.

However, Iran's ballistic and cruise missile forces, the unconventional capabilities of Iranian naval forces, and Iran's relationships with non-state actors like Hezbollah are thought by many experts to pose a credible and dangerous threat in the minds of Saudi security officials. Saudi Arabia, as a longstanding military ally of the United States, is likely viewed by Iranian policy makers as a potential staging ground or facilitator for attacks on Iran and a potential target for retaliation against Iran's enemies by virtue of the international community's dependence on Saudi oil exports. As such, Saudi officials reportedly fear that Iran could attack in the event Iran were to face a military confrontation with the United States or Israel, even if Saudi Arabia had not been involved in the planning or execution of a military operation.

Prospects

The rivalry inherent to the Iranian-Saudi relationship appears natural given that the two states are emerging powers seeking to maximize their interests in a volatile, economically important region and on the world stage. The vulnerability of both countries' energy assets and the unique constraints imposed by religious factors may help mitigate the likelihood of direct conflict, in spite of economic competition and apparent sectarian tensions between the two. Saudi-Iranian political tensions have flared in the past to the point of sparking limited military engagements, but over time Saudi and Iranian leaders consistently have found means of defusing their disagreements before these crises have escalated into broader conflict. To the extent that political developments in Iran empower figures intent on asserting Iranian influence in Iraq, the Gulf, and the Levant without regard for the views or interests of Arab states, Saudi Arabia can be expected to use its considerable economic and political influence to resist Iranian encroachment. To the extent that more accommodating, pragmatic figures prevail, Saudi leaders can be expected to continue limited engagement with Iran, in light of persistent concerns about Iran's regional ambitions. Developments in Iraq will shape Saudi and Iranian leaders' decision making about their own bilateral relationship.

Saudi Arabia's prospective response to the acquisition of a nuclear weapon by Iran has long been a matter of intense debate and conjecture among observers and policy makers. Speculative predictions aside, history and recent policy statements suggest that if Saudi leaders decide that a Iranian nuclear weapon would have a significant deterrent effect on the United States or otherwise intolerably alter the balance of power in the Gulf, then Saudi Arabia would take decisive action to secure its national interests as it has in the past, whether unilaterally or in cooperation with other governments. Most Gulf experts expect that Saudi Arabia's response would be a critical factor in other regional actors' decisions about a possible Iranian nuclear weapon's capability.

Qatar[12]

Perspectives and Interests

Since the Iranian revolution, Iran and Qatar have maintained positive relations, in spite of periods when Iran's relationships with the Arab Gulf states otherwise foundered, such as during the Iran- Iraq war and tanker war of the 1 980s. Qatari officials have met frequently with members of Iran's government in Iran and in Qatar in recent years, and the Qatari government regularly advocates for increased dialogue between the GCC states, other Arab states, and Iran. Iranian President Mahmoud Ahmedinejad attended the December 2007 GCC summit in Doha at the invitation of Qatari Emir Hamad bin Khalifa Al Thani. He also attended a January 2009 summit on Gaza sponsored by the emir. The emir in turn visited Iran in November 2009 for consultations on bilateral and regional issues. In a March 2009 interview with a German newspaper, the emir explained Qatar's current perspective on the region and on Iran by saying,

> "We are a small country and we can live with anything around us. We will not be an enemy to anybody, but of course we will not allow anybody to use us against others. We will not, for example, stand with America against Iran. For sure. Iran never bothered us, it never created a problem for us... It will be hard for the Gulf countries to be with Iran against the United States. And I believe Iran knows this."[13]

These remarks, coupled with Qatari decisions to host Iranian leaders and to encourage Arab solidarity with Hamas during the January 2009 Gaza war have led some observers to argue that Qatar is working in opposition to the efforts of Saudi Arabia and Egypt and in favor of Iran. Qatari officials largely reject analyses that divide the region into opposing camps and argue that engagement, dialogue, and collective approaches to regional security problems between Arab states and Iran may offer opportunities to avert further tension and conflict. These arguments and positions are consistent with the Qatar' government's reputation for favoring independent policies and attempting to assert a leadership role consistent with its growing economic clout, in spite of its small population and very limited military capabilities.

Policy Priorities

Qatar's foreign policy priorities reflect its leaders' desire to maintain their country's independence, security, and freedom of action among more powerful competing regional and international actors, including the United States. Like other Arab Gulf states, Qatar's economic growth and diversification is in many ways dependent on the maintenance of stability in the Gulf region. Thus it views potential conflict, whether initiated by Iran or by others, as undesirable. Statements from Qatari leaders suggest that Doha views Iran as an ascendant regional power that cannot be ignored or fully contained by non-military means, and thus Qatar prioritizes engagement with Iran and its potential adversaries. Qatar's recent diplomatic activities, including its mediation of Lebanon's political deadlock in early 2008 and its advocacy on behalf of Hamas in January 2009, have been viewed by many regional observers as consistent with Iran's priorities, although Qatari leaders have described their regional diplomacy as driven by traditional Arab nationalist concerns. In July 2006, Qatar was the sole member of the United Nations Security Council to oppose Security Council Resolution 1696, which called on Iran to "suspend all enrichment-related and reprocessing activities, including research and development, to be verified by the IAEA," and proposed potential sanctions should Iran refuse.

Economic and Security Concerns

According to the IMF, the value of Iranian-Qatari trade was estimated at $57 million in 2007 and $75 million in 2008.[14] Iran and Qatar share the large North Field/South Pars natural gas deposit off the Qatari coast. Most of the gas in the field lies in Qatar's territorial waters (approximately 900 trillion cubic feet), with Iran's waters possessing the remainder (approximately 280 trillion cubic feet). Qatar's share of the field is the basis for the country's status as holding the third largest natural gas reserves in the world. Qatari liquefied natural gas exports brought an estimated $35.6 billion in export revenue to the country in 2008.[15]

With small and lightly equipped armed forces, Qatar effectively relies upon the U.S. armed forces stationed in the country for its defense. However, the presence of U.S. forces also creates a potential flashpoint vis-à-vis Iran; in the event of U.S.-Iranian hostilities, U.S. military facilities in Qatar would be critical for U.S. command and control purposes and thus could be likely targets of Iranian attack. The Chief of Staff of the Qatari Armed Forces Major General Hamad bin Ali al Attiyah travelled to Iran in July 2009 and held security talks with Iranian defense officials, including the commander of the Iranian Revolutionary Guard Corps.

Prospects

Unlike the other GCC states, Qatar has an enduring economic and security linkage to Iran, by virtue of the shared energy resources in the countries' contiguous waters. Without access to the shared gas deposit or under conditions where gas production facilities created with massive state investments were threatened with attack, Qatar's economy and fiscal position could suffer greatly. Qatar has maintained a policy of engagement with Iran and has strengthened bilateral ties as Iran's influence relative to other regional actors has grown in recent years. Absent a change in the nature and senior clerical leadership of the Iranian government, political changes among Iran's elected leadership are unlikely to jeopardize or significantly alter Iranian-Qatari relations. In late June 2009, Qatari Prime Minister and Foreign Minister Sheikh Hamad bin Jassem bin Jabr Al Thani characterized Iran's post-election disputes as "an internal matter because we must respect the right of each state to solve its own problems. The Iranians will decide how to resolve their problems among themselves, and I am certain that they will bypass this crisis."[16] A more moderate government in Tehran could empower Qatari efforts to promote GCC engagement with as a means of preventing conflict.

Qatari officials have simultaneously pursued a policy of rapprochement with Saudi Arabia, bringing an end to a series of long running political and boundary disputes, and with other Gulf states, building transportation and energy linkages to Bahrain, the United Arab Emirates, and Oman. Qatar's policy of attempting to "not be an enemy to anybody" appears sustainable unless drastic changes in security conditions compel Qatari leaders to choose among friends.

Bahrain[17]

Perspectives and Interests

As the rulers of a small state among larger regional and international powers, Bahrain's Sunni Arab monarchy historically has depended on good relations with external actors as the ultimate guarantee of its stability and security. Bahrain's current foreign relations reflect dynamics common to the country's history: the government of Bahrain seeks to maintain the country's security and independence through alliances with fellow Arab states, through a policy of engagement and non-antagonism toward Iran, and through the support of a powerful extra- regional actor, the United States. As an international hub for business and banking, Bahrain's economic success depends upon its image as a secure environment for investment and commerce. The potential for disruptive regional developments or conflict and the island's perennially disgruntled Shiite majority are the two principal concerns of Bahrain's ruling elite.

Bahrain's ruling family, the Al Khalifa, first established control over Bahrain and its predominantly Shiite population in the 1780s, after overcoming and expelling Persian outposts on the island. The Al Khalifa family subsequently sought alliances to secure itself from the predations of several regional powers, including Persia, until ultimately agreeing to make Bahrain a British protectorate in 1861.[18] Persian officials contested Bahrain's sovereignty repeatedly during the 19th and 20th centuries, most notably in the early 1930s, when Reza Shah contested the right of Bahraini officials to grant oil concessions to U.S. and British interests, and in 1957, when a bill was submitted to the Iranian Majlis (legislature) to make Bahrain a province of Iran. Prior to Bahrain's independence from Britain in 1971, Iran reasserted its claim to Bahrain, and the United Nations Secretary General dispatched a representative to determine the views of Bahrainis, who found that the island's residents overwhelmingly favored independence from all outside powers, including Iran. The findings were endorsed by the United Nations Security Council in Resolution 278 and Iran's legislature ratified the resolution, in effect relinquishing all claims to Bahrain.[19]

While these issues were formally settled nearly forty years ago, concerns that the claims will be revived have arisen from time to time based on comments by officials and clerics associated with the Islamic Republic of Iran. The most recent example occurred in February and March 2009, when media reports that a former speaker of the Iranian parliament and then-aide to Iran's Supreme Leader had referred to Bahrain as Iran's 14th province sparked a regional controversy. In response, the Iranian Foreign Ministry repeatedly reasserted Iran's respect for Bahrain's sovereignty and independence alongside Bahraini officials, amid condemnations from a number of other Arab states. In spite of Iranian government assurances, the remarks were seized upon by Arab governments and observers who are convinced that Iran harbors hostile intentions toward its neighbors and have been concerned about perceived Iranian interference in Arab affairs in recent years. Bahrain's leaders, like those of other Arab Gulf states, have responded cautiously to Iran's nuclear program and the sectarian tension that has accompanied conflict in Iraq and rise of the Shiite Arab political parties since the fall of Saddam.

Policy Priorities

Bahrain's limited resources and large Shiite population, some of whom are of Persian ethnicity, create unique challenges for the country's leaders as they view their relationship with Iran and events in the region. In the past, Bahrain's rulers have accused Iran of supporting pro-Iranian proxy groups against the Bahrain government, and Bahraini concerns about the potential for Iranian-supported unrest have been amplified in recent years amid sectarian violence in Iraq and resurgent protests by Shiite groups in Bahrain. Riots in 2009 mirrored similar events in the mid- 1990s that produced accusations of Iranian interference, although reporting suggests the political disputes driving the more recent unrest are based on long-standing unresolved domestic grievances and government reactions rather than widespread pro-Iranian sentiment.

Bahrain's leading Shiite opposition party, Al Wefaq, remains engaged in the political process and expressed concern about Iranian comments concerning Bahrain's sovereignty in early 2009. The party also played a mediating role following the December 2008 arrests of Shiite activists accused of plotting bombing attacks on Bahrain's national day, helping to secure the release of rival Shiite leader Hassan Mushaima. In November 2009, Sunni politicians criticized Al Wefaq after the Shiite party's members in the lower house of parliament refused to support a resolution endorsing Saudi Arabia's military campaign against the Al Houthi fighters accused of infiltrating the kingdom from northern Yemen.[20] The controversy reignited concerns about sectarian divisions among Bahrainis, although both the royal court and Al Wefaq have issued statements underscoring the linkage between Saudi and Bahraini security. Al Wefaq and Mushaima's hardline Al Haq movement will compete for influence among Bahrain's Shiite majority in the run-up to parliamentary elections scheduled for 2010, although it remains unclear whether Al Haq will formally participate or seek to put pressure on Al Wefaq to reinstate its boycott in light of continuing disillusionment among Shiites. Al Wefaq has delayed confirming that it will participate in the election, citing concerns about the overall effectiveness of the parliamentary system and continued allegations of sectarian discrimination. Bahrain's monarchy and Sunni community are likely to continue to closely monitor developments among leading Shiites for signs of Iranian influence or agitation.

Economic and Security Concerns

Iranian-Bahraini trade is limited; the IMF estimated its 2007 value at $166 million and $177 million in 2008.[21] Negotiations for a potential natural gas agreement for Bahrain to import Iranian gas to meet growing domestic energy demand was temporarily placed on hold following the sovereignty controversy in early 2009. Under the terms of the agreement, Bahrain and Iran would build a pipeline to enable Bahrain to import 28 million cubic meters per day of gas over 25 years.[22]

As stated above, Bahrain's primary security concerns are domestic and relate to Iran only to the extent that Iranian leaders may seek to exacerbate existing tensions between Bahrain's Sunni monarchy and its majority Shiite population. Bahrain relies on its relations with the United States and Saudi Arabia for its external security. Like Qatar, Bahrain hosts major U.S. military facilities, specifically the forward headquarters for the U.S. Navy component of U.S. Central Command, and may fear a potential retaliatory attack in the case of hostilities involving the United States or Israel and Iran.

Prospects

Suspicions of Iran among Bahrain's leaders appear deeply ingrained, and are amplified in instances where Bahrain's leaders perceive Iran to be pursuing hegemonic or sectarian policies. Political changes in Iran as a result of the disputed 2009 election could mitigate some, but not all of Bahrain's concerns. Acquisition of a nuclear weapon by Iran would likely deepen Bahrain's reliance on the United States, although trends and reactions among the Gulf Cooperation Council states would also exert significant influence on Bahrain's response. Iran appears poised to continue its efforts "to consolidate and deepen relations with all nations in the Persian Gulf, especially Bahrain,"[23] as a means of minimizing the prospects for collective GCC action that could harm its interests.

The United Arab Emirates[24]

Perspectives and Interests

Like the other Gulf states, the individual emirates of the United Arab Emirates (UAE) have had complex relationships with Iran historically, marked by changing alliances and, in some cases, contested sovereignty. On a national basis, the UAE government has viewed Iran simultaneously both as a potentially hostile neighbor and as an important commercial partner since the formation of the UAE in 1971. The seven constituent emirates' relations with Iran have proven complex, with some, such as Ras Al Khaymah and Abu Dhabi, having long held more negative views of Iran and its intentions, and others, such as Dubai and Sharjah, taking more accommodating positions based on shared commercial and demographic ties.

Persian and Iranian interaction with the Arab Trucial States, as the emirates were collectively known prior to the formation of the UAE in 1971, was critical in their early economic and political development and shaped interactions and rivalries between the emirates as the new state emerged. In 1971, Iran, then ruled by U.S.-backed Shah Mohammed Reza Pahlavi, seized two islands, Greater and Lesser Tunb, from the emirate of Ras Al Khaymah, and established a military outpost on the largely uninhabited island of Abu Musa under a bilateral agreement with the emirate of Sharjah. In April 1992, Iran exerted control of the remainder of Abu Musa. The dispute over the sovereignty of the islands has persisted over the last nearly 40 years, and frequently has enflamed tensions between the UAE, Arab states, and Iran. In October 2008, the UAE and Iran signed an agreement to establish a joint commission to resolve the islands dispute; that agreement came two months after the UAE protested Iran's opening in August 2008 of administrative and maritime security offices on Abu Musa. The United States is concerned about Iran's control over the islands, but takes no position on the sovereignty of the islands.

In a March 2009 interview, UAE President Sheikh Khalifa bin Zayed Al Nahyan explained the UAE government's views on the islands dispute and the Iranian nuclear program:

> "As a matter of principle, we do not condone the use of force in solving international disputes no matter how far away the location of this dispute may be. How much more so, when it is next door! We always stress the need to listen to the sense of reason in resolving the differences on Iran's nuclear program, which should be by peaceful means. We still hope these efforts will succeed. We also hope that all parties will exercise self-restraint and meet the demands of the international community on this issue...
>
> We hope that our brothers and neighbors [sic] Iranians will respond to our demands by handing over the Islands to the UAE. Our request is not an impossible one (to accept), since we are only asking that our legitimate rights to the three islands of Abu Musa, Greater Tunb Greater and Tunb Lesser be restored. We are looking forward to retrieving our sovereignty over the Islands through peaceful approach and dialogue. We have said repeatedly that the UAE will accept any ruling by the International Court of Justice, whether in our favor or not."[25]

In December 2009, the leaders of the GCC states reiterated their support for UAE sovereignty over the islands and called for Iran to accept mediation or ICJ adjudication of the islands dispute. Iran's Foreign Ministry responded by asserting Iran's ownership of the islands "forever."[26] On December 23, UAE Foreign Minister Sheikh Abdullah bin Zayed al Nahyan stated that "They [Iran] call the [islands] issue a misunderstanding and we call it occupation. However, we should not view Iran's continuous occupation of the UAE islands as a barrier for developing economic ties between the two countries. We even hope that such ties will reach a level through which we can resolve the dispute, not the other way around."[27]

Policy Priorities

Like Saudi Arabia, the UAE's policy priorities wih regard to Iran are multifaceted. In general, Emirati officials stress that they are seeking to avoid circumstances that would lead to regional conflict in which Iran could attack UAE territory. Specifically, they are seeking to engage with Iran on key disputes and cooperate with international partners to stem the advance of Iranian regional influence. The UAE's economic potential and planned growth depends on security and regional stability, and UAE leaders accordingly promote peaceful resolutions to regional disputes, even as they prepare to minimize the threat that regional security disruptions and military threats could post to the UAE. Tangible expressions of these priorities are visible in UAE support for the Obama Administration's outreach to Iran and calls for a mediated resolution to the islands dispute. These initiatives are paired with UAE political and financial support for the Palestinian Authority, endorsement of the Arab League peace proposal to Israel, and the UAE's diplomatic engagement and debt forgiveness toward Iraq, all of which attempt to balance countervailing Iranian efforts.

Economic and Security Concerns

Iran-UAE economic relations are well developed. The IMF estimates the value of bilateral trade at $5.9 billion in 2007 and $7.74 billion in 2008.[28] Dubai has long served as a particularly important commercial center for Iranian traders and businessmen, and Iranian merchants make significant profits bringing goods back and forth across the Gulf to Emirati ports. A number of Iranian banks operate branches in Abu Dhabi and Dubai, which U.S. officials suspect have become increasingly important nodes for the Iranian banking system as it seeks to maintain access to international financial markets amid tightening multilateral banking sanctions. It remains unclear what impact, if any, Dubai's debt challenges and subsequent financial bailouts by Abu Dhabi will have on political relations within the federation or what effect any changes could have on the UAE's relations with Iran.

The UAE, under the auspices of the Abu Dhabi Executive Authority, also has begun to move forward with plans to build nuclear power stations, and has sought to position its program as a counterexample to Iran's by agreeing to forego the development of indigenous uranium enrichment and fuel reprocessing capabilities. Ironically, the willingness of international partners to support the UAE nuclear program has been undermined by instances in which Iran and other nuclear proliferation customers and suppliers have used the UAE as a transit, shipping, and financial hub.

The UAE, particularly Abu Dhabi, has long feared that the large Iranian-origin community in Dubai emirate (est. 400,000 persons) could pose a "fifth column" threat to UAE stability. Military cooperation and arms sales form a key pillar of U.S.-UAE relations. The UAE hosts frequent port calls and shore visits for U.S. naval vessels and allows the U.S. military to use Al Dhafra air base in support of a variety of missions in the U.S. Central Command (CENTCOM) area of operations. In 2007 and 2008, the Bush Administration notified Congress of over $19.4 billion in potential arms sales to the UAE, including what would be the first overseas sale of the Terminal High Altitude Air Defense system, an anti-missile system well suited for responding to potential Iranian threats.[29]

Prospects

UAE-Iranian relations are shaped by tensions inherent to interactions between a small, heterogeneous federation and a more powerful, ambitious, ideologically motivated neighbor. Each side views the bilateral relationship through the lenses of their economic interdependence, their open territorial disputes, their ethnic differences, and sectarian divisions. Emirati authorities allowed public protests at the Iranian consulate in Dubai in relation to post-election disputes in Iran, and subsequent political changes in Iran as a result of the election dispute have the ability to amplify or reduce the extent to which the UAE views Iran as a threat. The UAE strongly opposes the militarization of Iran's nuclear program and would likely seek greater security coordination with the Gulf Cooperation Council or a clear commitment of protection from the United States. The prospect remains that the UAE could alter its decision to forego domestic uranium enrichment or plutonium reprocessing technology at some time in the future, which could signal pursuit of a more independent option, although doing so would risk harming UAE-U.S. relations. Refined petroleum product sanctions legislation pending in the U.S. Congress (see H.R. 2194, S. 908, and S. 2799) could affect firms operating in the UAE, as well as proposed U.S.-UAE nuclear cooperation.

Kuwait[30]

Perspectives and Interests

Kuwait's relationship with and perceptions of Iran have generally been a function of Kuwait's core concerns about Iraq, Kuwait's larger neighbor which invaded and occupied it from August 1990 until February 1991. During the rule of Saddam Hussein in Iraq, Kuwait considered Iran a counterweight to Iraqi power in the Gulf region, and most strategists in Kuwait did not view Tehran as the potential regional hegemon that some of its Gulf allies have. Some of its Gulf neighbors criticized Kuwait for attempting to use Iran and Iranian-supported movements to weaken Saddam Hussein. During the 1 990s, Kuwait often hosted pro-Iranian Iraqi Shiite oppositionists against Saddam, including those of the Supreme Council for the Islamic Revolution in Iraq (SCIRI), which is now a major Shiite party in Iraqi politics and has changed its name to the Islamic Supreme Council of Iraq (ISCI).

Policy Priorities

In keeping with Kuwait's overall perceptions and strategy, Iran-Kuwait relations are relatively normal. High level visits are routine, including parliamentary exchanges. In early 2008, the two formed an Iran-Kuwait Higher Committee to continue building relations. Kuwaiti refineries supply gasoline to Iran, which must import about 30% of its gasoline needs. The two are attempting to resolve their common maritime border, a pre-requisite for the proposed joint development of the disputed Durra offshore oil field, which also straddles the Saudi maritime border.

Kuwait has also taken a moderate approach to Iran's nuclear program. While the Kuwaiti government has stated that it is committed to complying with all U.N. Security Council Resolutions, including resolution 1801 which includes sanctions on Iran[31], it has also cautioned against an escalation to conflict. Speaker of the Kuwaiti National Assembly Jassem al Kharafi stated that "there are provocative Western statements, and Iran responds in the same way....I believe that a matter this sensitive needs dialogue not escalation."[32]

Economic and Security Concerns

So acute were Kuwait's fears of Saddam Hussein that it curried favor with pro-Iranian Iraqi Shiite parties even though these same Shiite groups had conducted attacks in Kuwait in the 1980s. The December 1983 bombings of the U.S. and French embassies in Kuwait and an attempted assassination of the Amir in May 1985 were attributed to the Iraqi Da'wa (Islamic Call) Party, the Shiite party of Iraqi Prime Minister Nuri al-Maliki. Seventeen Da'wa activists were arrested for these attacks. Da'wa activists also hijacked a Kuwait Airlines plane in 1987. These acts in the 1980s were perceived by many as an effort by Tehran – using these Iraqi allies – to pressure Kuwait into ending its support of Iraq during the Iran-Iraq war. At that time, Iran was viewed by Kuwait and the other Gulf states as the larger threat in the Gulf. During 1987-88, the United States protected Kuwaiti oil tankers against Iranian attack. Kuwait's perception changed when Saddam turned against the Gulf states by invading Kuwait in August 1990. In May 2001, Kuwait publicly apologized for supporting Iraq during the Iran-Iraq war.

Iran and Kuwait also have limited trade, approximately $43 million in 2008.[33]

Prospects

Some Kuwaiti strategists, such as former Ambassador to the United States Shaykh Saud al Nasser Al Sabah, have questioned Kuwait's stance as naive and potentially dangerous.[34] These observers question Iran's motives and believe that Kuwaiti leaders mistakenly do not perceive that Iran is slowly seeking to establish hegemony in the Gulf. Kuwait has not publicly accused Iran of attempting to support Kuwaiti Shiites (who are about 30% of Kuwait's population) as a potential internal opposition in Kuwait, but some believe Iran is looking for opportunities to strengthen Shiites in Kuwait to ensure that Kuwait maintains a relatively friendly posture towards Iran. Others say that Iran has no opportunity to support Shiites in Kuwait as an opposition movement because Kuwaiti Shiites are relatively well integrated into Kuwait's society and economy, and have fewer grievances than do Shiites in other states of the Gulf. On July 18, 2008, Kuwait named its first ambassador to Iraq since the 1990 Iraqi invasion—Ali al Momen, a retired general. Momen is a Shiite Muslim, and his appointment signaled Kuwait's acceptance that Iraq is now dominated politically by Shiites.

Oman[35]

Perspectives and Interests

Of the Gulf states, Oman is perceived as politically closest to and the least critical of Iran. Its leader, Sultan Qaboos bin Said Al Said, has often pursued foreign policies outside an Arab or Gulf consensus, and Qaboos sees no inconsistency between Oman's alliance with the United States and its friendship with Iran. This relationship has proved useful to the United States in the past; Oman was an intermediary through which the United States returned Iranian prisoners captured during U.S.-Iran skirmishes in the Persian Gulf in 1987-88. Oman's attempts to steer a middle ground caused problems for Oman in April 1980 when, within days of signing an agreement allowing the United States military to use several Omani air bases, the United States used these facilities—reportedly without prior notification to Oman—to launch the abortive mission to rescue the U.S. Embassy hostages seized by Iran in November 1979.[36]

Policy Priorities

The question many observers ask is why is Oman not as wary of Iran as are the other GCC states. Oman has no sizable Shiite community with which Iran could meddle in Oman, so the fear of Iranian interference is less pronounced. There are also residual positive sentiments pre-dating Iran's Islamic revolution. Oman still appreciates the military help the Shah of Iran provided in helping end a leftist revolt in Oman's Dhofar Province during 1964-1975. Others attribute Oman's position on Iran to its larger concerns that Saudi Arabia has sought to spread its Wahhabi form of Islam into Oman, and Oman sees Iran as a rival to and potential counterweight to Saudi Arabia.

Economic and Security Concerns

Oman reportedly is discussing a security pact with Iran, although the scope is as yet undefined.[37] In addition, Oman's government is said to turn a blind eye to the smuggling of a wide variety of goods to Iran from Oman's Musandam Peninsula territory. The trade is illegal in Iran because the smugglers avoid paying taxes in Iran, but Oman's local government collects taxes on the goods shipped.[38] Bilateral trade between Oman and Iran was approximately $1.45 billion in 2008, and consists mostly of natural gas exports from Iran to Oman.[39]

Oman's position on Iran's nuclear program is consistent with the general trend of Oman-Iran relations. On October 1, 2009, Omani Foreign Minister Yusuf bin Allawi bin Abdallah stated that "the Arabs and any Arab have no interest in being hostile to Iran," adding that "the entire world calls for a peaceful solution" to the international dispute over the nature of Iran's nuclear program.[40]

Prospects

Some accounts say that Oman is in the process of drawing closer to Iran than it has previously. Oman, as do the other GCC states, publicly opposes any U.S. attack on Iran's nuclear facilities, and has rebuffed efforts by the other Gulf states to persuade Oman to distance itself from Iran politically.

Iraq[41]

Perspectives and Interests

Since the fall of Saddam Hussein, Iran has sought to shape and influence the post-Saddam political structure to Iran's advantage. Iran succeeded in that strategy during 2004-2007, when Iraq was highly unstable and when it appeared, at times, that the U.S. effort to secure and democratize Iraq were failing. As Iraq stabilized during 2008, Iraqi nationalism strengthened and Iran came to be seen by many Iraqis, both Sunni and Shiite, as contributing to sectarian conflict. Iraqi leaders continue to take Iran's interests into account, but they no longer reflexively support Iranian positions.

Policy Priorities

Several of Iran's interests have been served by post-Saddam Iraqi leaders. This continuing Iranian influence might be reflected in Iraq's announcement in December 2009 that it would relocate the 3,000 Iranian oppositionists who live at "Camp Ashraf," near the Iran border, to a detention center in southern Iraq. These oppositionists had been invited to set up camp in Iraq in 1986, from where they could launch incursions into Iran, but the current, relatively pro-Iranian central government does not want to host this group any longer.

Iran attempted, but failed, to derail a U.S.-Iraq Status of Forces Agreement (SOFA) that authorizes the U.S. military presence beyond December 31, 2008. Senior Iranian leaders publicly opposed the pact as an infringement of Iraq's sovereignty—criticism that masked Iran's fears the pact is a U.S. attempt to consolidate its "hold" over Iraq and encircle Iran militarily. This criticism did not derail the accord, but might have contributed to insistence by Iraqi leaders on substantial U.S. concessions to a final draft agreement. In the end, Iran's concerns were attenuated by a provision in the final agreement (passed by Iraq's parliament on November 27, 2008 and now in force as of January 1, 2009) that U.S. forces could not use Iraqi territory as a base for attacks on any other nation. This provision is perceived by some as a statement that Iraq does not support military action against Iran's nuclear program.[42]

During exchanges of high-level visits in July 2005, Iraqi officials took responsibility for starting the 1980-1988 Iran-Iraq war, indirectly blamed Saddam Hussein for using chemical weapons against Iranian forces during the war, signed agreements on military cooperation, and agreed to open Iranian consulates in Basra, Karbala, Irbil, and Sulaymaniyah. In response to U.S. complaints, Iraqi officials subsequently said that any Iran-Iraq military cooperation would not include Iranian training of Iraqi forces. On May 20, 2006, Iraq's Foreign Minister, Hoshyar Zebari, supported Iran's right to pursue "peaceful" nuclear technology.[43]

On the other hand, Iran has not returned the 153 Iraqi military and civilian aircraft flown to Iran at the start of the 1991 Gulf War, and Iraqi leaders demand their return. Iraqi officials also have refused to expel the Party for a Free Life in Kurdistan (PJAK), an Iranian Kurdish separatist group, which Iran says is staging incursions into Iran from Iraqi territory. On February 5, 2009, that group was named by the U.S. Treasury Department as a terrorism supporting entity under Executive Order 13224.

Most territorial issues that have contributed to past disputes were resolved as a result of an October 2000 rededication to recognize the *thalweg*, or median line of the Shatt al Arab waterway as the water border (a provision of the 1975 Algiers Accords between the Shah of Iran and the Baathist government of Iraq, abrogated by Iraq prior to its September 1980 invasion of Iran.) The water border is subject to interpretation, but the two sides agreed to renovate water and land border posts during the March 2008 Ahmadinejad visit to Baghdad. In February 2009, Foreign Minister Zebari urged Iran to move forward with these demarcations, suggesting Iranian foot- dragging to resolve an issue whose ambiguity now favors Iran.

Economic and Security Concerns

The key concern of the central government is Iran's separate relationship with Shiite factions and militias. These factions are political opponents of the government of Prime Minister Nuri alMaliki and their serve militias serve as a limitation on full government security control, particularly in the south. The most prominent such faction is that of Moqtada Al Sadr. His political ties to Iran were initially limited because his family remained in Iraq during Saddam's rule. Still, the Sadr clan has ideological ties to Iran; Moqtada's cousin, Mohammad Baqr Al Sadr, founded the Da'wa Party and was a political ally of Ayatollah Khomeini when Khomeini was in exile in Najaf (1964-1978). Iran came to see political value and potential leverage in Sadr's faction—which has 30 total seats in parliament, a large and dedicated following among lower- class Iraqi Shiites, and which built a 60,000 person "Mahdi Army" (Jaysh al-Mahdi, or JAM) militia after Saddam's fall.

Perceiving the JAM as useful against the United States in the event of a U.S.-Iran confrontation, in 2005, Iran began arming it through the Revolutionary Guard's "Qods (Jerusalem) Force," the unit that assists Iranian protégé forces abroad. During 2005-6, the height of sectarian conflict in Iraq, Badr fighters in and outside the ISF, as well as JAM militiamen, were involved in sectarian killings of Sunnis, which accelerated after the February 2006 bombing of the Al Askari Mosque in Samarra.

The sectarian conflict empowered Shiite militias such as the JAM, but the arbitrary administration of justice and sense of constant conflict created by the militias triggered a popular backlash against them and against Iran. This was demonstrated in the January 31, 2009 provincial elections, which represented a clear setback for Iran and its interests. The Islamic Supreme Council of Iraq (ISCI), traditionally close to Iran politically and formerly an ally of Maliki's Da'wa Party, was hoping to sweep the elections in the Shiite south, but it did not come in first in any Shiite province. Sadrist candidates also fared generally poorly. In most of the Shiite provinces, the slate of Prime Minister Nuri al-Maliki—who is relatively pro-Iranian but whose party does not have a militia and whose slate ran on a platform of rule of law—came in first. The Sadrist faction and ISCI have forged a coalition with several other parties ("Iraqi National Alliance") to compete against Maliki in the March 7, 2010 national elections that will determine the next four year government.

The Defense Department's latest "Measuring Stability and Security in Iraq" report, dated September 2009, appears to reflect a continued U.S. concern about Iran's support for Shiite the report did not repeat previous assertions that Tehran is also improving the training and weapons systems received by the proxy militants.

Suggesting the degree to which the Iraqi government still views Iran as a benefactor, Maliki has visited Iran four times as Prime Minister to consult on major issues and to sign agreements. On March 2-3, 2008, Iranian President Ahmadinejad visited Iraq, a first since the 1979 Islamic revolution. In conjunction, Iran announced $1 billion in credits for Iranian exports to Iraq (in addition to $1 billion in credit extended in 2005, used to build a new airport near Najaf, opened in August 2008, which helps host about 20,000 Iranian pilgrims per month who visit the Imam Ali Shrine there). Suggesting Iran's earlier generosity is being reciprocated, in February 2009, the Iraqi government awarded a $1 billion contract to an Iranian firm to help rebuild Basra, and to repair ancient Persian historical sites in southern Iraq.[45] The the two countries now conduct about $4 billion annually in bilateral trade, according to Iraq's Trade Minister[46], and the February 2009 visit of Iranian Foreign Minister Mottaki resulted in a plan to increase that trade to $5 billion annually through increases in oil and electricity-related trade.[47]

Prospects

Iran's influence in Iraq remains substantial, but might be beginning to wane. The Shiite militias that Iran has supported are far weaker than they were two years ago. Iran's influence could fall further if Maliki's coalition prevails in the March 7, 2010 election and he continues to assert Iraq's independence and sovereignty from all influences, including U.S. and Iranian. Some experts have long predicted that Iran's influence would fade as Iraq asserts its nationhood, as the security situation has improved, and as Arab-Persian differences reemerge. Many experts point out that Iraqi Shiites generally stayed loyal to the Iraqi regime during the 1980-1988 Iran-Iraq war. Najaf, now relatively secure and prosperous, might eventually meet pre-war expectations that it would again exceed Iran's Qom as the heart of the Shiite theological world.

On the other hand, U.S. forces will be drawing down to about 50,000 by August 2010, and some fear that this will expose vulnerabilities among government forces that allow Shiite militias and Sunni insurgent groups to flourish again and challenge stability. If the security situation deteriorates sharply as the U.S. withdraws, Iranian influence could experience a resurgence – assuming the current government in Iran fends off a major challenge by its own opposition.

Turkey[48]

Perspectives and Interests

Turkey and Iran share an almost 500 kilometer (310 mile) border that was established in the 17th century, and they have not been to war since then. Over the years, however, their bilateral relations have been characterized by both conflict and collaboration.[49] Tensions sometimes surfaced from the neighbors' competing regional ambitions and from their rival forms of Islam: most Turks are Sunnis, while most Iranians are Shiites. After Iran declared itself an Islamic Republic in 1979, some predicted a worsening of relations because the Turkish Republic established in 1923 had abolished the caliphate, the office of the Prophet Muhammad's successors, and adopted a constitution that guaranteed secularism as a basic principle of the state. However, Ankara's pragmatic policy of accepting and officially recognizing the new Islamic Republic speedily and focusing on economic relations proved the forecasters wrong.

The ruling Justice and Development Party (AKP) in Turkey has Islamist roots and a foreign policy doctrine of seeking "zero problems" with neighbors and of nurturing beneficial relations with all, including Iran. Powered by a robust economy, the AKP government has continued the realistic pragmatism or pronounced self-interest of its predecessors toward Iran. Since AKP came to power in 2002, Turkish-Iranian relations have expanded markedly. Officials have exchanged numerous visits, culminating in Iranian President Mahmud Ahmadinejad's visit to Turkey in August 2008. The AKP government hosted him in Istanbul, thereby working around Ahmadinejad's antipathy to Turkish secularism by enabling him to avoid a usually obligatory visit in the capital of Ankara to the mausoleum of Mustafa Kemal Ataturk, the founder of the Turkish Republic. Turkish President Abdullah Gul reciprocated by visiting Iran for a regional summit in March 2009, when he met both Supreme Leader Ayatollah Ali Khamene'i and President Ahmadinejad.

Turkey's pragmatism or *realpolitik* was evident in official reactions to Iran's June 12, 2009, presidential election as President Gul and Prime Minister Recep Tayyip Erdogan were among the first international leaders to congratulate Ahmadinejad on his re-election. Foreign Minister Ahmet Davutoglu later declared controversies over the outcome to be an internal Iranian affair. AKP's domestic critics charged that these "reflexive and premature" actions may have undermined Turkey's stature and credibility as an interest in stability embodied in the status quo appeared to trump values.[50] Prior to visiting Iran in October 2009, Prime Minister Erdogan told the British newspaper, *The Guardian*, "There is not doubt he (Ahmadinejad) is our friend.... As a friend, so far we have good relations and have no difficulty at all."[51]

Policy Priorities

Turkey seeks to further regional stability and its own national interests in its relations with Iran. Ankara has made common cause with Tehran in seeking to preserve the territorial integrity of Iraq in order to prevent its division into ethnic states that might serve as a model for separatists. Both Turkey and Iran have separatist/terrorist foes who attack them from safe havens in northern Iraq—the Kurdistan Workers Party (PKK) and the Party for a Free Life in Kurdistan (PJAK), respectively— and both place a high priority of combating these threats. At the same time, Turkish officials have encouraged Iraqi Kurds to play a greater role in

Baghdad to help counter what the Turks fear might become excessive Iranian influence over a Shiite-led Iraqi government.[52] Ankara also may believe that greater involvement in the central government might moderate the Iraqi Kurds' separatist inclinations.

Turkish officials state that Iran has the right to develop nuclear energy for peaceful purposes and have called on Tehran to cooperate with the International Atomic Energy Agency (IAEA) in order to demonstrate that its nuclear program has peaceful intentions. Prime Minister Erdogan has criticized the international community for its "double standards" in targeting Iran's nuclear program while ignoring Israel's nuclear arsenal. He almost always mentions Israel (if not by name, then as "the country in the region with nuclear arms") when defending Iran, which he does frequently.[53] For example, after discussing Iran with President Obama at the White House on December 7, 2009, the Prime Minister said, "We do not want to see a country in our region possessing nuclear weapons and we want the countries in the region who have nuclear weapons to be rid of them."[54]

Turkey seeks to have the dispute between Iran and the international community solved diplomatically. Erdogan considers the idea of a military attack on Iran to be "an insanity" and has warned Israel of "a response equal to an earthquake" if it used its relationship with Turkey, referring to Turkish airspace to "wage aggression on a third party," i.e., Iran.[55] In October 2009, Turkey cancelled Israel's participation in an annual NATO military exercise in Turkey ostensibly because of continuing public anti-Israel sentiment resulting from the December 2008-January 2009 Gaza conflict. Some analysts suggested that, in addition, Turkey did not want to give Israel an opportunity to rehearse flying in Turkish airspace near the Iranian border. Turkey also opposes the imposition of sanctions on Iran which might harm Turkey's interests because it is a neighbor and economic partner of Iran. It is likely to abstain should the U.N. Security Council vote on sanctions as in November 2009, when the IAEA passed a resolution demanding that Iran immediately freeze operations at a previously secret uranium enrichment plant. These misgivings or disagreements concerning approaches to thwart Iran's nuclear ambitions aside, Turkey still does not want Iran to develop nuclear weapons and thereby upset the regional balance of power.

Finally, access to Iran's energy resources is a high priority for Turkey, which imports 70% of all the energy it consumes. Turkey depends on Russia for 68% of its gas supplies and wants retain access to Iran for much of the rest and to lessen that dependence.

Economic and Security Concerns

Turkish-Iranian relations have a very strong economic component. About 1.5 million Iranian tourists visit Turkey annually, visa-free. Trade is growing and reached $10 billion annually in 2008, with Iranian exports of oil, oil products, and gas to Turkey accounting for $7.2 million of the total.[56] Officials of both governments have said that they hope to increase trade to $30 billion a year in the next few years.[57] A pipeline commissioned in 2001 carries natural gas from Tabriz to Ankara. In 2007, Turkey and Iran signed a memorandum of understanding (MOU) for the state-run Turkish Petroleum Corporation (TPAO) to be granted the right to develop natural gas fields in South Pars, to extract up to 20 billion cubic meters (bcm) of additional gas, and to transport it via a new 1,850 kilometer pipeline to Turkey. Turkey is to invest an estimated $3.5 billion and receive 50% of the gas produced. Both governments hope that the new pipeline will eventually link with the planned 3,300-kilometer Nabucco pipeline. Scheduled to be completed in 2014, Nabucco is intended to carry natural gas from the Caspian/Central Asian region via Georgia and Turkey to Austria, bypassing

Russia. Iranian gas has the potential to make Nabucco more viable especially if Russia dissuades the Central Asian states from using it and China competes for their resources as well. Turkey and Iran have formed a joint company to transfer the gas to Europe. However, the European partners in Nabucco (Hungary, Bulgaria, Romania, Germany, and Austria) have declared, "No Iranian gas will be accepted unless the nuclear problem is solved" and U.S. Special Envoy for Eurasian Energy Ambassador Richard Morningstar has stated, "At present, we do not support Iran's participation in the project."[58] Turkey opposes all energy-related sanctions on Iran mainly because of its energy needs.

In addition, in 2007, Turkey signed an MOU to build three natural gas-fired power plants in Iran and to import 3 to 6 billion kilowatt hours of electricity annually. The two neighbors also have plans for an ambitious new road and rail transportation network to link the Turkish Black Sea port of Trabzon and the Iranian Persian Gulf port of Bandar Abbas, and to establish a free industrial zone on their border.

In private, Turkish officials have voiced some security concerns about a nuclear-armed Iran and about the impact that such a development would have on the regional balance of power. They note that Turkey is Iran's closest neighbor and easily within range of its missiles -- even though Iran has not threatened Turkey. These concerns may have prompted Turkey's possible purchase of U.S. Patriot air defense missiles.[59] As noted above, Prime Minister Erdogan and President Gul have criticized the West's policy on the issue and charged it with "double standards," suggesting that Iran is being judged more harshly than presumed nuclear power Israel. In November 2008, Erdogan told a Brookings Institution audience, "We do not find it correct to tell just one country to scrap nuclear weapons. We do not think this is an honest approach. Whoever has nuclear weapons should scrap them first then let us all be rid of them."[60] The two leaders have repeatedly put Turkey forward as a possible mediator between Iran and the United States and Turkey accepted an IAEA suggestion that it act as a repository for Iran's uranium, but Iran rejected the idea.[61] Ahmadinejad has said that there is no need for Turkish or any other mediation. President Gul noted "the need for the Western world to understand Iran's security apprehensions about its regime" as well as Iran's "need to persuade the Western world that it is not seeking the nuclear weapon and that all its researches are within the peaceful framework."[62]

Due to their common security concerns about Kurdish separatists, the Turkish and Iranian armed forces have conducted joint operations against the PKK and PJAK in northern Iraq. Prime Minister Erdogan has said that cooperation with Iran in dealing with terrorism will continue.

Prospects

Turkey is likely to consult closely with like-minded Arab Sunni powers, such as Saudi Arabia and the United Arab Emirates, concerning the impact of Iran's nuclear weapons' ambitions on the regional balance of power. Should Iran acquire nuclear arms, Turkey could, as a NATO member, rely on NATO defense guarantees if it believes them to be credible.[63] If it does not have that belief, Turkey could develop its own nuclear weapons program. Turkey already has plans for nuclear power plants, the technical abilities needed for a weapons program, and some uranium resources. At the same time as it pursues this path, Ankara is likely to continue to cultivate good relations with Tehran in line with its "zero problems" approach to foreign policy and because of its energy needs and economic interests.

Afghanistan[64]

Perspectives and Interests

As it attempts to stabilize Afghanistan, nearly eight years after the United States helped Afghan militias overthrow the Taliban, the Obama Administration has seen Iran as potentially helpful – or at least not an obstruction -- to its strategy for Afghanistan. The U.S. Special Representative for Afghanistan and Pakistan, Ambassador Richard Holbrooke, has advocated a "regional" component of the strategy, which focuses primarily on Pakistan but also envisions cooperation with Iran to help keep Afghanistan calm.

Policy Priorities

Still, Iran and U.S. interests in Afghanistan, while in many ways coincident, are not identical. Iran perceives its key national interests in Afghanistan as exerting its traditional influence over western Afghanistan, which Iran borders and was once part of the Persian empire, and to protect Afghanistan's Shiite minority. Iran's assistance to Afghanistan has totaled about $1.1 64 billion since the fall of the Taliban, mainly to build roads and schools and provide electricity and shops to Afghan cities and villages near the Iranian border. This makes Iran among the top financial donors to Afghanistan and is in many ways supportive of the U.S. policy of attempting to stabilize Afghanistan in part through economic development. Iran did not oppose Karzai's firing of Iran ally Ismail Khan as Herat governor in September 2004, although Iran has opposed the subsequent U.S. use of the Shindand air base,[65] located in Herat Province, which Iran fears the United States might use to attack or conduct surveillance against Iran.

During his visit to the United States in May 2009, Karzai said he had told both the United States and Iran that Afghanistan must not become an arena for the broader competition and disputes between the United States and Iran.[66] In public statements, in part because of the economic development work done by Iranian firms, President Hamid Karzai has, at times, called Iran a "friend" of Afghanistan. In June 2009, Karzai[67] congratulated Iranian President Mahmoud Ahmadinejad for his re-election at a time when many Iranians took to the streets to dispute his victory. Similarly, Karzai's August 2009 re-election bid was flawed by charges of widespread fraud, yet Ahmadinejad congratulated him for a victory on September 19, 2009 – long before it was clear that a second round election run-off would not be held. The two leaders, along with the President of Pakistan, have formed a tripartite summit process to discuss regional issues; the last meeting was in May 2009, hosted in Tehran by Ahmadinejad.

At other times, the two countries have had disputes over Iran's efforts to expel Afghan refugees. About 1.2 million remain, mostly integrated into Iranian society, and a crisis erupted in May 2007 when Iran expelled about 50,000 into Afghanistan. About 300,000 Afghan refugees have returned from Iran since the Taliban fell.

Economic and Security Concerns

The United States has reserved its strongest objections to Iran's shipment of weapons into Afghanistan. This could represent an Iranian attempt to build influence with armed opposition factions in Afghanistan, through which Iran might be able to retaliate against the United States in the event of U.S.-Iran conflict. The State Department report on international terrorism for 2008, released April 30, 2009, said Iran continues to provide some training to and ships arms to "selected Taliban members" in Afghanistan. Weapons provided, according to the State Department report, include mortars, 107mm rockets, rocket-propelled grenades, and plastic explosives. Several shipments of such weapons were captured by the U.S. military in Afghanistan in 2007. Secretary of Defense Gates testified before the Senate Armed Services Committee in late January 2009 that the Defense Department had seen a slight increase in Iranian shipments of arms into Afghanistan in the few preceding months. On December 17, 2009, U.S. Ambassador to Afghanistan Karl Eikenberry said that "Iran or elements within Iran have provided training assistance and some weapons to the Taliban."[68]

Iranian aid to Taliban fighters puzzle some experts since these shipments would appear to jeopardize Iran's relations with the Karzai government. Iran actively helped put together that government, in cooperation with the United States – at the December 2001 "Bonn Conference." In addition, Iran has traditionally supported Persian-speaking non-Pashtun factions in Afghanistan, who would presumably be suppressed and marginalized by any new Taliban-led regime in Afghanistan. Iran saw the Taliban regime, which ruled during 1996-2001, as a threat to its interests in Afghanistan, especially after Taliban forces captured Herat (the western province that borders Iran) in September 1995. Iran subsequently drew even closer to the ethnic minority- dominated Northern Alliance than previously, providing its groups with fuel, funds, and ammunition.[69] In September 1998, Iranian and Taliban forces nearly came into direct conflict when Iran discovered that nine of its diplomats were killed in the course of the Taliban's offensive in northern Afghanistan. Iran massed forces at the border and threatened military action, but the crisis cooled without a major clash, possibly out of fear that Pakistan would intervene on behalf of the Taliban. Iran offered search and rescue assistance in Afghanistan during the U.S.-led war to topple the Taliban, and it also allowed U.S. humanitarian aid to the Afghan people to transit Iran.

Prospects

Others see Iran as a marginal player in Afghanistan, because it is identified primarily with nonPashtuns and its links to Taliban fighters are tenuous and sporadic. Those who take this view question whether U.S. engagement with Iran would contribute much to solving the core problems plaguing the U.S. mission there. Still others believe that talks with Iran on Afghanistan could lead to broader U.S.-Iran talks, or potentially even open up the possibility of using Iran as a supply line for non-U.S. NATO forces in Afghanistan. Secretary of State Clinton made a point of inviting Iran to the U.N.-led meeting on Afghanistan at the Hague on March 31, 2009. However, since then, Iran has been faced with a growing and increasingly strong democratic opposition movement and the Obama Administration might be re-thinking its degree of engagement with the current regime. In addition, Iranian leaders have not accepted U.S. and partner country proposals to formulate a mechanism to ensure that Iran's nuclear program is for purely civilian and peaceful purposes.

Egypt[70]

Perspectives and Interests

Throughout history, Egypt and Iran have, at times, been fierce rivals, a natural outgrowth of the region's balance of power. Egypt envisions itself as the standard-bearer of Arab nationalism, and Persian Iran serves as a foil. During the Cold War, Egypt was militarily aligned with the Soviet Union while Iran was a U.S. client state. Then, in the late 1970s, as a result of the Camp David Peace Accords and the Iranian revolution, Egypt and Iran essentially traded places in their regional allegiances. Egypt's peace treaty with Israel resulted in a much closer relationship with the United States, while Iran's revolutionary theocratic government perceived the United States, its moderate Arab allies, and Israel as its primary adversaries in the Middle East, and Iran developed a closer relationship with Russia. For over 30 years, this pattern has persisted and, in recent years, new dimensions have been added to the Egyptian-Iranian rivalry.

Iran and Egypt severed diplomatic ties in 1980, a year after the Iranian revolution. Iran not only objected to Egypt's peace treaty with Israel, but also to its hosting of the deposed Shah and its support for Iraq during the 1980-1988 Iran-Iraq war. As a provocation, Iran applauded the assassination of former Egyptian President Anwar Sadat, naming a street after the assassin (Khalid Islambouli). The Egyptians have insisted that this street be renamed and the mural of Islambouli along side it be removed before normal ties can be restored.

Policy Priorities

Currently, Egypt is concerned about Iran's support for Palestinian militants, particularly Hamas, Iran's influence in Iraq, and Iran's nuclear program. Hamas's control of the Gaza Strip poses a challenge for neighboring Egypt. Hamas's call for armed resistance against Israel and its alleged Iranian financial and military support[71] runs counter to Egypt's foreign policy, which is largely based on its peace treaty with Israel and friendly relations with the United States.

A nuclear-armed Iran and its effect on the regional balance of power is a pressing security concern. Egypt firmly opposes Iran's nuclear ambitions, and, as is the case with its stance toward Israel's clandestine nuclear program, Egypt has called for a "nuclear-free zone" in the Middle East. Egypt is a signatory to the Nuclear Non-Proliferation Treaty (NPT) and has pledged not to develop weapons programs of its own. It also has rebuffed U.S. talks of a nuclear shield protecting Gulf states and possibly Egypt from an Iranian attack.

In 2006, the Mubarak government announced its own intention to develop a civilian nuclear energy program.[72] To date, progress on its development has been slow, and most experts expect Although Egypt may have legitimate energy shortfalls that are driving the pursuit of nuclear energy, most analysts suspect that concern over Iran's quest for nuclear weapons is behind the Egyptian initiative.

Economic and Security Concerns

Between 2007 and 2008, for reasons not entirely clear, Egypt and Iran began a dialogue to tentatively explore improving bilateral relations. During that period, Iran had been reaching out to a number of Sunni Arab states, as some commentators called it a charm offensive designed to assuage fears of its regional ambitions and nuclear program. Egypt may also have been looking to raise eyebrows in U.S. policymaking circles, hoping that its independent initiative with Iran might draw more Bush Administration attention and political support at a time when relations had been strained due to U.S. concerns about human rights in Egypt.

In December 2007, former Iranian National Security Council Chief Ali Larjani, a close aide to Ali Khamanei, visited Egypt and held talks with President Mubarak. As a follow up, on January 30, 2008, Mubarak held talks with Iran's then Majles (parliament) Speaker Gholam Ali Haddad Adel in Cairo. Adel was the first senior Iranian parliamentary official to conduct high-level talks with Egyptian counterparts in three decades. At the end of March 2008, Former Iranian President Mohammed Khatami visited Cairo for additional discussions.

However, the supposed Egypt-Iran rapprochement was short-lived, as neither side appeared ready to reconcile differences. In July 2008, an Iranian group, the Committee for Commemoration of Martyrs of Global Islamic Movement, re-edited an old *Al Jazeera* documentary on the murder of former Egyptian President Anwar Sadat and released it publicly as a new documentary entitled, "Execution of a Pharaoh." The film positively portrayed Sadat's assassin as a martyr. Although Iran attempted to distance itself from the film, relations again soured. In October 2008, Egyptian Foreign Minister Ahmad Abu-al Ghayt warned Iran that anyone "who intervenes in Egypt's internal affairs will not be happy with the response they receive. The Iranians cannot interfere in our internal affairs."[73]

Although Egyptian-Iranian relations have been cool for decades, tensions remained relegated to the diplomatic and cultural spheres. Iran and Egypt maintain a limited economic relationship, with bilateral trade estimated at $99 million in 2008.[74] However, in April 2009, the discovery of an alleged Hezbollah military cell in Egypt significantly heightened tensions. On April 8, 2009, the Egyptian government declared that it had uncovered a 49-person Hezbollah "cell" clandestinely operating in Egypt. According to authorities, cell members had been monitoring ship traffic at the Suez Canal and were planning terrorist attacks against Sinai tourist resorts, particularly those frequented by Israelis. Egypt also accused Hezbollah of smuggling weapons to Hamas along the Egypt-Gaza border and spreading "Shi'ite ideology" inside Egypt. On April 10, Hezbollah chief Sheikh Hassan Nasrallah acknowledged that one of the plotters in custody had been dispatched to Egypt to conduct "reconnaissance" for Hezbollah.

Prospects

The revelation of a Hezbollah cell serves Egyptian interests in several ways.[75] First, it draws a sharp contrast between it and Iran, the primary U.S. and Israeli adversary in the region. By demonstrating that Egypt is a direct target of Iran's regional meddling, Egypt may hope to rally other moderate Arab states behind it, while placing Iran's Arab allies (such as Hezbollah, Hamas, Syria, and Qatar) on the defensive. Second, Egyptian leaders had been eager to retaliate against Iranian-backed Hezbollah after the Lebanese Shiite organization called for the overthrow of the Mubarak regime for its alleged lack of support to Palestinians in Gaza during Israel's Operation Cast Lead between December and January 2009.

Nevertheless, by the end of 2009, tensions in the Egyptian-Iranian relationship had eased, as evident by the December 2009 meeting between Iranian Parliament Speaker Ali Larijani and President Mubarak in Cairo. In a news conference following their meeting, Larijani said that "As for the economic relationship, there is a positive tone from the two sides." According to one report, he also remarked that "Israel was the Islamic world's main enemy, and that Iran and Egypt had the same strategy with regard to the Palestinian cause but different ways of implementing the strategy."[76] One unnamed Egyptian official claims that during their meeting, Larijani proposed to improve Iranian-Arab relations, saying "the message is offering a new Iranian approach to resolve outstanding issues."[77] Most analysts remain skeptical of the Iranian proposal, suggesting that it may be another "charm offensive" similar to previous attempts mentioned above.

Overall, so long as Iran pursues a nuclear program and continues to strongly back Hamas and Hezbollah, Egypt will feel threatened and will work to counterbalance Iranian policy. However, a direct confrontation appears highly unlikely. For now, Iran will use non-state actors to provoke and pressure Egypt, while the Mubarak government will continue to rally other Sunni Arab states around its mantle of leadership to keep Iran in check. Egypt also will continue to demand that Israel and the United Sates prioritize the Arab-Israeli peace process in order to reduce the allure of Iran's so-called axis of resistance.

Syria[78]

Perspectives and Interests

For over 30 years, close Syrian-Iranian relations have been a mainstay of Middle East power politics. Starting with the 1979 Iranian revolution and spanning the 1980-1988 Iran-Iraq war, the arming and training of Shiite militias in Lebanon after Israel's invasion in 1982, and the maturation of Palestinian militant groups such as Hamas over the last decade, Syria-Iran ties have grown stronger, as both governments have built an alliance based on shared strategic interests rather than shared cultural and religious affinities.[79] Though their partnership has changed over the years, with Syria now serving as the junior partner, both sense that their self-described "axis of resistance" is becoming more powerful, as their non-state proxies, Hezbollah and Hamas, exercise more influence on the politics of the region.

Nevertheless, many observers continue to question the permanence of a Syrian-Iranian alliance, as some analysts assert that Syrian foreign policy is essentially pragmatic rather than revolutionary. They argue that should a solution to the Israeli-Palestinian conflict emerge, Syria would end its policy of resistance and join other Arab states in making peace with Israel. Other experts suggest the foundation of the Syrian-Iranian relationship—a shared concern over Iraq, support for Hezbollah in Lebanon, and countering Israel—is deeply rooted in the geopolitics of the region and cannot be easily overturned.

Policy Priorities

From a military and economic standpoint, Syria is a weak state, but its active support of Palestinian, Lebanese, and Iraqi militants/terrorist groups gives it a disproportionate regional role. Syria is surrounded by powerful U.S-allied neighbors (Israel and Turkey and Iraq) whom Syria seeks to counter through its own alliances. Though Syria's self image is pan-Arab and the majority of its citizens are Sunni Arabs, predominantly Persian Shiite Iran has a similar foreign policy outlook, creating the foundation for close relations.

The Asad regime's primary policy priority is to control Lebanon either directly or indirectly. Many hard-line Syrian nationalists consider their smaller, weaker neighbor to be an appendage of a greater Syrian nation and an artificial French colonial creation. In order to wield substantial influence in the byzantine world of Lebanese confessional politics, Syria needs allies, particularly now that it no longer occupies the country. Iranian-backed Hezbollah, the Lebanese Shiite terrorist group/militia/political party/charitable organization, serves as Syria's primary local partner. Without Hezbollah, Syria would have far more difficulty influencing Lebanese politics.

The Syrian-Hezbollah partnership also is valuable to Iran. According to the U.S. State Department's 2008 Country Reports on Terrorism, Syria allowed Iran to use its territory as a transit point for weapons bound for Hezbollah. Hezbollah provides Iran with an entree into the Levant, allowing it to project power far beyond its immediate borders and to threaten Israel by proxy. As long as Israel still occupies the Golan Heights, Syrian leaders apparently believe that this serves Syrian interests as well.

In 2009, Israeli and other foreign governments accused Syria of continuing to serve as an Iranian conduit for weapons shipments to Hezbollah. In November 2009, Israeli forces siezed a freighter named the *Francop* en route from Iran to the Syrian port of Latakia which contained, according to reports, thousands of medium-range 107- and 122-millimeter rockets, armor-piercing artillery, mortar bombs, hand grenades, and ammunition for Kalashnikov rifles.

Economic and Security Concerns

Though the Syrian-Iranian relationship is primarily a diplomatic alliance, Iranian trade with and investment in Syria (or at least the appearance of them) have somewhat expanded in recent years, perhaps partially in response to Western policymakers' attempts to woo Syria away from Iran. In the financial sector, Iran has stated its intention to establish a joint Iranian-Syrian bank, possibly involving Bank Saderat and the Commercial Bank of Syria – entities which have been sanctioned by the U.S. Treasury Department. In the manufacturing and industrial sectors, the Iran Khodro Industrial Group has established two car assembly plants in Syria. Iranian companies also have invested in concrete production, power generation, and urban transportation. In the energy sector, Syria, Iran, Venezuela, and Malaysia established a joint petroleum refinery in Homs, Syria. In addition, Iran, Turkey, and Syria reached a new natural gas deal that would allow Iran to export 105 billion cubic feet of natural gas annually to Syria via Turkey. Despite increased Iranian investments, the overall volume of Iranian-Syrian trade remains low. According to the *Economist Intelligence Unit*, bilateral trade may total between just $160 and $400 million.[80]

Prospects

Barring a major change in Lebanese affairs or a breakthrough in Israeli-Palestinian peace negotiations, Syrian-Iranian relations will most likely remain strong. As an indication of their enduring ties, both countries signed a defense cooperation agreement in December 2009, despite many Arab and Western attempts to divide them.

Nevertheless, some experts suggest that the alliance has its weak points, and that Western and moderate Arab governments should try to exploit them. In October 2009, King Abdullah of Saudi Arabia paid an historic visit to Syria that was interrupted by many as a return to somewhat normal Saudi-Syrian relations. As a result of the king's visit, some observers anticipate that Saudi investment in Syria may resume or even increase.[81]

Although it is difficult to discern the true state of Iranian-Syrian relations due to the opaque nature of both regimes, tensions may have developed over the issue of Syrian peace talks with Israel. After Syria attended the November 2007 U.S.-sponsored Annapolis peace conference, one Syrian media outlet asserted that it was Syria's right to pursue its own interests, stating that it was "fine for Syria to knock at doors that appear closed, as there is often someone inside to open [them]."[82] According to a report by the Washington Institute for

Near East Policy, "Iranian discussions. In June 2008, a senior advisor to Supreme Leader Ayatollah Khameini cautioned Syria of the consequences of peace on its relations with Tehran."[83]

The Saudi media has focused on exploiting tensions in Iranian-Syrian relations. In 2008, the London-based, Saudi-owned *Al Hayat* pan-Arab daily noted that Syrian President Bashar al Asad's recent visit to Tehran had been a "failure" in reassuring Iran of his intentions regarding indirect Syrian-Israeli peace talks. According to the report, "sources told *Al Hayat* that these reports contain information, not sheer speculation or analysis, that Syrian President Bashar al Asad's recent visit to Tehran was not successful with regard to the stand on the Syrian-Israeli negotiations.... The same reports added that the Iranian concerns prompted Iran to ask the Syrian side a lot of questions during al Asad's visit, which did not end in an agreement. In fact, these reports used the phrase 'the failure of the visit.'"[84]

The future direction of Hezbollah may hold the key to the strength of the Syrian-Iranian alliance. The group has multiple aims, as it seeks to balance an anti-Israel, pro-Iranian revolutionary regional agenda while appearing to uphold both Lebanese national interests and the independent interests of its Shiite constituents. Sometimes it succeeds in merging these agendas, as when Hezbollah claims it is acting as a national liberation movement struggling to free Lebanon from Israeli occupation, even after Israel's 2000 withdrawal from the south. Other times, particularly after its 2006 war with Israel, critics of Hezbollah have been successful in blaming it for wreaking havoc on the state itself and serving as a pawn of foreign, in this case Iranian and Syrian, interests.

Although many analysts charge that Hezbollah's ties to Iran are immutable, others believe that Hezbollah seeks greater independence from its Iranian and, to a lesser extent, Syrian patrons. According to one RAND study, "Hezbollah statements suggest that it does not consider its interests to be in perfect alignment with those of Iran, and its behavior reaffirms this assessment—Hezbollah continues to focus its energies on internal Lebanese politics."[85] For now, Hezbollah remains a hybrid organization with a militia, an intelligence apparatus, terrorist capabilities, charities, private companies, religious institutions, and a political party. For Hezbollah to evolve into a strictly non-violent movement, a Lebanese-Israeli peace treaty would have to be signed. Should that occur, however unlikely, some experts assert that without a common enemy (Israel) binding them together, Iran, Syria and Hezbollah's interests would diverge, and Syria would perceive Hezbollah more as a competitor for control over the Lebanese political scene. In this scenario, Syria and Iran would find themselves without a common proxy advancing their mutual interests.

Lebanon[86]

Perspectives and Interests

Lebanon, and in particular Lebanon's Shiite population, have looked to Iran for financial support and political backing since (at least) 1982. At the time of the Iranian Revolution, Lebanon was engulfed in a civil war (1975-1990). As part of his policy to export the revolution, the founder of the Islamic Revolution of Iran, Ayatollah Ruhollah Khomeini, reached out to Lebanon's Shiites, who had long felt underserved and underrepresented in Lebanon. During the Israeli invasion of Lebanon in 1982, Iran sent a contingent of Pasdaran security forces into Lebanon. The force armed and trained Shiite militia groups that later formed the terrorist organization Hezbollah, and provided medical attention and other services to Lebanese affected by the Israeli invasion.

Iran's support for Lebanese Shiites during the civil war cemented a partnership that both sides consider mutually beneficial. Hezbollah requires outside funding and military support and Iran requires a proxy to pressure Israel and the United States. Iran is one of a number of regional actors vying for influence in Lebanon, and Lebanon's policy priorities reflect this reality.

Policy Priorities

During the Syrian occupation of Lebanon (1976-2005), Lebanese-Iranian relations paralleled Syria's relationship with Iran. Since Syrian withdrawal from Lebanon in 2005, Lebanon's politics have reflected the sectarian realities in Lebanese politics and Lebanon's policy toward Iran has changed little. Iranian support for Shiites in Lebanon (and Hezbollah in particular) serves as a counterpoint to Saudi Arabian support for Sunni groups. This foreign patronage, when considered along with Lebanon's consensus government, requires that any Lebanese government maintain a friendly relationship with all regional actors to avoid upsetting the delicate political balance among its religious sects and political parties.

Some analysts argue that Syria's withdrawal from Lebanon left a power vacuum that has been filled by Iran via its proxy Hezbollah. Others argue that, despite initial concerns following Hezbollah's 2008 siege of Beirut, the outcome of the June 2009 parliamentary elections represented a setback for Iranian influence in Lebanon and in the Levant.[87] Regardless, as long as Lebanese politics includes a stake for Shiites and, most of all, Hezbollah, the Lebanese government, whatever its composition, will likely maintain a friendly orientation toward Iran. The Lebanese government has supported Iran's right to peaceful nuclear energy and has not articulated any official concerns about a possible Iranian nuclear weapons program.

Economic and Security Concerns

Trade between Iran and Lebanon is limited. The International Monetary Fund (IMF) estimated it at $192 million in 2007 and $247 million in 2008.[88] Iran and Lebanon also established a joint economic commission to expand economic cooperation and bilateral ties. During a meeting in March 2009, then-Lebanese Prime Minister Fouad Siniora stated that "There are lots of grounds for the growth and expansion of commercial, industrial, infrastructure, and tourism cooperation between the two countries, and our relations have to expand on a daily basis, therefore."[89]

Official trade statistics do not include Iranian support for Hezbollah, which many analysts expect is substantial. Prior to Lebanon's June 7, 2009 parliamentary elections, Iran announced that it would provide Hezbollah and its allies with $600 million in aid, heightening concerns about Iran's material support for Hezbollah.[90]

Other events indicate that Iran might also aim to increase its influence among non-Shiites in Lebanon. Lebanon's primary security concern is Israel. In spite of efforts on the part of the Lebanese government and the international community to strengthen the Lebanese Armed Forces, many Lebanese perceive Hezbollah as the best line of defense against possible Israeli attacks along Lebanon's southern border. In what appeared to be an attempt to improve the standing of Hezbollah and its allies ahead of the parliamentary elections, Iran reportedly offered to provide arms and financial support to the Lebanese Armed Forces "without conditions." No official agreement materialized.[91]

Prospects

Since the civil war ended in 1990, Hezbollah, backed by Iranian largesse, has expanded its role in Lebanese politics. Many analysts, and some among Lebanon's non-Shiite groups, argue that Hezbollah's 2006 war with Israel and 2008 siege of Beirut demonstrate its growing strength in Lebanese domestic politics and its ability to act as a spoiler of Western interests in the region. These analysts have expressed concerns about the future of stability in Lebanon and the region if Hezbollah were backed by the promise of an Iranian nuclear device.

In Lebanon, Sunnis and some Christians have expressed similar fears.[92] As the regional influence of Iran grows, so does Hezbollah's strategic depth. Lebanese politics and policies are built around the national memory of the civil war, and any prospect for a change in Lebanese politics or a shift of power balance in the region underscores fears that Lebanon could again become a theater of regional conflict, especially if international efforts to curb Iran's nuclear program fail, or if Israel decides to take military action against Iran.

Palestinians[93]

Perspectives and Interests

Since its 1979 Islamic Revolution, Iran has at least rhetorically, and at times materially, supported the Palestinian national cause. Because Iran and its population were relatively remote from the Arab-Israeli conflict—Iran does not border Israel or the Palestinian territories, it had not been a party to any of the Arab-Israeli wars, and most Iranians are not Arab—many analysts believe that the Islamic Republic's adoption of the Palestinian cause after the 1979 revolution was calculated to persuade Sunni and Shiite Arab populations throughout the region that the Iranian regime more truly embodies the principles of Islamic leadership than the traditional Sunni Arab states of the region.[94] Other reasons—geopolitical competition with Israel and the United States, sympathy for the Palestinians as "victims of neo-colonialism" (given Iran's sensitivity to foreign involvement in its own affairs), religious and civilizational opposition to a Jewish/Zionist stronghold in a predominantly Muslim region—also are possible.

Dating back to when the late Yasser Arafat and the Palestine Liberation Organization (PLO) were in exile, the Palestinians have been historically ambivalent about openly accepting Iranian support for their national cause. While Arafat courted Ayatollah Khomeini's support at times,[95] he preferred to associate himself publicly with fellow Sunni Arab leaders (including Iran's enemy Saddam Hussein), and later developed greater ties with the West and engaged Israel through the Oslo "peace process." Arafat's engagement of Israel led Iran to refocus its efforts on influencing Palestinian groups that rejected Oslo—particularly Hamas, but also Palestinian Islamic Jihad and others—and that sought to derail efforts to forge peace with Israel on terms that they and Iran found objectionable. Since then, Hamas has grown significantly in influence—from the political margins to rivaling Arafat's Fatah movement in preeminence.

Mahmoud Abbas, Arafat's successor as PLO Chairman, Palestinian Authority (PA) President, and the head of Fatah, is clearly opposed to Iranian influence in Palestinian politics. From the viewpoint of Abbas and his allies, Iran has sowed factional and geographical division among Palestinians at a time when assembling credible, unified leadership to deal with Israel is vitally important. Analysts might conclude that the threat Iran poses to Israel—with its nuclear program and its support of militant groups such as Hamas and Hezbollah—has greatly increased the difficulty of Abbas's task of marshaling and sustaining international political will sufficient to persuade Israel to (1) abandon its control over Palestinian territory and (2) agree to Palestinian statehood in both principle and fact. Official representatives of the PLO and PA limit their statements on Iran to its role in internal Palestinian affairs, and thus have not taken a public position on the nuclear issue.

Some Palestinians who are skeptical of the Arab-Israeli peace process, however, believe that Iranian support for Palestinian militants and Hezbollah provides needed leverage with Israel that the United States and Europe are unlikely to deliver to Abbas. Yet, even though Hamas welcomes Iranian assistance, and even though Iran's reputation among Arab populations has arguably been bolstered in recent years by its anti-Western and anti-Israel positions and rhetoric, many believe that Hamas and Iran intentionally maintain a measure of distance from one another. An alternate interpretation is that they merely understate the extent of their ties. They appear to understand the importance of Hamas maintaining an image among its domestic constituents as an authentic Palestinian offshoot of the Muslim Brotherhood, instead of as an Iranian proxy—owing to the ethnic, sectarian, and linguistic differences between Palestinians (who are predominantly Sunni Arabs) and Iranians (who are mostly Shiite and non-Arab).

Policy Priorities

Iran's future influence over the Palestinian political scene seems tied to Hamas's fortunes, which have been on the rise since Hamas's political emergence in the late 1980s (and were accentuated by its victory in Palestinian Legislative Council elections in 2006). By consolidating its control over Gaza and pursuing popular support through resistance to Israel, Hamas appears to seek legitimacy by establishing its indispensability to any Arab-Israeli political arrangement. Many analysts believe that Hamas hopes to leverage this indispensability into sole or shared leadership of the PA in both the West Bank and Gaza—either through a unity arrangement with Abbas and his Fatah movement, or through presidential and legislative elections (which were supposed to take place in January 2010 under PA law, but have been postponed pending factional agreement on conditions for holding them)—and to gain membership in or somehow supplant the PLO, which remains internationally recognized as the legitimate representative of the Palestinian people.

Since its takeover of Gaza, however, some polls indicate that Hamas's popularity has suffered. Some analysts attribute this to doubts among Palestinians that Hamas is as incorruptible or as committed to ordinary people's best interests as was thought in 2006, partly due to the realities of governing and to certain of Hamas's practices (i.e., enabling/profiting from the smuggling of goods through tunnels from Egypt, provoking harm to Gazan civilians by firing on Israeli targets from dense urban populations during the 2008-2009 Gaza conflict).

Abbas and Fatah hope to regain influence in Gaza and to neutralize Hamas's ability to act as a peace process spoiler. To that end, they have alternated between, and sometimes have simultaneously pursued, (1) mobilization of international support for a Palestinian state to undercut Hamas's appeal to Palestinian peace process skeptics and (2) engagement in intermittent, Egyptian-brokered national unity discussions with the aims of integrating Hamas more fully into PA institutions and of ending or reducing Hamas's dependence on Tehran.

Various U.S. and international policymakers, including Secretary of State Hillary Rodham Clinton, have said or implied that organizational fissures may exist, particularly between Hamas's Gaza-based leadership and its leadership-in-exile—viewed as more closely tied to Iran—in Damascus, Syria.[96] Some believe that these potential fissures could be exploited by promising Gazan Hamas leaders greater engagement and other incentives in return for moderating their goals and tactics. Others have said that Hamas is more united than it seems, and that it benefits from the portrayal of its leadership as divided because this perception provides Hamas with greater flexibility in dealing with both Western actors who hold out hope of its moderation and its Syrian and Iranian allies who are reminded not to take its rejectionist stance for granted.

Economic and Security Concerns

The Gaza Strip is at the epicenter of economic and security concerns over Iranian influence on Palestinian life. Because Gaza and the West Bank are part of a customs union controlled by Israel, the Palestinians do not conduct formal trade with Iran. Nevertheless, possible Iranian-supported smuggling of weapons, cash, and other contraband into the Gaza Strip, along with Iranian training for Hamas militants, is believed by many to reinforce both Hamas's ability to maintain order and control over Gaza and its population, and Palestinian militants' ability to fire mortars and rockets into Israel.[97] Some reports say that contributions from Iran range from $20-30 million annually,[98] supplementing the funds Hamas receives from private individuals and organizations from the Palestinian diaspora and greater Arab and Muslim worlds (particularly in Saudi Arabia and other Gulf states).[99] The deputy leader of the Iran-backed Hezbollah movement in Lebanon told the *Financial Times* in May 2009 that Hezbollah has been providing "every type of assistance" to Palestinians in Gaza, including military assistance, for some time.[100] In addition, Hezbollah has acted in some ways as a mentor or role model for Hamas, which has sought to emulate the Lebanese group's political and media success.[101] During a December 2009 visit to Tehran, Hamas politburo chief Khaled Meshaal (who is based in Damascus) said, "Other Arab and Islamic states also support us ... but the Iranian backing is in the lead, and therefore we highly appreciate and thank Iran for this."[102]

The situation in Gaza came to a head with the December 2008-January 2009 conflict between Hamas and Israel, leading to the death and injury of hundreds of Gazan civilians, the displacement of thousands more, massive destruction of public and private infrastructure, and a general deterioration in quality of life. In the conflict's aftermath, dilemmas remain over how to reconstruct Gaza, support the recovery of its people, weaken Hamas's control, and end smuggling. Some advocate opening Gaza's border crossings for commerce to ease the economic pressures that may encourage smuggling; some advocate internationally coordinated anti- smuggling operations; some advocate both. In January 2009, the U.S interdiction of the Cypriot- flagged ship *Monchegorsk* in the Red Sea after it reportedly left Iran with weapons-related equipment and the Israeli bombing of an apparent arms-smuggling convoy in Sudan moving in the direction of the Egypt-Gaza border were signs of possible Iranian involvement in smuggling—perhaps in collusion with other states and non-state actors.[103] Although construction materials are generally not being allowed into Gaza through the border crossings, Iran has proposed its own reconstruction plans and claims to be distributing funds to Gazans affected by the conflict.[104] These plans may reflect Iranian ambition to compete—in concert with Hamas— against the PA, Gulf Arab states, and the international donor community for patronage and public support among Palestinians and other Arabs in the region.

Prospects

How Iranian influence on the Palestinians is likely to play out could depend in large part on events over the next several months. It is unclear how the popular unrest in Iran that has followed its June 2009 presidential elections might affect the Iranian regime's willingness and ability to exercise influence in the wider region and the strategic approach taken toward the Iranian- Palestinian linkage by the United States and Israel. Thus far, the Obama Administration has suggested that progress in the Arab-Israeli peace process (with the Palestinians and perhaps also with Syria and Lebanon) could improve the prospects of both countering Iran's nuclear threat and reducing its support of Hamas and Hezbollah, while Israel seems less inclined to pursue Arab- Israeli peace until the Iranian problems are addressed directly. Iran's internal political discord has complicated prospects for direct U.S.-Iran diplomacy aimed at resolving the nuclear issue. As a consequence, the U.S. focus on advancing the Arab-Israeli peace process could intensify. Alternatively, concerns about Iran's unpredictability might foster more of a "wait-and-see" attitude by the United States and other key actors with respect to the peace process and other diplomatic or strategic options in the region—possibly ceding the initiative to Palestinian militants, Hezbollah, or other potential spoilers.

Some claim that a conciliatory tone that some detect from Hamas, particularly since Barack Obama became President, may be due to the movement's calculation that cultivating an image of reasonableness presently serves its interests in light of (1) the diplomatic climate following President Obama's inauguration, (2) Israeli deterrence of Hamas-generated violence in the aftermath of the Gaza conflict, and/or (3) geopolitical changes affecting Hamas's principal benefactors in the region—Syria, Hezbollah, and Iran.[105] Those who are more skeptical of Hamas's intentions have countered that nothing of substance has changed in Hamas's existing positions, and that any reasonable-sounding statements are best explained as a ploy to give the impression of moderation.[106]

Israel[107]

Perspectives and Interests

From its founding in 1948 until the fall of Mohammed Reza Shah Pahlavi in 1979, Israel had good relations with Iran as, in the 1950's, it pursued a policy of trying to surround its Arab enemies with friends in the "periphery," including Iran, Turkey, and Ethiopia. Israel provided the Shah with weapons and trained his secret police, the infamous SAVAK, and Iran provided Israel with oil, even during the Arab oil embargo after the October 1973 War.[108]

Ayatollah Ruhollah Musavi Khomeini, founder of the Islamic Republic of Iran in 1979, rejected Israel's right to exist and ended all bilateral cooperation. In the early years of the

Republic, Israel generally ignored Khomeini's rhetoric because it viewed Saddam Hussein in Iraq as the greater threat. Moreover, Israel indirectly served Iran's interests in 1981, when it bombed Iraq's Osirak nuclear reactor, and is said to have secretly supported Iran briefly in the mid-1980's during the Iran-Iraq War (1980-1988).[109]

Yet, also in the 1980's, Israel began to perceive Iran as a threat as Tehran provided ideological inspiration and military support for the founding of the Lebanese Hezbollah, which later attacked Americans and Israelis in the region, and Jews abroad. This threat perception grew as Israel increasingly confronted Iranian-supported violent Palestinian terrorist groups (Hamas and Palestine Islamic Jihad) which rejected the existence of Israel and sought to sabotage the peace process.[110]

In October 2005, shortly after taking office, Iranian President Mahmud Ahmadinejad is said to have called for Israel to be "wiped off the map," and he has since repeatedly expressed virulently anti-Israel sentiments. Israel perceives an existential threat from an Iran whose officials have these views plus an intent to develop nuclear weapons. Israeli officials believe that a nuclear Iran could pose a direct threat to Israel, provide a nuclear shield for terrorists, and possibly provide them with a nuclear weapon.[111]

In a November 15, 2009, speech, Israeli Prime Minister Binyamin Netanyahu laid out his views regarding Iran's nuclear potential. He said

> Iran's pursuit of nuclear weapons threatens our security, peace in the Middle East, and global stability. With nuclear weapons, its powers of destruction, already considerable, would grow immensely. The moderates in the Middle East would be weakened and extremists strengthened. Other countries in the region would join the race for nuclear weapons. An Iranian regime that pledges to wipe Israel off the map would work day and night to undermine any attempt to advance peace between Israel and its neighbors – whether it is peace with the Palestinians, with Syria, and with anyone else.
>
> In contrast, if Iran's nuclear ambitions are thwarted, peace would be given a dramatic boost. Hezbollah and Hamas would be considerably weakened and moderate forces within the region would quickly become ascendant. That is why the fate of Iran's nuclear program is a true turning point in history. It would significantly influence our ability to achieve a stable and secure peace in the Middle East.[112]

Policy Priorities

Stopping Iran from acquiring nuclear weapons is Israel's number one foreign policy priority. The Israeli government insists that Iran is an international, not just an Israeli problem. Like his predecessors, Prime Minister Netanyahu said that he intended to enlist an international front to increase sanctions on Iran and preserve Israel's security interests.[113] His government is trying to prod the United States and other Western governments to progress from dialogue, to harsher sanctions, to military action if Iran continues to refuse to abandon uranium enrichment. Israel also hopes to influence Russia and China in order to end their obstruction of harsher U.N. sanctions against Iran. It particularly seeks to dissuade Russia from selling advanced S-300 anti-aircraft missiles to Iran, thereby enabling it to thwart an attack on its nuclear installations. As an interim measure, on October 31, 2009, Netanyahu endorsed a U.S. proposal to have Iran move enriched uranium outside of Iran as "a positive first step" in the effort "to unite the international community to address the challenge of Iran's attempts to become a nuclear military power." Israel's Defense Minister Ehud Barak opined that the agreement would set Iran back by about a year, but added "there is a drawback" in that it "recognized that Iran enriches uranium, on a low level, on its soil for peaceful purposes. This is problematic for us." He insisted, "what is required is a halt to enrichment in Iran, not just an export of the enriched material to build fuel rods." His views reflect those of other Israelis who regarded the proposed agreement as a retreat from the demand that Iran stop all uranium enrichment.[114] In the end, the views of Israeli officials did not matter as Iran rejected the proposal.

Israeli officials have been skeptical about the Obama Administration's outreach toward and possible engagement with Iran. Defense Minister Barak said, "if there is an engagement, we believe it should be short in time, well-defined in objectives, followed by sanctions." Many times, he has reaffirmed that Israel is taking "no options off the table," signaling that a military strike is among its policy choices.[115]

The priority that Israel gives to Iran lowers the priority it accords to the Arab-Israeli peace process. Because of the perceived Iranian threat, Israeli officials are wary of the possible establishment of a Palestinian state that would be vulnerable to takeover by Iranian-supported Hamas – thereby creating what Prime Minister Netanyahu calls "Hamastan," an Iranian proxy, on Israel's borders. Israeli leaders link movement on the Syrian-Israeli peace track partly to Syria's distancing itself from its ally Iran, again noting that it is essential to keep Iran away from Israel's northern border.

Economic and Security Concerns

Israel has no economic relations with Iran and, therefore, has few, if any, direct economic concerns. It is aware, however, that should Iran block the Straits of Hormuz and interfere with oil shipments from the Gulf in retaliation for an attack, then Israel's Western allies would be harmed, and Israel could be affected as a result.

Israel's security concerns are more immediate. Iran's ongoing arming of Hamas, Palestine Islamic Jihad, and Hezbollah is a threat to Israel's security. Israel wants Egypt and the United Nations to impede the smuggling of Iranian arms into Gaza and Lebanon, respectively. On at least five occasions, Israel has seized ships that it says were smuggling Iranian weapons. Foremost, as noted above, Israel believes that an Iran possessing nuclear arms would threaten its security and existence.

Prospects

Israel is keeping "all options on the table." It has been willing to give the United States and others in the international community a chance to engage in a dialogue with Tehran to see if incentives would induce Iran to stop enriching uranium or to enrich it outside of the country so that nuclear fuel could be monitored and not diverted from peaceful purposes to a weapons program. If dialogue does not work within a limited period of time, however, Israel expects the international community to impose rapidly escalating sanctions on Iran.

As 2009 drew to a close, Israeli officials and commentators noted that President Obama said that he would give Tehran until the end of the year to comply with international demands regarding its nuclear program. Since Iran has not complied, the Israelis expect the United States and the other members of the P5+1 (United Kingdom, France, Russia, China, and Germany) to ask the U.N. Security Council to endorse harsher sanctions in January 2010.

Should sanctions not work, Israel has indicated that it is preparing/prepared to take armed action. Israel already may have signaled its readiness to thwart Iran's nuclear ambitions by military means if diplomacy fails. On September 6, 2007, the Israeli Air Force carried out an air raid against a site in northeastern Syria. U.S. officials later confirmed that it was a nuclear reactor.[116] Then, on June 20, 2008, the *New York Times* reported that the Israeli Air Force had conducted a major exercise about 900 miles west of Israel, comparable to the distance planes would have to fly to strike Iran's uranium enrichment plant at Natanz.[117] In June and July 2009, Israel sent a submarine capable of launching a nuclear missile and several missile class warships through the Suez Canal into the Red Sea, in deployments that some observers suggested were preparation for a possible attack on Iran's nuclear facilities.[118]

While displaying its ability to attack Iran, Israel also has been reinforcing its defenses against an Iranian attack. It has proceeded with development, improvement, and successful testing of the Arrow anti-ballistic missile.[119] In October 2009, Israel and the United States held one of their regular joint biennial military exercises, called Juniper Cobra, to work on integrating their weapons, radars, and other systems. This time, it was a large exercise, involving 17 U.S. naval ships, one of which was armed with the Aegis Ballistic Missile Defense System, 1,400 U.S. European Command (EUCOM) servicemen and an equal number of IDF forces, and it tested the U.S. and Israeli air-defense systems and their interoperability. Juniper Cobra was considered yet another signal to discourage Tehran.

Experts appear to agree that an Israeli strike on Iran would be a complicated undertaking and carry a risk of asymmetric retaliation against both Israel and the United States, its closest ally, by Iranian-allied non-state actors.[120] There is some question as to whether it would be possible for Israel to attack Iran without U.S. permission, given U.S. control of Iraqi airspace which Israeli planes might have to transit en route to Iran, and possibly without more sophisticated U.S. weaponry than Israel now possesses. Furthermore, because Iranian nuclear facilities are dispersed, multiple air raids would be required, perhaps diminishing the chances of success. Some analysts believe that a successful strike would set back Iran's nuclear program for only a few years. Given the closeness of U.S.-Israeli relations and reported warnings by CIA Director Leon Panetta of U.S. expectations of advance notice, it is likely that Israel would inform and consult Washington before attacking Iran.[121]

Finally, there are those who contend that the danger to Israel from a nuclear-armed Iran is overstated because Iran would not want to risk a response from Israel's own unacknowledged nuclear arsenal -- a powerful deterrent.[122] Some conclude that Israel and the international community should become reconciled to the possibility of a nuclear-armed Iran and put aside other concerns. It is uncertain if the Netanyahu government would heed this advice.

Caspian Neighbors[123]

Iran's neighbors in the Caspian Sea region include Russia, the South Caucasian states of Armenia and Azerbaijan, and the Central Asian states of Kazakhstan and Turkmenistan. Russia is the dominant player in relations with Iran. Armenia and, to a lesser degree, Kazakhstan, have aligned themselves with Russian policy toward Iran. A major proportion of the world's Azerbaijanis (estimates range from 6-12 million), and about 200,000 Armenians reside in Iran. Ethnic Azerbaijanis are Iran's largest ethnic minority, constituting almost one-third of its population. More ethnic Turkmen reside in Iran and Afghanistan—over three million—than in Turkmenistan. The leaders of Kazakhstan, Turkmenistan, and Azerbaijan publicly embrace Islam but display hostility toward Islamic fundamentalism. Most of the people in Kazakhstan and Turkmenistan are Sunni Muslims. About three-fourths of the population of Azerbaijan is Shiia, and about one- fourth is Sunni. Among the Russian citizens living in the Caspian region, most are Russian Orthodox Christians, although a large proportion are Sunni or Sufi Muslims.

Policy Priorities

Iran has traditionally had friendly relations with Armenia and both have at times joined in opposing Turkish and Azerbaijani interests in the region. Armenia's relations with Iran are focused on trade, since its borders with Turkey and Azerbaijan are closed as a result of the unresolved Armenia-Azerbaijan conflict over Azerbaij an's breakaway Nagorno Karabakh (NK) region. As a result of the conflict, Armenian NK forces occupy areas along the border with Iran. Iran has an official policy of neutrality regarding the NK conflict and has offered to mediate the conflict. Islamic Shiite fundamentalists in Iran have urged Iran's government to forego its policy of neutrality in the NK conflict and to embrace solidarity with Shiites in Azerbaijan.

Energy security has been one of Armenia's main concerns, since it has been dependent on gas shipments from Russia through a pipeline that transits Georgia. Russia's fractious relations with Georgia have often jeopardized these shipments, causing Armenia to look to Iran for gas supplies.

Iran and Azerbaijan have differed on such issues as border delineation in the Caspian Sea, Iran's objections to Azerbaijani security ties with the United States, and Azerbaij an's objections to Iranian trade ties with Armenia. Some observers have suggested that Iran's increased acrimony with the United States in recent years may have been a spur to its efforts to improve official relations with Azerbaijan, in order either to encourage Azerbaijan to be a mediator or to urge it not to permit U.S. basing.

Azerbaijan and Iran have normal ties at the official level, but some in Azerbaijan have questioned whether Iran really supports the continued sovereignty and independence of the country. As an independent country, Azerbaijan stirs the aspirations of ethnic cohorts residing in Iran for greater rights or even secession. Iran has limited trans-Azerbaijani contacts to discourage the spread of ethnic consciousness among its "Southern Azerbaijanis," and has heavily criticized politicians in Azerbaijan who advocate separatism in Iran.[124] The example of the assertion of Kurdish ethnic rights in post-Saddam Iraq in 2003 has galvanized some Azerbaijanis who propagandize for greater rights for "Southern Azerbaijanis." Alternatively, officials in Azerbaijan at times have alleged that elements in Iran have fostered Islamic fundamentalism among the Shiia population or have sponsored terrorism.[125]

Since 2006, many in Azerbaijan increasingly have been concerned about Iran's arrests of ethnic Azerbaijani civil rights advocates and alleged separatists, including Abbas Lisani. Azerbaijani- Iranian relations were roiled at the end of 2007 by the conviction in Azerbaijan of fifteen individuals on charges of collaborating with the Islamic Revolution Guards Corps to plan a coup and carry out terror operations. After the Azerbaijani National Security Ministry released details of the case, the Iranian Foreign Ministry denied any Iranian involvement and termed the case a scheme by Israel and the United States to harm Azerbaijani-Iranian relations. In mid-2008, relations were further strained after the arrest of six individuals on charges of collaborating with the Islamic Revolution Guards Corps and Lebanon's Hizballah to attack the Israeli embassy in Baku.[126]

Movement in 2009 toward rapprochement between Armenia and Turkey may have contributed to some countervailing moves by Azerbaijan to improve relations with Iran, although Turkey has reassured Azerbaijan that such rapprochement will not make headway until Armenian forces withdraw from areas around the disputed Nagorno Karabakh region. Although a disagreement with Turkey over prices and transit fees for gas appeared to be the primary motive, the Armenia- Turkey rapprochement may have been a factor in Azerbaij an's agreement in November 2009 to boost gas exports to Iran. At the same time, Iran announced that it would lift visa requirements for Azerbaijani visitors (Turkey immediately made a similar offer to Baku).

Russia's ties with Iran have been both cooperative and competitive, and are grounded in Russia's drive to regain a prominent, if not superpower, status in international relations, to establish trade and transport links to the Persian Gulf, to coordinate oil and gas export policies as a cartel, and to counter U.S. influence in the Middle East. Russia's sizeable arms sales and nuclear technology transfers to Iran have raised regional concerns among such countries as Azerbaijan, Iraq, and Saudi Arabia, as well as wider international concern. Russia and Iran also want to limit Turkey's role in the region, which they view as an avatar of U.S. and NATO interests.

Russian perceptions of the Iranian nuclear threat and its policies toward Iran are driven by a number of different and sometimes competing factors. In January 1995, Russia signed an agreement to build a nuclear power plant at Bushehr and to provide other assistance for an Iranian civilian nuclear program. Moscow has maintained that its cooperation with Iran's civilian nuclear program is legal, proper, and poses no proliferation threat.After Iran's clandestine program to master the entire nuclear cycle became public in 2002 with an announcement by Iranian dissidents that Tehran had built an underground enrichment plant, Russia withheld delivery of nuclear fuel for the Bushehr reactor until the two sides agreed in 2005 that spent reactor fuel would be returned to Russia for reprocessing. Following further revelations about Iran's nuclear enrichment program, Russia joined in approving a series of limited U.N. Security Council sanctions on trade with Iran's nuclear infrastructure and a freeze on trade with and the assets of certain Iranian entities and individuals.[127] The delivery of Russian fuel for the Bushehr reactor was completed in January 2008, but the reactor has not yet begun to operate.

On September 21, 2009, Iran informed the IAEA that it had been building a second uranium enrichment plant near the city of Qom. Many observers raised fears that the disclosure was further evidence that Iran intended to build nuclear weapons. In a meeting with concerned nations on October 1, 2009 (the so-called P-5 plus one, consisting of the United States, United Kingdom, France, Russia, China, and Germany), Iran agreed to a late October IAEA inspection of the Qom enrichment site and initially appeared positive toward a plan to export most of its low-enriched uranium to other countries to be further enriched to fuel the Tehran Research Reactor. After inspecting the enrichment plant, the IAEA concluded that the plant was in the advanced stage of completion and that Iran's efforts to hide the plant for years heightened IAEA concerns that other nuclear facilities were being hidden. Russia reportedly mediated with Iran to urge it to accept the research reactor fuel deal. In mid-November 2009, Russia announced that it was further delaying the start-up of the Bushehr reactor, perhaps indicating some Russian pressure on Iran to accept the research reactor fuel deal.[128] On November 18, however, Iran rejected the research reactor fuel deal. In December 2009, Russia rejected international calls for added U.N. sanctions on Iran, with Prime Minister Putin declaring that Russia had no evidence that Iran intended to produce nuclear weapons.[129]

Since the early 1 990s, Iran and Russia have used the issue of the status of the Caspian Sea to hinder Western oil development efforts. With Russia's adoption of a more conciliatory stance regarding Caspian seabed development, Iran in 2001 became isolated in still calling for the Sea to be held in common, or alternatively for each of the littoral states to control 20% of the Sea (and perhaps, any assets). In 2007, Iran declined Russia's call for forming a Russia-dominated joint Caspian naval task force, but joined Russia in opposing any naval presence by non-littoral states. Among other recent differences of viewpoint between Iran and Russia, Iran objected to then- President Putin's offer to the United States in June 2007 to make the Gabala radar site in Azerbaijan available for tracking missile launches from Iran.

Some observers suggest that one reason Iran has opposed a settlement of the legal status of the Caspian Sea has been its opposition to the construction of trans-Caspian oil and gas pipelines from Kazakhstan and Turkmenistan to Azerbaijan that would not transit Iranian territory. While Russia also opposes such pipelines, it has joined other littoral states in calling on Iran to resolve the legal status of the sea. Kazakh President Nursultan Nazarbayav has urged Iran to agree to a median-line delineation of Caspian Sea borders rather than demand territorial concessions through Iran and enhanced trade as incentives to an agreement. Turkmenistan may seek to settle on sea borders as part of its seemingly increased interest in a possible trans-Caspian gas pipeline. In October 2009, Iran lodged strong diplomatic protests following a meeting between the littoral states on energy cooperation that excluded it. Iranian Foreign Minister Manuchehr Mottaki warned the littoral states that "before the final decision on the legal regime of the Caspian Sea is made, Iran will not permit the exploration and exploitation of energy sources in the 20 percent section belonging to other countries."[130] This statement was viewed by observers as referring to future energy development, since all the littoral states except Iran have offshore energy projects underway.

Economic and Security Concerns

Iran maintains bilateral trade with each of its Caspian neighbors, but trade with Russia, valued at $4.33 billion in 2008, is more developed than the other relationships.[131] On March 19, 2007, Armenia's then-President Robert Kocharyan and Iranian President Mahmoud Ahmadinejad inaugurated an 88-mile gas pipeline from Tabriz in Iran to Kadjaran in Armenia. Work was completed on the second section of the pipeline, a 123 mile section from Kadjaran to Ararat, in December 2008. The Russian-controlled ArmRosGazprom joint venture built this second section and operates the pipeline. Initial deliveries reportedly are 10.6-14.1 billion cubic feet of gas per year, with plans for more gas deliveries in future years. Some of this gas will be used to generate electricity for Iran and Georgia, but the remainder eventually may satisfy all Armenia's consumption needs, alleviating its dependence on Russian gas transported via Georgia.

Iran has argued for some time that Azerbaijan would most benefit financially by cooperating in building energy pipelines to Iran. At the end of 2005, Azerbaijan began sending up to about 35 million cubic feet of gas per day through a section of Soviet-era pipeline to the Iranian border at Astara in exchange for Iranian gas shipments to Azerbaij an's Nakhichevan exclave. In November 2009, Azerbaijan and Iran signed an agreement to boost

Azerbaijani gas exports. In late March 2009, Azerbaijan's state-owned SOCOR energy firm announced that it was holding talks with Russia's state-controlled Gazprom gas firm on the refurbishment of the gas pipeline from Russia to Astara (including the part now used by Azerbaijan), in order to facilitate a Russian gas swap arrangement with Iran. In October 2009, however, Azerbaijan and Russia signed a gas supply agreement that would use a section of this pipeline, but would reverse its flow to permit exports from Azerbaijan to Russia.

Seeking alternatives to pipeline routes through Russia, in December 1997 Turkmenistan opened the first pipeline from Central Asia to the outside world beyond Russia, a 125-mile gas pipeline linkage to Iran. Turkmenistan provided 282.5 bcf of gas to Iran in 2006 and reportedly a larger amount in 2007. At the end of 2007, however, Turkmenistan suddenly suspended gas shipments, causing hardship in northern Iran. Turkmen demands for higher payments were the main reason for the cut-off. Gas shipments resumed in late April 2008 after Iran agreed to a price boost. In July 2009, the two countries agreed to build a second pipeline to increase gas shipments.

Prospects

According to many observers, Iran appears likely to continue to build good relations with the Caspian regional states, and to not permit the export of Islamic extremism to damage correct state-to-state relations. All the Caspian littoral states have pledged not to permit the establishment of airbases that could be used for operations against any other littoral state, and the Collective Security Treaty Organization (to which all Iran's northern neighbors belong except Azerbaijan) forbids the presence of non-member state bases.[132] On other issues, it is possible that Iranian- Azerbaijani relations might become more fragile if civil dissent increases among some ethnic Azerbaijanis in Iran. According to analyst Mark Katz, Iran and Russia are likely to continue their uneasy "contentious cooperation" in regional affairs as long as both countries view the United States as a major opponent.[133] In the wake of the August 2008 Russia-Georgia conflict, several observers suggest that Russia is accelerating its efforts to reduce or eliminate U.S. influence in the wider Caspian region. Greater Russian influence in the region could contribute in the future to greater contention in Russian-Iranian relations over energy routes, regional security, nuclear technology-sharing, and other issues. More broadly, a possibly deteriorating security situation in Afghanistan might contribute to rising cross-border terrorism and trafficking in weapons, drugs, and weapons of mass destruction in the Caspian region.

ISSUES FOR CONGRESSIONAL CONSIDERATION[134]

Although the Obama Administration may share many goals of the previous administration on Iran, it also sees the need for new strategies and approaches. The Obama Administration advocated a policy of engagement with Iran to determine the nature of its nuclear program and address other subjects of international concern. While post-election turmoil in Iran delayed these efforts temporarily, the Administration pursued engagement through the P5+1 framework. The first meeting took place on October 1, 2009 and President Obama called it a "constructive beginning." As the talks continued, however, prospects for an agreement appeared to diminish.

The United States, Israel, and the EU proposed the end of 2009 as a "firm" deadline for Iran to demonstrate its willingness to cooperate on the nuclear issue. That deadline has lapsed with no visible progress toward a resolution and the Administration is now working with its P5+1 partners to determine a course of action for 2010. It is widely expected that the group will pursue a fourth round of sanctions through the U.N. Security Council with the goal of targeting the ruling elite in Tehran. U.S. Secretary of State Hillary Clinton said on January 12, 2010 that "It is clear that there is a relatively small group of decision makers inside Iran... They are in both political and commercial relationships, and if we can create a sanctions track that targets those who actually make the decisions, we think that is a smarter way to do sanctions. But all that is yet to be decided upon." Clinton also said the administration's thinking developed as part of consultations with a wide range of other countries and that the U.S. remains interested in engaging with Iran, even as it considers ways to pressure Tehran through sanctions.

Possible Regional Implications

Regardless of how they decide to proceed, any actions on the part of the Obama Administration, Congress, or the international community, and any developments in or provocations by Iran, will have implications for U.S. interests in the region as Iran's neighbors react and reevaluate their policies accordingly. Questions remain about the course of U.S. and international efforts to resolve the issue of Iran's uranium enrichment program: Will the U.N Security Council pass additional sanctions? Will member states enforce those sanctions? Can sanctions be effective to deter Iran from pursuing a nuclear weapons program? How will sanctions affect engagement with Iran and how might they increase or diminish the prospects for a negotiated resolution to Iran's nuclear program? How should the international community evaluate the effectiveness of sanctions? Is there a deadline for sanctions to yield results? What are the options of sanctions and continued engagement fail?

Regardless of the answers to these questions, most analysts agree that sanctions are the logical next step and that if they fail the U.S. and the international community could be forced to weigh the costs of a preemptive strike against the implications of a nuclear Iran. In any case, the policies pursued by the United States and the international community will continue to affect regional approaches toward Iran, and could have implication for other U.S. and international interests in the Middle East.

Of Increased Sanctions

While attention in the United States tends to focus on the response of European countries to expanded unilateral sanctions or the likelihood that Russia and China would join an international effort to impose sanctions on Iran, many of Iran's neighbors would also be affected. Iran has strong economic relations and shared economic interests with many of its neighbors that could be complicated by efforts to further isolate it. It is unclear whether Iran's neighbors would stop trade or forgo plans to cooperate in the area of resource exploitation in the face of international condemnation. The United Arab Emirates (UAE), for example, is among Iran's major gasoline suppliers by virtue of the fact that much of the refined petroleum products that Iran imports transit storage facilities in the UAE en route to Iran. Turkey and

Armenia depend on cooperation with Iran to reduce their dependence on Russia for energy resources. Expanded sanctions could force Iran's neighbors to choose between cooperating with the international community and their own economic well-being.

Of a Preemptive Strike

Engagement and sanctions are both aimed at alleviating tensions over Iran's nuclear program, but many also view them as the best hope for preventing a new war in the Middle East. Israeli Prime Minister Binyamin Netanyahu has made it clear that "all options remain on the table" for dealing with Iran, including the military option. So far, the Obama Administration has as well. They have also both referred to the end of 2009 as a deadline for Iran to demonstrate its willingness to cooperate with the international community on the nuclear issue. As the deadline fast approaches, Iran's Arab neighbors, the Gulf States in particular, appear nervous, weighing the cost of a regional war against the danger of a nuclear Iran, while calculating the long term political viability of the Iranian regime in light of continuing domestic protests.

Some argue that tension between Iran and Israel could bring Israel and/or the United States and Iran's Arab neighbors closer together, perhaps even to some level of cooperation. Others caution that any Israeli strike could outrage Iran's Arab neighbors, and that the conflict would become regional and factious. The security of U.S. military personnel, facilities, and material in neighboring countries is also of concern to U.S. decision makers and regional leaders.

Of a Nuclear Iran

Most regional states (with a few noteworthy exceptions) are concerned primarily with avoiding potential conflicts with Iran that could lead to military action or regional instability. Some might even prefer to learn to live with a nuclear Iran than to endure a regional war to prevent one. The primary concern among policy makers is the potential for a nuclear arms race in the Middle East, which would under undermine regional stability and run counter to the Obama Administration's long term vision of a world without nuclear weapons and its shorter term strategy to reduce the number of strategic warheads and missiles and to end the production of fissile material. [135] U.S. Secretary of State Hillary Clinton's remark about possibly protecting the Gulf states under a "defense umbrella" was perceived by some as a tacit acceptance of the prospect of a nuclear Iran. Others saw it as an effort to mitigate the risk of a nuclear arms race—highlighting concerns that some of Iran's neighbors might pursue their own nuclear programs if they become convinced that Iran's nuclear aspirations cannot be checked. [136] In the interim others have highlighted the dangers of a de facto regional conventional arms race, as Iran's Gulf Arab neighbors take steps to upgrade and expand their military forces as a deterrent and Iraq continues its efforts to reconstitute and reequip its military.

End Notes

[1] Prepared by Casey Addis, Analyst in Middle Eastern Affairs, January 2010.
[2] Some analysts also include Qatar on the side of Iran.

[3] According to the CIA World Factbook, Iran has a population of over 66 million, ranking it 20th in the world, and an area of 1.6 billion square kilometers, ranking it 25th in land mass. Iran also ranks in the top five when it comes to proven oil reserves and natural gas production.

[4] Energy Information Administration (EIA), "Country Analysis Briefs: Iran," 2007.

[5] "Global Trends 2025: A Transformed World," National Intelligence Council Report, November 2008.

[6] Secretary of Defense Robert Gates testified before the Senate Armed Services Committee on January 27, 2009 that the Defense Department had seen a slight increase in Iranian shipments of arms into Afghanistan in recent months, but also that the flow of Iranian weapons into Afghanistan remains at a small level. In attempting to explain the continuing shipments, some experts believe that Iran's policy might be shifting somewhat to gain leverage against the United States in Afghanistan (and on other issues) by causing U.S. combat deaths, but not so extensive as to risk a Taliban return to power. See Secretary Gates' testimony at http://armed-services.senate.gov/Transcripts/2009/01%20January/A%20Full%20Committee/09-02%20-%201-27-09.pdf

[7] Prepared by Christopher Blanchard, Analyst in Middle Eastern Affairs, December 2009.

[8] Saudi Foreign Minister Prince Saud Al Faisal stated in March 2009 following a visit from Iranian Foreign Minister Manouchehr Mottaki that, "although we [Saudi Arabia] appreciate the Iranian support for Arab causes, we believe that this support should be channeled through the Arab legitimacy, be consistent with its goals and positions, express its support for it and not be a replacement for it."

[9] "Saudi Arabia's Al Faysal, UK's Miliband Comment on Mideast Peace Process, Issues," OSC Report GMP20090409825006, April 9, 2009.

[10] Prince Saud al Faisal, Statement to the 64th Session of the U.N. General Assembly, September 26, 2009.

[11] International Monetary Fund (IMF), *Direction of Trade Statistics*, Islamic Republic of Iran, September 2009.

[12] Prepared by Christopher Blanchard, Analyst in Middle Eastern Affairs, December 2009.

[13] "Qatari Emir Views Foreign Investments, Change in Economic Powers, Mideast Peace," OSC Report EUP20090329499001, March 29, 2009.

[14] International Monetary Fund (IMF), *Direction of Trade Statistics*, Islamic Republic of Iran, September 2009.

[15] Vernon Silver and Henry Meyer, "Sheikh Who Backed Barclays Gets Another Shot With Qatar's Money," *Bloomberg*, May 12, 2009.

[16] *BBC Monitoring Middle East*, "Shaykh Hamad Bin-Jasim Bin Jabr Al Thani, Premier discusses Qatari mediation, Al-Jazeera, ties with Egypt, Israel, Saudi" June 26, 2009.

[17] Prepared by Christopher Blanchard, Analyst in Middle Eastern Affairs, December 2009.

[18] Majid Khadduri, "Iran's Claim to the Sovereignty of Bahrayn," *American Journal of International Law*, Vol. 45, No. 4 (Oct., 1951), pp. 631-647.; and, J. B. Kelly, "The Persian Claim to Bahrain," *International Affairs*, Vol. 33, No. 1 (Jan., 1957), pp. 51-70.

[19] For more information on this process, see Husain Al Baharna, "The Fact-Finding Mission of the United Nations Secretary-General and the Settlement of the Bahrain-Iran Dispute, May 1970," *International and Comparative Law Quarterly*, Vol. 22, No. 3 (Jul., 1973), pp. 541-552; Edward Gordon, "Resolution of the Bahrain Dispute," *American Journal of International Law*, Vol. 65, No. 3 (Jul., 1971), pp. 560-568; and, United Nations Security Council, Notes by the Secretary General, S/9726 and S/9772.

[20] Habib Toumi, "Al Wefaq blasted for stand on Al Houthi issue," *Gulf News* (Dubai), November 15, 2009.

[21] International Monetary Fund (IMF), *Direction of Trade Statistics*, Islamic Republic of Iran, September 2009.

[22] Geoff King, "Iran says not officially told Bahrain has suspended gas talks," *Platts Commodity News*, February 22, 2009.

[23] Iranian Foreign Minister Manuchehr Mottaki quoted in *Al Arabiya* "Bahrain and Iran declare 'good' ties after crisis," February 26, 2009.

[24] Prepared by Christopher Blanchard, Analyst in Middle Eastern Affairs, December 2009.

[25] *Emirates News Agency (WAM)*, "UAE President: Doha Summit an Opportunity to Mend Arab Fences," March 25, 2009.

[26] *Emirates News Agency (WAM)*, "GCC summit issues final communiqué" December 16, 2009; and, *Islamic Republic News Agency*, "Iran reiterates ownership of Persian Gulf islands," December 16, 2009.

[27] SABA Online (Yemen News Agency), "They Call It Misunderstanding... We Call It Occupation, Says Sheikh Abdullah," December 23, 2009.

[28] International Monetary Fund (IMF), *Direction of Trade Statistics*, Islamic Republic of Iran, September 2009.

[29] Information about notifications of proposed U.S. arms sales is available from the U.S. Defense Cooperation Agency at: http://www.dsca.mil/PressReleases/36-b/36b_index.htm.

[30] Prepared by Kenneth Katzman, Specialist in Middle Eastern Affairs, December 2009.

[31] U.S. Open Source Center (OSC) Document GMP20081002966020, "Kuwait in Compliance with UNSC Iran Sanctions Resolution Interior," *KUNA*, October 2, 2008.

[32] "Kuwaiti Parliament Speaker Says the West is 'Provoking' Iran On Nuclear Issue," *Associated Press*, July 14, 2008.

[33] International Monetary Fund (IMF), *Direction of Trade Statistics*, Islamic Republic of Iran, September 2009.

[34] CRS conversations with Shaykh Saud al Nasser Al Sabah. 1997 – 2006.

[35] Prepared by Kenneth Katzman, Specialist in Middle Eastern Affairs, December 2009.

[36] CRS conversations with U.S. Embassy officials in Oman. 1995-2003.
[37] Slackman, Michael. "Oman Navigates Risky Strait Between Iran and Arab Nations." *New York Times*, May 16, 2009.
[38] Ibid.
[39] International Monetary Fund (IMF), *Direction of Trade Statistics*, Islamic Republic of Iran, September 2009.
[40] U.S. Open Source Center (OSC) Document GMP20091001825001, "Omani Foreign Minister on Relations with Iran, Israel, Hamas, GCC," *Al-Hayah Online* (London), October 1, 2009.
[41] Prepared by Kenneth Katzman, Specialist in Middle Eastern Affairs, December 2009.
[42] For example, see "Joint Statement by Gulf States, Egypt, Jordan, Iraq, and U.S.: Ministers Reaffirm Commitment to Promote Regional Peace, Security," U.S. Department of State, available online at http://www.america.gov/st/texttrans-english/2008/September/20080925155930eaifas0.7949945.html.
[43] "Clarification Statement" issued by Iraqi Foreign Minister Hoshyar Zebari. May 29, 2006.
[44] The full text of the report is available at http://www.defense pubs/pdfs/9010_Report_to_Congress_Nov_ 09.pdf
[45] "Iran Offers $1 Billion Loan for Iraq Projects," *Reuters*, March 1, 2008.
[46] See Gina Chon, "Iran's Cheap Goods Stifle Iraq Economy, *Wall Street Journal*, March 18, 2009.
[47] "Iraq-Iran Trade Meeting Pledges $5 Billion," UPI.com, February 12 ,2009.
[48] Prepared by Carol Migdalovitz, Specialist in Middle Eastern Affairs, December 2009.
[49] See also Gokhan Cetinsaya, "Essential Friends and Natural Enemies: the Historic Roots of Turkish-Iranian Relations," *Middle East Review of International Affairs*, an online journal, Vol. 7. No. 3, September 2003.
[50] "FM Urges Iranians to Accept Election," *Hurriyet Daily News*, June 23, 2009, and Ilhan Tanir, "Davutoglu, the Architect, Miserably Fails to Deliver," *Hurriyet Daily News*, June 27, 2009.
[51] Robert Tait, "Iran is our Friend, Says Turkish PM Alongside Swipe at Disdainful EU," *The Guardian*, October 26, 2009.
[52] Anonymous comments of Turkish official, April 20, 2009.
[53] "PM Visits Iran, Receives Praise over Nuke Row, Israel," *Hurriyet Daily News*, October 27, 2009; "Turkish PM: West Treats Iran Unfairly," Agence France Presse, October 26, 2009.
[54] Andrew Tully, "Obama, Turkish PM Agree to Tackle Iran," http://www.rferl.org, December 8, 2009.
[55] "Turkish PM Warns Against Attack on Iran," *Hurriyet Daily News*, September 27, 2009l, "Turkey Warns IAF Against Using Airspace," *Jerusalem Post*, December 9, 2009.
[56] Barcin Yinanc and Mustafa Oguz, "Turkey Rolls its Diplomatic Dice," *Turkish Daily News*, August 14, 2008.
[57] "Iran, Turkey Keen to Boost Trade Exchange," Xinhua News Agency, October 28, 2009.
[58] "Austria Says Turkey's Position in Nabucco Limited," *Turkish Daily News*, May 23, 2008 and "Turkish Minister, US Envoy Discuss Gas Pipeline Project," Anatolia News Agency, June 4, 2009
[59] The U.S. Department of Defense Security and Cooperation Agency notified Congress of the possible missile sale worth $7.8 billion on September 9, 2009.
[60] Transcript of speech accessible via http://www.brookings.edu.
[61] During her visit to Turkey in March 2009, Secretary of State Hillary Rodham Clinton told a television interviewer, "We are going to ask for your help in trying to influence Iranian behavior." Borzou Daragahi and Ramin Mostaghim, "U.S.-Turkey-Iran Talks Envisioned; 'The Term 'Mediation" is Used,'" *Los Angeles Times*, March 10, 2009. U.S. Ambassador to Turkey James Jeffrey reported that President Gul had conveyed a message from Washington to Tehran during his March 2009 visit to Iran that the United States is "serious on talking about issues like Afghanistan and Iraq." "Turkish President Sends Message of U.S. Sincerity to Iran," *Hurriyet Daily News*, March 12, 2009.
[62] Interview with President Abdullah Gul by Ghassan Sharbil, date not given, *Al-Hayat*, May 13, 2009, Open Source Center Document, GMP20090513825009.
[63] Turks might be skeptical of NATO's guarantee because some NATO members (Germany, France, Belgium) were reluctant to assist Turkey before the war against Iraq in 2003, and only after considerable pressure from other members did the alliance deploy AWACS early warning planes and, on its behalf, the Netherlands sent Patriot missiles to Turkey. NATO's response was more united before the first Gulf war in 1991, when several member states sent warplanes, men, and missiles to defend Turkey and deter Saddam Hussein.
[64] Prepared by Kenneth Katzman, Specialist in Middle Eastern Affairs, December 2009
[65] Rashid, Ahmed. "Afghan Neighbors Show Signs of Aiding in Nation's Stability." *Wall Street Journal*, October 18, 2004; CRS conversations with Afghan observers and international officials in Herat, October 2009.
[66] Comments by President Karzai at the Brookings Institution. May 5, 2009.
[67] Afghan President Congratulates Ahmadinejad on Victory", Fars News Agency, June 20, 2009; "International Protests Over Iran Election Crackdown", Agence France-Press, June 15, 2009
[68] Comments by Ambassador Eikenberry on Radio Free Europe/Radio Liberty "Radio Azadi." RFE/RL press release, December 17, 2009.
[69] Steele, Jonathon, "America Includes Iran in Talks on Ending War in Afghanistan." *Washington Times*, December 15, 1997.
[70] Prepared by Jeremy M. Sharp, Specialist in Middle Eastern Affairs, December 2009.

[71] In the aftermath of Israel's Operation Cast Lead in Gaza between December 2008 and January 2009, Hamas reportedly sought Iranian military assistance in replenishing and upgrading its stockpiles. According to one report in *Jane's Defence Weekly*, an arms convoy destroyed by Israeli aircraft while transiting through Sudan on its way to the Egypt-Gaza border was carrying Iranian-supplied Russian Igla-1E (SA-16 'Gimlet') and Igla (SA-18 'Grouse') surface-to-air missiles (SAMs) as well as what the security and intelligence sources said were Stinger missiles. See, "Iran was Source of Hamas SAMs Destroyed in Sudan Airstrike," *Jane's Defence Weekly*, April 3, 2009.

[72] Egypt's nascent nuclear program was frozen in 1986 following the accident at the Chernobyl power plant in the Ukraine; however, it maintained a small experimental nuclear reactor. In May 2009, the International Atomic Energy Agency (IAEA) reported that it had found traces of highly enriched uranium in Egypt. Egypt is a signatory to the Nuclear Non-Proliferation Treaty (NPT) that allows for the peaceful production of nuclear energy. In 2005, the IAEA investigated Egypt's nuclear activities and concluded that Egypt had conducted atomic research but that the research did not aim to develop nuclear weapons and did not include uranium enrichment. Egypt admitted to failing to disclose the full extent of its nuclear research activities to the IAEA.

[73] "Egypt Wary of Iran's Perceived Growing Influence in Region," *Open Source Center*, November 5, 2008, pp. GMP20081105425001 Egypt, Iran -- OSC Report in English.

[74] International Monetary Fund (IMF), *Direction of Trade Statistics*, Islamic Republic of Iran, September 2009.

[75] The cell's "discovery" also comes nearly two weeks after CBS News reported that, in January 2009 - at the height of Israel's Operation Cast Lead in Gaza - the Israeli Air Force allegedly had conducted an air strike against trucks driving from Sudan to Egypt, carrying Iranian-supplied weapons bound for Hamas militants. News of Israel's air strike may have temporarily embarrassed Egypt, which, as a result, may have been eager to demonstrate its resolve to act decisively against Iranian intelligence and weapons smuggling in its sphere of influence.

[76] "Iran Speaker Positive on Egypt Investment Cooperation," *Reuters*, December 21, 2009.

[77] "Iran Makes New Bid for Improving Ties with Arabs," *Associated Press*, December 21, 2009.

[78] Prepared by Jeremy M. Sharp, Specialist in Middle Eastern Affairs, December 2009.

[79] Jubin M. Goodarzi, *Syria and Iran: Diplomatic Alliance and Power in the Middle East* (New York: Tauris Academic Studies, 2006).

[80] "Syria economy: Iran bank deal?," *Economist Intelligence Unit*, October 14, 2008.

[81] "Syria and Saudi end tariff war," *The National (UAE)*, November 2, 2009.

[82] Open Source Center Report, " Iran-Syria -- Leaders Hail Ties; Syrian-Israeli Talks Cause Concern," August 8, 2008, IAP20080808570001 Iran-Syria -- OSC Report in English.

[83] David Schenker, *Decoupling Syria from Iran: Constraints on U.S.-Syrian Rapprochement*, Washington Institute for Near East Policy, Jerusalem Issue Briefs, December 2008.

[84] BBC Monitoring Middle East, "Iran concerned about Israel-Syria talks Arabic article," August 10, 2008, Al-Hayat website, London, in Arabic 10 Aug 08/BBC Monitoring.

[85] RAND, *Dangerous but not Omnipotent: Exploring the Reach and Limitations of Iranian Power in the Middle East*, 2009.

[86] Prepared by Casey L. Addis, Analyst in Middle Eastern Affairs, December 2009.

[87] For official election results, see http://www.elections.gov.lb/. For a detailed analysis of the election outcome, see Richard Chambers, "Lebanon's June 7 Elections: The Results," International Foundation for Election Systems (IFES). Available online at http://www.ifes.org/files/IFES_LebanonReview060709Results.pdf.

[88] International Monetary Fund (IMF), *Direction of Trade Statistics*, Islamic Republic of Iran, September 2009.

[89] U.S. Open Source Center (OSC) Document IAP20090312950001, "Lebanese PM Stresses Importance of Strengthening Economic Ties with Iran," Tehran *IRNA,* March 12, 2009.

[90] U.S. Open Source Center (OSC) Document IAP20081216605003, "Iran Offers $600 million in Election Financial Aid to Lebanese Hizballah," *Tabnak* in Persian, December 15, 2008.

[91] "Hezbollah: Iran to support Lebanon," AlJazeera.net, May 30, 2009.

[92] See, for example, U.S. Open Source Center (OSC) Document GMP20090615966007, "Lebanese Divided over Iran's Presidential Election," *The Daily Star* (Beirut), June 15, 2009 and David Samuels, "The Year of the Elephant," *The New Republic*, May 20, 2009.

[93] Prepared by James Zanotti, Analyst in Middle Eastern Affairs, December 2009.

[94] Iran's elite "Quds Force" unit of the Iranian Revolutionary Guard Corps, which is responsible for training Iran-allied paramilitary groups throughout the region, is named after the Arabic/Persian word for Jerusalem ("Quds" or "Ghods")—a sign that Iran identifies its own strategic interests with the broader struggle throughout the Muslim world to "liberate" Jerusalem.

[95] For example, Arafat and the PLO reportedly assisted forces opposed to the Shah's rule, and after the Iranian revolution's success in 1979, Khomeini transformed the vacant Israeli embassy in Tehran into an embassy for the PLO.

[96] In testimony before the House Appropriations Subcommittee on State, Foreign Operations and Related Programs, Secretary Clinton said, "In fact, we think there is some divisions between the Hamas leadership in Gaza and in

Damascus. There's no doubt that those in Damascus take orders directly from Tehran." Transcript of Subcommittee hearing: "Supplemental Request," April 23, 2009.

[97] According to the State Department, in 2008, "Iran remained a principal supporter of groups that are implacably opposed to the Middle East Peace Process. Iran provided weapons, training, and funding to HAMAS and other Palestinian terrorist groups, including Palestine Islamic Jihad (PIJ) and the Popular Front for the Liberation of Palestine-General Command (PFLP-GC). Iran's provision of training, weapons, and money to HAMAS since the 2006 Palestinian elections has bolstered the group's ability to strike Israel." U.S. Department of State, "Country Reports on Terrorism 2008," Chapter 3, available at http://www.state.gov/s/ct/rls/crt/2008/122436.htm. See also Marie Colvin, "Hamas Wages Iran's Proxy War on Israel," *The Sunday Times* (UK), March 9, 2008.

[98] See Council on Foreign Relations Backgrounder, "Hamas," available at http://www.cfr.org/publication/8968/#p8; Matthew Levitt, "The Real Connection Between Iran and Hamas," *Counterterrorism Blog*, available at http://counterterrorismblog.org/2009/01/the_real_connection_between_ir.php.

[99] See Don Van Natta, Jr., with Timothy L. O'Brien, "Flow of Saudi Cash to Hamas Is Under Scrutiny by U.S.," *New York Times*, September 17, 2003.

[100] Anna Fitfield, "Hizbollah Confirms Broad Aid for Hamas," *Financial Times*, May 12, 2009.

[101] Several of Hamas's current leaders were deported by Israel from the West Bank and Gaza to southern Lebanon in December 1992. Not only did they persevere and bond through the hardships of a winter in exile, but they also cultivated relations with and received mentorship from Hezbollah before being repatriated to the West Bank and Gaza by Israel in February 1993 as a result of pressure from human rights organizations and the United States. See Paul McGeough, *Kill Khalid: Mossad's Failed Hit ... and the Rise of Hamas*, Crows Nest, Australia: Allen & Unwin, 2009, p. 68.

[102] Transcript of remarks by Khaled Meshaal, *Al Jazeera TV*, December 15, 2009, Open Source Document GMP20091215648001 (translated from Arabic).

[103] Possible Iranian/Hezbollah weapons smuggling to Palestinians can be traced at least as far back as to the January 2002 case of the *Karine A*, a Palestinian merchant vessel carrying 50 tons of weapons (including Katyusha rockets and anti-tank missiles) that was seized by the Israeli navy in the Red Sea during the second Palestinian *intifada*.

[104] Iranian Press TV reported in July 2009 that Iran had given money to over 100 families in Gaza who had lost a family member or their home in the conflict to allow them to build temporary housing: "Bypassing government bureaucracy, the Martyrs' Foundation of the Islamic Republic of Iran has worked in partnership with the local Ansar Charity Institute to provide the necessary assistance." "After Israeli War, Iran Moves to Rebuild Gaza," aljazeera.com (citing Iranian *Press TV*), July 29, 2009. See also David Rosenberg and Saud Abu Ramadan, "Gaza Rebuild Splits Palestinians as Iran, U.S. Clash," *Bloomberg*, March 2, 2009.

[105] Some speculate that Syria may be encouraging Hamas, to whose exiled leadership it provides safe haven, to at least appear more reasonable while Syria pursues a possible improvement in ties with the United States. Elections in Lebanon and Iran in June may have—for the time being—turned the primary focus of both Hezbollah and the Iranian regime to jockeying for power internally.

[106] See Matthew Levitt, "Score One for 'Hamaswood,'" Middle East Strategy at Harvard, August 11, 2009, available at *http://blogs.law.harvard.edu/mesh/2009/08/score-one-for-hamaswood/*.

[107] Prepared by Carol Migdalovitz, Specialist in Middle Eastern Affairs, December 2009.

[108] For background, see Trita Parsi, *Treacherous Alliance: the Secret Dealings of Israel, Iran, and the United States*, New Haven: Yale University Press, 2007.

[109] Ibid., and Orly Halpern, "Israeli Experts say Middle East was Safer with Saddam in Iraq," *Forward*, January 5, 2007, who notes that Shimon Peres briefly advocated support for Iran at that time.

[110] Hezbollah, Hamas, and Palestine Islamic Jihad (PIJ) are on the U.S. State-Department-designated Foreign Terrorist Organizations (FTOs). he annual State Department *Country Reports on Terrorism*, accessible via http://www.state.gov, notes that Iran provides financial, military, and training support to these groups.

[111] For example, see remarks of Prime Minister Binyamin Netanyahu after meeting with President Obama on March 18, 2009.

[112] Full text of speech to Saban Forum accessible at Israeli Ministry of Foreign Affairs website, November 15, 2009, http://www.mfa.gov.il.

[113] "Policy Speech by PM Netanyahu at Special Knesset Session," accessible via Israeli Ministry of Foreign Affairs website, July 22, 2009, http://www.mfa.gov.il.

[114] Ethan Bronner, "Netanyahu Supports Plan to Transfer Iran's Uranium," *New York Times*, October 31, 2009, Herb Keinon, et.al., "Barak: Vienna Proposal Will Only Delay Iranian Nuclear Program by a Year," *Jerusalem Post*, October 23, 2009.

[115] Greg Jaffe, "US and Israel Differ on Strategy if Iran Talks Fail; Leaders Agree Goal is to Bar Nuclear Arms," *Washington Post*, July 28, 2009, Richard Boudreaux, "Gates' Israel Trip Aims to Ease Iran Worries," *Los Angeles Times*, July 28, 2009.

[116] On April 24, 2008, then-National Security Advisor Stephen Hadley, CIA Director Michael Hayden, and Director of National Intelligence Mike McConnell presented evidence to congressional committees that the Israeli

[117] Michael R. Gordon and Eric Schmitt, "U.S. Says Exercise by Israel Seemed Directed at Iran," *New York Times*, June 20, 2008.
[118] Sheera Frenkel, "Israeli Navy in Suez Canal Prepares for Potential Attack on Iran," http://www.timesonline.co.uk, July 16, 2009.
[119] The Arrow is partly funded by the United States. For FY2009, Congress appropriated $74,342,000 for the Arrow Missile Defense Program, of which $13,076,000 is for producing Arrow components in the United States and Israel. P.L. 111-118, the Department of Defense Appropriations Act, 2010, signed into law on December 19, 2009, provides $72,306,000 for the Arrow program, of which $25 million is for producing components.
[120] See for example, Abdullah Toukan, *Study on a Possible Israeli Strike on Iran's Nuclear Development Facilities*, Center for Strategic and International Studies, March 16, 2009.
[121] "Senior Israel Source on CIA's Visit: No Plan to Surprise US with Iran Action," Israel-OSC Summary of multiple Israeli media reports, Open Source Center Document GMP20090514739002, May 14, 2009.
[122] Warren P. Strobel, "Dangers of Nuclear Iran may be Overstated," *Pittsburgh Post-Gazette*, November 18, 2007.
[123] Prepared by Jim Nichol, Specialist in Russian and Eurasian Affairs, December 2009.
[124] Analyst Brenda Shaffer argues that Iran tacitly supports the continuation of the NK conflict by assisting Armenia, since the conflict constrains Azerbaijan's ability to foster ethnic nationalism among Azerbaijanis in Iran and makes war-torn and poverty-stricken Azerbaijan appear less inviting as a homeland. Brenda Shaffer, *Borders and Brethren: Iran and the Challenge of Azerbaijani Identity*, Cambridge, Mass., MIT Press, 2002, pp. 136-140.
[125] Cameron Brown, *The Middle East Journal*, Autumn 2004, pp. 576-597; Brenda Shaffer, *Borders and Brethren: Iran and the Challenge of Azerbaijani Identity*, Cambridge, Mass., MIT Press, 2002.
[126] Open Source Center. *Central Eurasia: Daily Report* (hereafter *CEDR*), June 10, 2009, Doc. No. CEP-950251; January 8, 2008, Doc. No. CEP-950009; December 17, 2007, Doc. No. CEP-950308; December 16, 2007, Doc. No. CEP-950073;. December 14, 2007, Doc. No. CEP-950356; August 15, 2007, Doc. No. CEP-950239; January 31, 2007, Doc. No. CEP-950234; November 1, 2006, Doc. No. CEP-950311; August 11, 2006, Doc. No. CEP-950113.
[127] See CRS Report RL32048, *Iran: U.S. Concerns and Policy Responses*, by Kenneth Katzman, by Kenneth Katzman.
[128] *U.S. Fed News*, November 16, 2009.
[129] *ITAR-TASS*, December 3, 2009.
[130] *Iran: Daily Report*, October 15, 2009, Doc. No. IAP-11002.
[131] International Monetary Fund (IMF), *Direction of Trade Statistics*, Islamic Republic of Iran, September 2009. Iran's bilateral trade with Armenia: $211 million in 2008; with Azerbaijan: $751 million in 2008; with Kazakhstan: $1.9 billion; and Turkmenistan: $1.82 billion.
[132] *Iran: Daily Report*, October 16, 2007, Doc. No. IAP-950137.
[133] Mark Katz, "Russian-Iranian Relations in the Ahmadinejad Era," *Middle East Journal*, Spring 2008.
[134] Prepared by Casey Addis, Analyst in Middle Eastern Affairs, January 2010.
[135] The text of President Obama's address to the U.N. General Assembly is available online at http://www.nytimes.com/2009/09/24/us/ politics/24prexy.text.html.
[136] See, for example, U.S. Open Source Center (OSC) Document EUP20090810167025, "Post-Election Protests Harm US's Iran Engagement Drive," Centre for European Reform, London, August 10, 2009.

(Note: The text at the top of the page, before footnote 117, reads: "target was a nuclear reactor. Hayden said that it could have produced enough material for at least one weapon, but expressed 'low confidence' that the site was part of a nuclear weapons program.")

Chapter 3

IRAN'S NUCLEAR PROGRAM: STATUS[*]

Paul K. Kerr

SUMMARY

Although Iran claims that its nuclear program is exclusively for peaceful purposes, it has generated considerable concern that Tehran is pursuing a nuclear weapons program. Indeed, the UN Security Council has responded to Iran's refusal to suspend work on its uranium enrichment and heavy-water nuclear reactor programs by adopting several resolutions which imposed sanctions on Tehran.

Despite this pressure, Iran continues to enrich uranium, install additional centrifuges, and conduct research on new types of centrifuges. Tehran has also continued work on its heavy-water reactor and associated facilities.

Whether Iran is pursuing a nuclear weapons program is, however, unclear. A National Intelligence Estimate made public in December 2007 assessed that Tehran "halted its nuclear weapons program," defined as "Iran's nuclear weapon design and weaponization work and covert uranium conversion-related and uranium enrichment-related work," in 2003. The estimate, however, also assessed that Tehran is "keeping open the option to develop nuclear weapons" and that any decision to end a nuclear weapons program is "inherently reversible." Intelligence community officials have reaffirmed this judgment on several occasions. Iranian efforts to produce fissile material for nuclear weapons by using its known nuclear facilities would almost certainly be detected by the IAEA.

Although Iran has cooperated with the International Atomic Energy Agency (IAEA) to an extent, the agency says that Tehran's action's have not been sufficient to alleviate all of the IAEA's concerns about Iran's enrichment and heavy-water reactor programs. The IAEA continues to investigate the program, particularly evidence that Tehran may have conducted procurement activities and research directly applicable to nuclear weapons development.

---

[*] This is an edited, reformatted and augmented version of a CRS Report for Congress publication dated December 2009.

BACKGROUND

Iran's nuclear program began during the 1950s. Construction of a U.S.-supplied research reactor located in Tehran began in 1960; the reactor went critical in 1967.[1] During the 1970s, Tehran pursued an ambitious nuclear power program; according to contemporaneous U.S. documents, Iran wanted to construct 10-20 nuclear power reactors and produce more than 20,000 megawatts of nuclear power by 1994. Iran actually began constructing a light-water nuclear power reactor near the city of Bushehr. Tehran also considered obtaining uranium enrichment and reprocessing technology.[2]

Iran also took steps to demonstrate that it was not pursuing nuclear weapons. For example, Tehran signed the nuclear Nonproliferation Treaty (NPT) in 1968 and ratified it in 1970. Iran also submitted a draft resolution to the UN General Assembly in 1974 that called for establishing a nuclear-weapons-free zone in the Middle East. Nevertheless, the United States was even then concerned that Iran could pursue a nuclear weapons program, as evidenced by U.S. intelligence reports from the mid-1970s.[3]

Iran cancelled the nuclear program after the 1979 revolution, but "reinstituted" the program in 1982, according to a 1988 CIA report.[4] A 1985 National Intelligence Council report, which cited Iran as a potential "proliferation threat," stated that Tehran was "interested in developing facilities that ... could eventually produce fissile material that could be used in a [nuclear] weapon." The report, however, added that it "would take at least a decade" for Iran to do so.[5]

The Iranian government says that it plans to expand its reliance on nuclear power in order to generate electricity. This program will, Tehran says, substitute for some of Iran's oil and gas consumption and allow the country to export additional fossil fuels.[6] Currently, a Russian contractor is completing the Bushehr reactor and Iran says it intends to build additional reactors to generate 20,000 megawatts of power within the next 20 years.[7] Iranian officials say that Tehran has begun design work on its first indigenously produced light-water reactor, which is to be constructed at Darkhovin.[8] Iran has told the IAEA that construction on the reactor is scheduled to begin in 2011; it will be commissioned in 2015. However, the head of Iran's Atomic Energy Organization, Ali Akbar Salehi, stated October 4, 2009, that the "assembly of this plant will take ten years."[9] According to an official associated with the project (plans for which predate the 1979 revolution), Iran anticipates that "foreign experts" will be involved.[10] Indeed, Salehi explained that other countries "can cooperate in building this plant."[11]

Iranian officials have repeatedly asserted that the country's nuclear program is exclusively for peaceful purposes. For example, Supreme Leader Ayatollah Ali Khamene'i declared during a June 3, 2008, speech that Iran is opposed to nuclear weapons "based on religious and Islamic beliefs as well as based on logic and wisdom." He added, "Nuclear weapons have no benefit but high costs to manufacture and keep them. Nuclear weapons do not bring power to a nation because they are not applicable. Nuclear weapons cannot be used." Similarly, Iranian Foreign Ministry spokesperson Hassan Qashqavi stated November 10, 2008, that "pursuance of nuclear weapons has no place in the country's defense doctrine."[12] President Mahmoud Ahmadinejad asserted during an April 9, 2009, speech that "those who accumulate nuclear weapons are backwards in political terms."[13]

However, the United States and other governments have argued that Iran may be pursuing, at a minimum, the capability to produce nuclear weapons. Discerning a peaceful nuclear program from a nuclear weapons program can be difficult because of much of the technology's dual-use nature. In addition, military nuclear programs may coexist with civilian programs, even without an explicit decision to produce nuclear weapons. Jose Goldemberg, Brazil's former secretary of state for science and technology, observed that a country developing the capability to produce nuclear fuel

> does not have to make an explicit early [political] decision to acquire nuclear weapons. In some countries, such a path is supported equally by those who genuinely want to explore an energy alternative and by government officials who either want nuclear weapons or just want to keep the option open.[14]

Some analysts argue that several past nuclear programs, such as those of France, Sweden, and Switzerland, illustrate this approach.[15]

The main source of proliferation concern is Tehran's construction of a gas-centrifuge-based uranium-enrichment facility. Iran claims that it wants to produce low-enriched uranium (LEU) fuel for its planned light-water nuclear reactors. Although Iranian officials have expressed interest in purchasing nuclear fuel from other countries, they assert that Tehran should have an indigenous enrichment capability as a hedge against possible fuel supply disruptions.[16]

Gas centrifuges enrich uranium by spinning uranium hexafluoride gas at high speeds to increase the concentration of the uranium-235 isotope. Such centrifuges can produce both LEU, which can be used in nuclear power reactors, and highly enriched uranium (HEU), which is one of the two types of fissile material used in nuclear weapons. HEU can also be used as fuel in certain types of nuclear reactors.[17] Iran also has a uranium-conversion facility, which converts uranium oxide into several compounds, including uranium hexafluoride.[18]

A heavy-water reactor, which Iran is constructing at Arak, has also been a source of concern. Although Tehran says that the reactor is intended for the production of medical isotopes, it is a proliferation concern because its spent fuel will contain plutonium well suited for use in nuclear weapons. Spent nuclear fuel from nuclear reactors contains plutonium, the other type of fissile material used in nuclear weapons. In order to be used in nuclear weapons, however, plutonium must be separated from the spent fuel—a procedure called "reprocessing." Iran has said that it will not engage in reprocessing.

In addition to the dual-use nature of the nuclear programs described above, Tehran's interactions with the International Atomic Energy Agency (IAEA) have contributed to suspicions that Tehran has a nuclear weapons program.[19] In the past, Iran has taken actions that interfered with the agency's investigation of its nuclear program, including concealing nuclear activities and providing misleading statements. Although the IAEA has gotten a more complete picture of Iran's nuclear program since its investigation began in 2002, the agency still wants Tehran to provide more information. Then-IAEA Director-General Mohamed ElBaradei explained in a June 2008 interview that

> they [the Iranians] have concealed things from us in the past, but that doesn't prove that they are building a bomb today. They continue to insist that they are interested solely in using nuclear power for civilian purposes. We have yet to find a smoking gun that would prove

them wrong. But there are suspicious circumstances and unsettling questions. The Iranians' willingness to cooperate leaves a lot to be desired. Iran must do more to provide us with access to certain individuals and documents. It must make a stronger contribution to clarifying the last unanswered set of questions—those relating to a possible military dimension of the Iranian nuclear program.[20]

The IAEA reiterated September 17, 2009, that it "has no concrete proof that Iran has or has ever had a nuclear weapons programme."

RECENT NUCLEAR CONTROVERSY

The recent public controversy over Iran's nuclear program began in August 2002, when the National Council of Resistance on Iran (NCRI), an Iranian exile group, revealed information during a press conference (some of which later proved to be accurate) that Iran had built nuclear- related facilities at Natanz and Arak that it had not revealed to the IAEA. The United States had been aware of at least some of these activities, according to knowledgeable former officials.[21]

States-parties to the nuclear Nonproliferation Treaty (NPT) are obligated to conclude a safeguards agreement with the IAEA. In the case of non-nuclear-weapon states-parties to the treaty (of which Iran is one), such agreements allow the agency to monitor nuclear facilities and materials to ensure that they are not diverted for military purposes. However, the agency's inspections and monitoring authority is limited to facilities that have been declared by the states-parties.[22] Additional protocols to IAEA safeguards agreements augment the agency's ability to investigate clandestine nuclear facilities and activities by increasing the agency's authority to inspect certain facilities and demand additional information from states-parties.[23] The IAEA's statute requires the agency's Board of Governors to refer cases of non-compliance with safeguards agreements to the UN Security Council. Prior to the NCRI's revelations, the IAEA had expressed concerns that Iran had not been providing the agency with all relevant information about its nuclear programs, but had never found Iran in violation of its safeguards agreement.

In fall 2002, the IAEA began to investigate Iran's nuclear activities at Natanz and Arak, and inspectors visited the sites the following February. The IAEA board adopted its first resolution, which called on Tehran to increase its cooperation with the agency's investigation and to suspend its uranium enrichment activities, in September 2003. The next month, Iran concluded an agreement with France, Germany, and the United Kingdom, collectively known as the "E3," to suspend its enrichment activities, sign and implement an additional protocol to its 1974 IAEA safeguards agreement, and comply fully with the IAEA's investigation.[24] As a result, the IAEA board decided to refrain from referring the matter to the UN Security Council.

Ultimately, the IAEA's investigation, as well as information Tehran provided after the October 2003 agreement, revealed that Iran had engaged in a variety of clandestine nuclear-related activities, some of which violated Iran's safeguards agreement. These included plutonium separation experiments, uranium enrichment and conversion experiments, and importing various uranium compounds.

After October 2003, Iran continued some of its enrichment-related activities, but Tehran and the E3 agreed in November 2004 to a more detailed suspension agreement. However, Iran resumed uranium conversion in August 2005 under the leadership of President Mahmoud Ahmadinejad, who had been elected two months earlier. Iran announced in January 2006 that it would resume research and development on its centrifuges at Natanz. In response, the IAEA board adopted a resolution February 4, 2006, that referred the matter to the Security Council. Two days later, Tehran announced that it would stop implementing its additional protocol.

In June 2006, China, France, Germany, Russia, the United Kingdom, and the United States, collectively known as the "P5+1," presented a proposal to Iran that offered a variety of incentives in return for Tehran taking several steps to assuage international concerns about its enrichment and heavy-water programs.[25] The proposal called on the government to address the IAEA's "outstanding concerns ... through full cooperation" with the agency's ongoing investigation of Tehran's nuclear programs, "suspend all enrichment-related and reprocessing activities," and resume implementing its additional protocol.

European Union High Representative for Common Foreign and Security Policy Javier Solana presented a revised version of the 2006 offer to Iran in June 2008.[26] Representatives from the P5+1 discussed the new proposal with Iranian officials in July 2008. Iran provided a follow-up response the next month, but the six countries deemed it unsatisfactory.[27] Tehran has told the IAEA that it would implement its additional protocol "if the nuclear file is returned from the Security Council" to the agency.[28] It is, however, unclear how the council could meet this condition. Iran's Minister for Foreign Affairs Manouchehr Mottaki told reporters October 7, 2009, that Iran is not discussing ratification of the Protocol.[29]

The 2006 offer's requirements have also been included in several UN Security Council resolutions, the most recent of which, Resolution 1835, was adopted September 27, 2008.[30] However, a November 2009 report from ElBaradei to the Security Council and the IAEA board indicated that Tehran has continued to defy the council's demands by continuing work on both its uranium enrichment program and heavy-water reactor program.[31] Iranian officials maintain that Iran will not suspend its enrichment program.

Iran issued another proposal in early September 2009, which described a number of economic and security issues as potential topics for discussion, but only obliquely mentioned nuclear issues and did not explicitly mention Iran's nuclear program.[32]

October 2009 Geneva Meeting[33]

After an October 1 meeting in Geneva with the P5+1 and Solana, Iranian officials repeatedly stated that Tehran would like future discussions about its September proposal. Nevertheless, during that meeting, Iranian officials agreed in principle to a proposal that would provide fuel enriched to 19.75% uranium-235 for Iran's U.S.-supplied Tehran Research Reactor, which produces medical isotopes and operates under IAEA safeguards. Iran asked the agency in June to provide a new supply of fuel for the reactor, which will run out of fuel in approximately 18 months. Subsequently, the United States and Russia presented a proposal to the IAEA (which the agency conveyed to Iran) for providing fuel for the reactor.

Iranian officials have stated that, absent an agreement with international suppliers, Iran will produce its own fuel for the reactor.

According to the proposal, Iran would transfer approximately 1,200 kilograms of its low-enriched uranium hexafluoride to Russia, which would either enrich the uranium to 19.75% uranium-235 or produce the LEU from Russian-origin uranium. Russia would then transfer the low-enriched uranium hexafluoride to France for fabrication into fuel assemblies. Finally, France would transfer the assemblies to Russia for shipment to Iran. Iran had, as of October 30, 2009, produced 1,763 kilograms of low-enriched uranium hexafluoride containing less than 5% uranium-235.[34]

Beginning October 19, 2009, Iranian officials met with officials from the IAEA, France, Russia, and the United States to discuss details of implementing the proposal, such as the fuel price, contract elements, and a timetable for shipping the fuel. ElBaradei announced October 21 the conclusion of a "draft agreement," which was drafted by the IAEA. Moscow, Paris, and Washington have all stated their support for the agreement. ElBaradei announced October 29 that he had received "an initial response" from Iran. However, Tehran has yet to give an official reply. Ambassador Ali Asghar Soltanieh, Iran's Permanent Representative to the IAEA, indicated during several interviews November 2 that Iran wants to discuss details of the agreement.[35] Tehran has agreed to "accept the essential elements" of the fuel supply proposal "but has also sought modifications to the formula," according to a November 10 Iranian television report.[36] However, Foreign Minster Mottaki stated November 18 that Iran would not agree to ship its LEU to another country for further enrichment.[37]

More recently, Iranian officials have suggested that Tehran would accept a compromise in which it would ship the LEU out of the country in phases. These officials have suggested that the LEU would be simultaneously exchanged for fuel on an Iranian island or in a third country, such as Turkey.[38] In any case, Tehran has not yet given an official response to the P5+1, Russian Foreign Minister Sergey Lavrov said December 28.[39] Iranian officials have stated that, in the event that it cannot obtain reactor fuel from abroad, Iran will produce the fuel on its own.[40]

The P5+1 planned to hold another meeting with Iran before the end of October, but no such meeting has taken place. Following a November 20 meeting, those countries issued a joint statement expressing disappointment with Tehran's failure to agree to another meeting or respond positively to the Tehran Research Reactor proposal. "We have agreed to remain in contact and expect a further meeting soon to complete our assessment of the situation and to decide on our next steps," the statement said. Since then, the P5+1 have indicated that they may impose additional sanctions on Iran through the UN Security Council. White House Press Secretary Robert Gibbs stated December 22 that "preparations have begun" for additional Security Council action.

Iran's Cooperation with the IAEA

Iran and the IAEA agreed in August 2007 on a work plan to clarify the outstanding questions regarding Tehran's nuclear program.[41] Most of these issues,[42] which had contributed to suspicions that Iran had been pursuing a nuclear weapons program, have essentially been resolved, but ElBaradei told the IAEA board June 2, 2008, that there is "one remaining major [unresolved] issue," which concerns questions regarding "possible military dimensions to Iran's nuclear programme." Iran maintains that it has not conducted any work on nuclear weapons.

Iran and the IAEA have had a series of discussions regarding these issues; based on recent reports from ElBaradei, the last meeting was held August 18-20, 2008. The agency has provided Iran with documents or (in some cases) descriptions of documents, which themselves were provided to the IAEA by several governments, indicating that Iranian entities may have conducted studies related to nuclear weapons development. The subjects of these studies included missile reentry vehicles for delivering nuclear warheads, uranium conversion, and conventional explosives used in nuclear weapons.[43] Iranian officials have claimed that the documents are not authentic,[44] but ElBaradei told the IAEA Board of Governors June 17, 2009, that, nevertheless, "there is enough in these alleged studies to create concern in the minds of our professional inspectors." ElBaradei reported in May 2008 that Iranian officials have acknowledged the accuracy of some of the information in the documents, but the activities described were, the Iranians said, exclusively for non-nuclear purposes. Tehran has provided some relevant information about these matters to the IAEA, but ElBaradei reported in August 2009 that the government still should "provide more substantive responses" to the IAEA, as well as "the opportunity to have detailed discussions with a view to moving forward on these issues, including granting the Agency access to persons, information and locations identified in the documents."[45]

The IAEA has asked Tehran about other information suggesting that the country may have pursued nuclear weapons, such as

- "information about a high level meeting in 1984 on reviving Iran's pre-revolution nuclear programme";
- "the scope of a visit by officials" associated with Iran's Atomic Energy Organization "to a nuclear installation in Pakistan in 1987";
- information on 1993 meetings between Iranian officials and members of a clandestine procurement network run by former Pakistani nuclear official Abdul Qadeer Khan; and
- information about work done in 2000 which apparently related to reprocessing.[46]

The agency also wants Iran to provide more information on nuclear-related procurement, production, and research activity by entities linked to Iran's military and defense establishments. These included attempts to obtain items, such as spark gaps, shock wave software, and neutron sources, which could be useful for developing nuclear weapons.[47] In addition, ElBaradei's May 2008 report notes that "substantial parts" of Iran's centrifuge components "were manufactured in the workshops of the Defence Industries Organization."

Furthermore, the IAEA has asked Tehran to provide additional information about the manner in which it acquired a document "describing the procedures" for reducing uranium hexafluoride to uranium metal, as well as "machining ... enriched uranium metal into hemispheres," which are "components of nuclear weapons."[48] Tehran has previously told the agency that it was offered equipment for casting uranium but never actually received it. According to Iran, its nuclear suppliers, many of whom were affiliated with the Khan network, provided the document in 1987 at their own initiative, rather than at Tehran's request. Islamabad has confirmed to the IAEA that "an identical document exists" in Pakistan.[49]

ElBaradei's November 2008 report points out that the IAEA, with the exception of the document related to uranium metal, has "no information ... on the actual design or manufacture by Iran" of components (nuclear or otherwise) for nuclear weapons.

That report, as well as subsequent reports from ElBaradei, also suggests that Iran and the IAEA are at an impasse. Indeed, ElBaradei told the Board of Governors November 26 that, absent further Iranian cooperation, the agency's investigation has "effectively reached a dead end." Tehran has not cooperated with the agency on these matters since ElBaradei's September 2008 report. Iranian officials have indicated that Tehran will not provide any further information to the agency.[50] Nevertheless, Iran has been cooperating with the agency in other respects, albeit with varying consistency. The IAEA has been able to verify that Iran's declared nuclear facilities and materials have not been diverted for military purposes. And Tehran has provided the agency with "information similar to that which Iran had previously provided pursuant to the Additional Protocol," ElBaradei reported in February 2008, adding that this information clarified the agency's "knowledge about Iran's current declared nuclear programme." Iran, however, provided this information "on an ad hoc basis and not in a consistent and complete manner," the report said.[51] Indeed, the IAEA requested in April 2008 that Iran provide "as a transparency measure, access to additional locations related ... to the manufacturing of centrifuges, R&D on uranium enrichment, and uranium mining." Tehran has not yet agreed to do so, however.

ElBaradei's February 2008 report underscored the importance of full Iranian cooperation with the agency's investigation, as well as Tehran's implementation of its additional protocol:

> Confidence in the exclusively peaceful nature of Iran's nuclear programme requires that the Agency be able to provide assurances not only regarding declared nuclear material, but, equally importantly, regarding the absence of undeclared nuclear material and activities in Iran ... Although Iran has provided some additional detailed information about its current activities on an ad hoc basis, the Agency will not be in a position to make progress towards providing credible assurances about the absence of undeclared nuclear material and activities in Iran before reaching some clarity about the nature of the alleged studies, and without implementation of the Additional Protocol.

The IAEA has also asked Iran to "reconsider" its March 2007 decision to stop complying with a portion of the subsidiary arrangements for its IAEA safeguards agreement.[52] That provision, to which Iran agreed in 2003, requires Tehran to provide design information for new nuclear facilities "as soon as the decision to construct, or to authorize construction, of such a facility has been taken, whichever is earlier." Previously, Iran was required to provide design information for a new facility only 180 days before introducing nuclear material into it.[53] If Tehran does not alter this decision, the agency will receive considerably later notice about the construction of future Iranian nuclear facilities. Indeed, invoking its March 2007 decision, Iran until recently failed to provide the IAEA with "preliminary design information" for the planned Darkhovin reactor. The IAEA first requested the information in December 2007; Tehran provided it in September 2009. Tehran has also refused to provide updated design information for the Arak reactor.

Iran had also refused to allow IAEA officials to conduct an inspection of the Arak reactor in order to verify design information that Tehran provided to the agency. ElBaradei argued in his June 2009 report that this continued refusal "could adversely impact the Agency's ability to carry out effective safeguards at that facility," adding that satellite imagery is insufficient because Iran has completed the "containment structure over the reactor building, and the roofing for the other buildings on the site." However, IAEA inspectors visited the reactor facility in August 2009 to verify design information, according to ElBaradei's report issued the same month. IAEA inspectors had last visited the reactor in August 2008.

In addition, Iran failed to notify the IAEA until September 2009 that it was constructing a uranium enrichment facility near the city of Qom. In a letter published October 1, the IAEA asked Iran to provide additional information about the facility, including "further information with respect to the name and location of the pilot enrichment facility, the current status of its construction and plans for the introduction of nuclear material into the facility." The letter also requested that Tehran provide IAEA inspectors with access to the facility "as soon as possible." ElBaradei announced during an October 4 press conference that IAEA officials would inspect the Qom facility October 25, citing the agency's need to understand its "relationship to Iran's nuclear program, its capacity and many other, technical questions." Agency officials inspected the facility and met with Iranian officials October 25-28. According to ElBaradei's November report, Tehran "provided access to all areas of the facility," which "corresponded with the design information provided by Iran" October 18. The next inspection of the facility was scheduled for the end of November 2009, the report said. Although Iran provided additional design information to the IAEA October 28, the agency still has questions about the facility's "purpose and chronology" and wishes to interview other Iranian officials and review additional documentation, according to ElBaradei's report. (For more details about the facility, see the "Qom Facility" section below.)

ElBaradei's report states that Iran has told the IAEA that it does not have any other undeclared nuclear facilities "currently under construction or in operation," but adds that the agency has asked Tehran to confirm that it has not "taken a decision to construct, or to authorize construction of, any other [undeclared] nuclear facility." ElBaradei told the IAEA Board of Governors November 26 that "Iran's late declaration of the new facility reduces confidence in the absence of other nuclear facilities under construction in Iran which have not been declared to the Agency." The IAEA board adopted a resolution November 27, 2009, describing Tehran's failure to notify the agency of the Qom facility as "inconsistent with" the subsidiary arrangements under Tehran's safeguards agreement.

ElBaradei's November report also points out that Iran has not provided the IAEA with requested information about its fuel fabrication plant.

STATUS OF IRAN'S NUCLEAR PROGRAMS

Some non-governmental experts and former U.S. officials have argued that, rather than producing fissile material indigenously, Iran could obtain such material from foreign sources.[54] A National Intelligence Estimate (NIE) made public December 3, 2007, states that the intelligence community "cannot rule out that Iran has acquired from abroad—or will acquire in the future—a nuclear weapon or enough fissile material for a weapon."[55] Similarly, during a press briefing that same day, a senior intelligence official characterized such acquisition as "an inherent option" for Iran. However, Tehran's potential ability to produce its own HEU or plutonium is a greater cause of concern; the official explained that "getting bits and pieces of fissile material from overseas is not going to be sufficient" to produce a nuclear arsenal.

Fuel Manufacturing Plant

Iran is continuing work on a fuel manufacturing plant that, when complete, is to produce fuel for the Arak and Darkhovin reactors.[56] The plant has produced fuel rods and appears to be nearly complete.[57]

Uranium Enrichment

Iran has a pilot centrifuge facility and a larger commercial facility, both located at Natanz. The latter is eventually to hold more than 47,000 centrifuges.[58] Former Vice President Gholamreza Aghazadeh, who also headed Iran's Atomic Energy Organization until July 2009, explained in February 2009 that Iran's goal is to install all of them by 2015.[59] Iran began enriching uranium in the facility after mid-April 2007; as of October 30, 2009, Tehran had produced an estimated total of 1,763 kilograms of low-enriched uranium hexafluoride containing less than 5% uranium-235.[60] This quantity of LEU, if further enriched, could theoretically produce enough HEU for a nuclear weapon.[61] However, an Iranian attempt to enrich this LEU would likely be detected by the IAEA. (This point is discussed in greater detail below.)

Individual centrifuges are linked together in cascades; each cascade in the commercial facility contains 164 centrifuges. According to ElBaradei's November 2009 report, Iran was, as of November 2, feeding uranium hexafluoride into 24 cascades (3,936 centrifuges) of first generation (IR-1) centrifuges and is operating at least another 12 cascades (1,968 centrifuges) without feedstock. Tehran is also installing and testing additional IR-1 centrifuges in the facility.[62]

Iran's efforts to augment the facility's enrichment capacity have slowed in recent months. For example, Iran was, as of November 2, feeding uranium hexafluoride into 656 fewer centrifuges than it was as of August 12. Additionally, the rate at which the government has been installing centrifuges has decreased, according to data from ElBaradei's last three reports. The head of Iran's Atomic Energy Organization, Ali Akbar Salehi, suggested during a September 22, 2009, press conference that Iran would slow down its installation of centrifuges at Natanz and "focus on research and development dimension in order to improve the quality of our productions."[63]

Iran is testing two other types of more advanced centrifuges in a pilot facility, which could increase the commercial facility's enrichment capacity.[64] Aghazadeh indicated this past February that at least one new type of centrifuge would be installed in the "near future,"[65] but the research on new centrifuges has apparently been less successful than Tehran's development of its IR- 1 centrifuge.[66] Nevertheless, Salehi stated in a December 18 interview that Iran hopes to have the new types of centrifuges operational by early 2011.[67]

In addition to its centrifuge work, Iran produced approximately 541 metric tons of uranium hexafluoride between March 2004 and August 10, 2009.[68] Prior to 2009, Tehran apparently improved its ability to produce centrifuge feedstock of sufficient purity for light-water reactor fuel;[69] whether Iran is currently able to produce feedstock pure enough for weapons-grade HEU is unclear.

A senior U.S. intelligence official said December 3, 2007, that a country needs to be able to "operate large numbers of centrifuges for long periods of time with very small failure rates" in order to be able to "make industrial quantities of enriched uranium." The NIE stated that Iran still "faces significant technical problems operating" its centrifuges. Since then, however, Iran's ability to operate its centrifuges appears to have improved, although, as of June 2009, its IR- 1 centrifuges continued to run below design capacity.[70] A report to Congress submitted by the Deputy Director for National Intelligence described the amount of LEU that Iran produced in 2008 as a "significant improvement" over the amount it had produced in 2007.[71] Indeed, data from IAEA reports demonstrate that the Natanz facility's rate of LEU production increased significantly between January and May 2008. Other analysts have reached similar conclusions. For example, a September 15, 2008, report from the Institute for Science and International Security (ISIS) says that Tehran's centrifuges "appear to be running at approximately 85 percent of their stated target capacity, a significant increase over previous rates."[72] A senior UN official reportedly offered a similar assessment that same month.[73] Moreover, a June 2009 ISIS report points out that, based on data from ElBaradei's report issued that month, Iran has improved its daily rate of LEU production by 20%.[74] That rate remained the same, according to data from ElBaradei's August report,[75] but has since increased slightly, according to data from ElBaradei's November report.

The extent to which Iran's progress is sustainable is open to question. Former Pakistani nuclear official Abdul Qadeer Khan described Pakistan's first-generation centrifuges as "unsuccessful" in a 1998 interview.[76] Furthermore, Mark Fitzpatrick of the International Institute of Strategic Studies observed that "[i]t can be years before it is clear whether and enrichment programme is working well," noting that centrifuges at a Japanese enrichment facility "started to crash seven years after installation."[77]

It is also worth noting that Iran's ability to produce additional feedstock for centrifuges may be hindered by its dwindling supply of uranium oxide; Tehran is apparently running out of foreign- supplied uranium oxide and, although Iran is producing more of the material from indigenously mined uranium,[78] it had not yet transferred any indigenously produced uranium oxide to its uranium conversion facility as of June 2009.[79] Whether this is still the case is unclear; ElBaradei's last two reports state that Iran has shipped samples of ammonium diuranate to the conversation facility, suggesting that Iran has not yet shipped large quantities of uranium oxide to the facility.

A senior intelligence official explained during the December 2007 press briefing that the "acquisition of fissile material ... remains the governing element in any timelines in which they'd have a nuclear device." Stating that "centrifuge enrichment is how Iran probably could first produce enough fissile material for a weapon," the 2007 NIE adds that "the earliest possible date Iran would be technically capable of producing enough HEU for a weapon is late 2009."[80] This date, however, "is very unlikely," the estimate says, adding that "Iran probably would be technically capable of producing enough HEU for a weapon sometime during the 2010-2015 time frame." But the State Department Bureau for Intelligence and Research, the estimate says, judges that Tehran "is unlikely to achieve this capability before 2013"[81] and all intelligence agencies "recognize the possibility that this capability may not be attained until *after* 2015."[82] Some independent experts have published estimates for the amount of time necessary for the Natanz facility to produce enough HEU for a weapon—a process that would require Iran to reconfigure the cascades, which are not currently configured to produce HEU, and further enrich the uranium.[83]

As noted, the above time frame assesses Tehran's capability to produce HEU from its Natanz facility. However, the 2007 NIE states that Iran "probably would use covert facilities—rather than its declared nuclear sites—for the production of highly enriched uranium for a weapon." Indeed, it is very difficult to divert without detection significant amounts of nuclear material from centrifuge facilities under IAEA safeguards. A 2004 CIA report concluded that "inspections and safeguards will most likely prevent Tehran from using facilities declared to the IAEA directly for its weapons program as long as Iran remains a party to the NPT."[84] Moreover, it would be extremely difficult to reconfigure the cascades in the Natanz facility without detection.[85] Although Tehran could end its cooperation with the IAEA and use its declared centrifuge facilities to develop fissile material, such an action would be virtually unprecedented.[86]

A senior intelligence official explained that Iran could use knowledge gained from its Natanz facilities at covert enrichment facilities. According to the NIE, a "growing amount of intelligence indicates Iran was engaged in covert uranium conversion and uranium enrichment activity," but Tehran probably stopped those efforts in 2003.

Qom Facility[87]

Despite the intelligence assessment described in the previous paragraph, Iran revealed that it was constructing a new gas-centrifuge-based enrichment facility in September 2009. Tehran provided some details about the facility to the IAEA in a September 21, 2009, letter. Four days after the IAEA received the letter, officials from the United States, Britain, and France revealed that they had previously developed intelligence on the facility. The three governments provided a detailed intelligence briefing to the IAEA after the agency received Iran's letter. U.S. officials have said that, despite its letter to the agency, Iran intended for the facility to be kept secret. As noted, the IAEA inspected the facility in October.

The United States has been "observing and analyzing the facility for several years," according to September 25, 2009, Obama administration talking points, which added that "there was an accumulation of evidence" earlier in 2009 that the facility was intended for enriching uranium. Some of this evidence apparently indicated that "Iran was installing the infrastructure required for centrifuges earlier this year." U.S. officials have not said exactly when Iran began work on the facility, which is "located in an underground tunnel complex on the grounds of an Islamic Revolutionary Guard Corps" base near the Iranian city of Qom.[88] According to ElBaradei's November report, Iran has informed the IAEA that construction on the site began in the second half of 2007. However, the agency has information that appears to contradict Tehran's claim and, as noted, has asked Iran to provide more information about the facility's chronology.[89]

President Obama stated September 25 that "the size and configuration of this facility is inconsistent with a peaceful program." But the administration's talking points were somewhat more vague, stating that the facility "is too small to be viable for production of fuel for a nuclear power reactor," although it "could be used" for centrifuge research and development or "configured to produce weapons-grade uranium." The facility "would be capable of producing approximately one weapon's worth" of HEU per year, depending on the type and performance of the installed centrifuges.

Iranian officials have said that the facility is for peaceful purposes and that Tehran has acted in accordance with its international obligations. The letter to the IAEA described the facility as a "new pilot fuel enrichment plant" that would produce uranium enriched to no higher than 5% uranium-235. Regarding the facility's secret nature, Iranian officials have argued that Tehran was not previously obligated to disclose it to the IAEA.[90] Furthermore, Iranian officials have stated on several occasions that the facility was concealed in order to protect it from military attacks.[91] According to ElBaradei's report, the facility is "at an advanced stage of construction," but Iran has neither installed centrifuges nor introduced nuclear material into the facility. Tehran plans to install 16 cascades with approximately 3,000 IR-1 centrifuges and is constructing support buildings at the facility. Iran told the IAEA that it plans to install IR-1 centrifuges, but added that "the facility could be reconfigured to contain centrifuges of more advanced types should Iran take a decision to use such centrifuges in the future," the report says. According to the United States, Tehran will not be able to begin enriching uranium in the facility before 2010. Iranian officials have told the IAEA that the plant "is planned to be operational in 2011."[92]

Possible Future Enrichment Facilities

In addition to the Qom facility, Iranian officials have indicated that Tehran intends to construct ten additional centrifuge plants—a goal that many analysts argue is virtually unachievable. Salehi stated December 18 that Iran is investigating locations for the sites.[93]

Iranian officials have denied that they have other undisclosed enrichment-related facilities[94] and no British, French, or U.S. officials have disclosed evidence of such Iranian facilities. However, UK Foreign Secretary David Miliband suggested in a September 28 television interview that Iran is engaged in other secret nuclear activities.[95] Similarly, Israeli Military Intelligence Chief Amos Yadlin suggested in December that Iran has been constructing covert nuclear facilities for a weapons program.[96] For its part, the November 2009 IAEA Board of Governors resolution stated that Iran's declaration of the Qom facility "reduces the level of confidence in the absence of other nuclear facilities and gives rise to questions about whether there are any other [undeclared] nuclear facilities under construction in Iran."

Plutonium

Iran acknowledged to the IAEA in 2003 that it had conducted plutonium-separation experiments—an admission which aroused suspicions that Iran could have a program to produce plutonium for nuclear weapons. The IAEA, however, continued to investigate the matter, and ElBaradei reported in August 2007 that the agency has resolved its questions about Iran's plutonium activities.[97]

The 2007 NIE stated that "Iran will not be technically capable of producing and reprocessing enough plutonium for a weapon before about 2015." But, as noted above, Iran says that it does not plan to engage in reprocessing, and numerous reports from ElBaradei have noted that the IAEA has found no evidence that Iran is engaging in any such activities.

Arak Reactor

Iran says that its heavy-water reactor, which is being constructed at Arak, is intended for the production of medical isotopes. According to a May 5, 2008, presentation by Ambassador Ali Asghar Soltanieh, Iran's Permanent Representative to the International Atomic Energy Agency, the reactor is to substitute for an "outdated" LEU-fueled research reactor in Tehran that has been in operation since 1967.98 [99] However, the reactor is a proliferation concern because its spent fuel will contain plutonium better suited for nuclear weapons than the plutonium produced by light- water moderated reactors, such as the Bushehr reactor. In addition, Iran will be able to operate the reactor with natural uranium, which means that it will not be dependent on supplies of enriched uranium. Salehi stated September 26, 2009, that the reactor would be "operational" within the next three or four years."[100]

Iran also has a plant for producing heavy water. According to ElBaradei's June 2009 report, satellite imagery indicates that the plant has been "operating intermittently" since February 2009. ElBaradei's report from that month stated that the plant was "in operational condition," but his two most recent reports have stated that the plant appears not to be operating.

ElBaradei's November report states that, during an October 25 inspection of Iran's uranium conversion facility, IAEA inspectors "observed 600 50-litre drums said by Iran to contain heavy water." The inspectors visited the facility in order to verify an updated Design Information Questionnaire submitted by Iran in August 2009 and observed the drums after gaining access to an area of the facility which agency inspectors had not previously visited. [101] The agency has asked Tehran to "confirm the number of drums and their contents, and to provide information on the origin of the heavy water."

Bushehr Reactor

Iran is also constructing near the city of Bushehr a 1,000-megawatt nuclear power reactor moderated by light water. The original German contractor, which began constructing the reactor in 1975, abandoned the project following Iran's 1979 revolution. Russia agreed in 1995 to complete the reactor, but the project has since encountered repeated delays. In February 2005, Moscow and Tehran concluded an agreement stating that Russia would supply fuel for the reactor for 10 years. Atomstroyexport sent the first shipment of LEU fuel to Iran on December 16, 2007, and the reactor received the last shipment near the end of January 2008. The fuel, which is under IAEA seal, will contain no more than 3.62% uranium-235, according to an Atomstroyexport spokesperson.[102]

According to ElBaradei's August report, loading fuel into the reactor was scheduled to take place during October and November 2009, but this has not yet occurred. Iranian and Russian officials had said that the reactor would begin operating by the end of 2009,[103] but Russian Minister of Energy Sergei Shmatko stated November 16, 2009, that the reactor would not start up in 2009.[104] Salehi stated December 18 that "[i]f no particular problems occur, we will witness the inauguration of the power plant within the next few months."[105] It is widely believed that Moscow may be delaying the project in order to increase political pressure on

Iran to comply with the Security Council resolutions, although both Russian and Iranian officials have attributed the current delay to technical issues.

The United States had previously urged Moscow to end work on the project, citing concerns that it could aid an Iranian nuclear weapons program by providing the country with access to nuclear technology and expertise.[106] However, U.S. officials said in 2002 that Washington would drop these public objections if Russia took steps to mitigate the project's proliferation risks; the 2005 deal requires Iran to return the spent nuclear fuel to Russia.[107] This measure is designed to ensure that Tehran will not separate plutonium from the spent fuel. Moscow also argues that the reactor will not pose a proliferation risk because it will operate under IAEA safeguards. It is worth noting that light-water reactors are generally regarded as more proliferation-resistant than other types of reactors.

Although the UN Security Council resolutions restrict the supply of nuclear-related goods to Iran, they do permit the export of nuclear equipment and fuel related to light-water reactors.

DOES IRAN HAVE A NUCLEAR WEAPONS PROGRAM?

In addition to the possible nuclear weapons-related activities discussed above, Iran has continued to develop ballistic missiles, which could potentially be used to deliver nuclear weapons. It is worth noting, however, that Director of National Intelligence Dennis Blair indicated during a March 10, 2009, Senate Armed Services Committee hearing that Iran's missile developments do not necessarily indicate that the government is also pursuing nuclear weapons, explaining that "I don't think those missile developments ... prejudice the nuclear weapons decision one way or another. I believe those are separate decisions." Iran is developing missiles and space launch vehicles "for multiple purposes," he added.

In any case, Tehran's nuclear program has also raised concerns for various other reasons. First, Iran has been secretive about the program. For example, Tehran hindered the IAEA investigation by failing to disclose numerous nuclear activities, destroying evidence, and making false statements to the agency.[108] Moreover, although Iran's cooperation with the agency has improved, the IAEA has repeatedly criticized Tehran for failing to provide the agency with timely access to documents and personnel.

Second, many observers have questioned Iran's need for nuclear power, given the country's extensive oil and gas reserves. The fact that Tehran resumed its nuclear program during the Iran-Iraq war has also cast doubt on the energy rationale. Furthermore, many countries with nuclear power reactors purchase nuclear fuel from foreign suppliers—a fact that calls into question Iran's need for an indigenous enrichment capability, especially since Russia has agreed to provide fuel for the Bushehr reactor. Moreover, although Tehran plans to develop a large nuclear power program, the country lacks sufficient uranium deposits—a fact acknowledged by Iranian officials.[109]

However, Iran maintains that its enrichment program has always been exclusively for peaceful purposes. Tehran argues that it cannot depend on foreign suppliers for reactor fuel because such suppliers have been unreliable in the past.[110] Iran also says that it has been forced to conceal its nuclear procurement efforts in order to counter Western efforts to deny it nuclear technology—a claim that appears to be supported by a 1997 CIA report.[111]

Aghazadeh has also argued that, although Iran does not need to produce fuel for the Bushehr reactor, the Natanz facility needs to be completed if it is to be able to provide fuel for the planned Darkhovin reactor.[112]

Although few experts argue that there is no evidence that Iran has pursued a nuclear weapons program, some have documented Tehran's projected difficulty in exporting oil and natural gas without additional foreign investment in its energy infrastructure.[113] And at least one expert has described Iran's inability to obtain nuclear fuel from an international enrichment consortium called Eurodif. During the 1970s, Iran had reached an agreement with Eurodif that entitled Iran to enriched uranium from the consortium in exchange for a loan.[114]

Iran's stated rationale for its Arak reactor has also been met with some skepticism. Tehran says it needs the reactor to produce medical isotopes and to replace the Tehran research reactor. However, that reactor is capable of producing such isotopes and has unused capacity. Furthermore, as noted, Iran has expressed the desire to obtain more fuel for the reactor. In addition, non-proliferation experts have argued that the new reactor would be unnecessary for producing such isotopes.[115]

The 2007 National Intelligence Estimate

According to the 2007 NIE, "Iranian military entities were working under government direction to develop nuclear weapons" until fall 2003, after which Iran halted its nuclear weapons program "primarily in response to international pressure." The NIE defines "nuclear weapons program" as "Iran's nuclear weapon design and weaponization work and covert uranium conversion-related and uranium enrichment-related work." It adds that the intelligence community also assesses "with moderate-to-high confidence that Tehran at a minimum is keeping open the option to develop nuclear weapons."[116] The NIE also states that, because of "intelligence gaps," the Department of Energy and the National Intelligence Council "assess with only moderate confidence that the halt to those activities represents a halt to Iran's entire nuclear weapons program."

The NIE also states that "Tehran's decision to halt its nuclear weapons program suggests it is less determined to develop nuclear weapons than we have been judging since 2005."[117] The change in assessments, a senior intelligence official said December 3, 2007, was the result of "new information which caused us to challenge our assessments in their own right, and illuminated previous information for us to be able to see it perhaps differently than we saw before, or to make sense of other data points that didn't seem to self-connect previously."

According to press accounts, this information included various written and oral communications among Iranian officials which indicated that the program had been halted.[118] The United States may also have obtained information from Iranian officials who defected as part of a CIA program to induce them to do so,[119] as well as from penetration of Iran's computer networks.[120] Additionally, the NIE also incorporated open-source information, such as photographs of the Natanz facility that became available after Iran allowed a tour by members of the press.

According to the 2007 NIE, the intelligence community assesses "with moderate-to-high confidence that Iran does not have a nuclear weapon." The community assesses "with low confidence that Iran probably has imported at least some weapons-usable fissile material," but still judges "with moderate-to-high confidence" that Tehran still lacks sufficient fissile material for a nuclear weapon.

On several occasions, the U.S. intelligence community has reaffirmed the 2007 NIE's assessment that Iran halted its nuclear weapons program but is keeping its options open.[121] For example, Leon Panetta, Director of the Central Intelligence Agency, did so in May 2009.[122] Moreover, press accounts indicated that, as of September 2009, the community did not believe that Tehran has restarted its weapons program.[123] The late-September revelation of the Qom facility has increased suspicions that Iran may have restarted its nuclear weapons program. As noted, U.S. officials have indicated that the facility is likely intended for a nuclear weapons program. Nevertheless, administration talking points made public September 25, 2009, stated that the community still assesses that "Iran halted its nuclear weapons program in 2003."

Other factors also suggest that Iran may not have an active nuclear weapons program. First, the IAEA has resolved several of the outstanding issues described in the August 2007 Iran-IAEA work plan and has apparently not found additional evidence of a nuclear weapons program. Indeed, the agency has not discovered significant undeclared Iranian nuclear activities for several years (although, as noted above, the IAEA's ability to monitor Iran's nuclear facilities has decreased). Second, Tehran, beginning in 2003, has been willing to disclose previously undeclared nuclear activities to the IAEA (though, as previously discussed, Iran has not been fully cooperating with the agency). Third, Iran made significant changes to the administration of its nuclear program in fall 2003—changes that produced greater openness with the IAEA and may have indicated a decision to stop a nuclear weapons program.[124]

Fourth, as noted above, Iranian officials have stated numerous times that Tehran is not seeking nuclear weapons, partly for religious regions—indeed, Khamenei has issued a fatwa against nuclear weapons, according to Iranian officials.[125] A change in this stance could damage Iranian religious leaders' credibility. Moreover, Mark Fitzpatrick of the International Institute of Strategic Studies argued in May 2008 that "given the pervasive religiosity of the regime, it is unlikely that Iran's supreme leader would be secretly endorsing military activity in explicit contradiction of his own religious edict."[126]

Fifth, Iranian officials have argued that nuclear weapons would not improve the country's national security because Iran would not be able to compete with the arsenals of larger countries, such as the United States.[127] Moreover, the U.S.-led spring 2003 invasion of Iraq, which overthrew Iraqi leader Saddam Hussein and thereby eliminated a key rival of Iran, may also have induced Tehran to decide that it did not need nuclear weapons.

Living with Risk

Other findings of the NIE indicate that the international community may, for the foreseeable future, have to accept some risk that Iran will develop nuclear weapons. According to the 2007 NIE, "only an Iranian political decision to abandon a nuclear weapons objective would plausibly keep Iran from eventually producing nuclear weapons—and such a decision is inherently reversible." The estimate also asserted that "Iran has the scientific, technical and industrial capacity eventually to produce nuclear weapons if it decides to do so," adding that, "since fall 2003, Iran has been conducting research and development projects with commercial and conventional military applications—some of which would also be of limited use for nuclear weapons."

This is not to say that an Iranian nuclear weapons capability is inevitable; as noted above, Iran does not yet have such a capability. But Tehran would likely need to accept additional constraints on its nuclear program in order to provide the international community with confidence that it is not pursuing a nuclear weapon.

Other Constraints on Nuclear Weapons Ambitions

Although the production of fissile material is widely considered to be the most difficult step in nuclear weapons development, Iran would, even with the ability to produce HEU, still face challenges in producing nuclear weapons, such as developing a workable physics package and effective delivery vehicles. A 1978 CIA report points out that there is a

> great difference between the development and testing of a simple nuclear device and the development of a nuclear weapons system, which would include both relatively sophisticated nuclear designs and an appropriate delivery system.[128]

Although developing and producing HEU-based nuclear weapons covertly would probably be Tehran's preferred option, such a path would present additional challenges. A 2005 report from the International Institute for Strategic Studies concluded that "an Iranian planner would have little basis for confidence that significant nuclear facilities could be kept hidden."[129] Tehran would need to hide a number of activities, including uranium conversion, the movement of uranium from mines, and the movement of centrifuge feedstock.[130] Alternatively, Tehran could import uranium ore or centrifuge feedstock, but would also need to do so covertly. Furthermore, Iran could produce only fairly simple nuclear weapons, which are not deliverable by longer-range missiles, without conducting explosive nuclear tests. Such tests, many analysts argue, would likely be detected.[131] It is also worth noting that moving from the production of a simple nuclear weapon to more sophisticated nuclear weapons could take several additional years.[132]

End Notes

[1] The United States and Iran signed a nuclear cooperation agreement in 1957; it entered into force in 1959. The two countries negotiated another such agreement during the 1970s, but it was never concluded. For a summary of these negotiations, see William Burr, "A Brief History of U.S.-Iranian Nuclear Negotiations," *Bulletin of the Atomic Scientists*, January/February 2009.

[2] For example, the United States was willing to supply Iran with reprocessing technology, according to 1975 and 1976 National Security Council documents. Tehran also had a 1976 contract for a pilot uranium-enrichment facility using lasers (see *Iran*, Report by the Director General, GOV/2007/58, November 15, 2007). Additionally, Iran had contemplated building its own enrichment facility, according to a 1976 State Department cable (U.S. Embassy Tehran Airgram A-76 to State Department, "The Atomic Energy Organization of Iran," April 15, 1976).

[3] *Prospects for Further Proliferation of Nuclear Weapons*, Special National Intelligence Estimate, August 23, 1974. A 1975 Department of State memorandum referred to the "uncertainty over" Iran's "long-term objectives despite its NPT status." ("Memorandum for the Assistant to the President for National Security Affairs: Department of State Response to NSSM 219 (Nuclear Cooperation with Iran)," April 18, 1975). A 1988 CIA report (*Middle East-South Asia: Nuclear Handbook*) indicated that Iran conducted nuclear weapons "design work," before the 1979 revolution.

[4] *Middle East-South Asia: Nuclear Handbook*, Central Intelligence Agency, May 1988.

[5] *The Dynamics of Nuclear Proliferation: Balance of Power and Constraints*, National Intelligence Council, September 1985.

[6] Iran's previous regime also made these arguments for pursuing nuclear power. For example, according to a 1976 State Department cable, the head of the Atomic Energy Organization of Iran cited them as reasons for starting an ambitious nuclear program. (U.S. Embassy Tehran Airgram A-76 to State Department, "The Atomic Energy Organization of Iran," April 15, 1976). Ambassador Ali Asghar Soltanieh, Iran's Permanent Representative to the International Atomic Energy Agency, has explained that nuclear power will only meet "perhaps a small portion" of the projected national electricity demand. "Interview with Iran's Ambassador to IAEA," Campaign Against Sanctions and Military Intervention in Iran, June 29, 2008 (published July 2, 2008). http://www.campaigniran.org/casmii/index.php?q=node/ 5439.

[7] "Iran to Follow Nuclear Timetable Regardless of IAEA Reports – Official," *Islamic Republic of Iran News Network*, February 25, 2009.

[8] "Iran Nuclear Spokesman Interviewed on Situation," *E'temad*, November 9, 2008. Iran has stated that construction on the 360 MW reactor is to start in 2013. The reactor is to be completed in 2016. See "Foreign Firms Interested to Build Darkhovin Nuclear Plant - Iran Official," *Mehr News Agency*, October 19, 2008, and "Bushehr Plant To Be Inaugurated By Mid October 2008 - Iranian Official," *Islamic Republic of Iran News Network*, January 30, 2008.

[9] "Iranian Nuclear Chief Salehi Describes Talks With IAEA Chief ElBaradei," *Tehran Vision of the Islamic Republic of Iran Network 1*, October 4, 2009.

[10] *Mehr News Agency*, October 19, 2008.

[11] *Tehran Vision of the Islamic Republic of Iran Network 1*, October 4, 2009.

[12] "Weekly Briefing of the Foreign Ministry Spokesman," November 10, 2008.

[13] *Islamic Republic of Iran News Network*, April 9, 2009.

[14] Jose Goldemberg, "Looking Back: Lessons From the Denuclearization of Brazil and Argentina," *Arms Control Today*, April 2006.

[15] See James Acton, "The Problem with Nuclear Mind Reading," *Survival*, February-March 2009, pp. 119-42; Paul M. Cole, "Atomic Bombast: Nuclear Weapon Decisionmaking in Sweden 1945–1972," The Henry L. Stimson Center, 1996; "Neutral States: Sweden and Switzerland," in T.V. Paul , *Power Vs. Prudence: Why Nations Forgo Nuclear* Weapons (Montreal: McGill University Press), 2000, pp. 84-98; and Bruno Tertrais, "Has Iran Decided to Build the Bomb? Lessons from the French Experience," January 30, 2007, available at http://www.carnegieendowment.org/ publications/index.cfm?fa=view&id=18993.

[16] "Soltaniyeh: Iran Has No Alternative But To Enrich Uranium," *Islamic Republic News Agency*, October 2, 2008; Paul Kerr, "U.S. Offers Iran Direct Talks," *Arms Control Today*, June 2006; "Interview with Iran's Ambassador to IAEA," 2008.

[17] Highly enriched uranium typically contains over 90% uranium-235, whereas low-enriched uranium used in nuclear reactors typically contains less than 5% uranium-235.

[18] For a detailed description of the nuclear fuel cycle, see CRS Report RL34234, *Managing the Nuclear Fuel Cycle: Policy Implications of Expanding Global Access to Nuclear Power*, coordinated by Mary Beth Nikitin.

[19] For a detailed description of Iran's compliance with its international obligations, see CRS Report R40094, *Iran's Nuclear Program: Tehran's Compliance with International Obligations*, by Paul K. Kerr.

[20] "Interview With IAEA Boss Mohamed ElBaradei," *Der Spiegel*, June 11, 2008.

[21] Gary Samore, Former Senior Director for Nonproliferation and Export Controls on the National Security Council, personal communication June 5, 2008; Director of Central Intelligence George J. Tenet, "DCI Remarks on Iraq's WMD Programs," February 5, 2004, available at https://www.cia.gov/news-information/speeches-testimony/2004/ tenet_georgetownspeech_02052004.html.

[22] The IAEA does have other investigative tools, such as monitoring scientific publications from member-states.

[23] NPT states are not required to conclude additional protocols. However, applicable UN Security Council resolutions require Iran to conclude such a protocol.

[24] The text of the agreement is available at http://www.iaea.org/NewsCenter/Focus/IaeaIran/ statement_iran21102003. shtml. Iran signed its additional protocol in December 2003, but has not ratified it.

[25] The proposal text is available at http://armscontrol.org/pdf/20060606_Iran_P5+1_Proposal.pdf. Prior to late May 2006, the United States refused to participate in direct talks with Iran about its nuclear program. In March 2005, Washington had offered some limited incentives for Iran to cooperate with the E3. (See Kerr, *Arms Control Today*, June 2006). For more information about the state of international diplomacy with Iran, see CRS Report RL32048, *Iran: U.S. Concerns and Policy Responses*, by Kenneth Katzman.

[26] The revised proposal text is available at http://www.auswaertiges-amt.de/diplo/de/Aussenpolitik/Themen/Abruestung/IranNukes/Angebot-e33-080614.pdf.

[27] Iran had also presented a proposal to the P5+1 in May 2008. See Peter Crail, "Proposals Offered on Iranian Nuclear Program," *Arms Control Today*, May 2008. The proposal text is available at http://www.iaea.org/Publications/ Documents/Infcircs/2008/infcirc729.pdf.

[28] *Implementation of the NPT Safeguards Agreement and Relevant Provisions of Security Council Resolutions 1737 (2006), 1747 (2007) and 1803 (2008) in the Islamic Republic of Iran*, Report by the Director General,

GOV/2008/4, February 22, 2008. [29] "Iranian FM: No Discussions on Joining Additional Protocol," *Fars News Agency*, October 7, 2009.

[30] The resolution text is available at http://un.org/News/Press/docs/2008/sc9459.doc.htm. The resolutions also require Iran to suspend work on its heavy water-related projects.

[31] *Implementation of the NPT Safeguards Agreement and Relevant Provisions of Security Council Resolutions 1737 (2006), 1747 (2007), 1803 (2008) and 1835 (2008) in the Islamic Republic of Iran*, Report by the Director General, GOV/2009/74, November 16, 2009.

[32] The proposal text may be found at http://documents.propublica.org/iran-nuclear-program-proposal#p=1.

[33] Unless otherwise noted, this section is based on an October 1, 2009, background briefing by senior U.S. officials; ElBaradei's remarks during an October 4, 2009 press conference; an October 13 French Foreign Ministry briefing; an analyst interview with a U.S. official; Mark Hibbs, "Six Nations Might Place Conditions on Reactor Fuel Supply to Iran," *Nuclear Fuel*, October 5, 2009; "Iran to Provide 20 % Fuel if Probable Deal with West Fails: AEOI," *Iranian Students News Agency*, October 10, 2009; and "Iran Foreign Ministry Spokesman's Weekly News Conference," *Iranian News Network Channel*, October 12, 2009.

[34] GOV/2009/74.

[35] Sylvia Westall, "Iran Wants New Nuclear Fuel Talks, Deepening Doubts," *Reuters*, November 2, 2009; "Iran to Seek Fuel Supply Guarantees in Next Round of Talks," *Press TV*, November 2, 2009; "Iran Ready for New Nuclear Talks 'as Soon as Possible': Envoy," *Agence France Presse*, November 2, 2009; "Iranian Representative to IAEA Rejects Miliband's Remarks on Nuclear Deal," *Al-Alam*, November 2, 2009.

[36] "Nuclear Negotiator Says Iran's Rights to be Defended," *Press TV*, November 10, 2009.

[37] "Iran not to Send Out Enriched Uranium for Swap: FM," *Iranian Students News Agency*, November 18, 2009.

[38] "Iran Says It Would Swap Nuclear Material With West in Turkey," *The Associated Press*, December 26, 2009; "Mottaki: Iran Ready for Simultaneous N. Fuel Swap," *Fars News Agency*, December 26, 2009.

[39] "Iran Taking Its Time to Respond to U.S. Talks Offer – Lavrov, " *Interfax*, December 28, 2009.

[40] "Spokesman: Iran Waiting for 5+1 Response to N. Fuel Swap, " *Fars News Agency*, December 24, 2009.

[41] The text of the work plan is available at http://www.iaea.org/ Publications/ Documents/Infcircs/2007/infcirc 711.pdf.

[42] These issues included plutonium experiments, research and procurement efforts associated with two types of centrifuges, operations of a uranium mine, and experiments with polonium-210, which (in conjunction with beryllium) is used as a neutron initiator in certain types of nuclear weapons.

[43] For more information about Iran's ballistic missile program, see CRS Report RS22758, *Iran's Ballistic Missile Programs: An Overview*, by Steven A. Hildreth.

[44] In a September 28, 2008 letter to the IAEA, Iran described some characteristics of the documents discussed above. The letter stated that some of the information from the United States was shown to Iranian officials as PowerPoint presentations. Additionally, some of the documents are "in contradiction with typical standard Iranian documentation" and lack "classification seals," the letter said. See, Permanent Mission of the Islamic Republic of Iran, *Explanatory Comments by the Islamic Republic of Iran on the Report of the IAEA Director General to the September 2008 Board of Governors* (GOV/2008/38), September 28, 2008. INFCIRC/737. Iran has complained that the IAEA has not provided Tehran with original versions of some documentation related to the alleged "military dimensions" of Iran's nuclear program. Several reports from ElBaradei have stated that the agency has not had permission to provide this documentation from the governments which provided it. In his November 2009 report, ElBaradei again called on such governments to authorize the IAEA to share additional information with Iran.

[45] *Implementation of the NPT Safeguards Agreement and Relevant Provisions of Security Council Resolutions 1737 (2006), 1747 (2007), 1803 (2008) and 1835 (2008) in the Islamic Republic of Iran*, Report by the Director General, GOV/2009/55, August 28, 2009.

[46] For a detailed discussion of this information, as well as the documents concerning Iran's nuclear weapons related studies, see *Implementation of the NPT Safeguards Agreement and Relevant Provisions of Security Council Resolutions 1737 (2006), 1747 (2007), and 1803 (2008) in the Islamic Republic of Iran*, Report by the Director General, GOV/2008/15, May 26, 2008. Excerpts of related internal IAEA documents are available at http://www.isis-online.org/ publications/iran/IAEA_info_3October2009.pdf and in George Jahn, "Nuke Agency Says Iran Can Make Bomb," *Associated Press*, September 17, 2009. A related discussion is found in Mark Hibbs, "Iran Plant Disclosure May Prompt IAEA to Focus on Weapons Data," *Nucleonics Week*, October 1, 2009.

[47] GOV/2008/4.

[48] GOV/2008/15.

[49] GOV/2008/15.

[50] "Iran not to Answer Calls Beyond NPT," *Fars News Agency*, November 20, 2008; "Tehran Will Have Comprehensive Interaction with IAEA: Official," *Islamic Republic News Agency*, November 19, 2008; INFCIRC/737.

[51] GOV/2008/4.

[52] According to the 2001 IAEA Safeguards Glossary, subsidiary arrangements describe the "technical and administrative procedures for specifying how the provisions laid down in a safeguards agreement are to be applied."

[53] For more detail about Iran's safeguards obligations and reporting requirements, see CRS Report R40094, *Iran's Nuclear Program: Tehran's Compliance with International Obligations*.

[54] See, for example, then-Undersecretary of State for U.S. Arms Control And International Security Robert Joseph's testimony before the Senate Committee on Foreign Relations, February 9, 2006; and then-Director of Research Institute for National Strategic Studies National Defense University Stephen Cambone's testimony before the Senate Committee on Governmental Affairs, September 21, 2000.

[55] Available at http://odni.gov/press_releases/20071203_release.pdf.

[56] "Aqazadeh: Iran Heralds Peaceful Nuclear Program," *Islamic Republic News Agency*, April 8, 2008.

[57] *Implementation of the NPT Safeguards Agreement and Relevant Provisions of Security Council Resolutions 1737 (2006), 1747 (2007), 1803 (2008) and 1835 (2008) in the Islamic Republic of Iran*, Report by the Director General, GOV/2009/35, June 5, 2009.

[58] GOV/2008/15. According to this chapter, Iran is planning to install 16 cascade units, each containing 18 164-centrifuge cascades. Tehran has previously told the agency that it intends to install over 50,000 centrifuges; see *Implementation of the NPT Safeguards Agreement in the Islamic Republic of Iran*, Report by the Director-General, GOV/2004/83. Gholamreza Aghazadeh, who headed Iran's Atomic Energy Organization, also said in February 2009 that Iran would install 50,000 centrifuges ("Iran to Follow Nuclear Timetable Regardless of IAEA Reports – Official," *Islamic Republic of Iran News Network*, February 25, 2009).

[59] *Islamic Republic of Iran News Network*, February 25, 2009.

[60] GOV/2009/74.

[61] The IAEA term for this amount of uranium is "significant quantity," defined as the "approximate amount of nuclear material for which the possibility of manufacturing a nuclear explosive device cannot be excluded." That amount is 25 kilograms of uranium-235. Some types of weapons could be developed using less uranium-235.

[62] GOV/2009/74.

[63] "Iran Scientists Build New Generation of Centrifuges - Nuclear Official," *Islamic Republic News Agency*, September 22, 2009.

[64] GOV/2009/74. A June 2009 from ElBaradei report stated that Iran was testing four other more-advanced centrifuges.

[65] *Islamic Republic of Iran News Network*, February 25, 2009.

[66] Analyst interview with U.S. official, June 25, 2009.

[67] "Iran to Produce New Generation of Centrifuges - Nuclear Chief," *Fars News Agency*, December 18, 2009.

[68] Based on data from GOV/2009/74.

[69] IISS Strategic Comments, "Nuclear Iran: How Close Is It?," September 2007, available at http://www.iiss.org/publications/strategic-comments/past-issues/volume-13-2007/volume-13-issue-7/nuclear-iran/; Paul Kerr, "Iran Continues Security Council Defiance," *Arms Control Today*, June 2007; analyst interview with State Department official October 28, 2008.

[70] Analyst interview with U.S. official, June 25, 2009.

[71] Unclassified Report to Congress on the Acquisition of Technology Relating to Weapons of Mass Destruction and Advanced Conventional Munitions, Covering 1 January to 31 December 2008. Available at http://www.dni.gov/ reports/ Unclassified%20Report%20to%20 Congress%20WMD%20Covering%201January%20to%2031%20December%20200 8.pdf.

[72] David Albright, Jacqueline Shire, and Paul Brannan, *IAEA Report on Iran: Centrifuge Operation Significantly Improving; Gridlock on Alleged Weaponization Issues*, September 15, 2008, available at http://www.isis-online.org/ publications/iran/ISIS_Report_Iran_15September2008.pdf. The report compares data from the previous IAEA reports about the amount of uranium hexafluoride fed into Iran's centrifuges.

[73] Peter Crail, "ElBaradei Says Iran Stalls IAEA Inquiry," *Arms Control Today*, October 2008.

[74] David Albright and Jacqueline Shire, *IAEA Report on Iran: Centrifuge and LEU Increases; Access To Arak Reactor Denied; No Progress on Outstanding Issues*, June 5, 2009. Available at http://isis-online.org/publications/iran/ Iran_IAEA_Report_Analysis_5June2009.pdf.

[75] David Albright, Paul Brannan, and Jacqueline Shire, IAEA Report On Iran: Centrifuges Increase; Rate of LEU Production Steady; Progress on Inspection Requests at Arak and Natanz; No Progress on Possible Military Dimensions, August 28, 2009. Available at http://www.isis-online.org/publications/ iran/Analysis_IAEA_Report.pdf.

[76] "A Talk with A.Q. Khan: Pakistan's Top Nuclear Scientist Talks About Nuclear Weapons," *Jane's Foreign Report*, July 24, 1998.

[77] Mark Fitzpatrick, *The Iranian Nuclear Crisis: Avoiding Worst-Case Outcomes*, Adelphi Paper 398, International Institute of Strategic Studies, May 2008, p. 50.

[78] David Albright, Jacqueline Shire and Paul Brannan, *Is Iran Running Out of Yellowcake?*, Institute for Science and International Security, February 11, 2009. Available at http://isis-online.org/publications/iran/Iran_Yellow

cake.pdf; Barak Ravid, "Israel Slams Clinton Statement on Nuclear Iran," *Haaretz*, July 22, 2009; Mark Fitzpatrick, Statement before the Senate Committee on Foreign Relations, March 3, 2009.

[79] Analyst interview with U.S. official, June 25, 2009.

[80] This time frame describes the point at which Iran could have enough HEU for a weapon, rather than when Iran could start producing HEU.

[81] In responses to Questions for the Record from the Senate Select Committee on Intelligence, which were made public in August 2009, the Director for National Intelligence stated that the Bureau continues to stand by this estimate.

[82] The time frame described in the 2007 NIE is the same as one described in a 2005 NIE.

[83] See, for example, R. Scott Kemp and Alexander Glaser, "Statement on Iran's Ability to Make a Nuclear Weapon and the Significance of the 19 February 2009 IAEA Report on Iran's Uranium-Enrichment Program," March 2, 2009 (available at http://www.princeton.edu/~rskemp/can-iran-make-a-bomb.pdf); R. Scott Kemp, "Update On Iran's Ability to Make a Nuclear Weapon and the Significance of the 5 June 2009 IAEA Report on Iran's Uranium-Enrichment Program," June 17, 2009; Albright and Shire, June 5, 2009; and David Albright, Paul Brannan, and Jacqueline Shire, *Nuclear Weapon Breakout Scenarios: Correcting the Record*, March 18, 2009 (available at http://www.isisnucleariran.org/assets/pdf/Correcting_the_Record.pdf).

[84] Unclassified Report to Congress on the Acquisition of Technology Relating to Weapons of Mass Destruction and Advanced Conventional Munitions, January 1-December 31, 2004, available at http://www.odni.gov/reports/2004_unclass_report_to_NIC_DO_16Nov04.pdf.

[85] For more details about cascade configuration, see Houston G. Wood, Alexander Glaser, and R. Scott Kemp, "The Gas Centrifuge and Nuclear Weapons Proliferation," *Physics Today*, September 2008; International Institute for Strategic Studies, *Iran's Strategic Weapons Programmes: A Net Assessment*, (UK: Routledge, 2005), pp. 53-54.

[86] No state that has been found in good standing with the IAEA has ever used this tactic. North Korea restarted its nuclear weapons program after announcing its withdrawal from the NPT in 2003, but the IAEA has never completed an assessment of that country's nuclear activities.

[87] Unless otherwise noted, this section is based on Iran's September 21, 2009 letter to IAEA and September 25 background briefings from U.S. officials, along with associated talking points.

[88] Despite its location, the United States assess that Iran's Atomic Energy Organization is responsible for the facility's "development."

[89] Majlis speaker Ali Larijani, who was formerly Iran's lead nuclear negotiator, indicated September 27 that Iran had been constructing the facility for approximately three years. ("Iran Speaker Says Country has Fully Mastered Nuclear Technology," *Islamic Republic News Agency*, September 27, 2009).

[90] For more information, see CRS Report R40094, *Iran's Nuclear Program: Tehran's Compliance with International Obligations*, by Paul K. Kerr.

[91] See, for example, "Iranian Nuclear Negotiator Says 5+1 Talks 'Positive'," *Islamic Republic of Iran News Network*, October 1, 2009.

[92] GOV/2009/74.

[93] *Fars News Agency*, December 18, 2009.

[94] See, for example, Press Conference with Manouchehr Mottaki, Minister for Foreign Affairs of The Islamic Republic of Iran, *Federal News Service*, October 1, 2009. [95] "UK Condemns Iran Missile Test," September 28, 2009. Available at http://www.fco.gov.uk/en/news/latest-news/? view=News&id=20915346.

[96] Naama Lani, "Yadlin: We Haven't Had Such a Calm Winter in Decades," *ynetnews*, December 15, 2009.

[97] Iran, Report by the Director General, GOV/2007/48, August 30, 2007.

[98] "Iran's Exclusively Peaceful Nuclear Programs and Activities," Briefing for NGOs, May 5, 2008, available at http://www.reachingcriticalwill.org/legal/npt/prepcom08/WP/iran_briefing.pdf.

[99] Despite this claim, Iranian officials stated in September 2009 that Iran needs to obtain more LEU fuel for the reactor. See "Iran Scientists Build New Generation of Centrifuges," September 22, 2009. [100] *Vision of the Islamic Republic of Iran Network 2*, September 26, 2009.

[101] CRS analyst interview with a U.S. official, December 17, 2009.

[102] "Atomstroyexport Completes Latest Shipment of Fuel to Bushehr Nuclear Plant," *Interfax*, December 28, 2007.

[103] "Envoy: Bushehr N. Plant to Go on Stream in Winter," *Fars News Agency*, July 21, 2009; "Russia Confirms Launch of Iranian Nuclear Reactor by Year End," *RIA Novosti*, July 22, 2009.

[104] "Bushehr NPP Won't be Launched in 2009 – Energy Minister," *Interfax*, November 16, 2009.

[105] *Fars News Agency*, December 18, 2009.

[106] For example, then- Deputy Assistant Secretary of Defense Marshall Billingslea testified before the Senate July 29, 2002, that the United States was "concerned that the Bushehr nuclear power project is, in reality, a pretext for the creation of an infrastructure designed to help Tehran acquire atomic weapons." Similar concerns are expressed in a 2005 State Department report (Adherence to and Compliance with Arms Control, Nonproliferation, and Disarmament Agreements and Commitments, U.S. Department of State, August 2005, p.77.) Then-Undersecretary of State for International Security and Arms Control John Bolton told the House International Relations Committee in June 2003 that Iran could build "over 80 nuclear weapons" if it had

[107] access to sufficient fuel, operated the reactor for five to six years, and chose to withdraw from the nuclear Nonproliferation Treaty (NPT). This estimate assumes that Iran possesses a reprocessing facility.

[107] Estimates for the length of time the spent fuel will have to stay in Iran to cool range from two to five years. See Paul Kerr, "Iran, Russia Reach Nuclear Agreement," *Arms Control Today*, April 2005.

[108] For example, Iran sanitized a facility where Iranian scientists had enriched uranium, falsely told the IAEA that it had not enriched uranium, and falsely claimed that it had not procured any foreign components for one of its centrifuge programs.

[109] *Iranian Students News Agency*, April 17, 2007; Thomas W. Wood, Matthew D. Milazzo, Barbara A. Reichmuth, and Jeffrey Bedell, "The Economics Of Energy Independence For Iran," *Nonproliferation Review*, Vol. 14, No. 1, March 2007.

[110] Paul Kerr, "News Analysis: Behind Iran's Diplomatic Behavior," *Arms Control Today*, June 2006. Perhaps significantly, Iranian officials argued for an independent fuel production capability during the 1970s; see U.S. Embassy Tehran Airgram A-76 to State Department, "The Atomic Energy Organization of Iran," April 15, 1976.

[111] The report says that Iran had responded to "Western counterproliferation efforts by relying more on legitimate commercial firms as procurement fronts and by developing more convoluted procurement networks."

[112] *Islamic Republic of Iran News Network*, February 25, 2009.

[113] See, for example, "U.S.-Iranian Engagement: The View from Tehran," International Crisis Group, June 2, 2009; Roger Stern, "The Iranian Petroleum Crisis and United States National Security," *Proceedings of the National Academy of Sciences of America*, January 2007; and George Perkovich and Silvia Manzanero, "Plan B: Using Sanctions to End Iran's Nuclear Program," *Arms Control Today*, May 2004. Projections of Iranian oil depletion are not new. A 1975 U.S. government report stated that "Iran has decided now to introduce nuclear power to prepare against the time – about 15 years in the future – when Iranian oil production is expected to begin to decline sharply." ("Report of the NSSM 219 Working Group Nuclear Cooperation Agreement with Iran," April 1975).

[114] Oliver Meier, "Iran and Foreign Enrichment: A Troubled Model," *Arms Control Today*, January/February 2006.

[115] Robert J. Einhorn, "Iran's Heavy-Water Reactor: A Plutonium Bomb Factory," November 9, 2006, available at http://www.armscontrol.org/pressroom/2006/20061109_Einhorn.asp?print.

[116] Prior to the NIE, some non-governmental experts had argued that Iran had stopped its nuclear weapons program. See, for example, Paul Kerr, "Divided From Within," *Bulletin of the Atomic Scientists*, November/December 2006; Jeffrey Lewis, "Iran Roundup: Negotiations and Wonkporn," July 27, 2005, available at http://www.armscontrolwonk.com/703/iran-roundup-negotiations-and-wonkporn; and George Perkovich, *Changing Iran's Nuclear Interests, Policy Outlook, Carnegie Endowment for international Peace*, May 2005, available at http://www.carnegieendowment.org/files/PO16.perkovich.FINAL2.pdf.

[117] Although the 2005 NIE stated that "Iran currently is determined to develop nuclear weapons despite its international obligations and international pressure," that assessment was somewhat qualified. Titled "Iran's Nuclear Program: At A Crossroads," the estimate stated that Iran was not "immovable" on the question of pursuing a nuclear weapons program and also addressed the possibility that Tehran may not have had such a program. Moreover, the word "determined" was used in lieu of "pursuing" a nuclear weapon because the authors believed the latter to be a stronger term. The NIE was issued as a Memorandum to Holders of NIE 2001-15HC, "Iran's Nuclear Weapons Program: Multifaceted and Poised to Succeed, But When?"

[118] Dafna Linzer and Joby Warrick, "U.S. Finds that Iran Halted Nuclear Arms Bid in 2003," *Washington Post*, December 4, 2007; Greg Miller, "Iran's Nuclear Ambitions on Hold, U.S. Agencies Conclude," *Los Angeles Times*, December 4, 2007; David E. Sanger and Steven Lee Myers, "Details in Military Notes Led to Shift on Iran, U.S. Says," *New York Times*, December 6, 2007; Peter Baker and Dafna Linzer, "Diving Deep, Unearthing a Surprise; How a Search for Iran's Nuclear Arms Program Turned Up an Unexpected Conclusion," *Washington Post*, December 8, 2007.

[119] Greg Miller, "CIA Has Recruited Iranians to Defect; The Secret Effort Aims to Undermine Tehran's Nuclear Program," *Los Angeles Times*, December 9, 2007.

[120] David Sanger and William Broad, "U.S. and Allies Press Iran over Nuclear Plant 'Deception'," *The New York Times*, September 26, 2009.

[121] See also the 2008 report to Congress submitted by the DDNI; February 12, 2009 testimony before the Senate Intelligence Committee by Director of National Intelligence Dennis Blair; "Annual Threat Assessment of the Intelligence Community for the Senate Intelligence Committee," February 12, 2009; and March 10, 2009 testimony before the Senate Armed Services Committee by Director of the Defense Intelligence Agency Michael Maples.

[122] "Remarks of Director of Central Intelligence Agency, Leon E. Panetta, at the Pacific Council on International Policy," May 18, 2009.

[123] Mark Hosenball, "Intelligence Agencies Say No New Nukes in Iran: Secret Updates to White House Challenge European and Israeli Assessments," *Newsweek*, September 16, 2009; David E. Sanger, "U.S. Says Iran Could Expedite Nuclear Bomb," *The New York Times*, September 10, 2009.

[124] This argument is explained in more detail in Kerr, *Bulletin of the Atomic Scientists*, 2006. For an in-depth discussion of Iran's nuclear decision-making process, see Abbas William Samii, "The Iranian Nuclear Issue and Informal Networks," *Naval War College Review*, Winter 2006.
[125] Statement by H.E. Dr. M. Javad Zarif, Permanent Representative of the Islamic Republic of Iran Before the Security Council, December 23, 2006.
[126] *The Iranian Nuclear Crisis*, p. 13.
[127] Soltanieh, June 29, 2008.
[128] Available at http://www.faqs.org/cia/docs/44/0000107983/html. For a more detailed discussion, see Office of Technology Assessment, *Technologies Underlying Weapons of Mass Destruction* (OTA-BP-ISC-115), December 1993.
[129] International Institute for Strategic Studies, p. 57.
[130] The 2005 IISS report also explains that concealing a plutonium-based nuclear weapons program would be even more difficult (pp. 62-63).
[131] For a detailed discussion of this issue, see Steven A. Hildreth, statement before the House Committee on Oversight and Government Reform, Subcommittee on National Security and Foreign Affairs, March 5, 2008, available at http://nationalsecurity.oversight.
[132] *Iran's Nuclear and Missile Potential: A Joint Threat Assessment by U.S. and Russian Technical Experts*, EastWest Institute, May 2009. pp. 5-6.

In: Iran: Issues and Perspectives
Editor: Stephen D. Calhoun

ISBN: 978-1-61728-007-8
© 2010 Nova Science Publishers, Inc.

Chapter 4

IRAN'S NUCLEAR PROGRAM: TEHRAN'S COMPLIANCE WITH INTERNATIONAL OBLIGATIONS[*]

Paul K. Kerr

SUMMARY

In 2002, the International Atomic Energy Agency (IAEA) began investigating allegations that Iran had conducted clandestine nuclear activities. Ultimately, the agency reported that some of these activities had violated Tehran's IAEA safeguards agreement. The IAEA has not stated definitively that Iran has pursued nuclear weapons, but has also not yet been able to conclude that the country's nuclear program is exclusively for peaceful purposes. The IAEA Board of Governors referred the matter to the U.N. Security Council in February 2006. Since then, the council has adopted five resolutions, the most recent of which (Resolution 1835) was adopted in September 2008.

The Security Council has required Iran to cooperate fully with the IAEA's investigation of its nuclear activities, suspend its uranium enrichment program, suspend its construction of a heavy-water reactor and related projects, and ratify the Additional Protocol to its IAEA safeguards agreement. However, a November 2009 report from then-IAEA Director-General Mohamed ElBaradei to the agency's Board of Governors indicated that Tehran has continued to defy the council's demands by continuing work on its uranium enrichment program and heavy-water reactor program. Iran has signed, but not ratified, its Additional Protocol.

Iran and the IAEA agreed in August 2007 on a work plan to clarify the outstanding questions regarding Tehran's nuclear program. Most of these questions have essentially been resolved, but ElBaradei told the agency's board in June 2008 that the agency still has questions regarding "possible military dimensions to Iran's nuclear programme." The IAEA has reported for some time that it has not been able to make progress on these matters.

---

[*] This is an edited, reformatted and augmented version of a CRS Report for Congress publication dated December 2009.

This chapter provides a brief overview of Iran's nuclear program and describes the legal basis for the actions taken by the IAEA board and the Security Council. It will be updated as events warrant.

INTRODUCTION

Iran ratified the nuclear Nonproliferation Treaty (NPT) in 1970. Article III of the treaty requires non-nuclear-weapon states-parties[1] to accept comprehensive International Atomic Energy Agency (IAEA) safeguards; Tehran concluded a comprehensive safeguards agreement with the IAEA in 1974.[2] In 2002, the agency began investigating allegations that Iran had conducted clandestine nuclear activities; the IAEA ultimately reported that some of these activities had violated Tehran's safeguards agreement. The agency has not stated definitively that Iran has pursued nuclear weapons, but has also not yet been able to conclude that the country's nuclear program is exclusively for peaceful purposes. The IAEA continues to investigate the program.

Following more than three years of investigation, the IAEA Board of Governors referred the matter to the U.N. Security Council in February 2006. Since then, the council has adopted five resolutions requiring Iran to take steps to alleviate international concerns about its nuclear program. This chapter provides a brief overview of Iran's nuclear program and describes the legal basis for the actions taken by the IAEA board and the Security Council.

Background

Iran's construction of a gas centrifuge-based uranium enrichment facility is currently the main source of proliferation concern. Gas centrifuges enrich uranium by spinning uranium hexafluoride gas at high speeds to increase the concentration of the uranium-235 isotope. Such centrifuges can produce both low-enriched uranium (LEU), which can be used in nuclear power reactors, and highly enriched uranium (HEU), which is one of the two types of fissile material used in nuclear weapons. HEU can also be used as fuel in certain types of nuclear reactors. Iran also has a uranium-conversion facility, which converts uranium oxide into several compounds, including uranium hexafluoride. Tehran claims that it wants to produce LEU for its current and future power reactors.

Iran's construction of a reactor moderated by heavy water has also been a source of concern. Although Tehran says that the reactor, which Iran is building at Arak, is intended for the production of medical isotopes, it is a proliferation concern because the reactor's spent fuel will contain plutonium well-suited for use in nuclear weapons. In order to be used in nuclear weapons, however, plutonium must be separated from the spent fuel—a procedure called "reprocessing." Iran has said that it will not engage in reprocessing.

Iran and the IAEA agreed in August 2007 on a work plan to clarify the outstanding questions regarding Tehran's nuclear program.[3] Most of these questions, which had contributed to suspicions that Iran had been pursuing a nuclear weapons program, have essentially been resolved. Then-IAEA Director-General Mohamed ElBaradei, however, told the IAEA board June 2, 2008, that there is "one remaining major [unresolved] issue," which concerns questions regarding "possible military dimensions to Iran's nuclear programme." A November 16, 2009, report[4] from ElBaradei to the Security Council and the IAEA board indicates that the agency has not made any substantive progress on these matters. Tehran has questioned the authenticity of some of the evidence underlying the agency's concerns and maintains that it has not done any work on nuclear weapons.

Iran has also expressed concern to the IAEA that resolving some of these issues would require agency inspectors to have "access to sensitive information related to its conventional military and missile related activities." The IAEA, according to a September 2008 report from ElBaradei, has stated its willingness to discuss with Iran

> modalities that could enable Iran to demonstrate credibly that the activities referred to in the documentation are not nuclear related, as Iran asserts, while protecting sensitive information related to its conventional military activities.[5]

Indeed, the agency says that it has made several specific proposals, but Tehran has not yet provided the requested information.

The most recent Security Council resolution (1835), adopted September 27, 2008, requires Iran to cooperate fully with the IAEA's investigation of its nuclear activities, suspend its uranium enrichment program, suspend its construction of a heavy-water reactor and related projects, and ratify the Additional Protocol to its IAEA safeguards agreement.[6] However, ElBaradei's November report indicated that Tehran has continued to defy the council's demands by continuing work on its uranium enrichment program and heavy-water reactor program. Iran disclosed to the IAEA in September 2009 that it has also been constructing a gas-centrifuge uranium enrichment facility near the city of Qom. Iranian officials have repeatedly stated that Iran will not suspend its enrichment program. Tehran has signed, but not ratified, its Additional Protocol.

Iran and the IAEA

As noted above, Iran is a party to the NPT and has concluded a comprehensive safeguards agreement. According to the IAEA, safeguards pursuant to such agreements

> are applied to verify a State's compliance with its undertaking to accept safeguards on all nuclear material in all its peaceful nuclear activities and to verify that such material is not diverted to nuclear weapons or other nuclear explosive devices.[7]

Comprehensive safeguards are designed to enable the IAEA to detect the diversion of nuclear material from peaceful purposes to nuclear weapons uses, as well as to detect undeclared nuclear activities and material.[8] Safeguards include agency inspections and monitoring of declared nuclear facilities.

The agency's inspections and monitoring authority in a particular country are limited to facilities that have been declared by the government. Additional Protocols to IAEA comprehensive safeguards agreements increase the agency's ability to investigate clandestine nuclear facilities and activities by increasing the IAEA's authority to inspect certain nuclear-related facilities and demand information from member states.[9] Iran signed such a protocol in

December 2003 and agreed to implement the agreement pending ratification. Tehran stopped adhering to its Additional Protocol in 2006.

The IAEA's authority to investigate nuclear-weapons-related activity is limited. ElBaradei explained in a 2005 interview that "we don't have an all-encompassing mandate to look for every computer study on weaponization. Our mandate is to make sure that all nuclear materials in a country are declared to us."[10] Similarly, a February 2006 report from ElBaradei to the IAEA board stated that "absent some nexus to nuclear material the Agency's legal authority to pursue the verification of possible nuclear weapons related activity is limited."[11]

The current public controversy over Iran's nuclear program began in August 2002, when the National Council of Resistance on Iran (NCRI), an Iranian exile group, revealed information during a press conference (some of which later proved to be accurate) that Tehran had built nuclear-related facilities that it had not revealed to the IAEA. The United States had been aware of at least some of these activities, according to knowledgeable former officials.[12] Prior to the NCRI's revelations, the IAEA had expressed concerns that Iran had not been providing the agency with all relevant information about its nuclear programs, but had never found the country in violation of its safeguards agreement.

In fall 2002, the IAEA began to investigate Iran's nuclear activities at the sites named by the NCRI; inspectors visited the sites the following February. Adopting its first resolution (GOV/2003/69)[13] on the matter in September 2003, the IAEA board called on Tehran to increase its cooperation with the agency's investigation, suspend its uranium enrichment activities, and "unconditionally sign, ratify and fully implement" an Additional Protocol.

In October 2003, Iran concluded a voluntary agreement with France, Germany, and the United Kingdom, collectively known as the "E3," to suspend its enrichment activities, sign and implement an Additional Protocol to its IAEA safeguards agreement, and comply fully with the IAEA's investigation.[14] As a result, the agency's board decided to refrain from referring the matter to the U.N. Security Council. As noted above, Tehran signed this Additional Protocol in December 2003, but has never ratified it.

Ultimately, the IAEA's investigation, as well as information Iran provided after the October 2003 agreement, revealed that Iran had engaged in a variety of clandestine nuclear-related activities, some of which violated the country's safeguards agreement (see **Appendix A**). After October 2003, Iran continued some of its enrichment-related activities, but Tehran and the E3 agreed in November 2004 to a more detailed suspension agreement.[15] However, Iran resumed uranium conversion in August 2005 under the leadership of President Mahmoud Ahmadinejad, who had been elected two months earlier.

On September 24, 2005, the IAEA Board of Governors adopted a resolution (GOV/2005/77)[16] that, for the first time, found Iran to be in noncompliance with its IAEA safeguards agreement. The board, however, did not refer Iran to the Security Council, choosing instead to give Tehran additional time to comply with the board's demands. The resolution urged Iran:

- To implement transparency measures ... [including] access to individuals, documentation relating to procurement, dual use equipment, certain military owned workshops and research and development locations;
- To re-establish full and sustained suspension of all enrichment-related activity;
- To reconsider the construction of [the] research reactor moderated by heavy water;
- To ratify promptly and implement in full the Additional Protocol;

- [T]o continue to act in accordance with the provisions of the Additional Protocol.

No international legal obligations required Tehran to take these steps. But ElBaradei's September 2008 report asserted that, without Iranian implementation of such "transparency measures," the IAEA "will not be in a position to progress in its verification of the absence of undeclared nuclear material and activities in Iran."

Iran announced in January 2006 that it would resume research and development on its centrifuges at Natanz. The next month, Tehran announced that it would stop implementing its Additional Protocol.

Potential Noncompliance Since September 2005

Iran further scaled back its cooperation with the IAEA in March 2007, when the government told the agency that it would stop complying with a portion of the subsidiary arrangements for its IAEA safeguards agreement.[17] That provision, to which Iran agreed in 2003, requires Tehran to provide design information for new nuclear facilities "as soon as the decision to construct, or to authorize construction, of such a facility has been taken, whichever is earlier." Since March 2007, Iran has argued that it is only obligated to adhere to the previous notification provisions of its subsidiary arrangements, which required Tehran to provide design information for a new facility 180 days before introducing nuclear material into it.

This decision has provided the basis for Iran's stated rationale for its refusal to provide the IAEA with some information concerning its nuclear program. For example, Tehran has refused to provide updated design information for the heavy water reactor under construction at Arak. Similarly, Tehran had refused to provide the IAEA with design information for a reactor that Iran intends to construct at Darkhovin. However, Iran provided the agency with preliminary design information in a September 22, 2009, letter; the IAEA has requested Tehran to "provide additional clarifications" of the information, according to ElBaradei's November report. Iran has also argued, based on its March 2007 decision, that its failure to notify the IAEA before September 2009 that it has been constructing a gas-centrifuge uranium enrichment facility near the city of Qom is consistent with Tehran's safeguards obligations. Exactly when Iran began work on the facility is not clear.

Both the 2007 decision, which the IAEA has asked Iran to "reconsider," and Tehran's refusal to provide the design information appear to be inconsistent with the government's safeguards obligations. Although Article 39 of Iran's safeguards agreement states that the subsidiary arrangements "may be extended or changed by agreement between" Iran and the IAEA, the agreement does not provide for a unilateral modification or suspension of any portion of those arrangements.[18,19] Moreover, the IAEA legal adviser explained in a March 2009 statement that Tehran's failure to provide design information for the reactors is "inconsistent with" Iran's obligations under its subsidiary arrangements. The adviser, however, added that "it is difficult to conclude that" Tehran's refusal to provide the information "in itself constitutes non-compliance with, or a breach of" Iran's safeguards agreement. Nevertheless, ElBaradei's November 2009 report described Tehran's failures both to notify the agency of the decision to begin constructing the Qom facility, as well as to provide the relevant design information in a timely fashion, as "inconsistent with" Iran's safeguards obligations. The report similarly described Iran's delay in providing design information for the Darkhovin reactor.

Iran's March 2007 decision also formed the basis for Tehran's refusal until August 2009 to allow IAEA inspectors to verify design information for the Arak reactor. This action also appeared to be inconsistent with Tehran's safeguards agreement. Article 48 of that agreement states that the IAEA "may send inspectors to facilities to verify the design information provided to the Agency"; in fact, the agency has a "continuing right" to do so, according to a November 2008 report from ElBaradei.[20] Moreover, the legal adviser's statement characterized Iran's ongoing refusal to allow IAEA inspectors to verify the Arak reactor's design information as "inconsistent with" Tehran's obligations under its safeguards agreement.[21] IAEA inspectors visited the reactor facility in August 2009 to verify design information, according to a report ElBaradei issued the same month.[22]

The IAEA board has neither formally found that any of the Iranian actions described above are in noncompliance with Tehran's safeguards agreement, nor referred these issues to the UN Security Council. The IAEA board adopted a resolution November 27, 2009, that described Iran's failure to notify the agency of the Qom facility as "inconsistent with" the subsidiary arrangements under Iran's safeguards agreement, but this statement did not constitute a formal finding of noncompliance.

Iran and the U.N. Security Council

As noted, Iran announced in January 2006 that it would resume research and development on its centrifuges at Natanz. In response, the IAEA board adopted a resolution (GOV/2006/14)[23] February 4, 2006, referring the matter to the Security Council and reiterating its call for Iran to take the measures specified in the September resolution. Two days later, Tehran announced that it would stop implementing its Additional Protocol.

On March 29, 2006, the U.N. Security Council President issued a statement, which was not legally binding, that called on Iran to "take the steps required" by the February IAEA board resolution. The council subsequently adopted five resolutions concerning Iran's nuclear program: 1696 (July 2006), 1737 (December 2006), 1747 (March 2007), 1803 (March 2008), and 1835 (September 2008). The second, third, and fourth resolutions imposed a variety of restrictions on Iran.

Resolution 1696 was the first to place legally binding Security Council requirements on Iran with respect to its nuclear program. That resolution made mandatory the IAEA— demanded suspension and called on Tehran to implement the transparency measures called for by the IAEA board's February 2006 resolution. Resolution 1737 reiterated these requirements but expanded the suspension's scope to include "work on all heavy water-related projects."

It is worth noting that the Security Council has acknowledged (in Resolution 1803, for example) Iran's rights under Article IV of the NPT, which states that parties to the treaty have "the inalienable right ... to develop research, production and use of nuclear energy for peaceful Purposes."[24]

AUTHORITY FOR IAEA AND U.N. SECURITY COUNCIL ACTIONS

The legal authority for the actions taken by the IAEA Board of Governors and the U.N. Security Council is found in both the IAEA Statute and the U.N. Charter. The following sections discuss the relevant portions of those documents.

IAEA Statute

Two sections of the IAEA Statute explain what the agency should do if an IAEA member state is found to be in noncompliance with its safeguards agreement.[25] Article III B. 4. of the statute states that the IAEA is to submit annual reports to the U.N. General Assembly and, "when appropriate," to the U.N. Security Council. If "there should arise questions that are within the competence of the Security Council," the article adds, the IAEA "shall notify the Security Council, as the organ bearing the main responsibility for the maintenance of international peace and security."

Additionally, Article XII C. states that IAEA inspectors are to report non-compliance issues to the agency's Director-General, who is to report the matter to the IAEA Board of Governors. The board is then to "call upon the recipient State or States to remedy forthwith any non-compliance which it finds to have occurred," as well as "report the non-compliance to all members and to the Security Council and General Assembly of the United Nations."

In the case of Iran, the September 24, 2005 IAEA board resolution (GOV/2005/77) stated that the board

> found that Iran's many failures and breaches of its obligations to comply with its NPT Safeguards Agreement, as detailed in GOV/2003/75 [a November 2003 report from ElBaradei], constitute non compliance in the context of Article XII.C of the Agency's Statute;

According to the resolution, the board also found

> that the history of concealment of Iran's nuclear activities referred to in the Director General's report [GOV/2003/75], the nature of these activities, issues brought to light in the course of the Agency's verification of declarations made by Iran since September 2002 and the resulting absence of confidence that Iran's nuclear programme is exclusively for peaceful purposes have given rise to questions that are within the competence of the Security Council, as the organ bearing the main responsibility for the maintenance of international peace and security.

ElBaradei issued the report cited by the resolution, GOV/2003/75, in November 2003.[26] It described a variety of Iranian nuclear activities, which are detailed in **Appendix A**, that violated Tehran's safeguards agreement. ElBaradei has since reported that Iran has taken corrective measures to address these safeguards breaches. As noted above, the 2005 resolution called on Iran to take a variety of actions that Tehran was not legally required to implement.

U.N. Charter and the Security Council

Several articles of the U.N. Charter, which is a treaty, describe the Security Council's authority to impose requirements and sanctions on Iran.[27] Article 24 confers on the council "primary responsibility for the maintenance of international peace and security." The article also states that the "specific powers granted to the Security Council for the discharge of these duties are laid down" in several chapters of the charter, including Chapter VII, which describes the actions that the council may take in response to "threats to the peace, breaches of the peace, and acts of aggression."

Chapter VII of the charter contains three articles relevant to the Iran case. Security Council resolutions that made mandatory the IAEA's demands concerning Iran's nuclear program invoked Chapter VII. Article 39 of that chapter states that the council

> shall determine the existence of any threat to the peace, breach of the peace, or act of aggression and shall make recommendations, or decide what measures shall be taken in accordance with Articles 41 and 42, to maintain or restore international peace and security.

Resolution 1696 invoked Article 40 of Chapter VII "in order to make mandatory the suspension required by the IAEA." As noted earlier, that resolution did not impose any sanctions on Iran. Article 40 states that

> the Security Council may, before making the recommendations or deciding upon the measures provided for in Article 39 [of Chapter VII], call upon the parties concerned to comply with such provisional measures as it deems necessary or desirable.

Resolutions 1737, 1747, and 1803, which did impose sanctions, invoked Article 41 of Chapter VII. According to Article 41, the Security Council

> may decide what measures not involving the use of armed force are to be employed to give effect to its decisions, and it may call upon the Members of the United Nations to apply such measures. These may include complete or partial interruption of economic relations and of rail, sea, air, postal, telegraphic, radio, and other means of communication, and the severance of diplomatic relations.

As noted above, Security Council resolution 1835 did not impose new sanctions, but reaffirmed the previous resolutions and called on Iran to comply with them. The sanctions imposed by those resolutions remain in place. The five permanent members of the council, along with Germany, are continuing to discuss the matter.

It is worth noting that Article 25 of the U.N. Charter obligates U.N. members "to accept and carry out the decisions of the Security Council."

HAS IRAN VIOLATED THE NPT?[28]

Whether Iran has violated the NPT is unclear. The treaty does not contain a mechanism for determining that a state-party has violated its obligations. Moreover, there does not appear to be a formal procedure for determining such violations. An NPT Review Conference would, however, be one venue for NPT states-parties to make such a determination.

The U.N. Security Council has never declared Iran to be in violation of the NPT; neither the council nor the U.N. General Assembly has a responsibility to adjudicate treaty violations. However, the lack of a ruling by the council on Iran's compliance with the NPT has apparently had little practical effect because, as noted above, the council has taken action in response to the IAEA Board of Governors' determination that Iran has violated its safeguards agreement.

Iran's violations of its safeguards agreement appear to constitute violations of Article III, which requires NPT non-nuclear-weapon states-parties to adhere to their safeguards agreements. Tehran may also have violated provisions of Article II which state that non-nuclear-weapon states-parties shall not "manufacture or otherwise acquire nuclear weapons or other nuclear explosive devices" or "seek or receive any assistance in the manufacture of nuclear weapons or other nuclear explosive devices."

As previously noted, the IAEA is continuing to investigate evidence of what ElBaradei described in June 2008 as "possible military dimensions to Iran's nuclear programme." Such activities may indicate that Tehran has violated both Article II provisions described above, but the IAEA has never reported that Iran has attempted to develop nuclear weapons.

Despite the lack of such an IAEA conclusion, a 2005 State Department report argued that the country had violated Article II of the NPT:

> The breadth of Iran's nuclear development efforts, the secrecy and deceptions with which they have been conducted for nearly 20 years, its redundant and surreptitious procurement channels, Iran's persistent failure to comply with its obligations to report to the IAEA and to apply safeguards to such activities, and the lack of a reasonable economic justification for this program leads us to conclude that Iran is pursuing an effort to manufacture nuclear weapons, and has sought and received assistance in this effort in violation of Article II of the NPT.[29]

The report also stated that Iran's "weapons program combines elements" of Tehran's declared nuclear activities, as well as suspected "undeclared fuel cycle and other activities that may exist, including those that may be run solely be the military."

The State Department's reasoning appears to be based on an interpretation of the NPT which holds that a wide scope of nuclear activities could constitute violations of Article II. The 2005 report states that assessments regarding Article II compliance "must look at the totality of the facts, including judgments as to" a state-party's "purpose in undertaking the nuclear activities in question." The report also includes a list of activities which could constitute such noncompliance.[30]

The 2005 State Department report cites testimony from then-Arms Control and Disarmament Agency Director William Foster during a 1968 Senate Foreign Relations Committee hearing.[31]

Foster stated that "facts indicating that the purpose of a particular activity was the acquisition of a nuclear explosive device would tend to show non-compliance" with Article II. He gave two examples: "the construction of an experimental or prototype nuclear explosive device" and "the production of components which could only have relevance" to such a device. However, Foster also noted that a variety of other activities could also violate

Article II, adding that the United States believed it impossible "to formulate a comprehensive definition or interpretation."

A November 2007 National Intelligence Estimate stated that "until fall 2003, Iranian military entities were working under government direction to develop nuclear weapons."[32] This past program could be a violation of Article II, although the estimate does not provide any detail about the program.

It is worth noting that the State Department's arguments appear to rely heavily on the notion that a state's apparent intentions underlying certain nuclear-related activities can be used to determine violations of Article II. This interpretation is not shared by all experts.[33]

APPENDIX A. IRANIAN NONCOMPLIANCE WITH ITS IAEA SAFEGUARDS AGREEMENT

The November 2003 report (GOV/2003/75) from IAEA Director-General ElBaradei to the agency's Board of Governors details what the September 2005 board resolution described as "Iran's many failures and breaches of its obligations to comply with its safeguards agreement."

The report stated that

> Iran has failed in a number of instances over an extended period of time to meet its obligations under its Safeguards Agreement with respect to the reporting of nuclear material and its processing and use, as well as the declaration of facilities where such material has been processed and stored.

The report detailed some of these failures and referenced other failures described in two earlier reports (GOV/2003/40 and GOV/2003/63) from ElBaradei to the IAEA board.[34]

According to GOV/2003/40, Iran failed to declare the following activities to the agency:

- The importation of natural uranium, and its subsequent transfer for further processing.
- The processing and use of the imported natural uranium, including the production and loss of nuclear material, and the production and transfer of resulting waste.

Additionally, Iran failed to

- declare the facilities where nuclear material (including the waste) was received, stored and processed,
- provide in a timely manner updated design information for a research reactor located in Tehran, as well as
- provide in a timely manner information on two waste storage sites.

GOV/2003/63 stated that Iran failed to report uranium conversion experiments to the IAEA. According to GOV/2003/75, Iran failed to report the following activities to the IAEA:

- The use of imported natural uranium hexafluoride for the testing of centrifuges, as well as the subsequent production of enriched and depleted uranium.
- The importation of natural uranium metal and its subsequent transfer for use in laser enrichment experiments, including the production of enriched uranium, the loss of nuclear material during these operations, and the production and transfer of resulting waste.
- The production of a variety of nuclear compounds from several different imported nuclear materials, and the production and transfer of resulting wastes.
- The production of uranium targets and their irradiation in the Tehran Research Reactor, the subsequent processing of those targets (including the separation of plutonium), the production and transfer of resulting waste, and the storage of unprocessed irradiated targets.

Iran also failed to provide the agency with design information for a variety of nuclear-related facilities, according to the report. These included the following:

- A centrifuge testing facility.
- Two laser laboratories and locations where resulting wastes were processed.
- Facilities involved in the production of a variety of nuclear compounds.
- The Tehran Research Reactor (with respect to the irradiation of uranium targets), the hot cell facility where the plutonium separation took place, as well as the relevant waste handling facility.

Additionally, the report cited Iran's "failure on many occasions to co-operate to facilitate the implementation of safeguards, through concealment" of its nuclear activities.

APPENDIX B. EXTENDED REMARKS BY WILLIAM FOSTER REGARDING POSSIBLE NPT ARTICLE II VIOLATIONS

On July 10, 1968, then-Arms Control and Disarmament Agency Director William Foster testified before the Senate Foreign Relations Committee about the NPT. In response to a question regarding the type of nuclear activities prohibited by Article II of the treaty, Foster supplied the following statement:

> Extension of Remarks by Mr. Foster in Response to Question Regarding Nuclear Explosive Devices
>
> The treaty articles in question are Article II, in which non-nuclear-weapon parties undertake 'not to manufacture or otherwise acquire nuclear weapons or other nuclear explosive devices,' and Article IV, which provides that nothing in the Treaty is to be interpreted as affecting the right of all Parties to the Treaty 'to develop research, production and use of nuclear energy for peaceful purposes...in conformity with Articles I and II of this Treaty.' In the course of the negotiation of the Treaty, United States representatives were asked their views on what would constitute the 'manufacture' of a nuclear weapon or other nuclear explosive device under Article II of the draft treaty. Our reply was as follows:

'While the general intent of this provision seems clear, and its application to cases such as those discussed below should present little difficulty, the United States believe [sic] it is not possible at this time to formulate a comprehensive definition or interpretation. There are many hypothetical situations which might be imagined and it is doubtful that any general definition or interpretation, unrelated to specific fact situations could satisfactorily deal with all such situations.

'Some general observations can be made with respect to the question of whether or not a specific activity constitutes prohibited manufacture under the proposed treaty. For example, facts indicating that the purpose of a particular activity was the acquisition of a nuclear explosive device would tend to show non-compliance. (Thus, the construction of an experimental or prototype nuclear explosive device would be covered by the term 'manufacture' as would be the production of components which could only have relevance to a nuclear explosive device.) Again, while the placing of a particular activity under safeguards would not, in and of itself, settle the question of whether that activity was in compliance with the treaty, it would of course be helpful in allaying any suspicion of non-compliance.

'It may be useful to point out, for illustrative purposes, several activities which the United States would not consider per se to be violations of the prohibitions in Article II. Neither uranium enrichment nor the stockpiling of fissionable material in connection with a peaceful program would violate Article II so long as these activities were safeguarded under Article III. Also clearly permitted would be the development, under safeguards, of plutonium fueled power reactors, including research on the properties of metallic plutonium, nor would Article II interfere with the development or use of fast breeder reactors under safeguards.'

End Notes

[1] Under the NPT, the five nuclear-weapon states are China, France, Russia, the United Kingdom, and the United States. All other parties are non-nuclear-weapon states.
[2] INFCIRC/214, available at http://www.iaea.org/Publications/Documents/Infcircs/Others/infcirc214.pdf.
[3] The text is available at http://www.iaea.org/Publications/Documents/Infcircs/2007/infcirc711.pdf.
[4] GOV/2009/74, available at http://isis-online.org/uploads/isis-reports/documents/IAEA_Report_Iran_16 November 2009pdf_1.pdf
[5] GOV/2008/38, available at http://www.iaea.org/Publications/Documents/Board/2008/gov2008-38.pdf.
[6] Iran is also constructing a plant for the production of heavy water.
[7] IAEA Safeguards Glossary. Comprehensive safeguards agreements are based on a model described in INFCIRC 153, available at http://www.iaea.org/Publications/Documents/Infcircs/Others/infcirc153.pdf.
[8] Ibid.
[9] Additional Protocols for an individual IAEA member state are based on the agency's Model Additional Protocol (INFCIRC/540), available at http://www.iaea.org/Publications/Documents/Infcircs/1997/infcirc540c.pdf. [10] "Tackling the Nuclear Dilemma: An Interview with IAEA Director-General Mohamed ElBaradei," February 4, 2005, available at http://www.armscontrol.org/act/2005_03/ElBaradei.
[11] GOV/2006/15, available at http://www.iaea.org/Publications/Documents/Board/2006/gov2006-15.pdf.
[12] Gary Samore, Former Senior Director for Nonproliferation and Export Controls on the National Security Council, personal communication June 5, 2008; Director of Central Intelligence George J. Tenet, "DCI Remarks on Iraq's WMD Programs," February 5, 2004, available at https://www.cia.gov/news-information/speeches-testimony/2004/ tenet_georgetownspeech_02052004.html.
[13] Available at http://www.iaea.org/Publications/Documents/Board/2003/gov2003-69.pdf.
[14] The text of the agreement is available at http://www.iaea.org/NewsCenter/Focus/IaeaIran/statement_iran 21102003.shtml.
[15] The text of the agreement is available at http://www.iaea.org/Publications/Documents/Infcircs/2004/ infcirc 637.pdf.
[16] Available at http://www.iaea.org/Publications/Documents/Board/2005/gov2005-77.pdf.

[17] According to the 2001 IAEA Safeguards Glossary, subsidiary arrangements describe the "technical and administrative procedures for specifying how the provisions laid down in a safeguards agreement are to be applied."

[18] See also GOV/2007/22, available at http://www.iaea.org/Publications/Documents/Board/2007/gov2007-22.pdf.

[19] Available at http://www.armscontrolwonk.com/file_download/162/Legal_Adviser_Iran.pdf.

[20] GOV/2008/59.

[21] Iran stated in an April 2007 letter to the IAEA that, given Tehran's March 2007 decision regarding the subsidiary arrangements to its safeguards agreement, such visits were unjustified.

[22] GOV/2009/55, available at http://www.iaea.org/Publications/Documents/Board/2009/gov2009-55.pdf.

[23] Available at http://www.iaea.org/Publications/Documents/Board/2006/gov2006-14.pdf.

[24] The treaty text is available at http://www.iaea.org/Publications/Documents/Infcircs/Others/infcirc140.pdf.

[25] The text of the IAEA Statute is available at http://www.iaea.org/About/statute_text.html.

[26] Available at http://www.iaea.org/Publications/Documents/Board/2003/gov2003-75.pdf.

[27] The text of the charter is available at http://www.un.org/aboutun/charter/.

[28] Portions of this section are based on interviews with U.N. and State Department officials.

[29] *Adherence to and Compliance with Arms Control, Nonproliferation and Disarmament Agreements and Commitments*, Department of State, August 2005, available at http://www.state.gov/documents/organization/52113.pdf.

[30] According to the report, such activities can include (1) the presence of undeclared nuclear facilities; (2) procurement patterns inconsistent with a civil nuclear program (e.g., clandestine procurement networks, possibly including the use of front companies, false end-use information, and fraudulent documentation); (3) security measures beyond what would be appropriate for peaceful, civil nuclear installations; (4) a pattern of Article III safeguards violations suggestive not of mere mistake or incompetence, but of willful violation and/or systematic deception and denial efforts aimed at concealing nuclear activities from the IAEA; and (5) a nuclear program with little (or no) coherence for peaceful purposes, but great coherence for weapons purposes.

[31] *Nonproliferation Treaty*, Senate Committee on Foreign Relations, Joint Committee on Atomic Energy [Part 1] July 10-12, 17, 1968; Session 90-2 (1968). The complete statement regarding Article II violations is in Appendix B.

[32] Available at http://www.dni.gov/press_releases/20071203_release.pdf.

[33] Personal communication with Andreas Persbo, Senior Researcher, the Verification Research, Training and Information Centre.

[34] Those reports are available at http://www.iaea.org/Publications/Documents/Board/2003/gov2003-40.pdf and http://www.iaea.org/Publications/Documents/Board/2003/gov2003-63.pdf.

In: Iran: Issues and Perspectives
Editor: Stephen D. Calhoun

ISBN: 978-1-61728-007-8
© 2010 Nova Science Publishers, Inc.

Chapter 5

IRAN SANCTIONS[*]

Kenneth Katzman

SUMMARY

Iran is subject to a wide range of U.S. sanctions, restricting trade with, investment, and U.S. foreign aid to Iran, and requiring the United States to vote against international lending to Iran. Several laws and Executive Orders authorize the imposition of U.S. penalties against foreign companies that do business with Iran, as part of an effort to persuade foreign firms to choose between the Iranian market and the much larger U.S. market. Most notable among these sanctions is a ban, imposed in 1995, on U.S. trade with and investment in Iran. That ban has since been modified slightly to allow for some bilateral trade in luxury and humanitarian-related goods. Foreign subsidiaries of U.S. firms remain generally exempt from the trade ban since they are under the laws of the countries where they are incorporated. Since 1995, several U.S. laws and regulations that seek to pressure Iran's economy, curb Iran's support for militant groups, and curtail supplies to Iran of advanced technology have been enacted. Since 2006, the United Nations Security Council has imposed some sanctions primarily attempting to curtail supply to Iran of weapons-related technology but also sanctioning some Iranian banks.

U.S. officials have identified Iran's energy sector as a key Iranian vulnerability because Iran's government revenues are approximately 80% dependent on oil revenues and in need of substantial foreign investment. A U.S. effort to curb international energy investment in Iran began in 1996 with the Iran Sanctions Act (ISA), but no firms have been sanctioned under it and the precise effects of ISA—as distinct from other factors affecting international firms' decisions on whether to invest in Iran—have been unclear. While international pressure on Iran to curb its nuclear program has increased the hesitation of many major foreign firms to invest in Iran's energy sector, hindering Iran's efforts to expand oil production beyond 4.1

---
[*] This is an edited, reformatted and augmented version of a CRS Report for Congress publication dated December 2009.

million barrels per day, some firms continue to see opportunity in Iran. This particularly appears to be the case for companies in Asia that appear eager to fill the void left by major European and American firms and to line up steady supplies of Iranian oil and natural gas.

Some in Congress express concern about the reticence of U.S. allies, of Russia, and of China, to impose U.N. sanctions that would target Iran's civilian economy. In an attempt to strengthen U.S. leverage with its allies to back such international sanctions, several bills in the 111th Congress would add U.S. sanctions on Iran. For example, H.R. 2194 (which passed the House on December 15, 2009), H.R. 1985, H.R. 1208, and S. 908 would include as ISA violations selling refined gasoline to Iran; providing shipping insurance or other services to deliver gasoline to Iran; or supplying equipment to or performing the construction of oil refineries in Iran. Several of these bills would also expand the menu of available sanctions against violators. A bill reported by the Senate Banking Committee, S. 2799, contains these sanctions as well as a broad range of other measures against Iran, including reversing previous easings of the U.S. ban on trade with Iran, and protecting investment funds from lawsuits for divesting from companies active in Iran. A growing trend in Congress is to alter some U.S. sanctions laws in order to facilitate the access to information of a growing student-led opposition movement in Iran, and to sanction firms that sell the regime internet-monitoring gear. Some see the various legislative proposals as supporting Obama Administration policy by threatening Iran with further isolation, while others believe such legislation would reduce European cooperation with the United States on Iran. Still others say these proposals could backfire by strengthening the political control exercised by Iran's leaders. For more on Iran, see CRS Report RL3 2048, *Iran: U.S. Concerns and Policy Responses*, by Kenneth Katzman.

OVERVIEW

This chapter analyzes various U.S. sanctions in place against Iran, and their relationship to each other as well as to U.N. sanctions imposed since 2006 because of Iran's continued nuclear program development. A particular focus of this chapter is the Iran Sanctions Act (ISA), which has been the focus of differences of opinion between the United States and its European allies. Some pending congressional proposals to expand ISA's application have also been the basis of discussion between the United States and other countries ("P5+1" multilateral working group on Iran—United States, France, Britain, Russia, China, plus Germany)—about possible new U.N. sanctions against Iran's energy sector. These international sanctions are under consideration because Iran has refused to accept details of a plan, reached during October 1, 2009, talks between Iran and the P5+1, to send most of its enriched uranium out of Iran for reprocessing into medical uses.

Although the Obama Administration has emphasized potential benefit of direct engagement with Iran, it has not altered any U.S. sanctions on Iran. President Obama renewed for another year the U.S. trade and investment ban on Iran (Executive Order 12959) in March 2009. Section 7043 of P.L. 111-8, the FY09 omnibus appropriation, (signed March 8, 2009) required, within 180 days, an Administration report on U.S. sanctions, including which companies are believed to be violators, and what the Administration is doing to enforce sanctions on Iran. That deadline was October 8, 2009; the required report has not been published to date. A provision of the FY2010 National Defense Authorization Act (Section 1241 of P.L. 111-84) requires an Administration report, not later than January 31, 2010, on U.S. enforcement of sanctions against Iran, and the effect of those sanctions on Iran.

The Iran Sanctions Act (ISA)

The Iran Sanctions Act (ISA) is one among many U.S. sanctions in place against Iran. However, it has attracted substantial attention because it authorizes penalties against foreign firms, and because several bills pending in the 111th Congress propose amending the Act to curtail additional types of activity, such as selling gasoline to Iran or associated shipping services. In the past, the parent countries of such firms, many of which are incorporated in Europe, have tended to object to sanctions such as ISA, even though European countries generally share the U.S. goal of ensuring that Iran does not become a nuclear power. American firms are restricted from trading with or investing in Iran under separate U.S. executive measures.

Originally called the Iran and Libya Sanctions Act (ILSA), ISA was enacted to complement other measures—particularly Executive Order 12959 of May 6, 1995, that banned U.S. trade with and investment in Iran—intended to deny Iran the resources to further its nuclear program and to support terrorist organizations such as Hizbollah, Hamas, and Palestine Islamic Jihad. Iran's petroleum sector generates about 20% of Iran's GDP, but its onshore oil fields and oil industry infrastructure are aging and need substantial investment. Its large natural gas resources (940 trillion cubic feet, exceeded only by Russia) were undeveloped when ISA was first enacted. Iran has 136.3 billion barrels of proven oil reserves, the third largest after Saudi Arabia and Canada.

In 1995 and 1996, U.S. allies did not join the United States in enacting trade sanctions against Iran, and the Clinton Administration and Congress believed that it might be necessary for the United States to try to deter their investment in Iran. The opportunity to do so came in November 1995, when Iran opened its energy sector to foreign investment. To accommodate its ideology to retain control of its national resources, Iran used a "buy-back" investment program in which foreign firms recoup their investments from the proceeds of oil and gas discoveries but do not receive equity. With input from the Administration, on September 8, 1995, Senator Alfonse D'Amato introduced the "Iran Foreign Oil Sanctions Act" to sanction foreign firms' exports to Iran of energy technology. A revised version instead sanctioning *investment* in Iran's energy sector passed the Senate on December 18, 1995 (voice vote). On December 20, 1995, the Senate passed a version applying the legislation to Libya as well, which was refusing to yield for trial the two intelligence agents suspected in the December 21, 1988, bombing of Pan Am 103. The House passed H.R. 3107, on June 19, 1996 (415-0), and then concurred on a slightly different Senate version adopted on July 16, 1996 (unanimous consent). It was signed on August 5, 1996 (P.L. 104-172).

Key Provisions/"Triggers" and Available Sanctions

ISA consists of a number of "triggers"—transactions with Iran that would be considered violations of ISA and could cause a firm or entity to be sanctioned under ISA's provisions. ISA provides a number of different sanctions that the President could impose that would harm a foreign firm's business opportunities in the United States. ISA does not, and probably could not legally or practically, compel any foreign government to take any specific action against one of its firms.

ISA requires the President to sanction companies (entities, persons) that make an "investment" of more than $20 million in one year in Iran's energy sector,[1] *or* that sell to Iran weapons of mass destruction (WMD) technology or "destabilizing numbers and types" of advanced conventional weapons.[2] ISA is primarily targeting foreign firms, because American firms are already prohibited from investing in Iran under the 1995 trade and investment ban discussed earlier.

Once a firm is determined to be a violator, ISA requires the imposition of *two* of a menu of six sanctions on that firm. The available sanctions the President can select from (Section 6) include (1) denial of Export-Import Bank loans, credits, or credit guarantees for U.S. exports to the sanctioned entity; (2) denial of licenses for the U.S. export of military or militarily useful technology; (3) denial of U.S. bank loans exceeding $10 million in one year; (4) if the entity is a financial institution, a prohibition on its service as a primary dealer in U.S. government bonds; and/or a prohibition on its serving as a repository for U.S. government funds (each counts as one sanction); (5) prohibition on U.S. government procurement from the entity; and (6) restriction on imports from the entity, in accordance with the International Emergency Economic Powers Act (IEEPA, 50 U.S.C. 1701).

Waiver and Termination Authority

The President has the authority under ISA to waive the sanctions on Iran if he certifies that doing so is important to the U.S. national interest (Section 9(c)). There was also waiver authority in the original version of ISA if the parent country of the violating firm joined a sanctions regime against Iran, but this waiver provision was made inapplicable by subsequent legislation. ISA application to Iran would terminate if Iran is determined by the Administration to have ceased its efforts to acquire WMD and is removed from the U.S. list of state sponsors of terrorism, *and* no longer "poses a significant threat" to U.S. national security and U.S. allies.[3] Application to Libya terminated when the President determined on April 23, 2004, that Libya had fulfilled the requirements of all U.N. resolutions on Pan Am 103.

Traditionally reticent to impose economic sanctions, the European Union opposed ISA as an extraterritorial application of U.S. law. In April 1997, the United States and the EU agreed to avoid a trade confrontation in the World Trade Organization (WTO) over it and a separate Cuba sanctions law, (P.L. 104-114). The agreement contributed to a May 18, 1998, decision by the Clinton Administration to waive ISA sanctions ("national interest"—Section 9(c) waiver) on the first project determined to be in violation—a $2 billion[4] contract (September 1997) for Total SA of France and its partners, Gazprom of Russia and Petronas of Malaysia to develop phases 2 and 3 of the 25-phase South Pars gas field. The EU pledged to increase cooperation with the United States on non-proliferation and counter-terrorism, and the Administration indicated future investments by EU firms in Iran would not be sanctioned.

ISA was to sunset on August 5, 2001, in a climate of lessening tensions with Iran and Libya. During 1999 and 2000, the Clinton Administration had eased the trade ban on Iran somewhat to try to engage the relatively moderate Iranian President Mohammad Khatemi. In 1999, Libya yielded for trial the Pan Am 103 suspects. However, some maintained that both countries would view its expiration as a concession, and renewal legislation was enacted (P.L. 107-24, August 3, 2001). This law required an Administration report on ISA's effectiveness within 24 to 30 months of enactment; that report was submitted to Congress in January 2004 and did not recommend that ISA be repealed. Currently, as discussed below, ISA is scheduled to sunset on December 31, 2011.

Iran Freedom Support Act Amendments

In addition to the amendments to ISA referred to above, P.L. 109-293, the "Iran Freedom and Support Act" (H.R. 6198) amended ISA by (1) calling for, *but not requiring*, a 180-day time limit for a violation determination; (2) recommending against U.S. nuclear agreements with countries that supply nuclear technology to Iran; (3) expanding provisions of the USA Patriot Act (P.L. 107-56) to curb money-laundering for use to further WMD programs; (4) extending ISA until December 31, 2011 (see above); and (5) formally dropping Libya and changing the name to the Iran Sanctions Act.

Earlier versions of the Iran Freedom and Support Act in the 109th Congress (H.R. 282, S. 333) were viewed as too restrictive of Administration prerogatives. Among the provisions of these bills not ultimately adopted included setting a 90-day time limit for the Administration to determine whether an investment is a violation (there is no time limit in the original law); cutting U.S. foreign assistance to countries whose companies violate ISA; and applying the U.S. trade ban on Iran to foreign subsidiaries of U.S. companies.

Effectiveness and Ongoing Challenges

The Bush Administration maintained that, even without actually imposing ISA sanctions, the threat of sanctions—coupled with Iran's reputedly difficult negotiating behavior, and compounded by Iran's growing isolation because of its nuclear program—slowed Iran's energy development.

However, the Obama Administration's overall policy approach contrasts with the Bush Administration approach by actively attempting to engage Iran in negotiations on the nuclear issue, rather than focusing only on increasing sanctions on Iran. That approach was not significantly altered in the context of the Iranian dispute over its June 12, 2009, elections. The Administration supported "crippling" new U.N. sanctions if Iran does not return to multilateral nuclear talks by September 24, 2009, but the Administration agreed to join P5+1 talks with Iran on October 1, 2009, and described the talks as constructive. A tentative nuclear agreement at that meeting appeared to forestall discussion of additional U.N. or multilateral sanctions, although Iran has, to date, not agreed to terms to implement its agreement to send out most of its enriched uranium to France and Russia for reprocessing (for later medical use). As of early December 2009, the issue of new international sanctions has returned to the forefront of U.S.-partner country discussions.

As shown in **Table 1** below, several foreign investment agreements have been agreed with Iran since the 1998 Total consortium waiver, but others have been long stalled. Some investors, such as major European firms Repsol, Royal Dutch Shell, and Total, have announced pullouts, declined further investment, or resold their investments to other companies. On July 12, 2008, Total and Petronas, the original South Pars investors, pulled out of a deal to develop a liquified natural gas (LNG) export capability at Phase 11 of South Pars, saying that investing in Iran at a time of growing international pressure over its nuclear program is "too risky." Also in 2008, Japan significantly reduced its participation in the development of Iran's large Azadegan field. Some of the void has been filled, at least partly, by Asian firms such as those of China and Malaysia. However, some of those agreements are being implemented only slowly and these companies are perceived as not being as technically capable as those that have withdrawn from Iran.

Table 1. Post-1999 Major Investments in Iran's Energy Sector
($20 million + investments in oil and gas fields only and refinery upgrades included.)

Date	Field/Project	Company(ies)	Value	Output/Goal
Feb. 1999	Doroud (oil)	Totalfina Elf (France) /ENI (Italy)	$1 billion	205,000 bpd
Apr. 1999	Balal (oil)	Totalfina Elf/ Bow Valley (Canada)/ENI	$300 million	40,000 bpd
Nov. 1999	Soroush and Nowruz (oil)	Royal Dutch Shell	$800 million	190,000 bpd
Apr. 2000	Anaran (oil)	Norsk Hydro (Norway) /Lukoil (Russia)	$100 million	100,000 (by 2010)
July 2000	Phase 4 and 5, South Pars(gas)	ENI	$1.9 billion	2 billion cu.ft./day(cfd)
Mar. 2001	Caspian Sea oil exploration	GVA Consultants (Sweden)	$225 million	?
June 2001	Darkhovin (oil)	ENI	$1 billion	160,000 bpd
May 2002	Masjid-e-Soleyman (oil)	Sheer Energy (Canada)	$80 million	25,000 bpd
Sep. 2002	Phase 9 + 10, South Pars (gas)	LG (South Korea)	$1.6 billion	2 billion cfd
Oct. 2002	Phase 6, 7, 8, South Pars (gas) (est. to begin producing late 08)	Statoil (Norway)	$2.65 billion	3 billion cfd
Jan. 2004	Azadegan (oil)	Inpex (Japan) 10% stake; China National Petroleum Co. agreed to develop "north Azadegan" in Jan. 2009	$200 million (Inpex stake); China $1.76 billion	260,000 bpd
Aug. 2004	Tusan Block	Petrobras (Brazil)	$34 million	?
Oct. 2004	Yadavaran (oil). Finalized December 9, 2007	Sinopec (China)	$2 billion	185,000 bpd (by 2011)
June 2006	Gamsar block (oil)	Sinopec (China)	$20 million	?
July 2006	Arak Refinery expansion	Sinopec (China)	$959 million	
Sept. 2006	Khorramabad block (oil)	Norsk Hydro (Norway)	$49 million	?
Mar. 07	Esfahan refinery upgrade	Daelim (S. Korea)		
Dec. 2007	Golshan and Ferdows onshore and offshore gas fields and LNG plant; modified but reaffirmed December 2008	SKS Ventures (Malaysia)	$16 billion	3.4 billion cfd
Totals:				
$29.5 billion investment				
Oil: 1.085 million bpd Gas: 10.4 billion cfd				

Table 1. (Continued)

Date	Field/Project	Company(ies)	Value	Output/Goal
Pending Deals/Preliminary Agreements				
Kharg and Bahregansar fields (gas)	IRASCO (Italy)	$1.6 billion	?
Salkh and Southern Gashku fields (gas). Includes LNG plant (Nov. 2006)	LNG Ltd. (Australia)	?	?
North Pars Gas Field (offshore gas). Includes gas purchases (Dec. 2006)	China National Offshore Oil Co.	$16 billion	3.6 billion cfd
Phase 13, 14 - South Pars (gas); (Feb. 2007). Deal cancelled in May 2008	Royal Dutch Shell, Repsol (Spain)	$4.3 billion	?
Phase 22, 23, 24 - South Pars (gas), incl. transport Iranian gas to Europe and building three power plants in Iran. Initialed July 2007; not finalized to date.	Turkish Petroleum Company (TPAO)	$12. billion	2 billion cfd
Iran's Kish gas field (April 2008)	Oman	$7 billion	1 billion cfd
Phase 12 South Pars (gas). Incl. LNG terminal construction (March 2009)	China-led consortium; project originally subscribed in May 2007 by OMV (Austria)	$3.2 billion	20 million tones of LNG annually by 2012
South Pars gas field (September 2009)	Petroleos de Venezuela S.A.; 10% stake in venture	$760 million $up to 6	
Abadan refinery upgrade and expansion; building a new refinery at Hormuz on the Persian Gulf coast (August 2009)	Sinopec	billion if new refinery is built	

Sources: CRS, GAO cited later, a wide variety of press announcements and sources, CRS conversations with officials of the State Department Bureau of Economics (November 2009), CRS conversations with officials of Embassies of the parent government of some of the listed companies (2005-2009). CRS has neither the authority nor the means to determine which of these projects, if any, might constitute a violation of the Iran Sanctions Act. CRS has no way to confirm the precise status of any of the announced investments, and some investments may have been resold to other firms or terms altered since agreement. In virtually all cases, such investments and contracts represent private agreements between Iran and its instruments and the investing firms, and firms are not necessarily required to confirm or publicly release the terms of their arrangements with Iran.

These trends have constrained Iran's energy sector significantly; Iran's deputy Oil Minister said in November 2008 that Iran needs about $145 billion in new investment over the next 10 years in order to build a thriving energy sector. As a result of sanctions and the overall climate of international isolation of Iran, its oil production has not grown—it remains at about 4.1 million barrels per day (mbd)—although it has not fallen either.

Some observers maintain that, over and above the threat of ISA sanctions and the international pressure on Iran, it is Iran's negotiating behavior that has slowed international investment in Iran's energy sector. Some international executives that have negotiated with

Iran say Iran insists on deals that leave little profit, and that Iran frequently seeks to renegotiate provisions of a contract after it is ratified.

Some analyses, including by the National Academy of Sciences, say that, partly because of growing domestic consumption, Iranian oil exports are declining to the point where Iran might have negligible exports of oil by 2015.[5] Others maintain that Iran's gas sector can more than compensate for declining oil exports, although it needs gas to re-inject into its oil fields and remains a relatively minor gas exporter. It exports about 3.6 trillion cubic feet of gas, primarily to Turkey. A GAO study of December 2007, (GAO-08-58), contains a chart of *post-2003* investments in Iran's energy sector, totaling over $20 billion in investment, although the chart includes petrochemical and refinery projects, as well as projects that do not exceed the $20 million in one year threshold for ISA sanctionability.

Since the Total/Petronas/Gazprom project in 1998, no projects have been determined as violations of ISA. Some of the projects listed in the GAO report and in **Table 1** below may be under review by the State Department (Bureau of Economic Affairs), but no publication of such deals has been placed in the *Federal Register* (requirement of Section 5e of ISA), and no determinations of violation have been announced. State Department reports to Congress on ISA, required every six months, have routinely stated that U.S. diplomats raise U.S. policy concerns about Iran with investing companies and their parent countries. However, these reports do not specifically state which foreign companies are being investigated for ISA violations. Some Members of Congress believe that ISA would have been even more effective if successive Administrations had imposed sanctions, and have expressed frustration that the Executive branch has not imposed ISA sanctions.

Energy Routes and Refinery Investment

ISA's definition of sanctionable "investment"—which specifies investment in Iran's petroleum resources, defined as petroleum and natural gas—has been interpreted by successive Administrations to include construction of energy routes to or through Iran—because such routes help Iran develop its petroleum resources. The Clinton and Bush Administrations used the threat of ISA sanctions to deter oil routes involving Iran and thereby successfully promoted an alternate route from Azerbaijan (Baku) to Turkey (Ceyhan). The route became operational in 2005. No sanctions were imposed on a 1997 project viewed as necessary to U.S. ally Turkey—an Iran- Turkey natural gas pipeline in which each constructed the pipeline on its side of their border. The State Department did not impose ISA sanctions on the grounds that Turkey would be importing gas originating in Turkmenistan, not Iran. However, direct Iranian gas exports to Turkey began in 2001, and, as shown in Table 1, in July 2007, a preliminary agreement was reached to build a second Iran-Turkey pipeline, through which Iranian gas would also flow to Europe. That agreement was not finalized during Iranian President Mahmoud Ahmadinej ad's visit to Turkey in August 2008 because of Turkish commercial concerns but the deal remains under active discussion. On February 23, 2009, Iranian newspapers said Iran had formed a joint venture with a Turkish firm to export 35 billion cubic meters of gas per year to Europe; 50% of the venture would be owned by the National Iranian Gas Export Company (NIGEC).

Iran-India Pipeline

Another pending deal is the construction of a gas pipeline from Iran to India, through Pakistan (IPI pipeline). The three governments have stated they are committed to the $7 billion project, which would take about three years to complete, but India did not sign a deal "finalization" that was signed by Iran and Pakistan on November 11, 2007. India had re-entered discussions on the project following Iranian President Mahmoud Ahmadinejad's visit to India in April 2008, which also resulted in Indian firms' winning preliminary Iranian approval to take equity stakes in the Azadegan oil field project and South Pars gas field Phase 12. India did not attend further talks on the project in September 2008, raising continued concerns on security of the pipeline, the location at which the gas would be officially transferred to India, pricing of the gas, tariffs, and the source in Iran of the gas to be sold. Perhaps to address some of those concerns, but also perhaps to move forward whether or not India joins the project, in January 2009 Iran and Pakistan amended the proposed pricing formula for the exported gas to reflect new energy market conditions. However, there has been no evident movement on the project since that time. During the Bush Administration, Secretary of State Rice, on several occasions "expressed U.S. concern" about the pipeline deal or have called it "unacceptable," but no U.S. official has stated outright that it would be sanctioned.

European Gas Pipeline Routes

Iran might also be exploring other export routes for its gas. A potential project involving Iran is the Nabucco pipeline project, which would transport Iranian gas to western Europe. Iran, Turkey, and Austria reportedly are negotiating on that project. The Bush Administration did not support Iran's participation in the project and the Obama Administration apparently takes the same view, even though the project might make Europe less dependent on Russian gas supplies. Iran's Energy Minister Gholam-Hossein Nozari said on April 2, 2009, that Iran is considering negotiating a gas export route—the "Persian Pipeline"—that would send gas to Europe via Iraq, Syria, and the Mediterranean Sea.

Iranian Refinery Construction

Iran has plans to build or expand, possibly with foreign investment, at least eight refineries in an effort to ease gasoline imports that supply about 30%-40% of Iran's needs. Construction of oil refineries or petrochemical plants in Iran—included in the referenced GAO report—might also constitute sanctionable projects because they might, according to ISA's definition of investment, "include responsibility for the development of petroleum resources located in Iran." **Table 1** provides some information on openly announced contracts to upgrade or refurbish Iranian oil refineries.

It is not clear whether or not Iranian investments in energy projects in other countries, such as Iranian investment to help build five oil refineries in Asia (China, Indonesia, Malaysia, and Singapore) and in Syria, reported in June 2007, would constitute sanctionable investment under ISA.

Significant Iranian Energy Purchase and Sale Agreements

Major energy deals with Iran that involve purchases of oil or natural gas from Iran would not appear to constitute violations of ISA, because ISA sanctions investment in Iran, not trade with Iran. However, CRS is in no way positioned to determine what projects might or might not constitute violations of ISA. Many of the deals listed in the chart later in this paper involve combinations of investment and purchase. In March 2008, Switzerland's EGL utility agreed to buy 194 trillion cubic feet per year of Iranian gas for 25 years, through a Trans-Adriatic Pipeline (TAP) to be built by 2010, a deal valued at least $15 billion. The United States criticized the deal as sending the "wrong message" to Iran. However, as testified by Under Secretary of State Burns on July 9, 2008, the deal appears to involve only purchase of Iranian gas, not exploration, and likely does not violate ISA. In August 2008, Germany's Steiner-Prematechnik-Gastec Co. agreed to apply its method of turning gas into liquid fuel at three Iranian plants. In early October 2008, Iran agreed to export 1 billion cu.ft./day of gas to Oman, via a pipeline to be built that would end at Oman's LNG export terminal facilities.

Gasoline Sales to Iran

Iran, as noted, is dependent on gasoline imports. Such sales to Iran are not currently banned by any U.N. resolutions, although such sales have recently become subject to some U.S. sanctions, as discussed below. As noted below, pending legislation is intended to impose even stiffer potential penalties on firms that sell gasoline to Iran.

There appears to be a relatively limited group of major gasoline suppliers to Iran. These are, according to a variety of sources, Vitol of Switzerland; Trafigura of Switzerland; Glencore of Switzerland; Total of France; Reliance Industries of India; Petronas of Malaysia; and Lukoil of Russia. Royal Dutch Shell of the Netherlands and British Petroleum of United Kingdom have been suppliers as well, although they reportedly have reduced supplies because of Iran's increasingly outcast international status. Petroleos de Venezuela might be affected because of its September 2009 deal to supply Iran with gasoline, as would state owned Chinese firms that reportedly now provide Iran with up to one third of its gasoline imports.[6]

Efforts in the 110th Congress to Expand ISA Application

In the 110th Congress, several bills contained numerous provisions that would have further amended ISA, but they were not adopted. H.R. 1400, which passed the House on September 25, 2007 (397-16), would have removed the Administration's ability to waive ISA sanctions under Section 9(c), national interest grounds, but it would not have imposed on the Administration a time limit to determine whether a project is sanctionable.

That bill and several others—including S. 970, S. 3227, S. 3445, H.R. 957 (passed the House on July 31, 2007), and H.R. 7112 (which passed the House on September 26, 2008)—would have (1) expanded the definition of sanctionable entities to official credit guarantee agencies, such as France's COFACE and Germany's Hermes, and to financial institutions and insurers generally; and (2) made investment to develop a liquified natural gas (LNG) sector in Iran a sanctionable violation. Iran has no LNG export terminals, in part because the technology for such terminals is patented by U.S. firms and unavailable for sale to Iran.

Among related bills in the 110th Congress, H.R. 2880 would have made sales to Iran of refined petroleum resources a violation of ISA, although some believe that a sanction such as this would only be effective if it applied to all countries under a U.N. Security Council resolution rather than a unilateral U.S. sanction. H.R. 2347, (passed the House on July 31, 2007), would protect from lawsuits fund managers that divest from firms that make ISA-sanctionable investments. (A version of this bill, H.R. 1327, has been introduced in the 111th Congress.)

In early 2009, there were some indications that congressional sentiment had some effect on foreign firms, even without enactment of significant ISA amendment in the 110th Congress. In January 2009, Reliance Industries Ltd of India said it would cease new sales of refined gasoline to Iran after completing existing contracts that expired December 31, 2008. The Reliance decision came after several Members of Congress urged the Exim Bank of the United States to suspend assistance to Reliance, on the grounds that it was assisting Iran's economy with the gas sales. The Exim Bank, in August 2008, had extended a total of $900 million in financing guarantees to Reliance to help it expand. However, some observers say Reliance continues to make such sales to Iran.

Legislation in the 111th Congress: Targeting Gasoline Sales

A number of ideas to expand ISA's application, similar to those that surfaced in the 110th Congress, have been introduced in the 111th Congress. The major bills in the 111th Congress, in general, seek to take advantage of Iran's dependence on imported gasoline. As noted, such sales to Iran are not currently sanctionable under ISA, according to widely accepted definitions of ISA violations. However, using U.S. funds to filling the Strategic Petroleum Reserve with products from firms that sell over $1 million worth of gasoline to Iran is now prevented by the FY20 10 Energy and Water Appropriation (H.R. 3183, P.L. 111-85, signed October 28, 2009).

In the aftermath of Iran's crackdown on post-June 12, 2009, presidential election protests, the House Appropriations Committee marked up a version of a FY20 10 foreign aid appropriation (H.R. 3081) that would deny Eximbank credits to any firm that sells gasoline to Iran, provides equipment to Iran that it can use to expand its oil refinery capabilities, or performs gasoline production projects in Iran. This provision was incorporated into the FY2010 consolidated appropriation (P.L. 111-117).

In April 2009, several bills were introduced—H.R. 2194, S. 908, H.R. 1208, and H.R. 1985—that would make sanctionable efforts by foreign firms to supply refined gasoline to Iran or to supply equipment to Iran that could be used by Iran to expand or construction oil refineries. Such activity is not now sanctionable under ISA. S. 908 and H.R. 2194—both titled the Iran Refined Petroleum Sanctions Act of 2009 (IRPSA)—would, in addition, expand the menu of sanctions to be imposed against violating firms. In both these bills, the new mandatory sanctions would include (1) prohibiting transactions in foreign exchange by the sanctioned firm; (2) prohibiting any financial transactions on behalf of the sanctioned firm; and (3) prohibiting any acquisitions or ownership of U.S. property by the sanctioned entity. H.R. 2194 was reported out by the House Foreign Affairs Committee on October 28, 2009, and included a requirement that no Executive agency of the U.S. government contract with firms that cannot certify that they are not supplying gasoline or refinery equipment to Iran (over $200,000 in value). H.R. 2194 was passed by the House on December 15, 2009 by a vote of 412-12, with four others voting "present" and six others not voting. The opposing and "present" votes included several Members who have opposed several post- September 11 U.S. military operations in the Middle East/South Asia region. H.R. 1208 contained numerous other provisions that were in several of the bills mentioned above in the 110th Congress, including eliminating the exemption in the trade ban that allows importation of Iranian luxury goods, and applying the trade ban to subsidiaries of U.S. firms (if those subsidiaries were used by the parent specifically to conduct trade with Iran).

Senate Sanctions Bill

A bill similar to the others above but with broader provisions, the "Dodd-Shelby Comprehensive Iran Sanctions, Accountability, and Divestment Act," (S. 2799), was reported to the full Senate by the Senate Banking Committee on November 19, 2009. In addition to containing provisions sanctioning gasoline and refinery equipment sales, and preventing U.S. government contracting with such supplier firms, the bill would restore the restrictions on imports from Iran that were lifted in 2000 (a provision introduced several times in other legislation in the past few years); would require the U.S. freezing of assets of any Iranians (including Revolutionary Guard Corps officers) who are involved in proliferation activity or furthering of acts of international terrorism; would apply the U.S. trade ban to foreign subsidiaries of U.S. firms (another provision introduced several times in the past few years); would ban U.S. government contracts with firms which sell Iran equipment that can be used to censor or monitor internet usage in Iran; and would protect investment managers who divest from firms which are undertaking activity that might constitute a violation of the other provisions of the bill. The bill would also authorize a new licensing requirement for exports to countries designated, under the bill, as "Destinations of Possible Diversion Concern" and which fail to cooperate to strengthen their export control systems thereafter. Such a provision is targeted at such countries as UAE, Malaysia, and others that have been widely cited in press reports as failing to block exports or re-exports of sensitive technologies to Iran and other countries.

It was reported by "The Cable" (Josh Rogin) on December 11, 2009[7] that the Obama Administration has sought to negotiate with the key Senators involved in S. 2799 on the grounds that the legislation might weaken allied unity on Iran at a crucial time in considering new international sanctions on Iran. The Administration reportedly wants greater ability to exempt from sanctions firms of countries that are cooperating against the Iranian nuclear program. The House bill, H.R. 2194, might have been viewed by the Administration as more narrowly focused and therefore less likely to trigger European opposition. This could explain why the Administration did not seek to block or slow a House vote on H.R. 2194.

Likely Effects of the Iran Refined Petroleum Sanctions Act

Some Members who have introduced or co-signed versions of the Iran Refined Petroleum Sanctions Act have said that although such legislation might appear to conflict with President Obama's diplomatic outreach to Iran, such bills might strengthen that approach by demonstrating to Iran that there are substantial downsides to rebuffing the U.S. overtures. Upon introducing H.R. 2194, Rep. Howard Berman, Chairman of the House Foreign Affairs Committee, said, "I fully support the Administration's strategy of direct diplomatic engagement with Iran, and I have no intention of moving this bill through the legislative process in the near future.... However, should engagement with Iran not yield the desired results in a reasonable period of time, we will have no choice but to press forward with additional sanctions—such as those contained in this bill—that could truly cripple the Iranian economy."

Attempting to restrict gasoline sales to Iran is a focus not only of U.S. legislation but also of discussions among the P5+1 about further sanctions should nuclear negotiations not produce significant or lasting results. There has been a debate over whether such a ban would accomplish significant goals in Iran. Some believe Iran's dependence on gasoline imports would, at the very least, cause Iran's government to have to spend more for such imports. Others, however, believe the government would not import more gasoline, but rather ration it or reduce subsidies for it in an effort to reduce gasoline consumption. Many believe that Iran has many willing gasoline suppliers who might ignore a U.S. law, and possibly even a U.N. resolutions along these lines. Iran and Venezuela (Petroleos de Venezuela S.A.) signed a gasoline supply deal in September 2009 that some see as a strategy by Iran to demonstrate the ineffectiveness of such a sanction. Still others believe that a gasoline ban would cause Iranians to blame the United States and United Nations for its plight and cause Iranians to rally around President Ahmadinejad, thereby rebuilding his popularity, which has suffered because of the 2009 election dispute. [8]

Administration Responses and Review[9]

In 2008, possibly sensing some congressional unrest over the fact that no energy investments in Iran have been penalized under ISA, Undersecretary of State for Political Affairs William Burns testified on July 9, 2008 (House Foreign Affairs Committee), that the Statoil project (listed in Table 1) is under review for ISA sanctions. Statoil is incorporated in Norway, which is not an EU member and which would therefore not fall under the U.S.-EU agreement in 1998 that indicated that EU firms would not be penalized under ISA. Burns did not mention any of the other projects, and no other specific projects have been named since. Nor was there a formal State Department determination on Statoil subsequently.

Possibly in response to the new legislative initiatives in the 111th Congress, and to an October 2009 letter signed by 50 Members of Congress referencing the CRS table below, Assistant Secretary of State for Near Eastern Affairs, Jeffrey Feltman, testified before the House Foreign Affairs Committee on October 28, 2009, that the Obama Administration would review investments in Iran for violations of ISA. Feltman testified that the preliminary review would be completed within 45 days (by December 11) to determine which projects, if any, require further investigation. The list of projects to be further scrutinized has not been released, to date.

State Department officials told CRS in November 2009 that any projects subjected to additional investigation would be determined, within 180 days (consistent with the Iran Freedom Support Act amendments to ISA discussed above) whether they constitute ISA violations or not. Feltman testified that preliminary reviews of some announced projects found that such announcements were for political purposes and did not result in actual investment. State Department officials told CRS in November 2009 that project involving Iran and Venezuela appeared to fall into the category of symbolic announcement rather than actual implemented projects. The State Department review will be conducted, in part, through State Department officials' contacts with their counterpart officials abroad and corporation officials.

Relationships to Other U.S. Sanctions

ISA is one of many mechanisms the United States and its European partners are using to try to pressure Iran. The following sections discuss other U.S. sanctions and measures to pressure Iran's economy.

Ban on U.S. Trade and Investment With Iran

On May 6, 1995, President Clinton issued Executive Order 12959 banning U.S. trade and investment in Iran.[10] This followed an earlier March 1995 executive order barring U.S. investment in Iran's energy sector. The trade ban was intended to blunt criticism that U.S. trade with Iran made U.S. appeals for multilateral containment of Iran less credible. Each March since 1995 (and most recently on March 11, 2009), the U.S. Administration has renewed a declaration of a state of emergency that triggered the investment ban. Some modifications to the trade ban since 1999 account for the trade between the United States and Iran. As noted, in the 111th Congress, H.R. 1208 would reimpose many of the trade restrictions.

The following conditions and modifications, as administered by the Office of Foreign Assets Control (OFAC) of the Treasury Department, apply:

- Some goods related to the safe operation of civilian aircraft may be licensed for export to Iran, and as recently as September 2006, the George W. Bush Administration, in the interests of safe operations of civilian aircraft, permitted a sale by General Electric of Airbus engine spare parts to be installed on several Iran Air passenger aircraft (by European airline contractors).
- U.S. firms may not negotiate with Iran or to trade Iranian oil overseas. The trade ban permits U.S. companies to apply for licenses to conduct "swaps" of Caspian Sea oil with Iran. However, a Mobil Corporation application to do so was denied in April 1999.
- Since April 1999, commercial sales of food and medical products to Iran have been allowed, on a case-by-case basis and subject to OFAC licensing. According to OFAC in April 2007, licenses for exports of medicines to treat HIV and leukemia are routinely expedited for sale to Iran, and license applications are viewed favorably for business school exchanges, earthquake safety seminars, plant and animal conservation, and medical training in Iran. Private letters of credit can be used to finance approved transactions, but no U.S. government credit guarantees are available, and U.S. exporters are not permitted to deal directly with Iranian banks. The FY2001 agriculture appropriations law (P.L. 106-387) contained a provision banning the use of official credit guarantees for food and medical sales to Iran and other countries on the U.S. terrorism list, except Cuba, although allowing for a presidential waiver to permit such credit guarantees. Neither the Clinton Administration nor the George W. Bush Administration provided the credit guarantees.

- In April 2000, the trade ban was further eased to allow U.S. importation of Iranian nuts, dried fruits, carpets, and caviar. The United States was the largest market for Iranian carpets before the 1979 revolution, but U.S. anti-dumping tariffs imposed on Iranian products in 1986 dampened of many Iranian products. The tariff on Iranian carpets is now about 3%-6%, and the duty on Iranian caviar is about 15%. In December 2004, U.S. sanctions were further modified to allow Americans to freely engage in ordinary publishing activities with entities in Iran (and Cuba and Sudan). As of mid-2007, the product most imported from Iran by U.S. importers is pomegranate juice concentrate. In the 110th Congress, H.R. 1400, S. 970, S. 3445, and H.R. 7112 would have re-imposed the full import ban.

Application to Foreign Subsidiaries of U.S. Firms

The U.S. trade ban does not bar subsidiaries of U.S. firms from dealing with Iran, as long as the subsidiary has no operational relationship to the parent company. Among major subsidiaries that have traded with Iran are the following:

- Halliburton. On January 11, 2005, Iran said it had contracted with U.S. company Halliburton, and an Iranian company, Oriental Kish, to drill for gas in Phases 9 and 10 of South Pars. Halliburton reportedly provided $30 million to $35 million worth of services per year through Oriental Kish, leaving unclear whether Halliburton would be considered in violation of the U.S. trade and investment ban or the Iran Sanctions Act (ISA)[11]—because the deals involved a subsidiary of Halliburton (Cayman Islands-registered Halliburton Products and Service, Ltd, based in Dubai). On April 10, 2007, Halliburton announced that its subsidiaries had, as promised in January 2005, no longer operating in Iran.
- General Electric (GE). The firm announced in February 2005 that it would seek no new business in Iran, and it reportedly wound down pre-existing contracts by July 2008. GE was selling Iran equipment and services for hydroelectric, oil and gas services, and medical diagnostic projects through Italian, Canadian, and French subsidiaries.
- Foreign subsidiaries of several other U.S. energy equipment firms are apparently still in the Iranian market. These include Foster Wheeler, Natco Group, Overseas Shipholding Group, [12] UOP (a Honeywell subsidiary), Itron, Fluor, Flowserve, Parker Drilling, Vantage Energy Services, Weatherford, and a few others.[13]
- An Irish subsidiary of the Coca Cola company provides syrup for the U.S.-brand soft drink to an Iranian distributor, Khoshgovar. Local versions of both Coke and of Pepsi (with Iranian-made syrups) are also marketed in Iran by distributors who licensed the recipes for those soft drinks before the Islamic revolution and before the trade ban was imposed on Iran.

In the 110th Congress, S. 970, S. 3227, S. 3445, and three House-passed bills (H.R. 1400, H.R. 7112, and H.R. 957)—would have applied sanctions to the parent companies of U.S. subsidiaries if those subsidiaries are directed or formed to trade with Iran. In the 111th Congress, H.R. 1208 contains a similar provision, as does the "Dodd Shelby Comprehensive

Iran Sanctions, Accountability, and Divestment Act," (S. 2799) reported to the Senate on November 19, 2009.

Treasury Department "Targeted Financial Measures"

Various "targeted financial measures" have been undertaken by the Treasury Department, particularly the office of Undersecretary of the Treasury Stuart Levey (who has remained in the Obama Administration). Since 2006, strengthened by leverage provided in five U.N. Security Council Resolutions, Levey and other officials have been able to convince numerous foreign banks that dealing with Iran entails financial risk and furthers terrorism and proliferation. Treasury Secretary Timothy Geithner has described Levey as having "led the design of a remarkably successful program"[14] with regard to targeting Iran's proliferation networks. The actions have, according to the International Monetary Fund, partly dried up financing for energy industry and other projects in Iran, and have caused potential investors in the energy sector to withdraw from or hesitate on finalizing pending projects. However, Treasury Department officials say that some of these efforts have gone as far as possible and they are evaluating new mechanisms, in concert with partner countries, to pressure Iran, and particularly its Revolutionary Guard, financially.

Treasury and State Departments officials, in April 17, 2008, testimony before the House Foreign Affairs Committee, said they had persuaded at least 40 banks not to provide financing for exports to Iran or to process dollar transactions for Iranian banks. Among those that have pulled out of Iran are UBS (Switzerland), HSBC (Britain), Germany's Commerzbank A.G and Deutsche Bank AG. U.S. financial diplomacy has reportedly convinced Kuwaiti banks to stop transactions with Iranian accounts,[15] and some banks in Asia (primarily South Korea and Japan) and the rest of the Middle East have done the same. The International Monetary Fund and other sources report that these measures are making it more difficult to fund energy industry and other projects in Iran and for importers/exporters to conduct trade in expensive items.

Some of these results have come about through U.S. pressure. In 2004, the Treasury Department fined UBS $100 million for the unauthorized movement of U.S. dollars to Iran and other sanctioned countries, and in December 2005, the Treasury Department fined Dutch bank ABN Amro $80 million for failing to fully report the processing of financial transactions involving Iran's Bank Melli (and another bank partially owned by Libya). In the biggest such instance, on December 16, 2009, the Treasury Department announced that Credit Suisse would pay a $536 million settlement to the United States for illicitly processing Iranian transactions with U.S. banks. Credit Suisse, according to the Treasury Department, saw business opportunity by picking up the transactions business from a competitor who had, in accordance with U.S. regulations discussed below, ceased processing dollar transactions for Iranian banks. Credit Suisse also pledged to cease doing business with Iran.

In action intended to cut Iran off from the U.S. banking system, on September 6, 2006, the Treasury Department barred U.S. banks from handling any indirect transactions ("U-turn transactions, meaning transactions with non-Iranian foreign banks that are handling transactions on behalf of an Iranian bank) with Iran's Bank Saderat (see above), which the Administration accuses of providing funds to Hezbollah.[16] Bank Sepah is subject to asset freezes and transactions limitations as a result of Resolution 1737 and 1747. The Treasury Department extended that U- Turn restriction to all Iranian banks on November 6, 2008.

Thus far, the Treasury Department has not designated any bank as a "money laundering entity" for Iran-related transactions (under Section 311 of the USA Patriot Act), although some say that step has been threatened at times. Nor has Treasury imposed any specific sanctions against Bank Markazi (Central Bank) which, according to a February 25, 2008, *Wall Street Journal* story, is helping other Iranian banks circumvent the U.S. and U.N. banking pressure. However, the European countries reportedly oppose such a sanction as an extreme step with potential humanitarian consequences, for example by preventing Iran from keeping its currency stable. S. 3445, a Senate bill in the 110th Congress, and a counterpart passed by the House on September 26, 2008, H.R. 7112, call for this sanction. The "Dodd-Shelby" bill, referenced above, in the 111th Congress has a similar provision. FY20 10 National Defense Authorization Act (H.R. 2647), as passed by the Senate, expresses the Sense of the Senate that the Administration sanction Iran's Central Bank if Iran does not negotiate in good faith to curb its nuclear program.

In enforcing U.S. sanctions, on December 17, 2008, the U.S. Attorney for the Southern District of New York filed a civil action seeking to seize the assets of the Assa Company, a U.K-chartered entity. Assa allegedly was maintaining the interests of Bank Melli in an office building in New York City. An Iranian foundation, the Alavi Foundation, allegedly is an investor in the building.

Terrorism List Designation-Related Sanctions

Several U.S. sanctions are in effect as a result of Iran's presence on the U.S. "terrorism list." The list was established by Section 6(j) of the Export Administration Act of 1979, sanctioning countries determined to have provided repeated support for acts of international terrorism. Iran was added to the list in January 1984, following the October 1983 bombing of the U.S. Marine barracks in Lebanon (believed perpetrated by Hezbollah). Sanctions imposed as a consequence include a ban on U.S. foreign aid to Iran; restrictions on U.S. exports to Iran of dual use items; and requires the United States to vote against international loans to Iran.

- The terrorism list designation restricts sales of U.S. dual use items (Export Administration Act, as continued through presidential authorities under the International Emergency Economic Powers Act, IEEPA, as implemented by executive orders), and, under other laws, bans direct U.S. financial assistance (Section 620A of the Foreign Assistance Act, FAA) and arms sales (Section 40 of the Arms Export Control Act), and requires the United States to vote to oppose multilateral lending to the designated countries (Section 327 of the Anti- Terrorism and Effective Death Penalty Act of 1996, P.L. 104-132). Waivers are provided under these laws, but successive foreign aid appropriations laws since the late 1980s ban direct assistance to Iran (loans, credits, insurance, Eximbank credits) without providing for a waiver.

- Section 307 of the FAA (added in 1985) names Iran as unable to benefit from U.S. contributions to international organizations, and require proportionate cuts if these institutions work in Iran. No waiver is provided for.
- The Anti-Terrorism and Effective Death Penalty Act (Sections 325 and 326) requires the President to withhold U.S. foreign assistance to any country that provides to a terrorism list country foreign assistance or arms. Waivers are provided.

U.S. sanctions laws do not bar disaster aid, and the United States donated $125,000, through relief agencies, to help victims of two earthquakes in Iran (February and May 1997), and another $350,000 worth of aid to the victims of a June 22, 2002, earthquake. (The World Bank provided some earthquake related lending as well.) The United States provided $5.7 million in assistance (out of total governmental pledges of about $32 million, of which $17 million have been remitted) to the victims of the December 2003 earthquake in Bam, Iran, which killed as many as 40,000 people and destroyed 90% of Bam's buildings. The United States military flew in 68,000 kilograms of supplies to Bam. In the Bam case, there was also a temporary exemption made in the regulations to allow for donations to Iran of humanitarian goods by American citizens and organizations. Those exemptions were extended several times but expired in March 2004.

Executive Order 13224

The separate, but related, Executive Order 13324 (September 23, 2001) authorizes the President to freeze the assets of and bar U.S. transactions with entities determined to be supporting international terrorism. This Order, issued two weeks after the September 11 attacks, was intended to primarily target Al Qaeda related entities. However, it has increasingly been applied to Iranian entities. Such Iran-related entities named and sanctioned under this order are in the tables at the end of CRS Report RL3 2048, *Iran: U.S. Concerns and Policy Responses*, by Kenneth Katzman. Those tables also include the names of Iranian entities sanctioned by the United Nations.

Proliferation-Related Sanctions

Iran is prevented from receiving advanced technology from the United States under relevant and Iran-specific anti-proliferation laws[17] and by Executive Order 13382 (June 28, 2005).

The Iran-Iraq Arms Nonproliferation Act (P.L. 102-484) requires denial of license applications for exports to Iran of dual use items, and imposes sanctions on foreign countries that transfer to Iran "destabilizing numbers and types of conventional weapons," as well as WMD technology.

The Iran Nonproliferation Act (P.L. 106-178, now called the Iran-Syria-North Korea Non- Proliferation Act) authorizes sanctions on foreign entities that assist Iran's WMD programs. It bans U.S. extraordinary payments to the Russian Aviation and Space Agency in connection with the international space station unless the President can certify that the agency or entities under its control had not transferred any WMD or missile technology to Iran within the year prior.[18] (A Continuing Resolution for FY2009, which funded the U.S. government through March 2009, waived this law to allow NASA to continue to use Russian vehicles to access the International Space Station.)

Executive Order 13382 allows the President to block the assets of proliferators of weapons of mass destruction (WMD) and their supporters under the authority granted by the International Emergency Economic Powers Act (IEEPA, 50 U.S.C. 1701 et seq.), the National Emergencies Act (50 U.S.C. 1601 et seq.), and Section 301 of Title 3, United States Code.

The George W. Bush Administration decided to impose sanctions for violations, and it sanctioned numerous entities as discussed below. The Obama Administration sanctioned several entities on February 2, 2009, suggesting it is continuing that policy. Iranian entities designated under these laws and orders are listed in the tables at the end of CRS Report RL3 2048, *Iran: U.S. Concerns and Policy Responses*, by Kenneth Katzman, which includes lists of other entities sanctioned by the United Nations and other U.S. laws and Executive orders.

Despite these efforts, Iran has used loopholes and other devices, such as front companies, to elude U.S. and international sanctions. Some of these efforts focus on countries perceived as having lax enforcement of export control laws, such as UAE and Malaysia. In some cases, Iran has been able, according to some reports, to obtain sophisticated technology even from U.S. firms.[19]

In addition, successive foreign aid appropriations punish the Russian Federation for assisting Iran by withholding 60% of any U.S. assistance to the Russian Federation unless it terminates technical assistance to Iran's nuclear and ballistic missiles programs.

Relations to International Sanctions

The U.S. sanctions discussed in this paper are more extensive than those imposed, to date, by the United Nations Security Council. However, some of the U.N. sanctions are similar to some unilateral U.S. sanctions and sanctions that have been imposed separately by U.S. allies. As part of a multilateral process of attempting to convince Iran to choose the path of negotiations or face further penalty, during 2006-2008, three U.N. Security Council resolutions—1737, 1747, and 1803—imposed sanctions primarily on Iran's weapons of mass destruction (WMD) infrastructure. While pressing for sanctions, the multilateral group negotiation with Iran ("P5+ 1 :" the Security Council permanent members, plus Germany) at the same time offered Iran incentives to suspend uranium enrichment; the last meeting between Iran and the P5+1 to discuss these issues was in July 2008. The negotiations made little progress, and then entered a hiatus for the U.S. presidential election, the establishment of the Obama Administration, and then the Iranian presidential election. Iranian entities and persons sanctioned by the United Nations are included in **Table 2** at the end of this paper.

As noted above, talks resumed on October 1, 2009, and were viewed as productive. However, Iran's refusal to agree to implementing terms has prompted renew discussions between the United States and its partners about new international sanctions. U.S. officials continue to assert that Iran must accept the terms by the end of 2009 or else face new international sanctions.

Previous P5+1 discussions have focused on a U.N. ban on gasoline sales to Iran might have been discussed, although comments by the Russian and French Foreign Ministers since

September 2009 suggest that support for such a step within the U.N. Security Council is lacking. Other ideas reportedly under discussion include a British proposal to ban worldwide investment in Iran's energy sector, which would represent a U.N. endorsement of the key concept of the Iran Sanctions Act, although this idea, too, appears to lack Russian or Chinese support. Proposals that appear to have Russian and Chinese support include a ban on transactions with a broader range of Iranian banks; sanctioning shipping insurance or other shipping facilitation services to Iran; and mandatory travel bans on certain regime officials, particularly those in the security forces. Some of these proposals might be intended to support the efforts of the growing domestic opposition in Iran.

The main provisions of the current U.N. sanctions are below.

SUMMARY OF PROVISIONS OF U.N. RESOLUTIONS ON IRAN NUCLEAR PROGRAM (1737, 1747, AND 1803)

Require Iran to suspend uranium enrichment

Prohibit transfer to Iran of nuclear, missile, and dual use items to Iran, except for use in light water reactors

Prohibit Iran from exporting arms or WMD-useful technology

Freeze the assets of 40 named Iranian persons and entities, including Bank Sepah, and several Iranian front companies

Require that countries exercise restraint with respect to travel of 35 named Iranians and ban the travel of 5 others

Call on states not to export arms to Iran or support new business with Iran

Call for vigilance with respect to the foreign activities of all Iranian banks, particularly Bank Melli and Bank Saderat

Calls on countries to inspect cargoes carried by Iran Air Cargo and Islamic Republic of Iran Shipping Lines if there are indications they carry cargo banned for carriage to Iran.

Efforts to Promote Divestment

A growing trend not only in Congress but in several states is to require or call for or require divestment of shares of firms that have invested in Iran's energy sector (at the same levels considered sanctionable under the Iran Sanctions Act).[20]

Legislation in the 110th Congress, H.R. 1400, did not require divestment, but requires a presidential report on firms that have invested in Iran's energy sector. Another bill, H.R. 1357, required government pension funds to divest of shares in firms that have made ISA-sanctionable investments in Iran's energy sector and bar government and private pension funds from future investments in such firms. Two other bills, H.R. 2347 (passed by the House on July 31, 2007) and S. 1430, would protect mutual fund and other investment companies from shareholder action for any losses that would occur from divesting in firms that have investing in Iran's energy sector.

In the 111th Congress, H.R. 1327 (Iran Sanctions Enabling Act), a bill similar to H.R. 2347 of the 110th Congress, was reported by the Financial Services Committee on April 28, 2009. It passed the House on October 14, 2009, by a vote of 414-6. A similar bill. S. 1065, has been introduced in the Senate. Some provisions along these lines are contained in the "Dodd-Shelby" bill mentioned above (S. 2799).

Efforts to Prevent Internet Monitoring by Iran

Another trend in the 111th Congress, after the Iran election dispute, has been efforts to promote internet freedom in Iran or prevent the Iranian government from censoring or controlling the internet, or using it to identify opponents. Subtitle D of the FY2010 Defense Authorization (P.L. 111-84), called the "Voice Act," contains several provisions to increase U.S. broadcasting to Iran and to identify (in a report to be submitted 180 days after enactment, or April 25, 2009) companies that are selling Iran technology equipment that it can use to suppress or monitor the internet usage of Iranians. S. 1475 and H.R. 3284, the "Reduce Iranian Cyber-Suppression Act," would authorize the President to ban U.S. government contracts with foreign companies that sell technology that Iran could use to monitor or control Iranian usage of the internet. Firms, including a joint venture between Nokia (Finland) and Siemens (Germany), reportedly sold such technology to Iran in 2008.[21] Some question whether such a sanction might reduce allied cooperation with the United States if allied companies are so sanctioned. Some provisions along these lines are contained in the "Dodd-Shelby" bill referenced above (S. 2799).

In line with this trend, in December 2009, OFAC altered U.S. regulations of the trade ban to allow Iranians to download free mass market software (such as that offered by Microsoft and Google) in order to facilitate internet communications, which is being used extensively by anti- regime activists. The ruling appears to incorporate the major features of a legislative proposal, H.R. 4301, the "Iran Digital Empowerment Act."

Blocked Iranian Property and Assets

Iranian leaders continue to assert that the United States is holding Iranian assets, and that this is an impediment to improved relations. A U.S.-Iran Claims Tribunal at the Hague continues to arbitrate cases resulting from the 1980 break in relations and freezing of some of Iran's assets. Major cases yet to be decided center on hundreds of Foreign Military Sales (FMS) cases between the United States and the Shah's regime, which Iran claims it paid for but were unfulfilled. About $400 million in proceeds from the resale of that equipment was placed in a DOD FMS account, and about $22 million in Iranian diplomatic property remains blocked, although U.S. funds have been disbursed—credited against the DOD FMS account—to pay judgments against Iran for past acts of terrorism against Americans. Other disputes include the mistaken U.S. shoot-down on July 3, 1988, of an Iranian Airbus passenger jet (Iran Air flight 655), for which the United States, in accordance with an ICJ judgment, paid Iran $61.8 million in compensation ($300,000 per wage earning victim, $150,000 per non-wage earner) for the 248 Iranians killed. The United States has not compensated Iran for the airplane itself. As it has in past similar cases, the Bush Administration opposed a terrorism lawsuit against Iran by victims of the U.S. Embassy Tehran seizure on the grounds of diplomatic obligation.[22]

Table 2. Entities Sanctioned Under U.N. Resolutions and U.S. Laws and Executive Orders (Persons listed are identified by the positions they held when designated; some have since changed.)

Entities Named for Sanctions Under Resolution 1737	
Atomic Energy Organization of Iran (AEIO) Mesbah Energy Company (Arak supplier)	Gen Hosein Salimi (Commander, IRGC Air Force)
Kalaye Electric (Natanz supplier))	Dawood Agha Jani (Natanz official)
Pars Trash Company (centrifuge program) Farayand Technique (centrifuge program)	Ali Hajinia Leilabadi (director of Mesbah Energy)
Defense Industries Organization (DIO)	Lt. Gen. Mohammad Mehdi Nejad Nouri
7th of Tir (DIO subordinate)	(Malak Ashtar University of Defence Technology rector)
Shahid Hemmat Industrial Group (SHIG)— missile program	Bahmanyar Morteza Bahmanyar (AIO official)
Shahid Bagheri Industrial Group (SBIG) - missile program	Reza Gholi Esmaeli (AIO official)
Fajr Industrial Group (missile program)	Ahmad Vahid Dastjerdi (head of Aerospace Industries Org., AIO)
Mohammad Qanadi, AEIO Vice President	Maj. Gen. Yahya Rahim Safavi (Commander in Chief, IRGC)
Behman Asgarpour (Arak manager)	
Ehsan Monajemi (Natanz construction manager)	
Jafar Mohammadi (Adviser to AEIO)	
Entities/Persons Added by Resolution 1747	
Ammunition and Metallurgy Industries Group (controls 7th of Tir)	Fereidoun Abbasi-Davani (senior defense scientist)
Parchin Chemical Industries (branch of DIO)	Mohasen Fakrizadeh-Mahabai (defense scientist)
Karaj Nuclear Research Center	Seyed Jaber Safdari (Natanz manager)
Novin Energy Company	
Cruise Missile Industry Group	Mohsen Hojati (head of Fajr Industrial Group)
Sanam Industrial Group (subordinate to AIO)	Ahmad Derakshandeh (head of Bank Sepah)
Ya Mahdi Industries Group	
Kavoshyar Company (subsidiary of AEIO)	Brig. Gen. Mohammad Reza Zahedi (IRGC ground forces commander)
Sho'a Aviation (produces IRGC light aircraft for asymmetric warfare)	Amir Rahimi (head of Esfahan nuclear facilities)
Bank Sepah (funds AIO and subordinate entities)	Mehrdada Akhlaghi Ketabachi (head of SBIG)

Table 2. (Continued)

Entities/Persons Added by Resolution 1747	
Esfahan Nuclear Fuel Research and Production Center and Esfahan Nuclear Technology Center Qods Aeronautics Industries (produces UAV's, para-gliders for IRGC asymmetric warfare) Pars Aviation Services Company (maintains IRGC Air Force equipment) Gen. Mohammad Baqr Zolqadr (IRGC officer serving as deputy Interior Minister) Brig. Gen. Qasem Soleimani (Qods Force commander)	Naser Maleki (head of SHIG) Brig. Gen. Morteza Reza'i (Deputy commander-in-chief, IRGC) Vice Admiral Ali Akbar Ahmadiyan (chief of IRGC Joint Staff) Brig. Gen. Mohammad Hejazi (Basij commander)
Entities Added by Resolution 1803	
Thirteen Iranians named in Annex 1 to Resolution 1803; all reputedly involved in various aspects of nuclear program Electro Sanam Co. Abzar Boresh Kaveh Co. (centrifuge production) Barzaganin Tejaral Tavanmad Saccal Jabber Ibn Hayan Khorasan Metallurgy Industries Niru Battery Manufacturing Co. (Makes batteries for Iranian military and missile systems) Safety Equipment Procurement (AIO front, involved in missiles)	Ettehad Technical Group (AIO front co.) Industrial Factories of Precision Joza Industrial Co. Pshgam (Pioneer) Energy Industries Tamas Co. (involved in uranium enrichment)
Entities Designated Under U.S. Executive Order 13382 **(many designations coincident with designations under U.N. resolutions)**	

Entity	Date Named
Shahid Hemmat Industrial Group (Iran)	June 2005, September 2007
Shahid Bakeri Industrial Group (Iran)	June 2005, February 2009
Atomic Energy Organization of Iran	June 2005
Novin Energy Company (Iran)	January 2006
Mesbah Energy Company (Iran)	January 2006
Four Chinese entities: Beijing Alite Technologies, LIMMT Economic and Trading Company, China Great Wall Industry Corp, and China National Precision Machinery Import/Export Corp.	June 2006
Sanam Industrial Group (Iran)	July 2006

Table 2. (Continued)

Entities Designated Under U.S. Executive Order 13382 (many designations coincident with designations under U.N. resolutions)	
Ya Mahdi Industries Group (Iran)	July 2006
Bank Sepah (Iran)	January 2007
Defense Industries Organization (Iran)	March 2007
Pars Trash (Iran, nuclear program)	June 2007
Farayand Technique (Iran, nuclear program)	June 2007
Fajr Industries Group (Iran, missile program)	June 2007
Mizan Machine Manufacturing Group (Iran, missile prog. Aerospace Industries Organization (AIO) (Iran)	June 2007
Korea Mining and Development Corp. (N. Korea)	September 2007
Islamic Revolutionary Guard Corps (IRGC)	September 2007
Ministry of Defense and Armed Forces Logistics	October 21, 2007
Bank Melli (Iran's largest bank, widely used by Guard); Bank Melli Iran Zao (Moscow); Melli Bank PC (U.K.)	October 21, 2007
Bank Kargoshaee	October 21, 2007
Arian Bank (joint venture between Melli and Bank Saderat). Based in Afghanistan	October 21, 2007
Bank Mellat (provides banking services to Iran's nuclear sector); Mellat Bank SB CJSC (Armenia). Reportedly has $1.4 billion in assets in UAE	October 21, 2007
Persia International Bank PLC (U.K.)	October 21, 2007
Khatam ol Anbiya Gharargah Sazendegi Nooh (Revolutionary Guard construction, contracting arm, with $7 billion in oil, gas deals	October 21, 2007
Oriental Oil Kish (Iranian oil exploration firm)	October 21, 2007
Ghorb Karbala; Ghorb Nooh (synonymous with Khatam ol Anbiya)	October 21, 2007
Sepasad Engineering Company (Guard construction affiliate)	October 21, 2007
Omran Sahel (Guard construction affiliate)	October 21, 2007
Sahel Consultant Engineering (Guard construction affiliate)	October 21, 2007
Hara Company	October 21, 2007

Table 2. (Continued)

Entities Designated Under U.S. Executive Order 13382 (many designations coincident with designations under U.N. resolutions)	
Gharargahe Sazandegi Ghaem	October 21, 2007
Bahmanyar Morteza Bahmanyar (AIO, Iran missile official, see above under Resolution 1737)	October 21, 2007
Ahmad Vahid Dastjerdi (AIO head, Iran missile program)	October 21, 2007
Reza Gholi Esmaeli (AIO, see under Resolution 1737)	October 21, 2007
Morteza Reza'i (deputy commander, IRGC) See also Resolution 1747	October 21, 2007
Mohammad Hejazi (Basij commander). Also, Resolution 1747	October 21, 2007
Ali Akbar Ahmadian (Chief of IRGC Joint Staff). Resolution 1747	October 21, 2007
Hosein Salimi (IRGC Air Force commander). Resolution 1737	October 21, 2007
Qasem Soleimani (Qods Force commander). Resolution 1747	October 21, 2007
Future Bank (Bahrain-based but allegedly controlled by Bank Melli)	March 12, 2008
Yahya Rahim Safavi (former IRGC Commander in Chief	July 8, 2008
Mohsen Fakrizadeh-Mahabadi (senior Defense Ministry scientist)	July 8, 2008
Dawood Agha-Jani (head of Natanz enrichment site)	July 8, 2008
Mohsen Hojati (head of Fajr Industries, involved in missile program)	July 8, 2008
Mehrdada Akhlaghi Ketabachi (heads Shahid Bakeri Industrial Group)	July 8, 2008
Naser Maliki (heads Shahid Hemmat Industrial Group)	July 8, 2008
Tamas Company (involved in uranium enrichment)	July 8, 2008
Shahid Sattari Industries (makes equipment for Shahid Bakeri)	July 8, 2008
7th of Tir (involved in developing centrifuge technology)	July 8, 2008
Ammunition and Metallurgy Industries Group (partner of 7th of Tir)	July 8, 2008
Parchin Chemical Industries (deals in chemicals used in ballistic missile programs)	July 8, 2008

Table 2. (Continued)

Entities Designated Under U.S. Executive Order 13382 (many designations coincident with designations under U.N. resolutions)	
Karaj Nuclear Research Center	August 12, 2008
Esfahan Nuclear Fuel Research and Production Center (NFRPC)	August 12, 2008
Jabber Ibn Hayyan (reports to Atomic Energy Org. of Iran, AEIO)	August 12, 2008
Safety Equipment Procurement Company	August 12, 2008
Joza Industrial Company (front company for Shahid Hemmat Industrial Group, SHIG)	August 12, 2008
Islamic Republic of Iran Shipping Lines (IRISL) and 18 affiliates, including Val Fajr 8; Kazar; Irinvestship; Shipping Computer Services; Iran o Misr Shipping; Iran o Hind; IRISL Marine Services; Iriatal Shipping; South Shipping; IRISL Multimodal; Oasis; IRISL Europe; IRISL Benelux; IRISL China; Asia Marine Network; CISCO Shipping; and IRISL Malta	September 10, 2008
Firms affiliated to the Ministry of Defense, including Armament Industries Group; Farasakht Industries; Iran Aircraft Manufacturing Industrial Co.; Iran Communications Industries; Iran Electronics Industries; and Shiraz Electronics Industries	September 17, 2008
Export Development Bank of Iran. Provides financial services to Iran's Ministry of Defense and Armed Forces Logistics	October 22, 2008
Assa Corporation (alleged front for Bank Melli involved in managing property in New York City on behalf of Iran)	December 17, 2008
11 Entities Tied to Bank Melli: Bank Melli Iran Investment (BMIIC); Bank Melli Printing and Publishing; Melli Investment Holding; Mehr Cayman Ltd.; Cement Investment and Development; Mazandaran Cement Co.; Shomal Cement; Mazandaran Textile; Melli Agrochemical; First Persian Equity Fund; BMIIC Intel. General Trading	March 3, 2009
Entities Sanctioned Under Executive Order 13224 (Terrorism Entities)	
Qods Force	October 21, 2007
Bank Saderat (allegedly used to funnel Iranian money to Hezbollah, Hamas, PIJ, and other Iranian supported terrorist groups)	October 21, 2007
Al Qaeda Operatives in Iran: Saad bin Laden; Mustafa Hamid; Muhammad Rab'a al-Bahtiyti; Alis Saleh Husain	January 16, 2009
Entities Sanctioned Under the Iran Non-Proliferation Act and other U.S. Proliferation Laws	
Norinco (China). For alleged missile technology sale to Iran.	May 2003

Table 2./ (Continued)

Entities Sanctioned Under the Iran Non-Proliferation Act and other U.S. Proliferation Laws	
Taiwan Foreign Trade General Corporation (Taiwan)	July 4, 2003
Entities Sanctioned Under the Iran Non-Proliferation Act and other U.S. Proliferation Laws	September 17, 2003
13 entities sanctioned including companies from Russia, China, Belarus, Macedonia, North Korea, UAE, and Taiwan.	April 7, 2004
14 entities from China, North Korea, Belarus, India (two nuclear scientists, Dr. Surendar and Dr. Y.S.R. Prasad), Russia, Spain, and Ukraine.	September 29, 2004
14 entities, mostly from China, for alleged supplying of Iran's missile program. Many, such as North Korea's Changgwang Sinyong and China's Norinco and Great Wall Industry Corp, have been sanctioned several times previously. Newly sanctioned entities included North Korea's Paeksan Associated Corporation, and Taiwan's Ecoma Enterprise Co.	December 2004 and January 2005
9 entities, including those from China (Norinco yet again), India (two chemical companies), and Austria. Sanctions against Dr. Surendar of India (see September 29, 2004) were ended, presumably because of information exonerating him.	December 26, 2005
7 entities. Two Indian chemical companies (Balaji Amines and Prachi Poly Products); two Russian firms (Rosobornexport and aircraft manufacturer Sukhoi); two North Korean entities (Korean Mining and Industrial Development, and Korea Pugang Trading); and one Cuban entity (Center for Genetic Engineering and Biotechnology).	August 4, 2006
9 entities. Rosobornesksport, Tula Design, and Komna Design Office of Machine Building, and Alexei Safonov (Russia); Zibo Chemical, China National Aerotechnology, and China National Electrical (China). Korean Mining and Industrial Development (North Korea) for WMD or advanced weapons sales to Iran (and Syria).	January 2007
14 entities, including Lebanese Hezbollah. Some werepenalized for transactions with Syria. Among the new entities sanctioned for assisting Iran were Shanghai Non-Ferrous Metals Pudong Development Trade Company (China); Iran's Defense Industries Organization; Sokkia Company (Singapore); Challenger Corporation (Malaysia); Target Airfreight (Malaysia); Aerospace Logistics Services (Mexico); and Arif Durrani (Pakistani national).	April 23, 2007
13 entities: China Xinshidai Co.; China Shipbuilding and Offshore International Corp.; Huazhong CNC (China); IRGC; Korea Mining Development Corp. (North Korea);	October 23, 2008

Table 2. (Continued)

Entities Sanctioned Under the Iran Non-Proliferation Act and other U.S. Proliferation Laws	
Korea Taesong Trading Co. (NK); Yolin/Yullin Tech, Inc. (South Korea); Rosoboronexport (Russia sate arms export agency); Sudan Master Technology; Sudan Technical Center Co; Army Supply Bureau (Syria); R and M International FZCO (UAE); Venezuelan Military Industries Co. (CAVIM);	
Entities Designated as Threats to Iraqi Stability under Executive Order 13438	
Ahmad Forouzandeh. Commander of the Qods Force Ramazan Headquarters, accused of fomenting sectarian violence in Iraq and of organizing training in Iran for Iraqi Shiite militia fighters	January 9, 2008
Abu Mustafa al-Sheibani. Iran based leader of network that funnels Iranian arms to Shiite militias in Iraq.	January 9, 2008
Isma'il al-Lami (Abu Dura). Shiite militia leader, breakaway from Sadr Mahdi Army, alleged to have committed mass kidnapings and planned assassination attempts against Iraqi Sunni politicians	January 9, 2008
Mishan al-Jabburi. Financier of Sunni insurgents, owner of pro-insurgent Al-Zawra television, now banned	January 9, 2008
Al Zawra Television Station	January 9, 2008
Khata'ib Hezbollah (pro-Iranian Mahdi splinter group)	July 2, 2009
Abu Mahdi al-Muhandis	July 2, 2009

End Notes

[1] The definition of "investment" in ISA (Section 14 (9)) includes not only equity and royalty arrangements (including additions to existing investment, as added by P.L. 107-24) but any contract that includes "responsibility for the development of petroleum resources" of Iran, interpreted to include pipelines to or through Iran. The definition excludes sales of technology, goods, or services for such projects, and excludes financing of such purchases. For Libya, the threshold was $40 million, and sanctionable activity included export to Libya of technology banned by Pan Am 103-related Security Council Resolutions 748 (March 31, 1992) and 883 (November 11, 1993). For Iran, the threshhold dropped to $20 million, from $40 million, one year after enactment, when U.S. allies did not join a multilateral sanctions regime against Iran.

[2] This latter "trigger" was added by P.L. 109-293.

[3] This latter termination requirement added by P.L. 109-293

[4] Dollar figures for investments in Iran represent public estimates of the amounts investing firms are expected to spend over the life of a project, which might in some cases be several decades.

[5] Stern, Roger. "The Iranian Petroleum Crisis and United States National Security," *Proceedings of the National Academy of Sciences of the United States of America*. December 26, 2006.

[6] Blas, Javier, Carola Hoyas, and Daniel Dombey. "Chinese Companies Supply Iran With Petrol." *Financial Times*, September 23, 2009.

[7] Exclusive: State Department Letter to Kerry Outlines "Serious Substantive Concerns" With Iran Sanctions Bill. http://thecable.foreignpolicy.com/posts/2009/12/11/exclusive_state_department_letter_to_kerry_outlines_serious_subst antive_concerns_wi

[8] Askari, Hossein and Trita Parsi. "Throwing Ahmadinejad a Lifeline." *New York Times* op-ed. August 15, 2009.

[9] Much of this section is derived from a meeting between the CRS author and officials of the State Department's Economics Bureau, which is tasked with the referenced review of investment projects. November 24, 2009.

[10] An August 1997 amendment to the trade ban (Executive Order 13059) prevented U.S. companies from knowingly exporting goods to a third country for incorporation into products destined for Iran.

[11] "Iran Says Halliburton Won Drilling Contract." *Washington Times*, January 11, 2005.

[12] Prada, Paulo, and Betsy McKay. Trading Outcry Intensifies. *Wall Street Journal*, March 27, 2007; Brush, Michael. Are You Investing in Terrorism? MSN Money, July 9, 2007.

[13] Officials of Fluor claim that their only dealings with Iran involve property in Iran owned by a Fluor subsidiary, which the subsidiary has been unable to dispose of. CRS conversation with Fluor, December 2009.

[14] Hearing of the Financial Services and General Government Subcommittee of the House Appropriations Committee, *Federal News Service*, May 21, 2009.

[15] Mufson, Steven and Robin Wright. "Iran Adapts to Economic Pressure." *Washington Post,* October 29, 2007.

[16] Kessler, Glenn. "U.S. Moves to Isolate Iranian Banks." *Washington Post*, September 9, 2006.

[17] Such laws include the Atomic Energy Act of 1954 and the Energy Policy Act of 2005 (P.L. 109-58).

[18] The provision contains certain exceptions to ensure the safety of astronauts, but it nonetheless threatened to limit U.S. access to the international space station after April 2006, when Russia started charging the United States for transportation on its Soyuz spacecraft. Legislation in the 109th Congress (S. 1713, P.L. 109-112) amended the provision in order to facilitate continued U.S. access and extended INA sanctions provisions to Syria.

[19] Warrick, Joby. "Iran Using Fronts to Get Bomb Parts From U.S." *Washington Post*, January 11, 2009; Institute for Science and International Security. "Iranian Entities' Illicit Military Procurement Networks." David Albright, Paul Brannan, and Andrea Scheel. January 12, 2009.

[20] For information on the steps taken by individual states, see National Conference of State Legislatures. State Divestment Legislation.

[21] Rhoads, Christopher. "Iran's Web Spying Aided by Western Technology." Wall Street Journal, June 22, 2009.

[22] See CRS Report RL31258, *Suits Against Terrorist States by Victims of Terrorism*, by Jennifer K. Elsea.

In: Iran: Issues and Perspectives
Editor: Stephen D. Calhoun

ISBN: 978-1-61728-007-8
© 2010 Nova Science Publishers, Inc.

Chapter 6

IRAN'S 2009 PRESIDENTIAL ELECTIONS[*]

Casey L. Addis

SUMMARY

On June 12, 2009, following a heated campaign between reformist candidate Mir Hussein Musavi and incumbent President Mahmoud Ahmadinejad, Iranians turned out in record numbers to vote in the presidential election. Shortly after the polls closed, the Interior Minister announced that President Ahmadinejad had been reelected by a 62% margin. The announcement was followed by allegations of vote rigging and election fraud and prompted supporters of leading reformist candidate Mir Hussein Musavi and others to hold public demonstrations in several major cities of a size and intensity unprecedented since the Iranian Revolution of 1979.

Despite a government ban on unauthorized public gatherings, protests reportedly have continued since the election. Restrictions on foreign and domestic journalists, reported disruptions of mobile phone networks, limited accessibility of some internet sites, mass arrests, and clashes between civilian protestors and Basij forces have garnered international attention and increased concerns about the Iranian government's apparent disregard for human rights and basic civil liberties.

Regardless of the actual election results, the Supreme Leader Khamenei, along with the Revolutionary Guard and the Basij, appear determined to impose the election outcome by force. The government crackdown on protestors appears to be effective, even as smaller gatherings have continued in Tehran and other major cities. Attention has now focused on the potential long-term effects of the post-election unrest on Iranian government and society, and what the outcome might mean for U.S. efforts to resolve the issues of Iran's nuclear program, its support for terrorism, and other national security concerns.

The Obama Administration's response has been cautious, but somewhat has hardened as reports of deaths, injuries, and mass arrests of Iranian citizens have increased. Many

---
[*] This is an edited, reformatted and augmented version of a CRS Report for Congress publication dated July 2009.

observers believe that President Obama is attempting to balance the need to condemn the violence against the protestors with the need to avoid the perception of U.S. interference, which some worry could prompt the Iranian government to clamp down further on freedom of expression or jeopardize U.S. efforts to engage Iran on the issue of its nuclear program.

RECENT DEVELOPMENTS

On June 29, the Guardian Council confirmed the validity of the election outcome despite ongoing complaints of irregularities from reformist candidates Mir Hussein Musavi and Mehdi Karrubi. In its official letter to the Interior Minister, the Council acknowledged "minor violations that happen in every election and can be ignored," but insisted that, after a recount of a randomly selected 10% of the votes, the results were valid.[1] Musavi, along with Karrubi and former President Mohammad Khatami have continued to reject the election results, and Musavi has called for "independent arbitration" of the election disputes.[2] Meanwhile, the government continues its crackdown on protestors in Tehran and elsewhere and continues to level accusations of "foreign interference" in Iran's domestic affairs by Great Britain and other Western countries.

On June 28, nine local staff members of the British embassy in Tehran were reportedly arrested for "inflaming post-election tensions in Iran."[3] In response, EU nations on July 3 summoned Iranian ambassadors and threatened to withdraw their ambassadors from Tehran if the employees were not released.[4] Since then, eight of the nine employees detained have reportedly been released, but one remains in custody. Senior Iranian cleric Ayatollah Ahmad Jannati announced during Friday prayers on July 3 that the remaining embassy staffers in custody would "inevitably be tried as they have made confessions."[5] Many observers view this move as part of an ongoing campaign by the Iranian government to blame the post-election protests on the West, and to use allegations of foreign interference to distract from the government's use of force against the demonstrators.

Supreme Leader Khamenei along with the military apparatus of the state appears willing and capable, at this point, of imposing the election outcome by force. While smaller protests have continued since the June 20 crackdown, most observers agree that Musavi and his supporters, at least in the short-run, cannot maintain their momentum as long as the Revolutionary Guard and Basij are deployed to stop demonstrations. Many analysts have turned their attention to the possible long-term implications of the post-election unrest on both the government of Iran and Iranian society.

Following the Guardian Council's announcement on June 29, fissures in the Iranian government appeared to surface, particularly within the clerical establishment. Initial speculation about tension within the government centered around Ali Akbar Hashemi Rafsanjani, who has in the past clashed with Khamenei and who initially was silent on post-election events. On June 29, however, Rafsanjani reportedly accepted the outcome of the election review and praised the Supreme Leader for extending the time allowed for the investigation.[6] While some observers view Rafsanjani's statement as an expression of support for Khamenei and an Ahmadinejad presidency, others suspect that Rafsanjani is acting out of his own self-interest, and is supporting the Guardian Council's decision to preserve his own political standing and protect himself and his family from possible action against them.[7] More recently, attention has focused on the holy city of Qom, where two prominent clerical groups have expressed opposing viewpoints on the election outcome. The Association of Researchers and Teachers of Qom Seminary expressed their disapproval of the Guardian Council's decision and urged the judiciary to release all detainees and arrest those responsible for "beating, death, and damage."[8] While some analysts perceive that the religious establishment is beginning to split, others downplay the statements of this group, citing that the most powerful and influential group, the Society of Scholars of Qom Seminary, has congratulated Ahmadinejad on his reelection and accepted the ruling of the Guardian Council.[9]

IRAN'S 2009 PRESIDENTIAL ELECTION

The reported outcome of the June 12, 2009 presidential election in Iran prompted public demonstrations in several major cities of a size and intensity unprecedented since the Iranian Revolution of 1979. The announcement that President Mahmoud Ahmadinejad was reelected by a 62% margin was followed by allegations of vote rigging and election fraud. Supporters of leading reformist candidate Mir Hussein Musavi and others staged large protests in the streets of Tehran and other major cities that have drawn international attention. The actions taken by the Iranian government in the hours following the election, ongoing demonstrations, arrests, and clashes between civilians and Iran's paramilitary Basij forces have led some observers to argue that Iran's political dynamics have shifted considerably, and that the relationship between the government of the Islamic Republic and its citizens has been fundamentally shaken. While some analysts have speculated about military coups, color revolutions, and the future of the Iranian regime, others have reserved judgment about the likelihood of various potential short term developments because of the unpredictability inherent in this dynamic situation. Iran's institutions and centralized decision making are opaque and the United States has not had a diplomatic presence in Iran since the Islamic Revolution in 1979, further limiting its understanding of the Iranian system. Outside observation and analysis is further hampered by the fact that the Iranian government has restricted access to foreign and domestic journalists and interrupted the availability of mobile phone service and various internet sites and services.

The long term effects of the election and its aftermath on Iran's political system and social contract are difficult to foresee. Short term, it appears that government has decided to impose the election outcome by force. As a result, many analysts agree that the events surrounding the 2009 Iranian presidential elections and aftermath have upset the balance between the official and civil spheres of Iranian society and will have long term implications for both the government and the people of Iran and for U.S. policy.[10]

CANDIDATES AND CAMPAIGNS

In 2009, nearly 500 candidates for Iran's presidency filed their candidacy with the Guardian Council.[11] On May 20, 2009, the council announced that four candidates had been approved: incumbent president Mahmoud Ahmadinejad, conservative Mohsen Reza'i, reformist Mir Hussein Musavi, and reformist Mehdi Karrubi.

Social and political restrictions are often eased in Tehran during campaign season, but observers remarked that public activity this year was notably more energetic than would be expected. Some attribute this shift to the four years of crackdowns on social freedoms that have characterized President Ahmadinejad's term in office.[12] Others attribute the pre-election atmosphere to increased public tension between the candidates in the days leading up to the election, when the campaign became increasingly acrimonious.

During the week of June 3, 2009, the candidates participated in six live debates. The debate between incumbent President Mahmoud Ahmadinejad and reformist candidate Mir Hussein Musavi was particularly heated, most notably because of Ahmadinejad's open criticism of Musavi's wife, Zahra Rahnavard.[13] The debates offered the public an opportunity to observe fierce exchanges between the candidates for the first time in a presidential election and reportedly were watched by 40 to 50 million viewers, according to Iranian media reports.[14]

On June 9, Ali Akbar Hashemi Rafsanjani, a former president who now heads two powerful oversight bodies, issued an open letter complaining about the silence of Khamenei following the "insults, lies, and false allegations" by Ahmadinejad during the campaign debates.[15] It is rare in Iran for senior leaders to publicly criticize the supreme leader and many observers viewed the letter as a reflection of the intensity of the campaigns. Others perceive that Rafsanjani, who is often at odds with the Khamenei and lost the 2005 presidential race to Ahmadinejad, may be interested in forming an alternate power center in the government. Rafsanjani later accepted the election results, perhaps out of political self-interest.

Musavi appeared to experience a surge in public support in the final days of the campaign. The night before the election, on June 11, Musavi supporters reportedly formed a human chain on a main thoroughfare through Tehran.[16] The mass rally prompted some analysts and observers to speculate that Ahmadinejad's chances at reelection were dwindling. Some reports that the rural and urban poor population of Iran was shifting its support away from Ahmadinejad also surfaced in the week before the election. Many attributed this to increases in inflation and unemployment, compounded by international sanctions and the global financial crises that had disproportionately affected the poor, despite increases in wages and pensions provided under the Ahmadinejad government.[17]

The large rallies in favor of Musavi during the last days of the campaign may have caused alarm among some factions of the Iranian government.[18] Prior to the election, Iranian Revolutionary Guard Corps (IRGC) commander General Mohammad Ja'fari publicly stated that any attempt at a velvet revolution in Iran would be crushed.[19] The statement further fueled speculation that the regime felt threatened by the apparent popularity of Musavi in the last days of the campaign.

As observers watched the campaign unfold, most predicted a close race between Musavi and Ahmadinejad and many anticipated that a run-off would be necessary to determine a winner. Many observers also agreed that voter turnout may tip the election in favor of Musavi. During past elections, low voter turnout has been due in part to boycotts on the part of reform-minded Iranians, including many Iranian Americans who are eligible to vote. The Iranian system, in which the Guardian Council chooses which candidates are eligible to run, has in the past led some Iranians to feel that they have no genuine choice among the candidates.

ELECTION AND RESULTS

On June 12, following the heated campaign between Musavi and Ahmadinejad, Iranians went to the polls. Record voter turnout was reported throughout the day and the Interior Ministry ordered that voting centers stay open to accommodate those waiting to vote.[20] Many observers were optimistic that pro-reform segments of the population, who had boycotted elections in the past, had gone to the polls in favor of Musavi. Large campaign rallies prior to the election had even sparked discussion of a possible "Green Revolution." As the polls closed, however, the prospects began to dim for a Musavi victory, and for a popularly-accepted election outcome. As the polls closed, police and Basij paramilitary forces reportedly were deployed throughout Tehran, locking down the Interior Ministry where votes were being counted. Internet sites and mobile phones were also reportedly disabled. Less than three hours after the polls closed, the Interior Ministry announced that the election results were in and that Mahmoud Ahmadinejad had won, capturing 62% of the vote. The Interior Ministry also reported that 39 million votes were cast (about 85% of Iran's eligible voters), an unprecedented turnout.[21]

Following the announcement by the Interior Ministry, Supreme Leader Ayatollah Ali Khamenei issued a statement congratulating President Ahmadinejad, which most observers interpreted as a certification of the election results. Khamenei said the "miraculous hand of God" was evident in the "great epic" of the election.[22] Both Ahmadinejad and Musavi claimed victory as the announcement was made, even before the Guardian Council certified the results.

ALLEGATIONS OF FRAUD

Since no independent international observers were present for Iran's elections, it is difficult to ascertain the extent of alleged vote rigging or election violations that may have taken place. The expulsion of most foreign journalists from Iran and the government's interruption of mobile and internet communication have further complicated efforts to gain a clear picture of the events surrounding the election and its aftermath.

While many democracy promotion groups and NGOs have criticized the elections process in Iran as undemocratic, most agree that Iran's election procedures have been relatively well codified and that the irregularities reported in this particular election were substantial.[23] However, in the 2009 presidential election, doubts about the wide margin of victory reported for Ahmadinejad have overshadowed a number of serious procedural irregularities reported on election day, which are the subject of the formal complaints filed by the defeated candidates.

The Guardian Council reportedly received and nearly 650 poll complaints from the three losing candidates. Musavi's formal complaints include: the heads of governors' offices sabotaged the issuance of identification cards to electoral observers before the ballots were collected and counted manually; ballot papers were not distributed properly in Shiraz and Tabriz; additional television campaigning was allowed for Ahmadinejad; the headlines of agencies including Rajanews, Fars, and IRNA focused on Ahmadinejad's victory in the election; and Article 40 of the Criminal Code regarding army-related crimes was broken through the involvement of Basij members in Ahmadinej ad's campaign meetings.[24] Karrubi expressed similar concerns.

Conservative candidate Mohsen Reza'i also filed formal complaints, which some have perceived as an indication that it is not just reformist candidates and supporters who are dissatisfied with the results. According to the official result totals he received 678,000 votes. He argues that he received between at least 5.3 and 7 million votes and that some estimates could be as high as 9 million. He says that his claim is based on his observers' reports from polling stations, information collected from 1,000 ballot boxes by his electoral headquarters, official opinion polls held in the country, and remarks addressed to him by voters and members of his electoral headquarters.[25]

Taken together, doubts about the margin of victory and concerns over perceived fraud stemming from procedural violations fueled the largest protests since the Iranian Revolution and stoked international concerns about the legitimacy of the election results. Initially, the candidates, the Iranian people, and many who followed the election expressed doubts that the record 39 million votes cast could have been counted in such a short time, especially in light of reports that voting times were extended. Others have pointed to additional irregularities. While individual reports are difficult to verify, some reports suggest that, in some cases, ballot boxes were picked up by Interior Ministry officials before polling places closed which would mark a change in election procedures whereby ballots are typically counted by officials at the local level.[26]

Khamenei urged the Guardian Council on June 15 to examine seriously the allegations of vote rigging, but urged the candidates to pursue their complaints through legal channels. He went on to state that the probe into vote-rigging allegations would be completed by June 25.[27] Musavi has said that invalidating the election is the only way to regain the people's trust in the regime and rejected outright the Guardian Council's offer to recount some of the votes.[28] Some observers dismissed the investigation into the election results as an attempt to provide a cooling off period for the demonstrators and dissatisfied public, rather than a legitimate review of the results.

On Saturday, June 20, the Guardian Council held a meeting with all presidential candidates to discuss the election outcome and fraud allegations. Reformist candidate Mir Hussein Musavi did not attend the meeting on Saturday on the grounds that he has already rejected any solution to the current stand-off other than a new election.[29] Reports circulated on Monday, June 22 that the number of ballots cast in at least 50 voting stations as reported by the government exceeds the number of registered voters in that area. The Guardian Council acknowledged the "irregularities," but insisted that they in no way would have changed the election outcome.[30]

Some observers argue that the election results could be valid, despite the appearance of irregularities. They support this assertion with the claim that the young, liberal demographic in Iran is much smaller than it is often portrayed and that Ahmadinejad enjoys widespread support among the rural and urban poor, a more significant group in terms of size. These analysts also question the reliability of the polls prior to the election that indicated a close race. Others say that Ahmadinejad is often underestimated, as he was in 2005, and that his message of piety and anticorruption coupled with his hard line on national security issues are both popular among the majority of Iranians. Others have argued that election fraud on such a massive scale would have involved many levels of the government and would be difficult to perpetrate and conceal.[31]

Other analysts assert that the allegations of fraud are likely true, and that the regime had motivation to interfere with the results. These analysts argue that the Iranian government might have felt sufficiently threatened by the success of Ahmadinejad's reformist opponents to mobilize a segment of the population that in large part boycotted the last elections. Some analysts have speculated that Khamenei engineered the election results in Ahmadinejad's favor so drastically in an effort to avoid a close election that could have been contested. Others argue that Khamenei wanted to send a political message to the U.S. and others that overtures to the Iranian public did not sway Iran from its policies—a commitment to the nuclear program and an approval of Ahmadinejad's inflammatory rhetoric about Israel—and that discussions with the U.S. are not perceived by the Iranian people as a coveted prize. Some agree that Khamenei miscalculated, either by misjudging popular opinion or out of paranoia over suspected regime change efforts on the part of the U.S. and the West.[32]

Regardless of the actual election results, the public demonstrations on election night and continued protests in major cities across Iran caused observers to speculate about how the standoff between the government and Musavi's supports would be resolved, and what the outcome might mean for U.S. efforts to resolve the issue of Iran's nuclear weapons program, its support for terrorism, and other national security concerns.

AFTERMATH

Demonstrations in Iran

Shortly after the election results were announced, Iran's interior ministry issued a ban on unauthorized public gatherings.[33] Despite the warning, protests reportedly continued every day in Tehran and other major cities—including Mashhad, Tabriz, Shiraz, and Isfahan, until the Basij crackdown on June 20.[34] Restrictions on journalists and government efforts to restrict telecommunications made it difficult to know the scope of the public protests, but most accounts indicate numbers in the hundreds of thousands or more in Tehran. A counter demonstration in support of President Ahmadinejad also was reported, but most estimates indicate that it was significantly smaller than those in protest of the results—less than 10,000 people. Some media outlets alleged that the images of the Ahmadinejad rally were doctored to inflate the apparent size of the crowd.[35] Smaller protests have reportedly continued since June 20, with estimates ranging from hundreds to thousands of people.

In his speech on Friday, June 19, Supreme Leader Khamenei demanded an end to the protests, reiterated his support for President Ahmadinejad, and accused foreign "enemies" of interfering in Iran's domestic affairs. Protests continued in Tehran and in other cities, however, and on Saturday, June 20, Iranian Basij and Revolutionary Guard forces reportedly used tear gas and live ammunition to disperse crowds. Ten deaths were reported, bringing the unofficial toll to at least 17, although many speculate that violence between police and military forces and the protestors may be more widespread and lethal than media reports indicate. On June 22, reports indicated that the Basij and Revolutionary Guard have been deployed throughout Tehran as the government crackdown on demonstrations continues to intensify. In addition, the Iranian government also appears to be continuing its arrests of reformist leaders. On June 21, members of former President Rafsanjani's family were reportedly arrested, causing speculation that rifts in Iran's religious leadership could be widening.[36]

Smaller protests have reportedly continued since June 20, with estimates ranging from hundreds to thousands of people. Reports of arrests, injuries, and deaths are difficult to substantiate, but have gained international attention and raised concerns about human rights and freedom of expression. As of July 1, according to the Iranian government, 627 people have been arrested and 27 have died since June 13. Most observers believe that the actual numbers are much higher.[37]

International Response

World wide, attention has focused on the events unfolding in Iran. Demonstrations took place in Western Europe and in other regions to protest the election outcome or the use of force against the demonstrators in Iran. Iranian expatriates also joined the protests. In the United Arab Emirates, protesters gathered in front of the Iranian consulate in Dubai to protest alleged election abuses. The consulate denied that any protests had taken place. After protests were held for five consecutive days, UAE authorities ordered the protestors to disperse.[38]

While some leaders offered congratulations to Ahmadinejad after the election,[39] others withheld their felicitations until the Guardian Council's election probe is completed. The international community, particularly the United States and the European Union, has now focused its attention on the public demonstrations in Iran, but most official statements have been cautious, likely to avoid the appearance of interference in Iran's domestic affairs. The European Union expressed concerns about the alleged irregularities, adding that it "expects the new Government of the Islamic Republic of Iran will take its responsibility towards international community and respect its international obligations."

Britain's Foreign Secretary David Miliband also expressed concerns about the elections in Iran, saying that Britain had "followed carefully, and admired, the passion and debate" during the election and that the reports of irregularities and accusations of fraud were "a matter for the Iranian authorities to address" and that "our priority is that Iran engages with the concerns of the world community, above all on the issue of nuclear proliferation."[40]

U.S. Response

The Obama Administration's response has been cautious. President Obama expressed "serious concern" about the events in Iran and the allegations of election fraud. He also indicated after the election that he would pursue his policy of engaging with Iran to find a solution to the nuclear issue regardless of the outcome of the election. Some analysts fear, however, that recent events have diminished the prospects for diplomacy, particularly as use of the Basij to violently confront civilian protestors renewed concerns about Khamenei's disregard for human rights and basic civil liberties.

At a State Department press conference on June 17, U.S. Secretary of State Hillary Clinton said that the people of Iran deserve to have their voices heard and votes counted, and reiterated the position of other Administration officials that it is for the Iranians to determine how best to resolve the current situation in Iran. She also expressed the Administration's intent to pursue engagement regardless of the election outcome.

The U.S. government's response has been praised by some who argue that avoiding any appearance of involvement or meddling in Iranian affairs is the most likely choice to avoid provoking a harsh response from the Iranian government, one that would likely further endanger the lives of the demonstrators. These arguments tend to highlight the nationalist tendencies of Iranians from all parts of the political spectrum, particularly with regard to the complex history of intervention by the United States and other powers in Iran's domestic affairs. Others have criticized President Obama's response as too conciliatory toward Iran's existing leadership, particularly what some view as a lack of a strong enough condemnation of the use of force against civilians.

On June 16, 2009, President Obama drew criticism after saying in an interview with CNBC and the *New York Times* that, from an American national security perspective, there may not be a significant difference between Ahmadinejad and Musavi. He went on to say that the United States is going to be dealing with an Iranian regime that has historically been hostile to the United States. Critics of the statement argue that the President may be viewing the events in Iran solely through the lens of the nuclear issue.[41] Other analysts have argued that if Obama does not offer a stronger statement on the current situation it may be perceived by Iranians as a green light for Khamenei and the IRGC to use force to dispel the demonstrations.[42]

On June 19, the U.S. House of Representatives passed 405-1 H.Res. 560, which expresses support for Iranian citizens and "condemns the ongoing violence against demonstrators by the Government of Iran and pro-government militias, as well as the ongoing government suppression of independent electronic communication." The Senate also passed two measures— S.Res. 193 and S.Res. 196—which express support for Iranian citizens who "embrace freedom, human rights, civil liberties and rule of law" and which express the sense of the Senate on freedom of the press, freedom of speech, and freedom of expression in Iran.

As the government crackdown against protestors increased, the Obama Administration's position on Iran somewhat hardened. President Obama on June 20 called upon the government of Iran to "stop all violent and unjust actions against its own people" and stated that, "The Iranian people will ultimately judge the actions of their own government. If the Iranian government seeks the respect of the international community, it must respect the dignity of its own people and govern through consent, not coercion."[43] On June 25, the Administration announced that it was withdrawing its prior invitation to Iranian diplomats for U.S. embassy Fourth of July parties, citing the recent events in Iran. Some observers believed that this small gesture indicates that the Administration is gradually moving away from its policy of engagement.[44] Many observers believe that President Obama is attempting to balance the need to condemn the violence against the protestors with the need to avoid the perception of U.S. interference, which some worry could prompt the Iranian government to clamp down further on freedom of expression as well as jeopardize U.S. efforts to engage Iran on the issue of its nuclear program.

POSSIBLE OUTCOMES AND IMPLICATIONS FOR U.S. POLICY

There is much debate about where the current situation in Iran could lead, with some experts predicting significant changes in Iran's political and social structure, and others arguing the Iranians at present do not appear to be seeking or experiencing a wholesale change in the basic nature of their government. Among those predicting significant change, some analysts are arguing a brewing "green revolution" is about to unfold in Iran. They cite the continued momentum of the protests, and say that the damage done by the regime to its own legitimacy is irreversible. Other observers have stated that the circumstances surrounding the election amount to a military coup, orchestrated by Khamenei and his allies in the military establishment. Both groups maintain that the current situation in Iran has caused or will cause significant changes that may even mean the end of the "Islamic Republic."[45]

At the opposite end of the spectrum are experts and practitioners who have argued that the public protests have more to do with Iranians' complaint that the Islamic Republic's electoral system was abused, rather than dissatisfaction with the notion of the Islamic Republic itself. These analysts tend to believe that some negotiated solution could possibly resolve the situation in Iran. Given the widespread popular dissatisfaction with the actions and statements of Supreme Leader Khamenei, it is possible that the doctrine of *velayet e faqih*[46] that undergirds the supreme leader's position may be losing more support among some Iranians.

As the Iranian government continues to use the Basij and Revolutionary Guard to enforce the election outcome, reports of arrests, injuries, and deaths fuel human rights concerns and diplomatic tensions. The long-term implications on U.S. policy of post-election unrest and government infighting in Iran are difficult to foresee.

Prospects for Engagement

The Obama Administration has maintained its commitment to engaging with Iran to resolve the issue of Iran's nuclear weapons program, its support for terrorism, and other national security concerns. Some analysts have speculated, however, that the long-term implications of the postelection events in Iran may complicate or alter the course of U.S. policy. Optimists consider the recent outpouring of public support for Musavi and calls for a new election from his supporters and some members of the clerical establishment as an indication that the Iranian public is no longer satisfied with the existing social contract, and may be less willing, as a result, to accept the international isolation that accompanies the government's position on the nuclear program, support for terrorism, and Ahmadinejad's rhetoric toward Israel. Even if the government manages to repress this popular opinion in the short run, some observers have acknowledged the possibility that, over the long run, the regime might not be sustainable against public unrest and widespread perceptions of illegitimacy.[47]

Skeptics see the recent events differently. Some argue that the engineered election outcome is a signal that Khamenei and the government establishment do not see engagement with the United States as a "prize to be won,"[48] and that no amount of diplomacy could change the perception that the United States is using the nuclear issue as a cover under which to pursue its real objective of regime change. As the Obama Administration works to strike a balance between not being perceived as interfering in Iranian affairs while appearing sympathetic to the civilian demonstrators, Khamenei has continued to accuse Western leaders of encouraging popular unrest. Continued calls for an end to the protests and warnings during his June 19 speech indicate, according to some analysts, that the Iranian government is prepared to take whatever means necessary to protect against a breakdown of the current system.[49]

While the Obama Administration has become increasingly willing to more harshly condemn the deaths and arrests of protestors and British embassy officials, it has not articulated a change in U.S. policy toward Iran. Some speculate that blatant human rights abuses on the part of the current government, coupled with criticism of its tempered response, could make it difficult for the Obama Administration to negotiate with Iran over its nuclear program and other issues. These democracy, and freedom of expression, and that this policy could alienate supporters of Musavi who have historically been more sympathetic to U.S. interests in the region.[50] Others argue that continuing on the path of engagement is the only viable mechanism for dealing with Iran's nuclear ambitions, and that all other issues are subordinate to the nuclear issue as time is short for reaching a solution.[51]

End Notes

[1] U.S. Open Source Center Document IAP20090629950144, "Iran: Guardian Council Approves Polls Despite 'Minor Violations,'" Tehran *Vision of the Islamic Republic of Iran Network 1* in Persian, June 29, 2009.

[2] U.S. Open Source Center Documents IAP20090628950063, "Iran: Musavi Wants Election Dispute Referred to Independent Arbitration," Tehran *Qalam* in Persian, June 27, 2009 and FEA20090702866255, "Iran: Reformists Reaffirm Rejection of Election, Security Crackdown," OSC Feature, July 2, 2009.

[3] U.S. Open Source Center Document IAP20090628950012, "Local Staff of British Embassy in Iran said Arrested," Tehran *Press TV Online* in English, June 28, 2009.

[4] U.S. Open Source Center Document EUP20090703102001, "EU Nations Summon Iranian Ambassadors Over British Embassy Detentions," Paris *AFP* (North European Service), July 3, 2009.

[5] U.S. Open Source Center Document IAP20090704950095, "MP: Iran Will Not Drop Charges Against Local Staff of British Embassy," Tehran *Fars News Agency*, July 4, 2009.

[6] U.S. Open Source Center Document IAP20090629950042, "Rafsanjani Terms Unrest in Iran Plot by Secretive Elements," Tehran *Fars News Agency*, June 29, 2009.

[7] On June 21, 2009, five members of Rafsanjani's family, including his daughter, were arrested but have since been released. See also, "Iran: Silence Highlights Regime Divisions," *Oxford Analytica*, June 29, 2009.

[8] U.S. Open Source Center Document IAP20090705950142, "Iranian Clerics Protest Against Election Result," *Advar News* in Persian, July 4, 2009.

[9] Ibid. See also, U.S. Open Source Center Document EUP20090705167008, "Two Clerical Bodies in Iran's Qom at Loggerheads Over Election Results," London *FT.com*, July 5, 2009.

[10] For more information and background on Iran, see CRS Report RL32048, *Iran: U.S. Concerns and Policy Responses*, by Kenneth Katzman.

[11] The Guardian Council is a 14-member body appointed by the supreme leader and responsible for overseeing elections, among other things.

[12] U.S. Open Source Center (OSC) Document IAP2009061295001, "Editorial Says Entire Nation Will Win With Musavi Victory In Iran's Election," *E'temad Online*, June 10, 2009. See also Robert F. Worth, "In Iran, Harsh Talk as Election Nears," *New York Times*, June 8, 2009.

[13] Musavi's wife, Zahra Rahnavard, a political scientist and former chancellor of Alzahra University in Tehran, played a visible role in his campaign and garnered much support from female voters, an unconventional role in Iranian politics as wives of candidates have not in the past appeared at campaign events.

[14] U.S. Open Source Center (OSC) Document FEA20090610861590 "Iranian Election TV Debates Signal More Balanced Coverage," *BBC Monitoring*, June 10, 2009.

[15] See "Iranian Conservative Media Angry as Rafsanjani Lays Into Ahmadinejad," *BBC Monitoring*, June 10, 2009 and U.S. Open Source Center (OSC) Document IAP20099610950037, "Iranian President to Reply to Accusations Raised in Debates," *IRNA*, June 10, 2009. See also Thomas Erdbrink, "Ex-Iranian President Criticizes Ayatollah," *New York Times,* June 10, 2009.

[16] Robert F. Worth and Nazila Fathi, "Huge Campaign Rallies Snarl Tehran," *New York Times*, June 11, 2009.

[17] See Thomas Erdbrink, "Rural Iran May Shift Its Loyalty, *Washington Post*, June 7, 2009.

[18] See, for example, Marc Lynch, "Could There Be a Musavi Effect?," *Foreign Policy*, June 10, 2009.

[19] U.S. Open Source Center (OSC) Document IAP20090611950041, "Iran: Candidate Musavi Warns Against IRGC, Basij 'Interference' in Election," *Farda* in Persian (Tehran), June 11, 2009.

[20] U.S. Open Source Center (OSC) Document IAP20090612950172, "Iranian Governors-General Authorized to Extend Voting Time," *Voice of the Islamic Republic Iran Radio* in Persian, June 12, 2009.

[21] U.S. Open Source Center (OSC) Document IAP2009061350119, *IRNA* (Tehran), June 13, 2009.

[22] U.S. Open Source Center (OSC) Document IAP2009061350138, "Leader Hails Iranians' Massive Turnout in Election," *Fars News Agency* (Tehran), June 13, 2009.

[23] For information on Iran's election law and procedures, see the International Foundation for Election Systems Election Guide for Iran, available at: http://www.electionguide.org/country-news.php?ID=103.

[24] U.S. Open Source Center (OSC) Document IAP20090615950012, "Musavi Files Formal Complaint Against Result in Iran's Presidential Election," *Fars News Agency* (Tehran), June 14, 2009.

[25] U.S. Open Source Center (OSC) Document IAP20090615950012, "Musavi Files Formal Complaint Against Result in Iran's Presidential Election," *Fars News Agency* (Tehran), June 14, 2009.

[26] See Eric Hooglund, "Iran's Rural Vote and Election Fraud," Tehran Bureau, June 17, 2009, available online at: http://tehranbureau.com/2009/06/17/irans-rural-vote-and-election-fraud/.

[27] U.S. Open Source Center (OSC) Document IAP20090615950044, "Iran's Supreme Leader Says Musavi's Letter to be Given Careful Consideration," *Islamic Republic of Iran News Network Television (IRINN)*, June 15, 2009.

[28] U.S. Open Source Center (OSC) Document GMP20090614647001, "Musavi Demands Elections Cancelled; Karrubi Rejects Ahmadinezhad's Win," *Al-Arabiyah* Television (Dubai), June 13, 2009.

[29] U.S. Open Source Center (OSC) Document IAP2009062011002, "Iran: Text of Musavi's Letter to the Guardian Council," Tehran *Qalam* (in Persian), June 20, 2009.

[30] U.S. Open Source Center (OSC) Document IAP20090622950080, "Iran Guardian Council Spokesman: 'No Major Violations' in Vote Counting," *Vision of the Islamic Republic of Iran Network 1*, June 22, 2009.

[31] See George Friedman, "Western Misconceptions Meet Iranian Reality," Stratfor Geopolitical Weekly, June 15, 2009.

[32] See, for example, Suzanne Maloney, "Reacting to Iran's Disputed Presidential Election Outcome," Brookings.edu, June 15, 2009, and Mehdi Khalaji, Patrick Clawson, Michael Singh, and Mohsen Sazegara, "Iran's 'Election': What Happened? What Does It Mean?, Washington Institute for Near East Policy, Policy Watch #1537: Special Policy Forum Report, June 18, 2009.

[33] U.S. Open Source Center (OSC) Document IAP20090613950098, " Iran's Interior Minister Warns Against Public Gatherings Without Permits," *Tehran Islamic Republic of Iran News Network Television (IRINN)*, June 13, 2009.

[34] "Iran Opposition Keeps Up Pressure," *BBC News*, June 16, 2009.

[35] David Clark Scott, "Iran's pro-Ahmadinejad media: Using Fake Crowd Photos?" *International News Editor*, June 17, 2009.

[36] Ali Akbar Hashemi Rafsanjani currently presides over the Assembly of Experts, a powerful body of clerics that has the authority to remove the supreme leader by a two-thirds vote.

[37] See, for example, ICHRI, available online at http://www.iranhumanrights.org/2009/06/list/.

[38] Nour Sumaha, "Dubai Bans Iran Protests," *The National* (Abu Dhabi), June 17, 2009.

[39] Among those offering congratulations were the leaders of Syria, Lebanon, Indonesia, the Palestinian Authority, Turkey, Afghanistan, Russia, China, Iraq, and Head of Supreme Iraqi Islamic Council Abdul Aziz al-Hakim.

[40] U.S. Open Source Center Document EUP20090614086006, "Britain's Miliband Comments on Iranian Election," *London Foreign and Commonwealth Office*, June 13, 2009.

[41] Helene Cooper and Mark Landler, "For Obama, Pressure to Strike Firmer Tone," *New York Times*, June 18, 2009. Karim Sadjadpour of the Carnegie Endowment for International Peace added that "up until now, the president had very thoughtfully calibrated his marks on Iran," but called this particular statement an "uncharacteristic and egregious error." Sadjadpour and others have expressed concerns that such statements make Obama appear unsympathetic to the Iranians who are risking their lives to protest the elections by saying that the outcome does not matter to the United States.

[42] See Mehdi Khalaji, Patrick Clawson, Michael Singh, and Mohsen Sazegara, "Iran's 'Election': What Happened? What Does It Mean?", Washington Institute for Near East Policy, Policy Watch #1537: Special Policy Forum Report, June 18, 2009.

[43] The President's Statement on Iran, June 20, 2009, available online at http://www.whitehouse.gov/blog/The-Presidents-Statement-on-Iran/.

[44] Peter Spiegel and Jay Soloman, "U.S. Retracts July 4 Invites it Gave Iran," *Wall Street Journal*, June 25, 2009.

[45] Ibid. See also Mohsen Makhmalbaf interview with *Foreign Policy*, June 2009. Available online at http://www.foreignpolicy.com/story/cms.php?story_id=5018.

[46] Velayet e faqih (Guardianship of the Jurisprudent) is the principle on which the Islamic Republic is based, whereby Islamic (Shariah) law governs society and a leading Islamic scholar (in Iran, the Supreme Leader) is the guardian of the law.

[47] See, for example, "U.S. Should React Cautiously to Iran's "Stolen Election," CFR Interview with Gary Sick, June 14, 2009 and Suzanne Maloney, "Reacting to Iran's Disputed Presidential Election Outcome."

[48] Mehdi Khalaji, Patrick Clawson, Michael Singh, and Mohsen Sazegara, "Iran's 'Election': What Happened? What Does It Mean?, Washington Institute for Near East Policy, Policy Watch #1537: Special Policy Forum Report, June 18, 2009.

[49] Ibid. See also, for example, Mehdi Khalaji, "Khamene'i's Coup," *Washington Post*, June 15, 2009

[50] See, for example, Michael Gerson and Roger Hertog, "Realism on Iran? It's Called Freedom," Washington Post, June 21, 2009.

[51] See, for example, Suzanne Maloney, "Diplomacy with Iran: The Show Must go On," ForeignPolicy.com, June 29, 2009.

In: Iran: Issues and Perspectives
Editor: Stephen D. Calhoun

ISBN: 978-1-61728-007-8
© 2010 Nova Science Publishers, Inc.

Chapter 7

IRAN'S ACTIVITIES AND INFLUENCE IN IRAQ[*]

Kenneth Katzman

SUMMARY

With a conventional military and weapons of mass destruction (WMD) threat from Saddam Hussein's regime removed, Iran seeks to ensure that Iraq can never again become a threat to Iran, either with or without U.S. forces present in Iraq. Some believe that Iran's intentions go well beyond achieving Iraq's "neutrality"—that Iran wants to try to harness Iraq to Iran's broader regional policy goals and to help Iran defend against international criticism of Iran's nuclear program. Others believe Iran sees Iraq as providing lucrative investment opportunities and a growing market for Iranian products and contracts. The violent unrest in Iran surrounding that country's June 12, 2009, presidential election has given Iran another reason to exercise influence in Iraq—to try to suppress Iranian dissidents located over the border inside Iraq.

Iran has sought to achieve its goals in Iraq through several strategies: supporting pro-Iranian factions and armed militias; attempting to influence Iraqi political leaders and faction leaders; and building economic ties throughout Iraq that might accrue goodwill to Iran. It is Iran's support for armed Shiite factions that most concerns U.S. officials. That Iranian activity has hindered—and continues to pose a threat to—U.S. efforts to stabilize Iraq, and has heightened the U.S. threat perception of Iran generally.

While some see Iran as having accomplished many of its key objectives in Iraq, others maintain that Iran has suffered key setbacks over the past year. Its protégé Shiite factions, formerly united, are increasingly competing with each other politically, and several are losing support among the Iraqi public. The most pro-Iranian factions generally fared poorly in the January 31, 2009, provincial elections.

Also see CRS Report RL32048, *Iran: U.S. Concerns and Policy Responses*, by Kenneth Katzman.

---

[*] This is an edited, reformatted and augmented version of a CRS Report for Congress publication dated July 2009.

BACKGROUND

Since the fall of Saddam Hussein, Iran has sought to shape and influence the post-Saddam political structure to Iran's advantage, although Tehran couches its policies in terms of friendship with Iraq and humanitarian assistance to the Iraqi people. During 2003-2005, Iran calculated that it suited its interests to support the entry of Iraqi Shiite Islamist factions into the U.S.-led election process, because the number of Shiites in Iraq (about 60% of the population) virtually ensured Shiite dominance of an elected government. To this extent, Iran's goals did not conflict with the U.S. objective of trying to establish representative democracy in Iraq. Iran helped assemble a Shiite Islamist bloc ("United Iraqi Alliance"), encompassing the Islamic Supreme Council of Iraq (ISCI), the Da'wa (Islamic Call) party, and the faction of the 35-year-old cleric Moqtada Al Sadr. This formidable bloc won 128 of the 275 seats in the December 15, 2005, election for a full-term parliament. Dawa senior leader Nuri al-Maliki was selected as Prime Minister; several ISCI figures took other leadership positions, and five Sadrists were given ministerial posts.

ISCI's leaders, including Ayatollah Mohammad Baqr Al Hakim, who was killed in an August 2003 car bomb in Najaf, had spent their years of exile in Iran and built ties to Iranian leaders.[1] His younger brother, Abd al Aziz al-Hakim, succeeded Mohammad Baqr. Hakim has acknowledged publicly that he is undergoing treatment for lung cancer and, should he pass from the scene, he is likely to be succeeded by his son, Amar al-Hakim. Finance Minister Bayan Jabr and other ISCI leaders, such as deputy president Adel Abd al-Mahdi and constitutional review commission chair Hummam al-Hammoudi, might compete for that leadership. Some predict ISCI might fracture.

ISCI's militia, the "Badr Brigades" (renamed the "Badr Organization"), had been recruited, trained, and armed by Iran's Revolutionary Guard Corps, the most politically powerful component of Iran's military, during the 1980-88 Iran-Iraq war. In that war, Badr guerrillas conducted attacks from Iran into southern Iraq against Baath Party officials, but did not shake the regime. After Saddam's fall, Iran continued to provide political, financial, and military support to ISCI and the Badr Brigades militia, which numbered about 15,000. During 2005-6, apparently with the active work of then Interior Minister Bayan Jabr, the militia burrowed into the Iraqi Security Forces (ISF), particularly the 22,000-member National Police, which reports to the Interior Ministry.

The Sadr faction's political ties to Iran were initially limited because his family remained in Iraq during Saddam's rule. Still, the Sadr clan has political and ideological ties to Iran; Moqtada's cousin, Mohammad Baqr Al Sadr, founded the Da'wa Party in the late 1950s and was a political ally of Ayatollah Khomeini when Khomeini was in exile in Najaf (1964-1978). Baqr Al Sadr was hung by Saddam Hussein in 1980 at the start of the Da'wa Party rebellion against Saddam's regime. Moqtada is married to one of Baqr Al Sadr's daughters.

Iran recognized political value and potential leverage in Sadr's faction—which has 30 total seats in parliament, a large and dedicated following among lower-class Iraqi Shiites, and which built an estimated 60,000-person "Mahdi Army" (Jaysh al-Mahdi, or JAM) militia after Saddam's fall. Since 2004, Sadr has alternately unleashed and reined in the JAM as part of a strategy of challenging what he sees as a U.S. occupation of Iraq. Although U.S. and Iraqi military operations repeatedly defeated the JAM, Iran perceived it as useful against the United States in the event of a U.S.-Iran confrontation, particularly for its ability to kill U.S. forces with rockets and other weaponry. In 2005, Iran began arming it through the Revolutionary Guard's "Qods (Jerusalem) Force," the unit that assists Iranian protégé forces abroad. During 2005-6, the height of sectarian conflict in Iraq, JAM militiamen, as well as Badr fighters in and outside the ISF, committed sectarian killings of Sunnis, which accelerated after the February 2006 bombing of the Al Askari Mosque in Samarra.

ASSERTIONS OF IRANIAN SUPPORT TO ARMED GROUPS

Iran's arming and training of Shiite militias in Iraq has added to U.S.-Iran tensions over Iran's nuclear program and Iran's broader regional influence, such as its aid to Lebanese Hezbollah and the Palestinian organization Hamas (which controls the Gaza Strip). U.S. officials feared that, by supplying armed groups in Iraq, Iran was seeking to develop a broad range of options that included: pressuring U.S. and British forces to leave Iraq; to bleed the United States militarily; and to be positioned to retaliate in Iraq should the United States take military action against Iran's nuclear program. However, as of early 2009, according to the Defense Department, "Tehran has selectively reduced the number of militants it supports."

At the height of Iran's support to Shiite militias, U.S. officials publicly discussed specific information on Qods Force aid to the JAM. One press report said there are 150 Qods and intelligence personnel there,[2] but some U.S. commanders who have served in southern Iraq said they believed that there were perhaps one or two Qods Force personnel in each Shiite province, attached to or interacting with pro-Iranian governors in those provinces. Qods Force officers often do not wear uniforms and their main role is to identify Iraqi fighters to train and to organize safe passage for weapons and Iraqi militants between Iran and Iraq, although some observers allege that Qods officers sometimes assisted the JAM in its combat operations. A study by the "Combatting Terrorism Center" at West Point, published October 13, 2008 ("Iranian Strategy in Iraq: Politics and 'Other Means'"), details this activity, based on declassified interrogation and other documents.

- On February 11, 2007, U.S. military briefers in Baghdad provided what they said was specific evidence that Iran had supplied armor-piercing "explosively formed projectiles" (EFPs) to Shiite (Sadrist) militiamen. EFPs have been responsible for over 200 U.S. combat deaths since 2003. In August 2007, Gen. Raymond Odierno, then the second in command (now overall commander in Iraq), said that Iran had supplied the Shiite militias with 122-millimeter mortars that are used to fire on the Green Zone in Baghdad. On August 28, 2008, the *Washington Times* reported that pro-Sadr militias were now also using "Improvised Rocket Assisted Munitions"—a "flying bomb" carrying 100 pounds of explosives, propelled by Iranian-supplied 107 mm rockets.
- On July 2, 2007, Brig. Gen. Kevin Begner said that Lebanese Hezbollah was assisting the Qods Force in aiding Iraqi Shiite militias, adding that Iran gives about $3 million per month to these Iraqi militias. He based the statement on the March 2007 capture of former Sadr aide Qais Khazali and Lebanese Hezbollah operative Ali Musa Daqduq. They were allegedly involved in the January 2007 killing of five U.S. forces in Karbala. On October 7, 2007, Gen. David Petraeus, then overall U.S.

commander in Iraq, told journalists that Iran's Ambassador to Iraq, Hassan Kazemi-Qomi, is himself a member of the Qods Force.

Continuing to present evidence of Iranian material assistance to Shiite militias, Gen. Petraeus testified on April 8-9, 2008, that Iran was continuing to arm, train, and direct "Special Groups"— radical and possibly breakaway elements of the JAM—and to organize the Special Groups into a "Hezbollah-like force to serve [Iran's] interests and fight a proxy war against the Iraqi state and coalition forces...."

Shiite Internecine Combat

The Gen. Petraeus testimony in April 2008 was delivered amidst a falling out between mainstream Shiite factions represented by Prime Minister Maliki, and the Sadr faction. This rift caused a dilemma for Iran, which considered both Shiite factions as its allies and protégés. The Iraqi Shiite split had been growing for about a year, but broke out into an all-out military struggle with the ISF offensive, launched by Maliki on March 26, 2008, to clear JAM militiamen from Basra, particularly the port area, which the JAM and other militias controlled for financial benefit. Maliki reportedly launched the Basra offensive, in part, to reduce Sadrist strength in provincial elections held on January 31, 2009. In the initial assault, the ISF units (dominated by Badr loyalists) partly collapsed—1,300 of the 7,000 additional ISF sent in for the assault did not fight. Later, U.S. and British forces intervened with air strikes and military advice, helping the ISF gain the upper hand and restore relative normality. Sadr agreed to an Iran-brokered "ceasefire" on March 30, 2008, but not to disarm. Some fighting and JAM rocketing of U.S. installations in Baghdad continued subsequently, in some cases killing U.S. soldiers, and U.S. forces continued to fight JAM elements in Sadr City until another Sadr-Maliki agreement on May 10, 2008. Subsequently, the ISF moved into Amarah unopposed on June 16, 2008, and quieted that city. Other arrests of Sadrists took place in Sadr's former stronghold of Diwaniyah, the capital of Qadisiyah Province.

As noted, the Basra battles were the most dramatic manifestation of a rift between Maliki and Sadr that had begun in 2007. In 2007, Maliki and ISCI—viewing Sunni insurgents as the major threat to their dominant positions—recognized the need to cooperate with the U.S. "troop surge" launched that year. That cooperation required them to permit U.S. forces to place military pressure on the JAM, which the United States considered a key threat equal to or in some instances greater than that posed by Sunni insurgents. In 2006, Maliki had been preventing such U.S. operations in an effort to preserve his alliance with Sadr. As a result of Maliki's shift in 2007, Sadr broke with him, pulled the five Sadrist ministers out of the cabinet, and withdrew his faction from the UIA. The rift widened throughout 2007 as JAM fighters battled Badr-dominated Iraqi forces, and U.S. and British forces, for control of such Shiite cities as Diwaniyah, Karbala, Hilla, Nassiryah, Basra, Kut, and Amarah. This also caused a backlash against Sadr among Iraqi Shiite civilian victims, particularly after the August 2007 JAM attempt to take control of religious sites in Karbala. The backlash caused Sadr to declare a six-month "suspension" of JAM activities. (He extended the ceasefire in February 2008 for another six months, although with the implicit understanding that it would be an indefinite suspension.) The intra-Shiite fighting expanded as Britain drew down its forces in the Basra area from 7,000 to 4,000 in concert with a withdrawal from Basra city to the airport, and the transfer of Basra Province to ISF control on December 16, 2007.

The Decline of Sadr and Implications for Iran

The Basra battles weakened Sadr politically, and his movement has not recovered to date. Sadr told his followers on June 13, 2008, that most of the JAM would now orient toward "peaceful activities," clarified on August 8, 2008, to be social and cultural work under a new movement called "Mumahidun," or "trail blazers;" and that a small corps of "special companies" (the U.S.- described Special Groups) would be formed from the JAM to actively combat U.S. (but not Iraqi) forces in Iraq. Subsequently, U.S. commanders began to observe new, smaller Shiite militias emerging, with names such as Asa'ib al-Haq, Keta'ib Hezbollah (Hezbollah Battalions); Sadr has publicly called on them to place themselves within the Sadrist fold, suggesting these groups are acting somewhat independently. He has also asked them to join a new armed wing, the "Promised Day Brigade," which could represent an organizational manifestation of the "Special Groups." Many of the exact relationships among these militia to each other, to Sadr, and to Iran and the Qods Force, remain unclear.

In the months leading up to the January 31, 2009, provincial elections, U.S. commanders in Iraq said they had seen a clear reduction of Sadrist militia activity. On August 18, 2008, the number two U.S. commander in Iraq, Lt. Gen. Lloyd Austin, said that many JAM fighters had gone to Iran temporarily for more training and resupply. In December 2008, Lt. Gen. Thomas Metz said that there was a marked decline in the number of explosive devices coming into Iraq from Iran.[3] The relative quiescence of the JAM could also explain why a U.S. briefing on new information on Iranian aid to the JAM, first expected in May 2008 but opposed by Iraqi leaders who do not want to draw Iraq into a U.S.-Iran dispute, was not held. Nor has there been further follow-up from an Iraqi parliamentary group that visited Iran to discuss the issue in April 2008, or from an Iraqi commission investigating Iran's aid to the JAM.

Implications of the Provincial Elections for Iranian Influence

Suggesting that he did not feel overly confident about Sadrist prospects in the January 31, 2009, elections, Sadr also announced in August 2008 that he would back technocrats and independents for upcoming provincial elections but not offer a separate "Sadrist" list. Iraq's election authorities published candidate lists, but Sadr representatives did not specify who specifically were Sadrist candidates. The slate that was most well-known for being pro-Sadr was the "Independent Liberals Trend" (list number 284).

Iran's political influence in Iraq was further jeopardized by a growing political rift between Maliki and his erstwhile political ally, ISCI. ISCI and Maliki's Da'wa Party have long been the core of the Shiite alliance that dominates Iraq, but they filed competing slates in the provincial elections. Maliki's slate was called the State of Law Alliance (slate no. 302), and ISCI's slate was the Shahid (Martyr) al-Mihrab and Independent Forces List (slate no. 290). ISCI activists assert that Maliki has surrounded himself with Da'wa veterans who have excluded ISCI from decision- making influence. Maliki, trying to compensate for Da'wa's organizational deficiencies, tried to align his party with tribal leaders in the south to win provincial council seats. The net effect was to introduce new splits in the Shiite bloc in Iraq and to cause Iran to have to choose among its various Shiite allies in Iraq.

To the extent that Maliki is less pro-Iranian than is ISCI or Sadr, the January 31, 2009, elections represented a clear setback for Iran and its interests. ISCI, which was hoping to sweep the elections in the Shiite south, did not come in first in any Shiite province. In most of the Shiite provinces, the Maliki slate came in first, and his slate won 28 out of the 57 seats on the Baghdad provincial council, and it won an outright majority in Basra—20 out of 35 seats on that provincial council. ISCI's best showing in the south was in Najaf, where it tied with the Maliki slate with 7 seats each on the 28-seat provincial council. ISCI has few opportunities to forge coalitions that will determine who will be governor of a particular province.

In many of the Shiite provinces of the south, the Sadrist list came in third. In Basra, the former JAM stronghold, the Sadrist list won only 2 out of the 35 seats. Still, in some provinces, Sadr's faction has been a coalition partner that helped determine provincial leaderships. Through coalition building, a Sadrist did gain the chairmanship of the provincial council of Babil Province.

The first Defense Department "Measuring Stability and Security in Iraq" report since the elections, released March 2009, acknowledged that Tehran suffered a setback in the elections, which were viewed as victories for parties favoring a strong central government, by stating that "Iraqi nationalism may act as a check on Iran's ambitions. ..." The report added that "Tehran has selectively reduced the number of militants it supports ... [h]owever, [it] has also simultaneously improved the training and weapons systems received by the proxy militants." Still, the report also said that Iran "continues to pose a significant challenge to Iraq's long-term stability and political independence ..." and that "Iran continues to support Sadr 's religious studies in Qom, Iran [where Sadr is believed to have been for at least a year]." Some might argue—and this is discussed in sections below—that Maliki and his faction are pro-Iranian as well, and therefore Maliki's strong showing in the provincial elections does not necessarily mean that Iran's influence in Iraq is diluted.

U.S. Efforts to Reduce Iran's Activities in Iraq

In addition to the U.S. and Maliki efforts against the JAM, U.S. forces arrested a total of 20 Iranians in Iraq, many of whom are alleged to be Qods Forces officers, during December 2006- October 2007. On August 12, 2008, U.S.-led forces arrested nine Hezbollah members allegedly involved in funneling arms into Iraq, and on August 29, 2008, U.S. forces arrested Ali Lami on his return to Iraq for allegedly being a "senior Special Groups leader." Five of the purported Qods Force members were arrested in January 2007 in the Kurdish city of Irbil, and three of those were held until July 2009. In July 2009, the three were handed over to Iraq in accordance with the provisions of the U.S.-Iraq Security Agreement, which took effect January 1, 2009, and which, among many major provisions, requires U.S. forces to turn over to Iraqi control all U.S.-held detainees. The three were immediately released by Iraq and returned to Iran. Iran maintained the three were diplomats, but the United States Central Command insists they were Qods Forces officers and that their holding was legitimate, even though they reportedly had not conducted any actual attacks on U.S. forces.

On March 24, 2007, with U.S. backing, the U.N. Security Council unanimously adopted Resolution 1747 (on the Iran nuclear issue), with a provision banning arms exports by Iran—a provision clearly directed at Iran's arms supplies to Iraq's Shiite militias and Lebanese Hezbollah. In 2007, the U.S. military built a base near the Iranian border in Wasit Province, east of Baghdad, to stop cross-border weapons shipments. In July 2008, U.S. forces and U.S. civilian border security experts established additional bases near the Iran border in Maysan Province, to close off smuggling routes.

In an effort to financially squeeze the Qods Force, on October 21, 2007, the Bush Administration designated the Qods Force (Executive Order 13224) as a provider of support to terrorist organizations. Also on October 21, 2007, the Administration designated the Revolutionary Guard and several affiliates, under Executive Order 13382, as proliferation concerns. The designations carry the same penalties as do those under Executive Order 13224. Neither the Guard or the Qods Force was named a Foreign Terrorist Organization (FTO)—recommended by the FY2008 defense authorization bill (P.L. 110-181).

Since January 2008, the Treasury Department has taken action against suspected Iranian and pro- Iranian operatives in Iraq by designating them as a threat to stability in Iraq under a July 17, 2007, Executive Order 13438. The penalties are a freeze on their assets and a ban on transactions with them. The most prominent entity designated is Khata'ib Hezbollah, mentioned above, which is a splinter faction of the JAM Special Groups. Khata'ib Hezbollah was designated under the Order on July 2, 2009, along with Abu Mahdi al-Muhandis, who allegedly facilitated Iranian weapons deliveries to the Special Groups and other Shiite militias. Al Muhandis was convicted by Kuwait of involvement in the Da'wa Party bombings in Kuwait in December 1983 (U.S. and French embassies there) and the May 1985 bombing of the Amir of Kuwait's motorcade (he was slightly injured in that attack).

Other persons and entities named under the order, in designations made on January 9, 2008, and on September 16, 2008, are a blend of Qods Force members and Iraqi Shiite militia figures. The designees include:[4] Ahmad Forouzandeh, Commander of the Qods Force Ramazan Headquarters, accused of fomenting sectarian violence in Iraq and organizing training in Iran for Iraqi Shiite militiamen; Abdul Reza Shahlai, a deputy commander of the Qods Force; Abu Mustafa alSheibani, the Iran-based leader of network that funnels Iranian arms to Iraqi Shiite militias; Isma'il al-Lami (Abu Dura), a Shiite militia leader—who has broken from the JAM—alleged to have planned assassination attempts against Iraqi Sunni politicians; and Akram Abbas al-Kabi, a JAM Special Groups leader.

Negotiations with Iran

The United States has also sought, at times, to directly engage Iran in an effort to refrain from activities that undermine stability in Iraq. The Bush Administration initially rejected the recommendation of the "Iraq Study Group" (December 2006) to include Iran in multilateral efforts to stabilize Iraq, in part because of concerns that Iran might use such meetings to discuss Iran's nuclear program. However, in a shift conducted in concert with the "troop surge," the United States attended regional (including Iran and Syria) conferences ("Expanded Neighbors Conference" process) in Baghdad on March 10, 2007, in Egypt during

May 3-4, 2007, and in Kuwait on April 22, 2008. Secretary of State Rice and Iranian Foreign Minister Mottaki held no substantive discussions at any of these meetings.

In a more pronounced shift, the Bush Administration agreed to bilateral meetings with Iran, in Baghdad, on the Iraq issue, led by U.S. Ambassador to Iraq Ryan Crocker and Iranian Ambassador Kazemi-Qomi. The first meeting was on May 28, 2007. A second round, held on July 24, 2007, established a lower-level working group; it met on August 6, 2007. Talks in Baghdad scheduled for December 18, 2007, were postponed because Iran wanted them at the ambassador level, not the working group level. On May 6, 2008, Iran said it would not continue the dialogue because U.S. forces are causing civilian casualties in Sadr City, although the Iranian position might have reflected a broader Iranian assessment that it needs to make no concessions to the United States in Iraq. During a visit to Iraq by Iranian Foreign Minister Manuchehr Mottaki on February 11, 2009, Mottaki ruled out new talks with the United States on Iraq, saying that improved security in Iraq made them unnecessary.

It is possible that the Iranian position reflects lack of a firm decision by Iran on how to respond to the Obama Administration's overtures toward Iran for a broader dialogue on the nuclear issue and other outstanding issues. The U.S. offer to resume multilateral negotiations with Iran remains, even after the June 12, 2009, disputed election and subsequent crackdown against protesters. However, suggesting a hardening of the Administration position in light of the Iranian crackdown, the Obama Administration has indicated that Iran must resume negotiations by late September 2009, or it would return to talks with its allies and other countries about imposing potentially "crippling" economic sanctions on Iran.

IRANIAN INFLUENCE OVER IRAQI POLITICAL LEADERS

Iran has tried to exploit its ties to Iraqi government leaders to try to build broad political and economic influence over outcomes in Iraq, although Iran's commerce with and investment in Iraq do not necessarily conflict with U.S. goals. A pressing concern for the United States was Iran's efforts to derail the U.S.-Iraq Security Agreement, mentioned above, that authorized the U.S. military presence beyond December 31, 2008. Senior Iranian leaders publicly opposed the pact as an infringement of Iraq's sovereignty—criticism that likely masks Iran's fears the pact is a U.S. attempt to consolidate its "hold" over Iraq and encircle Iran militarily. This criticism might have contributed to insistence by Iraqi leaders on substantial U.S. concessions to a final draft agreement. As an example of the extent to which Iran was reputedly trying to derail the agreement, Gen. Odierno said on October 12, 2008, that there were intelligence reports suggesting Iran might be trying to bribe Iraqi parliamentarians to vote against it. In the end, Iran's concerns were attenuated by a provision in the final agreement (passed by Iraq's parliament on November 27, 2008, and now in force as of January 1, 2009) that U.S. forces could not use Iraqi territory as a base for attacks on any other nation. Iranian opposition was also reduced by U.S. agreement to an Iraqi demand to set a timetable (end of 2011) for a full withdrawal of U.S. forces from Iraq. However, even after the pact took effect, Iran's Supreme Leader Ali Khamene'i (January 5, 2009) warned Maliki that the United States cannot be trusted to implement its pledges under the pact.

In accordance with the entry into force of the Agreement, Iraq has a greater degree of input over U.S. operations in Iraq. Iran has apparently sought to use this change to try to eliminate its Iraq- based opposition. There are 3,400 members of the Iranian opposition People's Mojahedin Organization of Iran (PMOI), a group allied with Saddam against Iran, at "Camp Ashraf" near the Iran border. Iran has urged Prime Minister Maliki and other pro-Iranian Shiite leaders in Iraq to expel the group, possibly including extraditing its members to Iran. Before and since the U.S.- Iraq Security Agreement took effect on January 1, 2009, Iraqi leaders, presumably reflecting Iran's orientation as well as their own resentment that the PMOI was close to Saddam politically, said the Ashraf activists were no longer welcome and need to leave Iraq. (Shiites and Kurds in Iraq say Saddam used PMOI forces to help put down uprisings by those communities after the 1991 Gulf war.) However, the State Department said in December 2008 that Iraqi leaders had pledged, in writing, to respect the residents' human rights and not to expel them or force them to go to Iran.

Still, under the provisions of the U.S.-Iraq Agreement, in February 2009, the ISF took control of the outer perimeter of Ashraf, with a small number of U.S. forces nearby but taking no active role in guarding the camp any longer. On July 28, 2009, the ISF attempted to assert its full control over Ashraf by establishing a police post inside its main gate, but the PMOI residents, although unarmed, resisted the ISF (mainly police), and altercations ensued. PMOI leaders say at least 10 residents have been killed in the violence, and numerous others injured. The U.S. position, articulated by Secretary of State Clinton on July 29, 2009, is that resolving the issue of Camp Ashraf and its residents is now an Iraqi matter.

The Iraqi move into Ashraf raises questions about whether the Iraqi government, now fully sovereign, might abrogate its pledges to the United States to treat the residents humanely. The options for the residents of Ashraf are unclear, as is their status under international law. About 200 have thus far have used U.N.-led processes to leave Iraq as refugees, but the remainder at Ashraf have refused to take advantage of these programs. The International Committee of the Red Cross (ICRC) representatives say Iraq is considering moving the camp into Anbar Province, far away from the Iranian border. Few countries will accept the PMOI activists as residents—a consequence of the PMOI designation by many countries (including the United States) as a terrorist organization. On January 26, 2009, the European Union removed the group from its list of terrorist organizations, potentially opening up avenues for arranging relocation of the Ashraf inhabitants to countries in Europe.

Longstanding Territorial and Property Disputes

Some of Iran's interests have been served by post-Saddam Iraqi leaders, although Iraqi nationalism that has been emerging since 2007 has reduced Iraq's pliability to compromise with Iran on longstanding disputes. During exchanges of high-level visits in July 2005, Iraqi officials took responsibility for starting the 1980-1988 Iran-Iraq war, indirectly blamed Saddam Hussein for using chemical weapons against Iranian forces in it, signed agreements on military cooperation, and agreed to Iranian consulates in Basra, Karbala, Irbil, and Sulaymaniyah. In response to U.S. complaints, Iraqi officials subsequently said that any Iran-Iraq military cooperation would not include Iranian training of Iraqi forces. On May 20, 2006, Iraq's Foreign Minister, Hoshyar Zebari, supported Iran's right to pursue "peaceful" nuclear technology.[5]

On the other hand, Iran has not returned the 153 Iraqi military and civilian aircraft flown to Iran at the start of the 1991 Gulf War, although it allowed an Iraqi technical team to assess the aircraft in August 2005. The ICRC is continuing to try to resolve the approximately 75,000 total Iranians and Iraqis[6] still unaccounted for from the Iran-Iraq war, although the two have continued to exchange bodies (most recently 241 exchanged in December 2008) and information when discovered. Another source of tension is Iran's allegation that Iraq is not doing enough to deny safe haven to the Party for a Free Life in Kurdistan (PJAK), an Iranian Kurdish separatist group, which Iran says is staging incursions into Iran. On February 5, 2009, that group was named by the U.S. Treasury Department as a terrorism supporting entity under Executive Order 13224.

Most territorial issues that have contributed to past disputes were resolved as a result of an October 2000 rededication to recognize the *thalweg*, or median line of the Shatt al Arab waterway as the water border (a provision of the 1975 Algiers Accords between the Shah of Iran and the Baathist government of Iraq, abrogated by Iraq prior to its September 1980 invasion of Iran.) The water border is subject to interpretation, but the two sides agreed to renovate water and land border posts during the March 2008 Ahmadinejad visit. In February 2009, Foreign Minister Zebari urged Iran to move forward with these demarcations, suggesting Iranian foot-dragging to resolve an issue whose ambiguity now favors Iran.

Economic Relations

Suggesting the degree to which the Iraqi government views Iran as a benefactor, Maliki has visited Iran four times as Prime Minister to consult on major issues and to sign agreements. The visits were: September 13-14, 2006, resulting in agreements on cross-border migration and intelligence sharing; August 8-9, 2007, resulting in agreements to build pipelines between Basra and Iran's city of Abadan to transport crude and oil products for their swap arrangements (finalized on November 8, 2007); June 8, 2008, resulting in agreements on mine clearance and searches for the few Iran-Iraq war soldiers still unaccounted for; and January 4-5, 2009, primarily to explain to Iran the provisions of the U.S.-Iraq pact but also to continue Iraqi efforts to buy electricity from Iran. On March 2-3, 2008, Ahmadinejad visited Iraq, a first since the 1979 Islamic revolution. In conjunction, Iran announced $1 billion in credits for Iranian exports to Iraq (in addition to $1 billion in credit extended in 2005, used to build a new airport near Najaf, opened in August 2008, which helps host about 20,000 Iranian pilgrims per month who visit the Imam Ali Shrine there). The visit also produced seven agreements for cooperation in the areas of insurance, customs treatment, industry, education, environmental protection, and transportation. In 2005, Iran agreed to provide 2 million liters per day of kerosene to Iraqis. Suggesting Iran's earlier generosity is being reciprocated, in February 2009, the Iraqi government awarded a $1 billion contract to an Iranian firm to help rebuild Basra, and to repair ancient Persian historical sites in southern Iraq.

Trade relations have burgeoned. As of the beginning of 2009, the two countries now conduct about $4 billion in bilateral trade, according to Iraq's Trade Minister, and the February 2009 visit of Iranian Foreign Minister Mottaki resulted in a plan to increase that trade to $5 billion annually through increases in oil and electricity-related trade. The two countries have developed a free trade zone around Basra, which buys electricity from Iran.

PROSPECTS

Iran's influence in Iraq remains substantial, as evidenced by Iraq's attempts to gain control over Camp Ashraf, but some aspects of Iranian influence—particularly its efforts to sustain Shiite militias—are waning. Some experts have long predicted that Iran's influence will gradually fade as Iraq asserts its nationhood, as the security situation has improved, and as Arab-Persian differences reemerge. Many experts point out that Iraqi Shiites generally stayed loyal to the Iraqi regime during the 1980-1988 Iran-Iraq war. Najaf, relatively secure and prosperous, might eventually meet pre-war expectations that it would again exceed Iran's Qom as the heart of the Shiite theological world. As noted, some of these trends are starting to appear, but it is unlikely that anything close to the enmity that existed when Saddam Hussein was in power will return.

End Notes

[1] In 1982, Mohammad Baqr was anointed by then Iranian leader Ayatollah Ruhollah Khomeini to head a future "Islamic republic of Iraq."

[2] Linzer, Dafna. "Troops Authorized To Kill Iranian Operatives in Iraq," Washington Post, January 26, 2007.

[3] Barnes, Julian. "U.S. Says Drop in Iraq Deaths Tied to Iranian Arms Cutback." Los Angeles Times, December 12, 2008

[4] Some persons designated under the Order are related to the Sunni insurgency in Iraq, and not to the Shiite militias that are a key subject of this paper.

[5] "Clarification Statement" issued by Iraqi Foreign Minister Hoshyar Zebari. May 29, 2006.

[6] ICRC estimates the number still unaccounted for as: 25,000 Iranians; and 50,000 Iraqis. June 2009.

INDEX

A

accessibility, x, 175
accounting, 79
acquisitions, 44, 155
Activists, 15, 16
acts of aggression, 139
advocacy, 67
age, 17
aggression, 63, 79, 139
agriculture, 22, 158
Air Force, 6, 95, 105, 166, 167, 169
airbases, 99
alternatives, 35, 99
ambassadors, 176
ambiguity, 76, 198
ammonium, 118
antagonism, 68
arbitration, 176
armed forces, 4, 18, 67, 80
arrest, 5, 6, 7, 16, 18, 48, 57, 97, 177
assassination, 5, 10, 19, 73, 83, 172, 195
assault, 192
assessment, 11, 18, 87, 113, 118, 119, 124, 129, 130, 196
assets, 19, 23, 24, 31, 36, 46, 50, 53, 54, 55, 65, 97, 98, 129, 156, 161, 162, 164, 165, 168, 195
atrocities, 36
attacks, 13, 15, 32, 36, 37, 38, 46, 57, 63, 65, 69, 73, 76, 84, 89, 120, 162, 190, 195, 196
authenticity, 134
authority, 4, 5, 19, 24, 56, 58, 111, 135, 138, 139, 148, 151, 162, 186
authors, 130
availability, 177

B

background, 106, 127, 129, 176, 186
backlash, 77, 192
ballistic missiles, 27, 47, 122, 163
banking, 26, 30, 68, 72, 160, 168
banks, vii, ix, 2, 19, 24, 26, 30, 46, 50, 51, 52, 72, 145, 158, 160, 163, 164
batteries, 44, 167
behavior, 46, 58, 87, 104, 149, 151
beliefs, 109
beryllium, 127
binding, 46, 87, 137
biological weapons, 27
black market, 19
blame, 28, 157, 176
blog, 187
blogger, 16
blogs, 16, 58, 106
blood, 26
bonds, 52, 148
border crossing, 91
border security, 30, 35, 195
borrowers, 9
breaches, 138, 139, 141
breakdown, 185
brothers, 30, 71
buffer, 22
bureaucracy, 106

C

campaigns, 178
candidates, 4, 8, 10, 16, 29, 56, 61, 77, 176, 178, 179, 180, 186, 193
capital markets, 52
carrier, 44

cartel, 97
cast, 11, 60, 122, 179, 180
casting, vii, 1, 114
CBS, 105
cell, 84, 105, 142
censorship, 13
certification, 32, 54, 179
channels, 64, 140, 180
charities, 87
charm, 83, 85
children, 14
CIA, 3, 58, 95, 102, 106, 109, 119, 122, 123, 125, 126, 130
CIS, 7
civil action, 161
civil liberties, x, 175, 183
civil rights, 96
civil society, 48, 49
civil war, 88, 89
clarity, 115
classes, 6, 10, 11
classification, 127
clients, 7
close relationships, 37
coercion, 183
coherence, 144
collaboration, 78
collusion, 92
commander-in-chief, 5, 167
commerce, 54, 68, 91, 196
Common Foreign and Security Policy, 112
communication, 13, 42, 139, 144, 179, 183
compensation, 165
competence, 138
competition, 30, 64, 65, 81, 89
competitor, 5, 87, 160
complement, 147
compliance, 22, 23, 26, 32, 65, 111, 126, 134, 137, 138, 140, 143
components, 6, 106, 114, 115, 130, 141, 143
composition, 12, 88
compounds, 110, 112, 133, 142
concentration, 110, 133
concrete, 30, 86, 111
confessions, 176
confidence, 39, 106, 116, 120, 123, 125, 138
configuration, 119, 129
conformity, 142
confrontation, 5, 10, 29, 39, 44, 64, 65, 76, 85, 148, 191
conjecture, 66
consciousness, 96
consensus, 25, 52, 74, 88

consent, 8, 147, 183
conservation, 158
consumption, 50, 98, 109, 152, 157
contingency, 45
contradiction, 124, 127
control, x, 2, 11, 14, 32, 35, 36, 54, 56, 67, 68, 70, 76, 83, 85, 87, 90, 91, 95, 98, 146, 147, 156, 162, 163, 165, 192, 194, 197, 199
conversion, viii, 22, 108, 110, 112, 114, 118, 119, 121, 123, 125, 133, 135, 142
conviction, 96
cooling, 180
corruption, 10
costs, 45, 100, 109
counterbalance, 85
covering, 48
crack, vii, 1
credentials, 17
credibility, 19, 78, 124
credit, 24, 30, 51, 52, 77, 148, 154, 158, 198
creditors, 52
criticism, xi, 5, 8, 9, 10, 16, 29, 46, 75, 158, 178, 183, 185, 189, 196
crude oil, 62
cruise missiles, 33, 44
CSS, 47
culture, 17, 56
currency, 160
customers, 72

D

danger, 95, 101
dating, 74
death, 4, 5, 12, 16, 91, 177
deaths, x, 11, 17, 102, 176, 182, 184, 185, 191
debt, 52, 72
debts, 9
decision makers, 100, 101
decision making, 66, 177
decision-making process, 131
decisions, ix, 18, 34, 66, 100, 122, 139, 145
defense, 8, 13, 19, 27, 30, 31, 33, 34, 35, 42, 45, 58, 67, 80, 86, 89, 95, 101, 103, 110, 114, 166, 195
definition, 50, 141, 143, 152, 153, 154, 172
delivery, 32, 33, 97, 125
democracy, 3, 7, 15, 40, 41, 45, 46, 47, 48, 49, 179, 185, 190
denial, 144, 148, 162
Department of Defense, 104, 106
Department of Energy, 123
deposits, 122
destruction, 91, 93

detainees, 14, 177, 194
detection, 33, 44, 119
detention, 14, 17, 18, 75
deterrence, 92
diamonds, 38
dignity, 183
directors, 19
disappointment, 9, 113
disaster, 161
disclosure, 61, 97
discrimination, 15, 17, 69
dismantlement, 32
displacement, 91
dissatisfaction, 184
diversification, 19, 67
division, 78, 90
domestic policy, 5
dominance, 190
donations, 162
donors, 32, 36, 81
doors, 87
draft, 25, 45, 75, 109, 113, 143, 196
drawing, 75, 77
drug smuggling, 36
drugs, 99
dumping, 158
duties, 139

E

early warning, 104
earth, 47
economic cooperation, 88
economic development, 81
economic growth, 67
economic resources, 63
electricity, 21, 52, 77, 80, 81, 98, 109, 126, 198, 199
embargo, 43, 93
employees, 176
empowerment, 64
Energy Policy Act of 2005, 58, 173
engagement, vii, viii, 1, 15, 23, 28, 34, 36, 38, 39, 40, 41, 59, 60, 61, 64, 66, 67, 68, 72, 82, 89, 91, 94, 99, 100, 146, 156, 183, 185
environment, 47, 68
environmental protection, 198
equity, 147, 153, 172
espionage, 16, 17
ethnic minority, 82, 96
ethnicity, 69
evil, viii, 2, 46
evolution, 40, 46
exaggeration, 44

execution, 65
exercise, xi, 46, 51, 71, 79, 85, 92, 95, 164, 189
expertise, 122
exploitation, 17, 98, 101
explosives, 35, 82, 114, 191
export routes, 153
exporter, 62, 152
exports, 21, 25, 29, 30, 32, 52, 53, 65, 67, 75, 77, 79, 97, 99, 147, 148, 152, 156, 158, 160, 161, 162, 195, 198
exposure, 12, 52
expulsion, 29, 179

F

fabrication, 113, 116
failure, 6, 47, 87, 113, 116, 118, 136, 137, 140, 142
faith, 16, 25, 161
family, 5, 14, 29, 37, 68, 76, 106, 177, 182, 185, 190
family members, 5, 14, 37
farmers, 9
fatwa, 124
fear, 17, 28, 32, 42, 43, 44, 56, 65, 70, 74, 77, 79, 82, 183
fears, 5, 14, 21, 28, 29, 34, 61, 63, 64, 73, 75, 81, 83, 89, 97, 196
feet, 67, 86, 98, 99, 147, 152, 153
finance, 158
financial institutions, 154
financial markets, 72
financial sector, 86
financial support, 71, 87, 89
financing, 23, 30, 51, 52, 54, 155, 160, 172
firms, ix, x, 19, 23, 53, 54, 73, 81, 130, 145, 146, 147, 148, 149, 151, 153, 154, 155, 156, 157, 158, 159, 163, 164, 171, 172
first generation, 117
flexibility, 14, 91
flight, 47, 50, 165
focusing, 25, 26, 78, 149
food, 158
foreign aid, ix, 38, 48, 49, 52, 53, 145, 155, 161, 163
foreign assistance, 149, 161
foreign banks, vii, 2, 160
foreign exchange, 155
foreign firms, ix, 53, 65, 145, 147, 148, 154, 155
foreign investment, ix, 123, 145, 147, 149, 153
foreign policy, 5, 19, 27, 67, 78, 81, 83, 85, 93
forgiveness, 72
fossil, 109
fraud, vii, x, 1, 9, 11, 81, 175, 177, 180, 181, 182, 186
free trade, 199

freedom, xi, 16, 17, 49, 67, 164, 176, 182, 183, 184, 185
freezing, 54, 156, 165
friendship, 74, 190
fruits, 158
frustration, 152
funding, 31, 45, 48, 58, 88, 105
funds, x, 38, 46, 48, 49, 61, 82, 91, 92, 146, 148, 155, 160, 164, 165, 166

G

gasoline, viii, x, 2, 23, 26, 28, 37, 38, 50, 54, 73, 101, 146, 147, 153, 154, 155, 156, 163
GDP, 9, 147
gender, 16
gender inequality, 16
generation, 7, 12, 21, 86, 118
genocide, 8
goals, vii, xi, 1, 18, 35, 40, 50, 59, 91, 99, 103, 156, 189, 190, 196
government procurement, 54, 148
government revenues, ix, 145
grand jury, 57
grants, 24
green revolution, 184
gross domestic product, 9
grouping, 7, 24, 35
growth, 19, 71, 88
guardian, 187
guidance, 30
gut, 20

H

hands, 8
harm, 46, 70, 79, 91, 97, 148
health, 47, 52, 53
health care, 47
hegemony, 5, 74
height, 40, 76, 88, 105, 191
hopes, 11, 46, 90, 93, 118
host, 66, 75, 77, 198
hostilities, 33, 43, 67, 70
hostility, 96
housing, 28, 37, 53, 106
hub, 63, 68, 72
human rights, x, 7, 17, 46, 49, 58, 84, 106, 175, 182, 183, 184, 185, 197
humanitarian aid, 82
hybrid, 87

I

ideal, 20
ideals, 19
identification, 180
ideology, 21, 27, 38, 84, 147
image, 10, 53, 68, 85, 90, 92
imagery, 116, 121
IMF, 67, 70, 72, 88, 103, 105, 107
implementation, 63, 115, 136, 142
imports, 38, 50, 54, 65, 79, 101, 148, 153, 154, 156
incentives, 22, 24, 25, 40, 91, 94, 98, 112, 127, 163
incumbents, 8
independence, 16, 29, 67, 68, 69, 77, 87, 96, 194
indication, 48, 86, 180, 184
indigenous, 72, 110, 122
indoctrination, 14
industrial sectors, 86
industry, 3, 147, 160, 198
ineffectiveness, 157
inflation, 9, 178
infrastructure, 26, 37, 43, 88, 91, 97, 119, 123, 130, 147, 163
insanity, 79
insecurity, 64
inspections, 21, 22, 24, 43, 50, 61, 111, 119, 134, 135
inspectors, 61, 111, 114, 116, 121, 134, 135, 137, 138
inspiration, 93
instability, 101
institutions, 19, 23, 87, 91, 161, 177
instruments, 151
insurance, x, 24, 26, 51, 52, 146, 161, 163, 198
integration, 21
integrity, 78
intelligence, 8, 10, 16, 19, 20, 30, 38, 45, 47, 58, 87, 104, 105, 109, 116, 118, 119, 123, 124, 147, 191, 196, 198
intentions, xi, 61, 69, 70, 79, 87, 92, 141, 189
interaction, 52, 70
interactions, 70, 72, 110
interdependence, 72
interest rates, 9
interference, xi, 12, 18, 21, 30, 31, 48, 61, 64, 69, 74, 176, 182, 183
International Covenant on Civil and Political Rights, 17
international diplomacy, 39, 127, 133
international financial institutions, 51
international investment, 151
international law, 197

International Monetary Fund, 65, 88, 103, 105, 107, 160
international relations, 97
international terrorism, 13, 27, 52, 53, 82, 156, 161, 162
internationalization, 51
internet, x, 146, 156, 164, 165, 175, 177, 179
interoperability, 95
intervention, 10, 183
interview, 20, 57, 66, 71, 110, 116, 118, 120, 127, 128, 129, 135, 183, 187
intifada, 106
investors, 149, 160
irradiation, 142
ISC, 131
isolation, x, 5, 6, 24, 146, 149, 151, 184
isotope, 110, 133

J

journalism, 17
journalists, x, 33, 175, 177, 179, 181, 192
judges, 17, 119, 124
judgment, viii, 108, 165, 177
judiciary, 4, 6, 17, 56, 177
justice, 77
justification, 140

K

kerosene, 198
killing, 13, 15, 52, 192

L

labor, 3, 7, 16, 49
land, 53, 76, 102, 198
language, 48, 49
lasers, 125
laws, ix, x, 52, 53, 58, 145, 146, 161, 162, 163, 173
lawyers, 56
leadership, 6, 19, 32, 34, 40, 64, 67, 68, 85, 89, 90, 91, 105, 106, 112, 135, 182, 183, 190
legislation, x, 4, 9, 13, 50, 53, 54, 56, 58, 73, 146, 147, 148, 154, 156
legislative proposals, x, 146
lending, ix, 24, 51, 52, 145, 161
lens, 183
letters of credit, 158
leukemia, 158
liberation, 27, 87
licenses, 148, 158

likelihood, 65, 100, 177
limitation, 51, 76
line, x, 5, 6, 18, 29, 30, 64, 76, 81, 82, 85, 89, 98, 146, 165, 181, 198
linkage, 67, 69, 92, 99
links, 34, 37, 82, 97
liquefied natural gas, 67
loans, 52, 53, 148, 161
local government, 75
loyalty, 19
lung cancer, 190

M

maintenance, 39, 67, 138, 139
major cities, x, 175, 177, 181
management, 53
manipulation, 2
manpower, 65
mantle, 85
manufacturer, 171
manufacturing, 19, 86, 115, 117, 128
market, ix, xi, 26, 65, 145, 153, 158, 159, 165, 189
market share, 65
markets, 9
marriage, 38
maturation, 85
measures, viii, x, 2, 39, 54, 136, 137, 139, 144, 146, 147, 157, 159, 160, 183
media, 6, 11, 19, 34, 36, 49, 64, 69, 87, 91, 106, 178, 181, 182, 186
median, 76, 98, 198
mediation, 67, 71, 80, 103
membership, 35, 52, 90
memory, 89
men, 5, 17, 31, 104
mentor, 6, 91
mentorship, 106
messages, 15, 46
migration, 58, 198
militarization, 72
military aid, 35
military pressure, 192
military spending, 65
militias, xi, 23, 27, 30, 43, 76, 77, 81, 85, 172, 183, 189, 191, 192, 193, 195, 199
mining, 115
minorities, 3, 15, 19, 35
minority, 16, 17, 36, 81
minority groups, 16
missions, 48, 72
misunderstanding, 71
mobile phone, x, 175, 177, 179

model, 78, 91, 143
moderates, 31, 93
momentum, 176, 184
money, 105, 106, 149, 160, 170
money laundering, 160
motivation, 181
motives, 74
movement, x, 2, 3, 4, 6, 7, 9, 12, 13, 15, 28, 41, 69, 74, 82, 87, 90, 91, 92, 94, 125, 146, 153, 160, 193
murder, 84
mutual respect, 64

N

naming, 83
narcotics, 54, 58
nation, 21, 41, 46, 76, 85, 109, 196
national emergency, 58
national interests, 27, 66, 78, 81, 87
national security, vii, x, 1, 4, 18, 43, 56, 58, 124, 148, 175, 181, 183, 184
National Security Council, 4, 5, 84, 125, 126, 144
nationalism, 75, 83, 107, 194, 197
NATO, 35, 79, 80, 82, 97, 104
natural gas, x, 29, 38, 62, 67, 70, 75, 79, 80, 86, 102, 123, 146, 147, 149, 152, 153, 154
negotiating, vii, 1, 52, 149, 151, 153
negotiation, 24, 143, 163
nerve, 26
newspapers, 16, 64, 152
nodes, 72
nuclear arms race, 101
nuclear talks, 22, 41, 42, 52, 149

O

objectives, xi, 18, 27, 39, 58, 94, 126, 189
obligation, 165
observations, 143
obstruction, 81, 93
oil production, ix, 130, 146, 151
oil revenues, ix, 9, 145
openness, 124
opinion polls, 180
oppression, 7
organ, 138
orientation, 88, 197
oversight, 5, 131, 178
ownership, 71, 103, 155

P

partnership, 22, 49, 85, 86, 88, 106
peace process, viii, 31, 39, 58, 59, 60, 63, 64, 85, 89, 90, 91, 92, 93, 94
peers, 4
penalties, ix, 53, 145, 147, 154, 195
pensions, 178
perceptions, 8, 15, 73, 97, 184
permit, 13, 20, 22, 23, 96, 98, 99, 122, 158, 192
personal communication, 126, 144
photographs, 123
physics, 125
planning, 43, 45, 65, 84, 128
plants, 86, 120, 153, 154
plutonium, 20, 72, 110, 112, 117, 120, 121, 122, 127, 131, 133, 142, 143
police, 6, 12, 14, 93, 179, 182, 197
policy choice, 20, 94
policy makers, 65, 66, 101
political leaders, xi, 189
political parties, 30, 61, 69, 88
political pluralism, 7
political power, 63
politics, 6, 34, 36, 61, 73, 85, 87, 88, 89, 90, 107, 186
polling, 11, 180
polonium, 127
poor, 10, 11, 15, 18, 178, 181
population, 8, 16, 17, 31, 34, 49, 67, 68, 69, 70, 74, 87, 89, 91, 96, 102, 178, 179, 181, 190
ports, 72
positive relation, 66
posture, 74
poverty, 107
power plants, 80, 151
pragmatism, 78
prayer, 11
prejudice, 122
presidency, 8, 22, 29, 31, 52, 177, 178
president, 5, 6, 10, 28, 31, 34, 178, 187, 190
pressure, viii, ix, 2, 3, 5, 21, 24, 25, 26, 43, 65, 69, 73, 85, 88, 98, 100, 104, 106, 108, 121, 123, 130, 145, 149, 151, 157, 160
prestige, 5
prices, 9, 43, 50, 51, 65, 97
prisoners, 74
probe, 47, 180, 182
production, 5, 20, 47, 54, 65, 67, 86, 101, 102, 104, 110, 114, 118, 119, 121, 125, 130, 133, 138, 141, 142, 143, 155, 167
productivity, 65
profit, 151

profits, 72
proliferation, 19, 30, 53, 54, 57, 58, 65, 72, 97, 109, 110, 121, 122, 123, 133, 148, 156, 160, 162, 182, 195
propaganda, 63
protocol, 111, 112, 115, 126, 135
prototype, 141, 143
public awareness, 16
public support, 13, 32, 92, 178, 184
purity, 26, 118

Q

quality of life, 91
questioning, 8
quotas, 52

R

race, 6, 9, 61, 62, 93, 101, 178, 181
radar, 33, 44, 45, 98
radio, 15, 49, 139
range, ix, x, 27, 33, 42, 43, 47, 53, 80, 86, 91, 96, 100, 125, 130, 145, 146, 163, 191
reality, 37, 88, 130
reason, xi, 71, 98, 99, 189
reasoning, 140
recognition, 36, 41
reconcile, 12, 84
reconciliation, 6
reconstruction, 92
recovery, 91
reelection, 9, 177, 178
refining, 28, 50
reflection, 19, 178
refugees, 58, 81, 197
regional policy, xi, 31, 189
regulations, ix, 145, 160, 162, 165
relationship, vii, viii, 28, 32, 38, 58, 59, 60, 65, 69, 72, 73, 74, 76, 79, 83, 84, 85, 86, 88, 116, 146, 159, 177
relaxation, 7
relevance, 141, 143
reliability, 181
relief, 53, 161
religion, 10, 16, 17
religiosity, 124
repair, 77, 198
repression, 7, 11, 16, 17
reprocessing, vii, 1, 23, 67, 72, 97, 109, 110, 112, 114, 120, 125, 130, 133, 146, 149
reputation, 67, 90

resale, 165
resentment, 197
reserves, 62, 67, 102, 122, 147
resistance, 7, 12, 14, 42, 83, 85, 90
resolution, 3, 7, 13, 18, 24, 26, 32, 49, 50, 51, 52, 60, 68, 69, 71, 73, 79, 100, 109, 111, 112, 116, 120, 127, 134, 135, 137, 138, 139, 141, 154
resources, 19, 21, 34, 61, 67, 69, 79, 80, 81, 101, 147, 152, 153, 154, 172
retaliation, 42, 43, 65, 94, 95
revenue, 65, 67
rhetoric, 63, 64, 90, 93, 181, 184
risk, 52, 54, 72, 95, 101, 102, 122, 124, 160
rods, 94, 117
royalty, 172
rule of law, 77, 183
runoff, 8, 10
rural areas, 11

S

sabotage, 93
safety, 158, 173
sales, viii, 2, 22, 23, 24, 26, 37, 38, 45, 51, 72, 97, 103, 154, 155, 156, 158, 161, 163, 171, 172
satellite, 47, 116, 121
school, 6, 81, 158
SCO, 35
search, 35, 82
searches, 44, 198
Secretary of Defense, 20, 32, 37, 40, 42, 43, 45, 82, 102, 130
Secretary of Homeland Security, 37
secularism, 78
seizure, 3, 53, 165
self-interest, 78, 177, 178
sensing, 9, 25, 157
sensitivity, 89
sentencing, 7
separation, 14, 112, 120, 142
sewage, 53
shape, 63, 64, 66, 75, 190
shares, vii, 1, 29, 54, 164
sharing, 30, 45, 99, 198
shock, 114
shoot, 39, 165
short run, 184
signs, 69, 92
Singapore, 57, 153, 171
skimming, 33
smoking, 111
smuggling, 19, 30, 75, 84, 91, 94, 105, 106, 195
soccer, 16, 29, 50

social behavior, 7
social contract, 177, 184
social structure, 184
social welfare, 9
software, 114, 165
soil, 94
solidarity, 64, 66, 96
sovereignty, 3, 29, 68, 69, 70, 71, 75, 77, 96, 196
space, 47, 122, 162, 173
space station, 162, 173
spectrum, 183, 184
speculation, 87, 176, 178, 182
speech, 8, 10, 11, 12, 13, 15, 28, 39, 40, 42, 93, 104, 106, 109, 181, 183, 185
sports, 50
stability, viii, 6, 28, 30, 31, 56, 59, 60, 61, 63, 67, 68, 71, 72, 77, 78, 89, 93, 101, 194, 195
stabilization, 36
standards, 65, 79, 80
state control, 5, 7, 10
state intervention, 6
statehood, 90
statistics, 88
stock, 22
stockpiling, 143
storage, 14, 101, 141, 142
strategies, xi, 59, 99, 189
strength, 3, 6, 27, 34, 87, 89, 192
stress, 71
students, 3, 6, 7, 17, 38
summer, 51
suppliers, 50, 72, 101, 113, 114, 122, 154, 157
supply, ix, 34, 37, 43, 58, 73, 82, 99, 110, 112, 113, 118, 121, 122, 125, 145, 149, 153, 154, 155, 157
supply disruption, 43, 110
suppression, 11, 13, 183
surveillance, 35, 81
suspects, 57, 148
sympathy, 15, 89

T

tactics, 12, 35, 44, 91
takeover, 2, 12, 13, 31, 90, 94
targets, 19, 27, 28, 36, 42, 53, 67, 91, 100, 142
tariff, 105, 158
teachers, 16, 17, 49
technical assistance, 57, 163
technology transfer, 97
telecommunications, 181
television, 15, 64, 104, 113, 120, 172, 180
television stations, 15
tension, 30, 66, 69, 101, 176, 178, 198

terminals, 154
territory, 32, 35, 71, 75, 76, 86, 90, 98, 196
terrorist organization, 13, 14, 19, 31, 63, 88, 147, 195, 197
thinking, 82, 100
threats, 18, 29, 63, 64, 71, 72, 79, 139
threshold, 152, 172
time frame, 20, 22, 25, 119, 129
timing, 12
tones, 151
torture, 18
tourism, 88
tracking, 98
trade agreement, 22, 52
trading, 9, 52, 147
traffic, 84
trafficking in persons, 17
training, 18, 19, 27, 30, 31, 35, 76, 77, 82, 85, 91, 105, 106, 158, 172, 191, 193, 194, 195, 197
transactions, 19, 23, 24, 31, 34, 50, 53, 147, 155, 158, 160, 162, 163, 171, 195
transparency, 115, 136, 137
transport, 79, 97, 151, 153, 198
transportation, 30, 68, 80, 86, 173, 198
transshipment, 35
trial, 17, 52, 147, 148
triggers, 147
trust, 14, 180
tumor, 31
turnout, 8, 178, 179

U

uncertainty, 61, 126
unemployment, 178
unions, 16
university students, 16
urban population, 91

V

vacuum, 88
vehicles, 114, 122, 125, 162
velvet, 178
venue, 140
vessels, 72
victims, 41, 89, 161, 165, 192
violence, xi, 12, 13, 30, 31, 64, 69, 92, 172, 176, 182, 183, 195, 197
visas, 23, 41
vision, 19, 55, 101
voice, 147

voters, 8, 179, 180, 186
voting, 11, 23, 56, 57, 155, 179, 180
voting times, 180
vulnerability, ix, 21, 65, 145

W

wages, 9, 178
weakness, 44, 48
wealth, 29
weapons of mass destruction, xi, 18, 39, 99, 148, 162, 163, 189
wear, 16, 191
wholesale, 56, 184
winning, 153
winter, 106
withdrawal, 32, 87, 88, 129, 193, 196
wives, 186
women, 3, 6, 10, 14, 16, 18
workers, 6, 16
working groups, 58
World Bank, 52, 53, 161
World Trade Organization, 22, 52, 148
World War I, 2
worry, xi, 176, 183
writing, 197